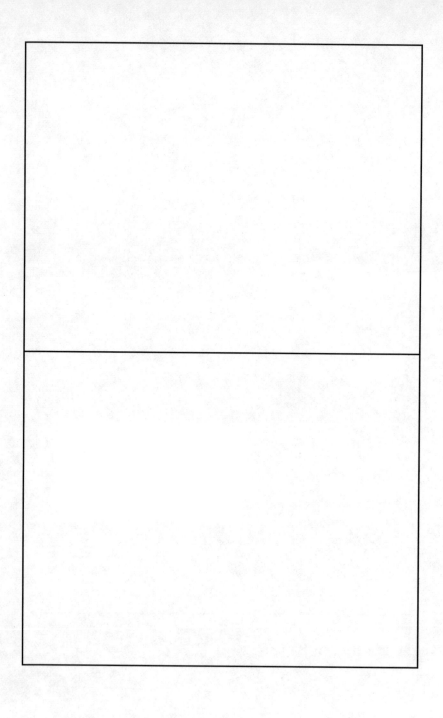

African Radio Narrations
and Plays

compiled and edited by Wolfram Frommlet

Nomos Verlagsgesellschaft
Baden-Baden

Publisher:
Nomos Verlagsgesellschaft GmbH & Co. KG., Postfach 610, 7570 Baden-Baden

in cooperation with
Radio Deutsche Welle, Training Centre (DWAZ) Postfach 100 444, 5000 Köln 1, Germany

(DWAZ publication No. 9)

Die Deutsche Bibliothek – CIP-Einheitsaufnahme

African radio narrations and plays / Compiled and ed. by Wolfram Frommlet.
– 1. Aufl. – Baden-Baden: Nomos Verl.-Ges., 1992
   ISBN 3-7890-2692-1
NE: Frommlet, Wolfram [Hrsg.]

Table of contents

plays

FOREWORD

The Radio Deutsche Welle Training Centre (DWAZ) is pleased to present – after "African Radio Plays" in 1991 – a second anthology of African writing; this time containing narrations and plays from 11 African countries.

For many years the promotion of culture, literature in particular, has become an integral part of training courses at the
DWAZ. This is a response to the fact that African societies are undergoing tremendous changes, both political and social. Every process of change ought to take place in culturally stable and aware societies, otherwise these changes could have devastating effects.

The narrations and plays in this anthology clearly prove that although African writers have a lot to contribute towards cultural identity and the search for culturally valuable developments, their problem lies in the distribution of their works. Radio could play a leading role in the dissemination of African literature. Too often we at the DWAZ heard African broadcasters complain about the lack of books, of printed literature in general and thus their difficulties in producing "literature on the air". This collection is aimed at relieving this problem to a certain extent.

The Deutsche Welle Radio Training Centre (DWAZ) would like to thank Wolfram Frommlet for collecting and editing this second anthology which hopefully will serve as a valuable Thesaurus in many African radio stations.

I sincerely hope that this anthology will not only find many interested readers, both in Africa and Germany but, moreover, that these narrations and plays will be produced and broadcasted all over the continent.

Winfried-Illo Graff
– Director DWAZ –

Cologne, May 1992

INTRODUCTION

Literature without publishers – readers without books

Manuscripts are piled up on shelves and in corners; dust has settled over them and some are yellowed with age. At the top are the latest arrivals – only a year old – while those at the bottom have been there for anything up to seven years. These manuscripts are from Tanzanian writers and are the ones which have at least managed to reach a publisher's office.

And most likely that's the end of the road for most of them, comments Walter Magoya, former editor of Tanzania Publishing House. There will be enough paper for only a handful of scripts, and the state publishing house does not have the financial means to pre-finance the binding and the printing of more than some five or six titles a year. The little financial return that comes back from the few bookshops does not even cover a minimum of the production costs since in a country like Tanzania, only subsidised books will find buyers. In a country where the price of school uniforms presents even a university lecturer on a "civil servant top salary" with problems, books are the last thing on the shopping list of an intellectual, let alone a worker or a farmer with a much lower income.

Where potential buyers are few, the number of copies has to be limited and this increases the production costs per book; thus a publisher like Walter Magoya has to think twice about the number of scripts he can risk publishing annually. That is why on average it takes five to seven years for an accepted script to reach a bookshop.

What's true for Tanzania is now true in most countries of the South, particularly in Africa – these countries are gradually regressing into pre-Gutenberg societies, without books, without literature. Without printed literature. Because there are as many themes as there are writers who transform them into poems and novels, short stories and plays.

While Hermamn Schulz, editor-in-chief of the Wuppertal based Peter Hammer Publishing House, was on his search for authors in Zaire, he spent some days in Kinshasa. He was interviewed by a radio reporter to whom he explained his interest in African literature and that he would greatly welcome meeting some of the young Zairean talents. The next morning hundreds of authors, complete with unpublished works, were waiting in an endless queue to see him. Nobody had read, checked, corrected, edited or critically assessed their scripts because even the capital of that vast country does not offer its national talents the necessary publishing facilities. Many in the queue had heard the radio interview in distant villages and small towns where no publisher would ever wittingly set foot and they had started the trip immediately in order to see the foreign publisher before he left. Some had written their scripts on waste paper or in exercise books and none had ever had the chance to exchange views and ideas with others since there is no organisation in a country like Zaire to arrange a writer's conference. Even if there were, the majority would not be able to afford the bus ticket to the capital.

In 1978, with German government funds, I was able to help organise a national writers' conference in Lusaka, Zambia, the first one since the country's independence in 1964.

For 14 years, the national publishing house NECZAM had not been able to raise the necessary funds to get the country's writers together.

Today at 'Kingstons', Lusaka's former and only bookshop, potatoes, cabbages and exercise books are sold. On the first floor, a few dusty copies of Kenneth Kaunda's "Letter to my children" are waiting for customers, certainly no longer very popular after KK's downfall in 1991. There are no other Zambian writers on sale, because either they are not sought after or they are not printed. There are no South African writers on sale, nor are there any novels from neighbouring Zimbabwe, although Chinjerai Hove's novel 'Bones' has received international awards and been translated into German and Dutch and although there is an an abundance of new African writing: Charles Mungoshi with his children's stories based on the rich legacy of oral literature, Dambudzo Marechera, Shimmer Chinodya, Stanley Nyamfukudza or Tsitsi Dangarembga whose novels are literary eye-openers on colonialism and the liberation struggle in the region: key novels on the spiritual and cultural impact of colonial domination of a people.

It is not thanks to its government that Zimbabwe is currently the home of Africa's most flourishing publishing scene. When it became clear that the young writers were not prepared to formulate psalms of praise to the ruling elite, there was no longer any money to spare from the government's coffers for the promotion of national literature. It is mostly the private and church initiatives which have had the economic and literary courage to publish contemporary literature which calls for a critical look at both national past and present. The fact that these books are not available in Zambia, and equally in Malawi, Kenya or Tanzania is not only a problem of foreign currency. In all these countries there are sufficient funds for the importation of US-American cultural trash for state-controlled TV and commercial cinemas. There is plenty of foreign reading material to be found also at Lusaka's 'Kingstons', for which, no doubt, precious foreign exchange had to be paid – for instance, 'Lady Di' cut-out picture books for children and the treacly old British 'Mother Goose' nursery rhymes, of no cultural relevance to Zambian children, 'Cosmopolitan' & the English versions of 'Vogue' and 'Bunte'. The customers are from the very same neo-bourgeois middle-class which Frantz Fanon so brillantly described in 'Black skin – white masks'.

Denying the allocation of foreign exchange for the importation of African literature which, in most cases, is critical and bitter about the post-independence era (Marechera, Ngugi Wa Thiongo, Chinua Achebe, to mention but a few) is an indirect implementation of state censorship. Yet there are both private and state-run publishing houses in Africa making serious efforts to provide a forum for national writers and to defend their critical views against state interference (Mocambique, Angola, Guinea Bissau, Tanzania, or the East African Publishing House in Nairobi). These are affected by the present economic crisis more than any other sector of African society.

Printed literature, including school books, has become a luxury everywhere in Africa, more difficult to obtain than clean drinking water.

Books are to do with bananas, with coffee, cocoa, sisal or cotton. Company fusions mean that increasingly fewer and simultaneously increasingly bigger food, textile and raw material corporations, trade outlets and restaurant chains compete with each other and – very much in the interest of their customers in the North – pay less to the producers of raw materials every year. Because the terms of trade constantly turn against these producers of raw materials, the countries of the South, Africa in particular, find themselves in a poverty striken economy. Between 50 and 70 % of foreign currency earnings from monocultural products are spent on debt repayment; this is no longer the exception but the rule for most African states.

The Structural Adjustment Programmes, forced upon African economies by the World Bank and the International Monetary Fund, always aim at the same results: everything which does not render a profit and which does not promise a quick return for repayment of debts and interest is thrown overboard.

Books do not make profits in Third World countries. On the contrary, they need subsidies which many of the young, post-independence governments granted for years – although at very low levels and often under the umbrella of state censorship or 'national guidance'. That now is out. Bankers are not interested in culture but in agriculture or, to be precise, in monocultures. These guarantee the flow of foreign currency to Africa, which is then pocketed again by the North for debt repayments or as investments into modernisation projects, which serve the same purpose.

When people in the rural areas have to wait for days for a bus connection into town, when Africans have to queue for mealie meal or cassava flour, when operations in provincial hospitals have to be carried out by candle light – then it is because the miserably small amount of foreign exchange which is left after the regular debt repayment is simply not enough for the importation of spare parts for buses, for a grain mill or a generator in the rural hospital.

How can a government be expected to consider the importation of books, of printing paper or even printing machines under such conditions?

"The people need so many basic things which we have to take care of that there is simply no money left for culture, although we are very much aware that a nation cannot develop without culture. But what can we do?", the Ugandan ambassador in Bonn recently told me.

For the third time within five years the Nobel prize for literature went to Africa – the first to be awarded was the Nigerian Wole Soyinka, followed by the Egyptian Nagib Machfus and the South African Nadine Gordimer.

Hundreds of African writers of similar reputation have received international awards before. Their works are to be found in libraries and specialised bookshops all over Europe but not in their home countries. Due to the lack of foreign currency they cannot be imported from neighbouring African states, let alone from Europe where the majority is still being published.

1990 was declared the "International Year of Literacy" by UNESCO – yet nowhere has the plan of the UN-organisation in charge of culture and education been implemented i.e. to establish small public libraries for the millions of people who, often at great pains and at the same time with so much enthusiasm, have learnt to read and write – libraries where they could find the literature which makes their history, the present and, hopefully, also their future more understandable to them.

Half of Africa's population is under the age of 18. This very same half is being pushed back into illiteracy, a whole generation is growing up without books and hence without history, without the stories about their own society, without visions. It is ironical that now, when the African continent is being shaken up by a second, post-colonial phase of liberation, the enormous breadth of its literature which could provide what the people need in their search for identity, in a new process of self-awareness and discovery, is not accessible to them. Even in wealthy South Africa the black majority population is not in a position to read what would be relevant to them at the dawning of a new, a post-apartheid society: Nadine Gordimer's novels which have the caliber to make the psychology of power, of oppression, of fear and racial hatred understandable to black South Africans and thus surmountable.
But then, in none of the so-called homelands or in the many crowded townships is there a bookshop or public library to be found. And even if there were, the majority of Blacks lack the educational skills and background which would enable them to read great African literature since most of it has been written in the former colonial language.

The South African poet Farouk Asvat (who was banned from 1973 -1978) once told me of the difficulties he encountered when trying to get his works both published and distributed: "Of course there are quite a lot of publishers in South Africa, but they are purely commercial. Others are non-profitmaking or are aimed at promoting alternative, independent culture. But personally I found great difficulties getting my works published. After my banning order was lifted I gave my manuscripts to several publishers and two years later, when they had said neither yes or no, I ended up borrowing money from people and publishing the book on my own."

Getting a loan for publishing from a bank anywhere in Africa is impossible. The reason given for refusal is that literature does not sell – an argument Farouk Asvat has heard more than once. Yet he believes it is a sham argument which he has disproved. "Most publishers are not prepared to publish generally more than 750 – 1000 copies of poetry. When I did my first collection I printed 2500 copies and sold them within six months. With my first collection of poetry I did a lot of readings in the townships with colleagues like Don Mattera and at every reading we used to sell copies of our books."

Farouk Asvat is closely associated with a fairly new movement in South Africa – "the popular culture" and thus he strongly believes that literature should be developed from within the people and consequently be distributed where they live.

"My main method of distribution was giving it to political organizations, civic associations, youth groups and individuals in the community. And I travelled all across the country."

Asvat's experiences clearly demonstrate the root of the project Nadine Gordimer intends to initiate and to sponsor with the lion's share of the Nobel prize money, a project which hopefully will give the signal for a new cultural policy even beyond the South African borders. Gordimer envisages the translation of both leading African and South African writing into the main South African Bantu languages (since they are largely understood in neighbouring Botswana, Lesotho, Swaziland and partly also in Namibia, Mocambique and Zimbabwe the translations will be readable for the Africans in those countries as well); the training of black writers in regular workshops (in the long-run a kind of academy) and consequently the promotion and support of new publication and distribution systems for their literature.

Not the only beacon of light in the literary scene in Southern Africa – once in a while culture is given a surprisingly quick push: in April 92, shortly after the second year of Namibia's independence, the new "Build a Book Cooperative" in Windhoek was able to launch five locally produced children books, and a few weeks later, in May, all Namibian writers, with the financial support of the Swedish International Development Agency, SIDA, gathered in Windhoek to discuss the perspectives and challenges of a national literature and publishing policy.

Hopeful developments, indeed, yet no reason to be blind to the over-all perspectives for African literature.

Apart from the financial aspects and the lack of distribution facilities, the rising rate of illiteracy and the poor quality of the formal educational system – mainly due to the economic crisis – hampers the reading skills of millions of Africans. Should they therefore have no access to contemporary African writing? I am convinced that this is the wrong attitude to take.

The answer to these problems could be radio. A cultural radio whose priority would be the promotion and distribution of the written arts.

The spoken word has a long-standing tradition in Africa and through radio, a fairly new cultural phenomena for the majority of Africans, writing, could be blended into a new form.

Due to its popularity, due to its advantage of reaching millions at fairly low costs (as compared to the elitist and culturally destructive medium television, compared even to and equal number of books), radio could take the lead in bringing African writers to the masses. Rarely radio in Africa has been seen as a means towards cultural identity and cultural conscientisation, but rather as a tool for political and developmental propaganda.

Within the many African radio stations I have worked I have never come across a library comprising of African literature, and amongst the many African broadcasters I have trained in the fields of cultural programmes there was the constant complaint that they had no access to the wealth of writing from their own vc continent. Thus this second anthology which consists of a cross section of African writing, suitable for broadcasting as well as relevant for the emancipation and cultural awareness for both rural and urban audiences.

A good number of the literary pieces are based on the great African oratory. Marti Tololwa Mollel not only takes us on a journey into the Massai myths and legends, but dismantles in "Rhino's Boy" the "primitivity" of an ethnic minority which has been the target for a rude and unscrupulous "integration and civilisation strategy" by the arrogant ruling elites both in Tanzania and Kenya.

In "Dendi" and "Adieu Innocence", in "Fetters Gone" and "Good-bye Ntombenhle" the rural population is being given back the dignity, pride and social responsibility which they have been deprived of by Western as well as African "development technocrats".
The old man in the village, the illiterate, "Pa Musa", analyses Africa's modernisation strategies with the very same sharpness the new elites are so much afraid of, that they cannot but discriminate the villagers as "stubborn and backward".
The Zulu culture as described by Mbukeni Herbert Mnguni in his poetic, almost lyric tenderness, is, in the present waves of violence in South Africa's townships, the proof that the cliché of the Zulu's as "bloodthirsty warriors" might be good for Chief Buthelezi and Western media but far from the ethnic truth.

As much as the "Champion Wrestler" and "Mother was a Great Man" are literary documents of traditions which always formed the framework of women's suppression, as much they give most detailed and sensitive insights into cultural value systems which, regardless of their need for change and adjustment, produce strong male and female individuals on both sides.
What seems to be striking in many of the narrations is the high degree of authenticity in the description of characters, of their feelings, emotions, their fears and joys. This holds through not only for the African characters, but in a master piece of psychological literature, in the portrayal of the white Afrikaander mentality in "Fire in the Fog".

Much has been written about the destructive impact of the post-colonial educational systems which, even three decades after the decolonialisation, go on destroying African minds and souls. Most of the fine academic works were of little relevance to those who unabatedly were the targets of mental brainwashing. Yet, the highlight of literary satire, "His Excellency's Visit", or "The benefit of knowledge", the plays "Walls" and "Converts" provide the kind of analysis which should result on the side of the listeners (respectively the readers) in a search for cultural identity. Identity which, like in Odun Balogun's "The early return" and "Mother and Son", can blend old and new, modern and traditional values, thus creating individuals who can stand solidly on a cultural lineage.

The rural-urban gap, the cultural disintegration, the class- barriers and the lack of appropriate educational schemes for the ever growing number of school-leavers provide the background for
"As the dust settled", and the plays "Tantine Madok", "Family Business" and "Palmwine and Peanut Soup".

"Family Business" and "Palmwine and Peanut Soup" represent a new approach towards dramatic arts: they are the result of creative and collective writing workshops in which one or two group members took the lead in drafting a story line, designing a plot and formulating scenes and dialogues, while the other members were asked to actively criticise phrases, emotions, the use of proverbs or the development of characters. This process of collective writing is intended to incorporate a variety of life experiences through the group members, and thus a high degree of credibility and immediate feed-back on language, plot and dramatic constellations.

In a very different way Khalid Al Mubarak's latest parabel "Tooth of Fire", on power and resistance, ideological mass hysteria, one-party dictatorships and cultural barbarism, – a kind of continuation of his play "The desert crocodile or why Allah stopped sending prophets" –, in a very different way this highlight of African dramatic art seems to me the result of a collective process:
Mubarak drew from the beauty of classical Arabic poetry as well as from the art and traditions of story telling; the narrator creates a permanent distancing effect and warns the audience not to get mixed up between political reality and dramatic events, this is clearly influenced by Bertolt Brecht's "Verfremdungs-Theory"; the content of the play is more than a parabel on Islamic fundamentalism. Books are burned in an Arabic environment, language is turned into a tool of demagogyand propaganda. Islamic context, solely? Weren't books burned in Nazi Germany as well, only some fifty years ago? Isn't language being turned into propaganda of consumerism and "free market demagogy" ? In the end traditional wisdom gains victory over the barbaric means of modern ideologists. Democracy, yes, but not a flat copy of Western models but one based on indigenous forms of cultural traditions.

However, the liberation of African societies from political supression will need the acknowledgment of the bitter realities in everyday lives of millions of people:
the fight for survival in African townships and compounds – the "Parking Boy" – environments; the daily city survival, the "Matatu Menace"; the male chauvinism with its traumatic after-effects for women – "Starlight"; the recognition of those affected by hunger, starvation and exodus – "It had a destiny" and "Remember, Mama"; a critical reflection on the recent past, the colonial terror and the freedom struggle – "Serpents in the sunshine" and "A scene from the past".

16

There is not one African literature, nor is there one African reality. The anthology's purpose is to deliberately expose potential listeners (and readers) to a facette of styles, various degrees of writing skills, and a range of topics, characters and settings.

Wolfram Frommlet

TOLOLWA M. MOLLEL

RHINO'S BOY
a Maasai story

FOREWORD

The narrative art among the Maasai is a highly valued element in social intercourse. Greetings, for instance, involve an exhaustive and unhurried narrative exchange of personal news, ranging from one's woes, the family's welfare to current affairs. The recounter elevates his narrative to a poetic and philosophical commentary on life in general, by interweaving illustrative proverbs, metaphors, sayings, and allegories from myth, tales, legends and past events. This helps to draw in the listener through the activation of a shared cultural experience. In general, poetry and thought in language spice up encounters between individuals and oil relationships. The listener intersperses the narrative with appropriate conventional words and sounds of response. Listening is an art. One is only as good a narrator as he is a listener. The Maasai regard any lengthy exchange between individuals as a verbal banquet; the experience is literally described as "eating words".

I have drawn inspiration for "Rhino's Boy" from this area of Maasai oral tradition. The rhythms, patterns of expression, and the manner of articulating life experiences in the tale derive from, and hopefully do credit to, the Maasai word art. My purpose has been to try and interpret, as authentically as possible, the Maasai world and ethos.

Years had gone by and the need to see the old man again was too strong to be ignored. My life, I felt, was at an impasse, imprisoned within a meaningless job and empty city existence. In the past, when I still had some freedom, regular visits to the old man had provided me with a sense of renewal, which I now felt was what I desperately needed. He had, with his calm, clear gaze into things, always inspired in me a resurgence of optimism and energy whenever I needed a boost. A word, a phrase, a proverb or song from him was enough to dispel the mist of despair and gloom, with refreshing insights into unexpected truths.

Several bus rides got me to the small town of Monduli, but I had to foot it up the mountains where the old man lived, a steep climb that, despite the cool mountain air, left me thoroughly drenched in sweat by the time I arrived at old ole-Meyan's homestead.

Time had taken its toll on the old man. Disease had become an occupant in the old homestead, the old man told me, and death a companion in his old age. Each year had seen the claiming of a child by death, so that now only one remained of the male offsprings borne him by his five wives. The old man saw it as a curse.

I tried to assuage his apprehensions. "It's mere ill fortune, nothing more." The old man laughed, a short painful burst. "I know bad luck when I see it," he replied. "This is nothing of the kind, it is a different matter."

He had been to oloiboni (a diviner and healer or medicineman), he said, and seen the root of his troubles; it was the medicineman who had saved him the boy still alive. "The boy was all but dead too," the old man said. "He had been sick for a long time and would be dead now were it not for the medicineman."

Later on I saw the survivor, as he laboured forth to come and sit at his father's feet. Sickness had thoroughly crippled him. His age was indeterminate – he could have been six, seventeen or fifty. He was childhood and old age in one. My face must have expressed my horror, for the old man hastened to say, "He's much, much better now. A few months ago you couldn't have looked at him. Each day brings a miracle. The medicineman knew his job."

Then, as I looked at the boy, into his blank, unblinking eyes, a most bewildering thing happened. Slowly but surely his face cracked into a painful glow; it was unmistakeable; he had smiled.

The next thing I knew was the old man violently tugging at me, his voice brimming with a babbling ecstasy.

"You have brought blessing into my homestead!" he beamed, and added that it was the first time the boy had smiled in ages.

I must say the old man's outburst completely caught me by surprise, but in a moment he had so infected me with his joy that suddenly there we were, two clowns roaring away, so consumed by our laughter that we failed to notice that the boy, too, had joined us. It was the boy's mother, old ole-Meyan's senior wife, drawn out of her hut by the noise of our merriment, who noticed the boy laughing. She broke into a long, piercing ululation.

In a while the homestead was afire with excitement and a crowd had formed about the boy. But a true miracle was to come. As the crowd watched, the boy suddenly pressed his hands on the ground and slowly lifted himself up. What happened next brought a stunned hush all round. Little by little the boy raised himself and, before we knew what was happening, he was on his feet and had made one wobbly step. Our disbelief could not have been more complete if it had been a corpse come alive.

Later in the evening, when I apologised to the old man for bringing along no gifts, he cut me short with a joyous chuckle. "Don't jest, child, don't jest. You brought us life, what better thing could we ask for?"

I should have slept well that night, knowing I had brought hope where none had been, life where death had lurked, but for some reason sleep was elusive. It must have been after dawn that sleep came finally, but I only was aware that I had at last fallen asleep when sounds outside woke me.

Something was up, I could tell as I got out, and immediately realised I was witnessing the beginning of a mourning. I did not need to be told who was being mourned, as I saw a group of women knotted around the forlorn figure of old ole-Meyan's senior wife.

"But only yesterday. . ." I stammered, my mind reeling in helpless incomprehension.

A tall, stooped elder cut me short with a dry bitter laugh. "Oi!" he went, "haven't you heard it said that the star is brightest during its fall?"

Old ole-Meyan stood at the doorway of his senior wife's hut, his face silent, immobile. I made my way through mourners to his side, then followed him as he wordlessly walked away out of the gate of the homestead into the morning sunlight, to the shade of a small stunted tree I remembered was his favorite. There we sat, each fixing his silence on the dust.

"I'll tell you a story. . ." the old man said at last. ". . .It's an old Maasai legend, about a boy and the rhino."

I had heard the story before, from the old man himself during my last visit almost a dozen years previously. Then it had been an idle tale to soothe the ears. But now, narrated against the background of the fresh calamity, it reminded me of an arrow trained on a difficult target across a dangerously overdrawn bow.

Time had gone by since the story was told anew to me, but over the years the tale has taken root and matured in my mind, prompting to be told. I hereby present it, blending my voice with that of old ole-Meyan.

One night long ago a baby boy was born, but just before his birth a prophecy had spoken of his death: "This little thing entering the world shall die killed by the rhino before he has turned a warrior; nothing else shall be instrument to his death, only to the rhino is being given the claim to his life. But should the impossible come to pass and he survives the rhino to become a seasoned warrior, then he shall live and live and live, and only a ripe old age shall rob him of breath!"

Shortly after the boy was born, two warriors said to themselves, "Oi! What is he, this one just born, that he should be invulnerable to everything but the rhino? Ha, we shall see the truth of this yet!"

So one night they slipped soundless as shadows into the hut of the newborn and bore him out to the bush and slashed open his front, all the way down to the base of the loins, a bold, even cut that had the entrails bared to the night chill.

The next morning when the baby was discovered missing, grief threw the mother into convulsions and the elders into a stunned uncomprehending silence. Never before had a day dawned to a hide empty of a newborn, and, instead of the little early morning chores, people had woken up to the task of wrestling with a mother caught in the throes of wild anguish. Could it, thought the elders, perhaps be that the rhino had already come? No, it couldn't be, it was not the rhino's way to snatch away little ones in the dead of the night. Or could it perhaps be that the prophecy was not true, and a leopard had unheard prowled away with the baby?

But grief or no grief, children must have milk, herds must be grazed, and, as usual, the herdboys set out for the pasturage. But they had not been away long before they were back, the missing baby in their hands. Breathless and dusty, they poured out their tale: "We were right in the thick of bush when of a sudden one of us howled, 'Fellows, is that which I hear not the wailing of a baby?' We all listened and true it was, and when we went thrashing around the undergrowth, sure enough, there was the little fellow very much breathing and kicking!"

When they had got over their bewilderment, the elders pressed closer. Was it real what they were seeing, or mere illusion, they wondered, squinting at the baby. But it was the baby alright, alive and whole, except for a thin, faint, almost unnoticeable line on his front, all that was left of the wound from the warriors' cut.

Now, the two warriors had all the while been silent, in all appearances bystanders as innocent as any. But seeing the mark on the baby, they of a sudden grew cold of body, remorse and fear assailing them. How could they have so foolishly pitted themselves against the prophetic pronouncement? Couldn't they have seen that it would be to no avail, that their swords were not the rhino, the only thing the boy need fear?

So by and by the two warriors found themselves recounting the tale of their reckless deed, sparing no detail and speaking in such hushed and truthful tones that the elders found no way to admonish them. They knew a straight word and respected the warriors for their forthrightness; in fact, in their hearts they thanked the two, for now there would be no more lingering doubt as to the potency of the prophecy. So, rather than pick a quarrel with the warriors, who had but acted as the venturesome creatures warriors will forever be, far better it was to think of what to do.

In this, however, the elders were divided. While a few urged some sort of action to prevent the prophecy from coming to pass, others considered as folly the question of pitting the land against a prophetic utterance, against what they saw must surely come to pass. It was a long, drawn out debate, with neither side backing down. And, in the end, a visit to the diviner was decided on as the only way to resolve the impasse. A few chosen elders were dispatched to oloiboni, who had this to say:

"In the wake of the boy's death, there will be but one more season of abundance before ill fortune sets in, a season of such abundance as has never been seen. Rain will bear down on earth, milk will flow, wombs will yield life, laughter and song will fill the air, the felling of bulls will shake the bush, all as never before. A time of thoughtless feasting and wild ceremony it will be, and the heavens will grow red and the earth green with the spirit of opulence. After the rains, for a time to come, the flourishing of things will continue. The blessings of the season – the flow of milk, the laughter and song, the slaughter of bulls – will diminish only gradually, and the wombs will not close all too suddenly."

"But soon the wetness of the earth will give way to a dry spell, and in the homesteads there will be jostling and cursing among the women over what few drops of milk the season will allow.

The new year, the following one, the next and the next and the next, seven altogether, these years, will be one unending season of hunger and sickness and death. The heavens will grow white with the venom of a deadly drought. A blade of grass will be something to fight over, and donkeys and carrion will be things for food."

The diviner concluded by saying that it was up to the elders and their agemates to see to it that the boy did not fall to the rhino; for, warned oloiboni, no charm, sacrifice or prayer would be potent enough to ward off the calamities that must follow the boy's death.

For those elders who stood for duelling with the prophecy, the visit to the diviner was clearly a victory. No longer now could those who were for giving in to the prophecy confidently say, "Let the boy die, what must pass must pass!" It was now known that this boy was no ordinary being; his blood was blood of the land, his death death of life, his doom doom for the living. He must not die.

Until he had become a full blown warrior, the elders decided, he must at all times be kept indoors under guard, out of the way of the rhino.

But as the baby began to crawl, he would not willingly be confined. Not even his mother's breast could reconcile him to his incarceration. At the enraged bellow of the bull, the barking of the dogs or the cackle of the warriors, the boy would be drawn into a yearning for that which lay beyond the hut and he would cry and cry and cry. The elders, gradually driven sick of the madness of a baby wailing the day long, and forgetting themselves in their want of peace, would blurt out to the mother, "Oi, let the little thing go wherever it pleases him!" But the mother at all times aware of what must not be, would softly murmur to the angry little man, "Quiet, quiet, little mouse of mine, for out there where you ache to go is the rhino out to get you!"

When the boy was old enough, a gap was made in his lower teeth, as is the custom, and not long after his ears were pierced and distended. But although this now meant he was old enough to be useful, he could not go with those of his age to the pasturage, and it was only through the accounts of others that he was able to learn something of the life of a herdboy in the bush.

He learned, for example, that out in the solitude of the bush, a boy and his herd make one close-knit family; that with eyes closed a seasoned herdboy could say of a particular cowbell, "There goes such and such a bull!" or "There comes the little spotty cow with a limp!", so accustomed does one become to the music of the bells and so distinctive does each cowbell sound. After a time, too, a herdboy could say of this or that cow encountered deep in the bush, "This one of such a brandmark belongs to Ilmasangwani clan", or, "This one bears the brandmark of the Ilparkeneti!" The tending of the goats, however, the boy learned, was infinitely different from that of cows. Goats are a troublesome breed, but deep out in the desolate spread of bush, a boy would single out a goat he could call his favourite, with which he could converse to enliven the lonely vigil in the wilderness.

Such accounts of a life, a world, he would never know as a child, gradually so filled the boy with an aching for open places that several times, in unthinking defiance, he attempted to break out of his captivity and throw himself after his agemates out in the bush, but each time he was lashed back to his hut by the warriors.

Thus did the seasons come and go, and by and by the circumcision season was due.

Overnight, tender boys of yesteryear turned into brooding youths pressing for a place among men, their manhood on fire to be trimmed. Under the stern patronage of the elders, the boys undertook an expedition to the diviner, who granted their demand for circumcision. He formally opened the new initiation season, signalling the start of the initiation rites and festivities, which would be crowned by the ultimate in manly feats, the barehanded wrestling down by the boys of a king bullock.

The boy's father, like the other fathers with sons marked for cutting, diligently performed the necessary rites, and the honey beer he brewed his fellow elders drank heartily, as if in celebration of a victory already achieved. A few more days, the elders could not help thinking, and the duel with the rhino would be over, with victory, god willing, going to them. This dream, however, they masked well, hiding it even from each other; for there is always something like being too hopeful, reasoned the good elders, and therein lies imprudence. After all, the awaited day was still far off, the days of danger many still, and who knew which one belonged to the rhino? Better then to sit out the remaining days with a calmness that says nothing of the ripples running deep in the soul; no need surely for premature rejoicing, for it brings nothing but ill-luck.

Days passed, and it was the boy's turn. A fresh branch of the sacred, scented oloirien tree planted by the boy's door, announced to all that his moment had come. The circumcisor had already arrived, a gangly, beggarly man of the Iltorobo tribe, who are poor cousins to the Maasai, hunters and despised by the cattle-owning Maasai for that. He had briefly visited the hut, to taunt the boy. The boy had said nothing but merely looked up at the loose ugly frame darkening the doorway.

To the boy, the circumcisor's bullying was really nothing new. The past few days had held nothing but ceaseless torment for him. Those youths who already had had their turn at the knife had run amok with the frenzy of their newly crowned manhood and were on a rampage in search of those of their brethren not yet circumcised. But all the hunted had gone into hiding, all except the unfortunate inmate who had no other sanctuary but the hut. The hunters had descended on him to punish him for all the others in hiding. They had cut him up with sticks and insults, spat on him, called him coward, piece of cowdung, donkey's skin, carrion, all the imaginable bad things deserved as a name by an untrimmed fellow.

But the boy had stoutly withstood the heat and not a word or whimper escaped him. What could he say?

Only a donkey clings forever to his foreskin; for a boy, a time comes when the foul piece of skin on him must become an unmentionable thing of the past. So torment is necessary, for the victim's anger at his tormentors lends him the necessary courage and determination to face the knife.

So the boy had known no peace. In the day he was assaulted, in the night he was sung to, counselling songs but studded with itching little insults that caused the insides to throb angrily.

And now this night before his seating, the singing and the taunting were at their most venomous, cutting so deep that the boy's usual equanimity crumbled. Angry hot veins stood out from neck to toe, and his body bunched up as a piercing, tearless burst tore out of his throat. But the singing continued, weaving into a single thing the victim's anguished scream and the twitching shadows of the night. And it was only the elders who noticed the boy's pain and remarked, "He's ready!"

At the hour of the buffalo, the boy washed in cold water in which was soaked a pain dulling plant, then he sat in the doorway to wait for sunrise. The singing was still going on but the taunts now only made him smile faintly to himself. He knew that later, when it was all over and the glory his, erstwhile tormentors would sing his honour.

His nerves tingled angrily as he made up his mind. He would think nothing of their tribute and neither would he allow himself to be in any way touched by the festivities that would follow.

At the hour of the red sky, the boy's mother opened the gate of the homestead, then fetched an ox-hide and placed it by the right hand post of the gate. The elders had been against such disregard for the rhino. They had preferred the darkness of the boy's own hut; however already there had gathered within and without the homestead, throngs and throngs of spectators who had streamed in from far and wide the night long, and they would not be deprived of a spectacle. They had laughed off the fears of the elders, patiently reminding them that it was not the rhino's way to come boring through gatherings in search of a victim.

So now, clean shaven, the boy strode out of his hut to the gate. The morning air made him blink but in a moment he had taken his place on the hide, looking a little too frail beside the menacing figure of the circumcisor. At the sight of the boy seated dazed on the hide, his legs pinned down straight out by two assistants, the Iltorobo man cackled madly, generally finding the spectacle most relishing. In his eagerness, he sang and juggled merrily with the dozen or so knives he had brought along. (Not that he would be needing them all, but the trick is to terrify the candidate out of his wits!)

24

In a little while, however, the excitement stirred by the circumcisor's clowning died down. And amidst the silence, the circumcisor crouched low over the boy's groin, and it was only his two assistants who could see his face, and part of his awesome arsenal – long, wild, hooked fingernails poised for action. Over the circumcisor's shoulder, the boy could see only a silent mist in place of the watching multitude, and was able to hear none of the hushed taunts that even at this supreme moment were stabbing at him.

Then came the pain – no, death itself! It leapt out in unrelenting searing surges that rolled down thick palls of darkness. Before the darkness however, the boy was able to see his father, all done up in his ceremonial garb, seated in the very front ranks of the watchers, and joy tumbled with pain in the boy. His father, he noted in sweet relief, had trusted that he had a bullock for a son, and had not like some fathers gone to hide in shameful fear that his son would soil his lineage by wincing at the knife. Well, thought the boy in the midst of his pain, be he a doomed, useless lout, he would prove worthy of his father.

And as the knife ripped his foreskin, it seemed as if something had turned him into a rock, so that when it was all over, he realised in disbelief that he had not winced, twitched or blinked; he had not moved a muscle.

He had remained completely immobile as he should. From somewhere a wave had descended to tide him over to manhood.

The songs of acclaim and ululations reached him from the mist and silence, to let him know that the rhino now had a full grown man to grapple with. The applause, however, meant nothing to him.

The elders knew this and kept their silence. No eulogies, the wise elders knew, are ever tribute enough for the fortitude marshalled against the knife; for the pain is a thing no words can grasp; it is a fire coursing through the crevices of the body, a digging into the entrails, a slaughter.

Afterwards the loose, shapeless Iltorobo man had flung down his knives and shuffled away. The boy, washed clean in milk, had picked up his ox-hide to go to his hut, his movements cool as those of to whom nothing at all has happened. But once back in his lair, alone, the tears had come finally, hot, gushing, maddened; but it mattered no more. After the outflow of his blocked anguish, he lay down, amidst his tears and vomit, the fire in his loins consuming him.

Now, days later he sat in his doorway, the pain blunted, his bow ready for birds who chanced to perch on the fence of the homestead.

His pride had not allowed him to accept the offer of birds from his fellow initiates, who foraged beyond the homestead in thickets abounding in mouse birds. The hunting therefore took him longer but finally he had a sufficient number of birds shot down, stuffed and fastened around his head in a crown decorated with ostrich plumes. The crown, a painted face, a long ceremonial garb and some ornaments, these make up the true fashion of the young initiates, who are called ilsipolio.

Though the boy's attire was now complete, he could not, like his fellow ilsipolio, go prancing around the land, displaying his glory for all to see, unleashing his newly found manhood on the uncircumcised, thrashing, cursing, debasing them as he had been debased. Of all the things denied him by the rhino, this he found to be most unfair and unbearable, and caused him such restlessness that it was all the elders could do to restrain him from breaking out of the hut.

"Only a few days remain," counselled the elders, "and they might yet be the most dangerous of all. Wait for a while longer and your days as olsipolio will be over, then as a seasoned warrior you will proclaim to the world what a man you are for beating the knife and also the rhino. Must you gamble away your life for a foolish and youthful vanity?"

And as the elders soothed him, the boy's yearning slowly subsided, and contentment seeped into him, as he thought to himself, "It's true what my fathers are saying. A few more days and I will shed this my crown of birds to become a true warrior. Indeed, what are a few more days?"

Thus pacified, the boy grew brighter of face, his person flooding with the sunlight of his contentment. And it seemed as if he had not known it himself, that he had needed someone else to reveal to him how few, how very few indeed, the days were before the years of danger come to a close and he gained his freedom. This simple truth was like a total discovery, consuming him and turning him into a person wholly new. His face lost its immobility as he gradually opened up. His fellow ilsipolio visited him more and more, for no longer was there now about him that earlier unapproachable air of doom. His mates now found it infinitely easier to regard him more as belonging to the living than to the rhino. And whereas before they had looked down on the hut as a coward's sanctuary, now they looked upon it as a shrine, a heroic arena where life was triumphing over death. No longer was its occupant a harbinger of woe in the land, a sower of sorrows for the living. He had become the embodiment of survival of a whole age group and generation. And in these the boy's last days in confinement, his fellow initiates decided they would abandon the bravado of their ilsipolio life to keep him company as tribute to his perseverance.

Thus did the boy live out his last days of confinement, and so rapidly did the days pass in the companionship of his fellow ilsipolio, that it seemed as if he had gone to sleep and only come awake the day before his deliverance, to murmur, disbelieving, "Tomorrow is the day!"

Now, on this day before his uncrowning, the morning dawned bright and clear, and it seemed as if the sun bursting out in all splendour, and the birds chirping cheerily in the windless morning, knew it was the boy's last day in confinement and were hailing him into the world. The preparations for the next day's festivities were complete. From every creek, path, hillock and ridge, streams of men and women and children, with donkeys and dogs, had been pouring in to pay homage. For the women, clad in annointed, bright red raiment, it was to celebrate a birth, a rebirth; they had come to share in a mother's joy. In the course of events they would fell an oily black ceremonial ram, and thanksgiving for a son granted life, for a land spared extinction, would be sung to Parmwain, lord of creation and the powers of the air, master of thunder and rain, morning star in highest heaven...

Despite the festive mood, anxiety lingered, a vague fear that the morrow might not come soon enough, and some of the elders were for uncrowning the boy that very day, turning him fully into a warrior without delay. But the majority of the elders, though just as anxious, would not have it.

"Why the haste?" they demanded. "Don't we all know that life cannot be hurried? What has happend to sour our decision? Is it perhaps the rhino, we fear it might yet strike?" Laughing nervously, the other elders backed down. "Alright, tomorrow be it!"

Their composure somewhat restored, the elders retreated from the sharpening edge of the sun, to a shade on a hillock overlooking the homestead. Not for them the clamour and bustle, they were too old. Let the youth take over; after all, it was their day, for the boy's victory belonged to the land, and who but the youth were the heartbeat of a people? Speechless, the elders looked down at the spectacle below them. Clearly it was difficult to imagine that there had ever been, or would ever be, such an astounding gathering of people. A pebble tossed into the air would not have found its way back to the ground. They were all here, men and women from all over Maasai country. The world, it seemed, had disgorged its peoples into this humble homestead, chosen for a few nights and days to be the centre of the universe. And still the earth was reverberating with a patter of a thousand thousand feet as the paths bore forth yet more crowds.

With more arrivals, singing rocked the air, a fiery multitudinous outpouring, coming forth as from a single mouth, filling like the river, the creeks and valleys, and like smoke rising to heaven, to Parmwain.

But of the dancing, all that the elders could observe was a massive heaving back and forth and over, of a giant human floodtide; it was impossible from their position to note the individual thrusts of the body into the air or the swaying of the shoulders and the neck, so numerously packed together were the dancers.

At the boy's hut, the throngs had massed up right against the walls, blocking the doorway and darkening the hut. Inside, taking no part in any way in the festivities, the boy sat silent surrounded by his fellow ilsipolio, equally silent; they would not leave him in these his last hours of confinement. He was one of their ranks, a pride to their age-set; in his life had dwelt the power over good and ill fortune, and it was only fitting that in these last moments they should join him in a silent tribute to victory. The bitterness of his incarceration had been his alone, but his victory would be their victory.

All of sudden, the tranquillity in the room was ripped apart. A strange note had punctured the festivities without. The ilsipolio whipped up their heads, violently jerked out of their reverie. They thrust themselves out as pandemonium tore the crowds asunder, and cries issued forth:

"Rhino, rhino!
Rhino, rhino!"

And through the scattering and crashing of bodies, the rhino was seen bearing down on the homestead. But it had not reached anywhere near when the warriors quickly formed a protective ring in front of the fence and made short work of the monster.

Amidst the din and dust of victory, the boy was borne aloft from the hut to where the rhino lay. And as the boy began a hero's dance, the fever in the celebrants reached a peak, for it was clear that the days in confinement had in no way crippled the boy, he was as nimble and spirited a dancer as any born of woman. From somewhere in him, a frenzy had started, and to a roar of applause he shot into the air like some wild buck, in total abandon. And too late he noticed his recklessness.

On the ground where the slain beast lay, blood from its wounds had made a large puddle, and when the possessed dancer came hurtling down, he landed splash into the puddle, slipping on the blood. Now, all in the barest flash of the moment, it occurred to the boy that he must save his pride, he must not allow himself to totter in front of all the girls and the warriors. In a twinkling of an eye, he decided that, to restore his poise, he must shoot back into the air. However, in so doing, he lost his balance irrecoverably and fell sprawling. A stunned hush seized the crowd.

The rhino usually dies on its belly, with its horn pointed to the heavens. In falling the boy had impaled himself on the horn.

The sun had disappeared under clouds, and as the loyal ilsipolio bore away their gored comrade to see what could be done to save him, thunder ripped the air and from a solemn sky, rain looked poised to pelt down.

The calmness in the old man's voice, as he brought the story to an end, was unnverving; it contrasted uncannily with the situation at hand. It turned the sounds of grief in the homestead into a thing far outside of him, a thing distant, like the wailing of the birds in the bush. He was beyond pain. The death of his male progeny, and especially of this last boy-child, was now but a source of knowledge for him, a fable that called for another, to confirm an ancient truth concerning man and fate. The old man had traded in his anguish for enlightened resignation.

A strong sense of loyalty prevented my immediate departure from the homestead. I hung around for another two days, feeling I had to do something but never really knowing what. I was consumed by a desire to reach out to the old man with some of the strength that he had so generously bestowed on me in the past.

But even as I burned with impotent concern, I knew he would be in no need of my strength. Finally I had to leave and I bade him farewell. His face unreadable, he wished me luck and called on Parmwain to go with me.

Leaving in mid afternoon, I made my descent at an easy, thoughtful pace, turning things over in my mind. The sun was going down as I came to the last bend in the path before the foot of the mountain. I chose a rock and sat on it. Below me the road to the city was visible for a good distance, a lonely stretch of murram pressing through the plains. The corrugated rooftops of the small town cast back at me the feeble rays from the dying sun, and I saw my elegant misgivings about life as petty and ineffectual. I suddenly wished I could stay in the mountains a lot, lot longer. The bush, I felt, was just waiting for me to be gone, to seal the path against me forever.

I lit a cigarette, then anxiously glancing up at the setting sun, quickly got up.

AYUK AUGUSTIN AYUK

THE WRESTLING MATCH
An Ejagham Tale

Achot eehh!

This is not the type of story you tell in a hurry. Oh no, Sir, it ain't. It's been told before? Oh yes; a thousand times.

So? Well, yes, the story has to do with that most important custom of African pastimes: wrestling.

So? Let's begin. Rather, let the story begin.

We need not go into details. We need not say that this particular sheep or this particular tiger cub lived centuries ago in the West African jungle villages of Ejagham. No, Sir, we needn't.

But we must be frank. We must be frank and say that at birth, Sheep's son was not much to look at. No, really not much to look at. Even its mother would have admitted that.

We must be frank. We must be frank and say that Sheep's son looked weak and helpless: a fireplace lover.

Its mother despaired. Its father despaired. Its sheep uncle, sheep aunt, sheep nephew and sheep niece all despaired.

All its sheep relatives on the father's side, and sheep relatives on the mother's side despaired. Not without reason. No; not without reason.

Oh, how hard the times were when the world was young! How harsh its people; how stringent their ways! Rather, how harsh the times! How tough the people had to be!

The lamb's mother, father, and aunts, and uncles and friends were all quake with fear for this reason. The laws of the land required that the two closest born must wrestle to the death on the day of their initiation into the clan.

And the closest born to baby sheep was none other than the Lion's cub.

Lion's cub! Oh, mine! Lion's cub! Was it ever so confident! Was it ever so sure of itself! It ran around, catapulted, summersaulted forward, summersaulted backward, tried to outsprint its shadow... and its parents cheered and cheered. Oh no, they had no fear at all. Their son was going to tear the sheep's kid into shreds on the day of the wrestling. Of that they had absolutely no doubt.

Meanwhile, the sheep's kid stayed beside its mother's fireside, shivering every now and then from a rising fever as the day of the wrestling drew nearer and nearer. Its mother kept weeping day in day out.

All her little son's attempt to comfort her were of no avail. "Be comforted," the shivering baby sheep pleaded "the day hasn't yet arrived."

"But it will," she wept, "It will."

The day arrived!

My word! The day arrived!

It started like any ordinary day: Crowing cocks and bleating sheep around the early hours; the waking sun already climbing overhead from its home behind the mountains; the waking populace running behind the houses to ease themselves and bathe in the stream on the forest's fringes. It was a day like any other.

With one exception: no-one went to the farm. Instead, the womenfolk hurried about in their kitchens, cooking delicious sauces of black freshwater snails and pounding the foofoo which would be eaten in celebration of the new entrant into the clan. The menfolk spent all day in the village hall, discussing, drinking palmwine and planning.

As the sun started its homeward journey and the birdfolk began preening themselves in preparation for the night, the menfolk emerged and set up the wrestling ring in front of the Ekwe Hall.

It was a small circle. Wrestling in those harsh times was not what it is today. It was not a sport. There was no canvass to prevent a fallen wrestler from sustaining injury. Instead... well, just listen.

At the middle of this small wrestling ring the men placed a broad, razor-sharp cutlass, its cutting edge pointing upward. Whoever lost in this wrestling match was not going to sustain injury: He was going to be carted away in two pieces...

The drummers started up. The drummers started up with a will. They pounded the drums. They beat the drums. They scooped the drums.

The lion delegation arrived, smiles on every face. The cub started limbering up. It started sprinting, racing its shadow up and down the village, wrestling the walls, the trees, wrestling almost ... itself.

The drummers went wild, the cub jumped into the ring and did a thousand summersaults. The crowd cheered and cheered and cheered.

And a question started creeping into every mind: where was the sheep's son? Where was the sheep's son, neighbours asked one another in amazement. Where was the sheep's son the elders asked. Where was sheep's son, father lion demanded loudly of no-one in particular, a little smile playing on his face.

Then the commotion began. Heads twisted to left, right ad behind, looking for the source of the confusion. Finally all eyes riverted toward the entry into the village. Impossible! They couldn't believe their eyes, and yet they knew they were not dreaming.

The transformation was incredible.

From a timid, shivering creature which would not quit its mother's fireside, the sheep's son had become a magnificient ram: its powerful horns coiled twice and reflecting the reddish glow of the setting sun with forbidding strength, its body covered by a thick coat of hair which dropped right down to the ground, its gait majestic. It threw its head from side to side as it cantered up, the wild music of combat coursing through its veins.

Woh!

My words!

The lion cub was struck speechless. Its pranks ceased instantly.

Woh!

The cub's parents could not believe their eyes. Their mouths drooped and for the first time fear for their son struck them.

"Let the wrestling start," the elders ordered.

The drummers were possessed by the spirit of drumming; the crowd was possessed by the spirit of wrestling: they all went wild.

The lion cub tried: there is no doubt about that. The cub unleashed its deadly claws and roared until the coconuts shook on the trees. And sprang...

But the magnificient ram was just too fit. With faultless grace it retreated to the edge of the circle. It stamped its right front hoof twice and the ground shook. As the lion cub sprang, the ram charged in one powerful, destructive rush.

Its horns caught the cub squarely on the chest and the other felt as if it had run into a rock. It went flying through the air like an arrow and fell on its back directly across the razor-sharp cutlass...

To deafening applause, the victorious ram was welcomed into the clan.

KALU OKPI

THE CHAMPION WRESTLER
Ndi-Oji-Abam, Eastern Nigeria, 1919

I sat there quietly watching father roast one of his few yams remaining from the last harvest. It was raining heavily outside and I could hear little children splashing about and playing in the rain. I wondered how they could do it. If I ventured out in that rain, I would catch a bad cold. But then I wasn't a child anymore. Besides, it was more cosy sitting here in father's hut, watching him roast one of his last yams over the wood-fire and anticipating one of the old stories he was going to tell me any minute now.

That he was going to tell me a story about my ancient forebears, I had no doubt. The problem was when he was going to do it. You never rushed father. He did everything in his own way. Slowly. He stretched out a bony hand into the fire and turned the yam. By now, I was no longer alarmed when father put his hand into the fire to turn a yam. His hand was fireproof. When he had turned the yam to his satisfaction, he retrieved his hand and wiped it on his wrapper. He looked at me with his rheumy eyes and sighed. I knew what was coming next and got up before he had a chance to open his mouth. As I walked across the room, I saw him nod to himself. I climbed into the mud-bed at the far end of the hut, reached up and unhooked his raffia-bag from the bamboo rafters. There was only one kola-nut left in the bag. I took out the kola-nut, hung up the bag again, climbed down the mud-bed, and handed the nut to father.

He took it without a word and began to peel the back off. I went back and sat down near the fire. The rain was still pounding outside and the children were still screaming their heads off. I was sitting in that room, just me and father, shut off from the rest of the world. Time seemed to have stood still. Suddenly, I understood why father never hurried over anything. There was always going to be another day. The rain was always going to fall and children were always going to play in the rain, whilst the elders sat in their huts roasting yams. There were always going to be yams to roast, too. That was the way life was. That was the way life was always going to be, so what was the reason to hurry?

Where were you hurrying to anyway? You were always going to be around until you died. Not a single day less. The gods and your forefathers decided when you were going to die. You had no hand in it. So what were you hurrying about? You couldn't die before your time anyhow.

"Kola is here, my son" I woke up from my reverie with a start. Father was offering me a piece of the kola which he had broken. I accepted it and bit off a small piece. I didn't like kola. It was too bitter, but you didn't refuse anything your father gave you. I sat there trying to hide my small piece of kola under my tongue while father put a whole lobe into his mouth and started chewing it noisily. We sat there chewing our kolas for a long time without saying anything.

After sometime, father turned the yam in the fire again, and then sat back to his kola once more. My patience wasn't as good as it used to be, so I did something which no good son should ever do.

"Tell me about the time when you were the champion wrestler of the clan," I said, interrupting father when he was still chewing his kola. He looked at me as if I had just defiled the Grove of the Ancestors at Atan. He kept on staring at me until I began to feel very ashamed of myself and lowered my face to the floor. It was very quiet all of a sudden in the hut.

After what seemed to me like two or three full moons, father spat into the fire and cleared his throat noisily.

"It is a long story," he said, as if nothing had happened. "It is a very long story."

I looked up and saw father looking at me with what practically amounted to a smile on his face. That surprised me because father never smiled unless he was marrying a new wife, and he hadn't taken a new wife for many a full moon now.

"It is a very long story," Father repeated once more. This time I could have sworn he really was smiling in spite of the fact that a virgin bride had not graced his inner mud-bed in a long time. I kept quiet and waited.

"It was the planting season before the gods took the sun away," said father, as if he were trying to convince himself that he really had the date right this time. As for me, I was never surprised by anything father said anymore. If he said that the gods took the sun away at one time long ago, then that was the way it must have been.

"Yes, that was the time," father said. "In those days, all the nine villages in the clan used to hold wrestling matches during the new yam festivals. The champions from every village then went to Ozu-Abam to wrestle for the Okpu-Agu prize. The final champion of the festivals won the prize and brought undying fame and glory to his village." Here father stopped and looked at me as if he expected me to say something. I didn't say anything. I just moved nearer to him on the mud-bed. He sighed and turned the yam in the fire over once more, feeling it to make sure it was roasting just the way he wanted it.

"In those days, I used to be a good wrestler," father said, and stared at me defiantly, as if challenging me to refute his claim. When I didn't say anything, he went on. "The year the gods took the sun away, I threw everybody in this village, and so became the village champion. I used to be as strong as a buffalo in those days, unlike the young men of today who do nothing but go to the whiteman's school and carry paper about. They are all women, that's what I say."

Father spat into the fire disdainfully. I knew he was referring to me. Ever since I had gone off to that Catholic school, father had started referring to me as a women. It pained him that a son of his had left the farms and gone off with the round-toed whiteman. Usually, I put up a big argument about how the new way was even better than yam farms, but today I did not say anything. I wanted to hear that story.

Father spat again and continued his story, after mumbling under his breath about the regrettable fact that his own son, of all people, had gone and become a pot-licking woman.

"I waited impatiently until the Eke-day when we were to go to Ozu-Abam and wrestle for the prize. The day dawned, and we set off for Ozu with our war-dance group in attendance. We were all dressed in George wrappers and gleaming matchets and leopard caps. As we went, the war-dance group played their ancient drums and the singer called on our forefathers to help us bring the prize home, and so win undying fame and glory for our village. We danced and chanted and brandished our matchets high in the harmattan air. Nobody dared walk on the same path as we did. They ran and hid themselves in the bush when they heard us approaching."

"The singer kept on calling on our ancestors and recounting their brave deeds in battle, and the drummers kept on pounding away at their Ikpirikpe drums. After sometime, the singer shouted my grand-father's name and began to recount his brave deeds ...

"Ekpo Kamalu Igiri-giri ...
He who is beautiful ...
And yet goes to farm!
He who killed a tiger with his bare hands!
Great judge ...
Who defeated even the gods in judgment!
Brave warrior ...
Always the first to capture a head in battle!
Will you let your grandson be thrown today?
If it had been you ...
No one would have been in doubt of the outcome.
But ...
Your son ...
Your son is strong ...
But he has too many wives
... your son is not a woman ...
– But –
He has broken too many virgins ..."

"I didn't like that at all!" Father shouted suddenly. "The Nkalu monkey was practically calling me a woman!" Father stopped, and began to breathe heavily. He was overcome with emotion at the distant memory of the Nkalu-monkey-singer insinuating that he was a woman of all things!

I hid a smile behind my hand and quietly gave thanks to the ancient singer who had had the nerve to call father a pot-licking and dish-washing female.

After sometime, father quieted down enough to continue the story.

"I flashed my machet in the air and answered the rash one thus:

"Hear me, my forebears!
Hai Omerigue!

34

Abam Onyerubi!
Have you forgotten so soon?
You too Igweola . . .
How could you forget?
Don't you remember how I threw . . .
China . . .
And Okorie
And Ojembe, the fast-footed one?
How could you forget so soon?
I might have broken many virgin maidens . . .
– But –
I am not a woman!"

"The rest of the war-dance group shouted my name with a voice like the mighty voice of the Thunder-god. They had not forgotten. And so we danced and sang to one another until we finally got to Ozu-Abam."

Father stopped talking and stared into the fire, as if he could see that far-gone day in the smouldering embers. After a long time, he sighed and coughed loudly.

I got up again and started walking towards the other end of the room. Father did not often cough without reason. Whenever he coughed like that, it could only mean one thing. He wanted his snuff-box. He thought it was more dignified than going to the trouble of asking one of his sons to get him his snuff-box. Besides, what did you have sons for, if they could not be trained to know that a long sigh meant a kola-nut, and that a loud cough meant the snuff-box?

I climbed into the mud-bed, got the snuff-box, climbed down, walked across the room and handed it to father. He took it from me and stared at it reverently for a while. I walked around the fire and sat down again. After sometime, father transferred the box to his left palm and started tapping on it with the fingers on his right hand.

He called on the spirits of his long departed ancestors to join him and partake of the snuff.

"Chief Okwara Igbonku.
Chief Omemgboji . . .
My fathers and ancestors . . .
Come and join me.
Snuff had come.
Let us have long life . . .
And . . .
Let our children be men.
Please my ancestors . . .
Let them be men!"

There it was again. Father never lost the slightest opportunity to remind me that I was now something less than a man. Sometimes, I felt like telling the Reverend father at the Seminary to go and marry his mother, just so I would become a man once more in the eyes of my father. It had gotten to the stage where I wasn't even sure what sex I was anymore. It certainly does something to a man to be called a woman by his own father, who should normally know about these things for sure. However, I didn't say anything. I really wanted to hear that story. I could always raise my objections later.

Father blew his nose loudly one last time, and closed the snuff-box firmly.

"When we got to Ozu, the sun-god was already in the middle of the heavens." Father continued, as if he had never stopped. "The market place was crowded with people from all the other clans in Abam. If you had thrown a handful of air into that market-place, it would have hit somebody. We danced around for a while and the people gave proper salutation and welcome. When the sun finally began to go down, we stopped dancing and gathered around the market square and the festivals began. The chief of Ozu took the place of honour with all his elders around him. The wrestling group saluted the chief and then started playing their drums and Ikoro." At this point of the story, father got to his feet and executed a few dignified steps around the smouldering fire. He smote his breasts, sighed wistfully, and sat down again.

"What happened after that"? I asked. That was another mistake. Rule number one in the unpublished manual of clan etiquette specifically states that a good son should never interrup his father. Father pretended he hadn't heard me and continued with his story.

"The first wrestlers were not important and they soon left the square for the real tournament to begin. Ogbuaja, from Atan jumped into the square, danced round the drummers, and stood in the middle of the arena waiting for any of the other village champions to dare to come out and face him. He was a big box and it took some time before anybody accepted his challenge. It was Okorie Ukate from Idima who finally jumped into the arena and stetched out his hands towards him. They sized each other up and then proceeded to join battle. The ground shook from their fierce combat. For a long time, none of them was able to throw the other. Finally, Ogbuaja crouched low, hefted Ukata off his feet and threw him bodily to the hard Ozu earth. The crowds cheered and screamed and Ukata was carried off the arena by his people.

"Ogbuaja stood there flushed with victory and shouted out a fierce challenge to the remaining village champions to come out and do battle with him. Nobody went out for a while, but finally Olugu of Ndi-Okereke jumped out and stretched out his hands towards the champion of the day. Olugu was a good wrestler in those days, but he was no match for Ogbuaja. They carried him out after Ogbuaja had thrown him right over his shoulder onto the ground. After that, Ogbuaja threw the next six opponents who came out to wrestle with him. By that time, the only other village champions left were Dimgba, the Ozu champion, and I, the Ndi-Oji champion.

"The chief of Ozu at this point got to his feet and made a startling announcement. Thinking that his village champion, Dimgba, was going to carry the day, he announced that in addition to the leopard cap and the eagle-feather that the final champion was to receive, he was going to give him the most beautiful virgin maiden in the whole of the Abam clan. He sent his men into the village and within a short time, they came back with what certainly looked like the most beautiful girl, not only in Abam, but in the whole world. Her breasts were pointed and her hips were full and ripe for a man. When I saw her, I jumped into the square immediately to do battle with Ogbuaja, but my townspeople held me back. They wanted me to wait and fight the final champion of the day. I restrained myself with difficulty and waited with my eyes still fixed on the virgin maiden standing behind the Chief's royal stool.

"The drummers started pounding their drums again, and Dimgba leapt into the square with Ogbuaja. The people shouted and roared and screamed until I thought the thunder-god was finally coming to destroy the world and carry us all to Ali-mong. Dimgba gripped Ogbuaja and tried to dash him to the ground, but it was no use. Ogbuaja was an old hand at the game. He knew all the tricks. He recovered quickly, turned quickly on his heel and spun Dimgba over his right shoulder. If Dimgba had not been such an expert wrestler, everything would certainly have been over then. As it was, he flipped over in the air and landed on his two feet. The crowd roared, and Ogbuaja stared at his opponent like a dizzy ox. That particular trick of his had never failed before. Nobody in the whole clan had ever been able to counter that trick of his before now. While he was still recovering from his surprise, Dimgba slid in under his guard and threw him with a lightning-god movement."

Father paused once more and coughed loudly again. I sighed and handed him his snuff-box. He certainly knew how to keep you in suspense. I could remember many past nights when he had temporarily halted a story at its very climax, then eaten a hearty and leisurely meal before picking up the story again, with me almost in tears waiting to hear what happened next.

This time, he went through the whole snuff ceremony again, before pinching the grey powdery stuff into his nostrils. I sat there shifting about impatiently on the mud-bed watching him blowing his nose noisily and belching a couple of times. When he finally started speaking again, he picked up the story right where he had stopped, as if there hadn't been any interruption at all.

"The crowd screamed and roared like the river god on a stormy night. The townsmen of Ogbuaja carried him off from the field of battle and Dimgba stood there preening himself like the Lekeleke-bird in the harmattan. Every once in a while he would look over to where the ripe virgin was standing behind the chief and smile a secret smile to himself. You didn't need to be a witch-doctor to know that he was thinking about just what he was going to do to her that very night, in the privacy of the wide mud-bed inside his inner room. Do you know what happened next, my son?" Father was back at his old tricks again. Anything to delay the climax of the story. I shook my head vehemently and motioned him to enlighten me.

"Well, my son, nothing happened next." I didn't believe that for a second. The old man certainly was tricky. He should have been a professional story-teller.

"Please father," I begged. "I will be a good son from now on. Please tell me what happened next!" He looked at me as if he did not believe me, but nevertheless he continued the story. I sighed gratefully to the gods.

"Well, to tell you the truth, son, I was not very anxious to go out there and tangle with Dimgba after having seen his biceps and what he did to Ogbuaja. But when I thought about how he was going to take that ripe virgin into his inner room that night, my blood began to boil. Besides, it had been such a long time since I last had a virgin on my mud-bed, and this was a special virgin, too. With these thoughts rushing through my head, I leapt into the arena and stretched out my hands towards Dimgba. His biceps were certainly bigger from so near, but my mind was on what I was going to do in the privacy of my inner room that night.

"I grabbed Dimgba and hurled him over my right left but it was no good. The master-wrestler did not fall. Instead, he managed to get underneath me and lifted me right up into the air. I saw the ground rushing past far below me and I started praying to my ancestors to receive my spirit. Dimgba could have thrown me there and then, but he wanted to show everybody that he could wrestle. He carried me round the arena with the crowd screaming for blood. My blood. I closed my eyes and commended my spirit again to the care of my forebears. I think Dimgba would have thrown me finally, had I not opened my eyes just then and seen the face of the ripe virgin. She was looking at me with tears in her eyes.

"To tell you the truth, I didn't know why she was looking at me like that. She probably thought I had a better mud-bed than Dimgba. Whatever the reason, however, that face gave me the courage I needed. I went limp in Dimgba's hands. He must have thought I was done for, because he started lowering me to the ground instead of throwing me. Suddenly, I flexed my muscles and put my right foot under Dimgba's knee. Before he knew it, I had swung him right over my shoulder and dashed him hard against the Ozu earth. The whole arena was very quiet when I straightened up. Not a single person spoke and the Ozu chief stood there staring unbelievingly at his champion on the ground.

"Suddenly, then Ozu people, who had just seen victory wrenched away from them, started fighting the people from my village. Some of them jumped into the arena and came for me. I grabbed one of the heavy drums and broke a few heads before deciding to get out of there before they killed me. I jumped onto the royal dais, grabbed my prize, the ripe virgin, and before anybody knew what was going on I was already halfway to Ndi-Oji with my prize firmly across my shoulders."

Father stopped speaking and I let out a deep sigh. That should have been the end of the story, but from the sly grin on father's face, I knew it wasn't. He was hiding something juicy from me.

He took the yam from the fire and started cleaning it. The sly grin was still on his face. Rule one or no rule one, I decided to ask him what was on my mind.

"Who was that woman, father?"

He looked up very surprised. That did it. I was sure now that he was hiding something from me.

"Who was that woman, father?" I asked again, staring him right in the eye.

He looked up and stared at me for a while.

"That woman," he began slowly, "that woman is your mother!"

That really should have been the end of the story except that about three market days later, I found myself reluctantly accompanying my mother to her cassava farm.

Walking behind her along the winding forest path, I began to think about the story my father had told me that rainy day in front of the wood-fire. There was something in the story which bothered me so I decided to ask mother about it.

"Mother" I said, clearing my throat.

"What is it?" mother asked without even turning her head.

I took a deep breath.

"You remember the day father threw Dimgba in that wrestling match at Ozu long ago and won you as a bride?"

She paused in her tracks but did not stop walking.

"I remember" she sighed.

It could have been my imagination, but I thought I heard a wistful tone in her voice.

"Just before father threw Dimgba, they were holding each other very close, weren't they?"

"Yes, what about it?"

"They were so close to each other and moving around all the time, so how did . . ."

Abruptly, mother stopped and turned all the way round to face me.

I halted hurriedly before I bumped into her.

She fixed me with piercing eyes for so long that I began to regret ever opening my big mouth.

"What do you want to know?"

"Which one of them were you looking at, father or Dimgba?"

Mother stared at me for a long time, then turned, and started walking down the path once more.

I couldn't be sure, but I could have sworn I saw tears deep in her eyes before she turned away. . . .

CATHERINE OBIANUJU ACHOLONU

MOTHER WAS A GREAT MAN

It was on a dry Harmattan evening. The leaves were already falling from the trees and the wind blew this way and that. But for the rustling whisper of trees bending to the wind, a big hush pervaded the village square as Oyidiya and her two daughters, Mmema and Ikonne, moved past and into the family compound. Neither of the three women spoke. Their heads were bowed low. Their minds were occupied by the same nagging feeling of guilt. They had gone too far. They had tried to rearrange the destiny imposed on Oyidiya by her chi and now they are learning the hard way.

Mmema and Ikonne were both married to prosperous and well-to-do husbands. Their husbands were both in the beer business. They were agents of several beer and mineral drink manufacturers and this yielded much money. Oyidiya was lucky with her daughters; they were rich and easily came to her assistance whenever she needed them. Mmema had been given to her husband Kaka twenty years earlier. Kaka was about thirty when he paid her bride price. Oyidiya still remembered the day she and Mmema went to the big Orlu market to sell palm kernels. Orlu is a small town in the Igbo heartland. Orlu people live on top of the hill about seven miles away from Mmema's people of Umuma who live in the valley. In those days if one wanted to get to the big Orlu market called Orie early enough, one set out at the first cock-crow. Then one would be sure to arrive there before the sun was overhead. Now the motor car has made every thing easy, Oyidiya thought.

The Orlu people were queer people. The people of Umuma did not trust them, they regarded them as semi-strangers who could not be trusted because they had opened up to the white man without reserve. They would even sell off the wares on your head while they talked and drank with you. The Orlu people on the other hand regarded the Umuma people as enemies of progress. Umuma people were timid and hateful; they hated to see progress and happiness in others. If an Umuma man saw that his neighbour's or brother's children were doing well in trade, he would quickly go to the witch doctor to prepare some poisonous concoctions to kill them with. In Umuma, if you made progress, you would keep it secret; an Umuma man who owned a car would never drive it home or that would be the last time his eyes would glimpse the sun.

These notwithstanding Oyidiya had given her first daughter, Mmema, a young girl of barely fourteen years, in marriage to Kaka. Many said it was because of Kaka's wealth, others said it was witchcraft. But Kaka had been spellbound by the beauty of this little tender thing whose skin was as smooth as a water pebble and as light as ripe banana fruits, and whose eyes twinkled as they told countless exciting stories. He had quickly paid the bride price and Mmema had been escorted to his home with Ikonne to keep her company. Then they had sealed the relationship by being wedded in the church. Ikonne grew into a very attractive young girl resembling Mmema as she grew, only she was taller and stronger looking. Kaka wanted to make sure that this little girl who had been almost a daughter to him would not get into wrong hands, so he got her attached to his bosom friend Odili, from a neighbouring village, who was also in the beer business. Now, both men were rich and their wives wielded economic power in their respective homes. Oyidiya was proud of her daughters and grateful that their high financial standing made it possible for her to realise her plans; and even though she had no son of her own, people respected her because of the prosperity of her daughters which was always felt around her. She had even taken the title of Lolo which was reserved only for rich women and women of high social standing. In Igboland, women who wielded much influence and power in their communities were rewarded with the Lolo title, especially if such women commanded respect and high regard.

As Oyidiya remembered the events of the past years, it struck her that she and her husband had almost exchanged roles. Nekwe, her husband, was a man who surpassed every woman in beauty. He was tall and skinny, with a skin as light as ripe udala fruits; and, as if to crown his beauty, Nekwe even had mbibi patterns on his face and arms – sketches carved into the skin and darkened with some black substance to enhance beauty. These scarification marks were often associated with vanity. Now, as the thought occurred to her, Oyidiya wondered why her husband, who was now dead, did not instead go for the ichi facial marks that were emblems of manhood, valour and productivity. But it would hardly have become him, she thought. Nekwe was not the manly type. Was it not she, Oyidiya, who had had to stand on her feet and defend her family whenever another family challenged it? How often did she have to defend her husband against his fellow men? Yes, the gods knew what they were doing. They always joined together in marriage people of opposing qualities and thus ensured harmony.

Oyidiya did not want to admit it, but now as she went through her life in her mind, she saw clearly that she had been the man of the house while her husband, Nekwe, had been the woman. Yes. She had even indulged in excesses, for which she was now paying. She felt a strong pang of guilt and remorse. She, Oyidiya had gone too far. She had not accepted her lot. She had forced the hand of her chi, her personal god that represented her destiny. And now this was the result.

Oyidiya walked faster. She thought her own guilt feeling surpassed those of her two daughters, who, in fact, had no hand in the decision that was now costing her her peace of mind, except perhaps in so far as they had given her the financial support with which she had realised her plans. Oyidiya walked faster still, then she stopped and turned round to face her two daughters.

"But I did the only thing any woman would have done under the circumstances. You are not blaming me, are you?" She burst out. "Nne, nobody is blaming you. Humphrey will come back. We shall do all in our power to see that they release him soon." Mmema did not even believe herself. Humphrey, she was sure, was going to face the firing squad for armed robbery.

"Kompin will die in that place, my spirit tells me he will not come out of it alive. And it is all my fault. If I had heeded to my chi."

Humphrey was Oyidiya's last child and only son. As the old woman could not pronounce the complicated white man's name, she called him Kompin. The tears were now running down her cheeks. Oyidiya was now very old, and she had suffered a lot, chasing after a male issue which always eluded her. She had had the misfortune of bearing exceptionally beautiful children, for the understanding was that such children were water spirits and never lived long. Oyidiya knew this, but what she could not understand was why it was only the male issues that turned out to be water spirits while her female issues all lived and bustled with excessive vitality. No, something else was responsible for the early deaths of all her male children. She was sure her husband's second wife, Njido, was responsible. Njido was a witch and was clearly eating off all her boys hoping to lay claim to their husband's property. Even now the cold war had begun. Njido and her wretched boys were claiming everything, and they had ensured that her only son Kompin was safely behind bars. They had bewitched him, she was sure of it. Why did I not think of this before? she questioned her mind. My chi has definitely fashioned me for great things, but Njido is bent on foiling it. Yes. My chi has fashioned me for greatness. . .

Oyidiya remembered, as she took the last steps towards her family compound, that she was a woman of no ordinary birth. Her parents had been rich and very prosperous. But what made her more proud was the fact that she was of royal birth. She was from a family of chieftains, and her father, Uloka, had earnestly desired her birth. In her village, no prospective chief would ever attain his royal stool unless he begot a daughter. A man's first daughter was his constant companion and bosom friend. When his wives quarrelled, his first daughter would be called in to descend sternly on them and sort out the quarrel. The first daughter of every Igbo family commanded a high position and pride of place, she was her father's "two legs" while the first son was his "right hand". In many parts of Igboland it was the first daughter who ate the best part of the meat whenever an animal was slaughtered in her father's compound. Oyidiya remembered the story her mother had told her of how her father had had to marry her as a second wife in the bid to get a daughter to complete the requirements of his chieftaincy title.

"Your father was rich, he had a large yam barn, a hard-working wife, four able-bodied sons and, above all, the royal blood of his ancestors flowed through his veins. But the elders were adamant. They would not hear of a chieftain without a daughter. 'That is the custom of Ikeduru', they insisted, 'and nobody will change it'".

She still remembered how she shook with fear as she stood by her father while he made his pledge to the elders; how she, a mere child of six, had had to put up with the discomfort of the heavy jigida[2] strings of disc-like beads on her hips and the ivory armlets and anklets that had darkened with age; she remembered, too, the discomfort of having to pronounce the difficult words that would give credence to her father's solemn pledge to the people of Ikeduru.

'But why a daughter?' Oyidiya had asked her mother. 'Surely a son would have been of greater importance. Our people only want sons.'

'Yes, they want sons, but they always say that to beget a daughter first is a blessing to the family. A daughter caters for the wellbeing of her parents in their old age, sons only care for their immediate families. They care little for their ageing parents. A son caters for continuity of the family name and external image, but a daughter caters for love, understanding and unity within the family circle. She brings the brethren together and sorts out their differences. Our people believe that it is almost a curse to beget only sons and no daughter. They will not put up with a chieftain who has no daughter. They say that his homestead is standing on spikes and sooner or later will be razed to the dust.'

So, whereas other girls of her age felt inferior to the boys, Oyidiya was treated with special preference. She did not have to put up with the absurdities that forbade women to whistle, or to climb trees, and because none of these sanctions were placed on her, she grew up with the exuberance and freedom that was allowed only to boys. She did not realise the difference in the sexes until the day she bled between her legs. She had gone on a cricket-hunting session with her friends most of whom were boys. Oyidiya sighted an ube[3] tree full of ripe fruits, and made straight for it climbing with youthful abandon. Then somebody, one of the boys, shouted –

'Oyidiya is bleeding. Oyidiya is bleeding between her legs.' She could not remember how she got down from that tree. The boys jeered at her all the way home. That was how she parted ways with her male companions, especially after she discovered from her mother that that awful experience would be repeating itself every seven market weeks.

That was many many years ago. Looking back Oyidiya thought what an irony of fate it was that she who had been a highly desired daughter should afterwards hang on the balance because she had no male issue.

Oyidiya was left with no choice but to do what in Igboland was reserved for women of high social and financial standing to which class she rightly belonged. She must have her own son and if he would not come from her own womb then some other woman would do so in her name and on her behalf. She summoned her husband's kinsmen and told them she was going to take a wife. The men said they were surprised she had waited so long to take that inevitable step. And so after series of visits with kegs of palm wine and presents to the Umuado village, Nekwe's kinsmen brought home to Oyidiya a young girl of sixteen, looking so ripe and full that one would have expected from her only male issues. But that was not to be, or maybe she did not stay long enough to find out. When her first two issues turned out to be girls, Oyidiya got impatient and sent her home to her parents. Then she married again, but this time the young woman was having difficulty in conceiving. Oyidiya invited a witch doctor to administer treatment to her, but, to her dismay and shame, the healer eloped with the young bride. Oyidiya was not one to brood over a shameless woman when she could marry into the house as many as she could. So she quickly married again, but this time, there was no Nekwe to supply the male seed. Nekwe was bitten by a snake on his way to the farm and died soon afterwards. But the new development did not dissuade Oyidiya from keeping the new wife. Afterall, what were a husband's male relations for if not to see to it that their dead brother's name was not buried with him. So the new wife bore her first issue which turned out to be twin girls; and she and her new babies did not outstay the night. They were quickly bundled back to the girl's parents. It was a pity the white man had put his nose in everything, otherwise mother and daughters would have been killed and thrown into the bad bush, Oyidiya had fumed.

Oyidiya was now quite old and physically weak but her heart was strong. She was bent on leaving behind her after her death, a son to claim her own share of her husband's property and to retain her homestead. She, Oyidiya, daughter of Uloka, would not leave this world without a son to repair and breed life into her hut. It was a pity that girls had to marry and leave their fathers' houses to breed life into other men's homes. If she did not have a son before her death her hut would be demolished and soon the children of the other wife of her husband would begin to farm on it. That was not to be. She, Oyidiya, was going to prevent that. Afterall was her name not Oyidiya – the one that resembled her husband, or rather the woman that resembled a man, she quickly corrected herself.

She had long forgotten about the second wife who had escaped with the witch doctor, and was recovering from the ill luck of the twin girls when, one day, a distant relative of her husband, who lived almost buried and forgotten in the far away town of Asaba across the great river about which she had only heard in stories of adventure, came home with the story that changed everything. Oyidiya's forgotten wife, Chitu, was living there and had long given birth to a baby boy by her witch doctor lover. Oyidiya smiled to herself. The gods had blessed her at last, for the son was hers. In fact all Chitu's children were hers, but she was not interested in the girls; all she wanted was the boy. In spite of his questionable breeding and heritage, Oyidiya wanted to hold him in her arms, to feel his young muscles, to smell his boyhood. Gradually the feeling grew into an ache, a longing. Oyidiya summoned the kindred of her husband and told them of the new development. Some thought it was not wise to bring in a son from the lineage of wizards; it would not go well, they argued. But there were many others who thought that the gods had finally heard Oyidiya's prayers. It was therefore agreed that the boy should be brought home, if necessary he would be abducted.

Oyidiya sent word to her daughters inviting them to give her financial support. She had to pay out a lot of money to the young men who undertook the journey. And so Humphrey was abducted and brought home to Oyidiya, who performed several sacrifices of appreciation to her chi and to Ogwugwu, the god of the village that catered for justice and fair play. Oyidiya remembered it all so vividly now as she pushed open the carved wooden door that led into the compound. Yes, she now had a son, but she had something else in addition, she had misery, frustration, even more – anxiety, for Kompin was an embodiment of all vices. He was a cheat, a liar, a thief, a glutton. Right from the first day he was brought into Oyidiya's home the little boy,

44

who was then barely four years old, had been caught eating the fish from the soup-pot and since that day he had never ceased to be in trouble. Now he was locked up in the white man's prison at Orlu. As soon as she heard the news Oyidiya had sent for her daughters, and though they had tried to bribe him out, it was all to no avail. Oyidiya was sure this was going to be the end of the boy and of the dream that had spurred her on and filled her with hope even at the most trying periods. He was going to be shot by the soldiers who now ruled the country. She too was tired, she had lost interest in living, but she would not give up the fight. She was going to retaliate from the grave against her husband's second wife who had taken the ground from under her feet. Oyidiya pushed at the carved wooden gate of the dwarf mud-wall which creaked open to allow them in. As she took the last few steps and disappeared into the cold dark interior of her thatched, mud-walled hut, she was oblivious to everything around her – she did not see her dog, Logbo, whimpering its welcome, she did not hear her two daughters calling her from behind, she was only conscious of a dry ache somewhere inside her head. Then she swooned and was about to fall when Ikonne caught her, and, tenderly, the two women laid their aged mother onto her bamboo bed. Oyidiya the fighter, the husband of three wives, the manly woman, was no more. But before she breathed her last, Oyidiya gave her last instructions to her daughters.

"I have fought a good fight. You two should not give up now. Before they shoot him, be sure to keep a wife here in his name. Then my life shall not have been in vain. The gods and my chi have fashioned me for great things." The two women exchanged glances.

"Mother was a great man," they both agreed. "We must prepare for her a befitting burial."

Notes

1 Nne   is an Igbo appellation for Mother.
2 Jigida   is a string of disc-like beads worn round the hips by young maidens.
3 Ube   tree is the native pear, the fruits of which ripen by becoming darker on the surface.

TITI ADEPITAN

ADIEU INNOCENCE

He sped through the narrow bush track between their house and the one next door, disregarding the slippery ground and the overgrown weeds which lashed at his shins. His father must not call a second time. Inside the house he stopped briefly in the parlour, and dashed off again, towards the small room at the back of the house. He was in time to save the old man another bellow and panting, and waited for what might follow. His fear was so much he did not even take a casual look at the stranger who sat in the room with his father, but he knew his mission.

"Where were you when I called?"

He had a strong urge to lie – to claim to have been tending the flock or sweeping the yard – but the steely stare of the old man compelled the truth.

"I was playing with the other boys."

"Playing with the other boys! After all my warnings?" The old man looked sideways at his guest as if inviting him to share in his sense of outrage at the filial intransigence, and turned again to Abiona, his son. "You are like the dog that must get lost: nothing will make it heed the hunter's whistle. But before you become too stiff for me to bend, I will leave one or two marks on you to show to your children."

The boy took two uncertain steps back before being halted by his father's stare.

"En-en, where do you think you are going? Afira, come and sit down here, if you don't want me to break every bone in your body. Omokomo!"

The boy sat down.

From a corner of the room the old man brought out a big, white, enamel plate and placed it before the boy. He looked at his guest and inquired:

"Arakunrin, what did you say your name was, o jare?"

"Jimoh Saliu."

The old man turned to his son again and, without being told, the boy adjusted his posture, now squatting on his heels.

"O ya, say after me:
Light is the glory of the sun
When day breaks
It blazes its light round the earth
When Light shines
Darkness scurries into hiding
Whatever is hidden in the affairs of Jimoh Saliu
May the rays of Light shine on it."

The boy repeated, more out of memory than from the old man's lead. He then stopped, looking into the plate. The room was silent. The old man sat immobile on his ramskin, his left palm cupping his chin, waiting for the message. On the small bench to his left the visitor also sat, bent forward, his eyes travelling from the boy's face to the empty, shiny enamel plate before him and back. After a full minute the deep concentration on the boy's face broke a bit, and he spoke.

"I see this man dressed in white robes".

"Unh-unh?" The old man.

"I see a crowd milling round him."

"Unh-unh?"

"They are laughing and joking with him."

"Unh-unh?"

"But the same people are splashing him with mud from behind, dirtying his white robes. He himself does not seem to know it, but he is not moving in any definite direction. Truly, the choice of which way to go has long been taken away from him. Now they are tossing him about: first this way, then that; all the time laughing and joking with him and splattering his white robes with mud. A voice tells me that the worms that are proving so destructive to the vegetable leaf are not attackers that come under the cover of darkness. They live right on the leaf itself."

The boy looked up.

"What else?"

"It is finished. That is all." He sat down.

The old man waited a while, tapping his outstretched left leg with his index finger. And then suddenly he looked up.

"Arakunrin, may our own never be difficult."

The stranger answered "Ase". "Your problem is ill-will." The old man tapped his leg again.

"What did I say? Your problem is ill-will – ill-will from the household where you were born; ill-will from enemies who flock about you as friends; ill-will from those who know what you are destined to become and are bent on reducing it to nothing more than a dream."

The visitor squirmed a bit in his seat and, his voice betraying his fear of the unknown, inquired: "Aafa, I do not understand."

The old man laughed: short and dry – the kind elders reserve for people who must be indulged because they have refused to grow. He turned to his son. "You, go out. And don't let me see you wandering about like an abandoned child again!". He then turned again to the visitor and spoke for quite a long while. By the time the man Jimoh Saliu left, the old man had told him what to do.

Baba Aafa, as he was called, was a sheep-drover. He shuttled between the northern parts of the country like Sokoto and Maiduguri where he bought his flocks, and the western cities of Ibadan and Ijebu-Ode where the sheep, rams and goats were in great demand. The peak periods then, as now, were the religious festivals like the Id-el-Kabir, Christmas and the New Year when adherents slaughtered rams either as a mark of worship or as a symbol of affluence. He always travelled by rail with his son and the flock from the north to Ibadan, from where the rest of the journey was made sometimes by road, sometimes on foot, to Ijebu-Ode. But occasionally, when

Abiona his son, complained of fatigue after a tedious journey Baba Aafa would first chide him before telling him stories of days gone by – days long before Abiona was born – when lorries were a rarity, when there was nothing like rail transportation, and Baba Aafa himself used to trek with his own father and the flock right from Sokoto or Maiduguri to Ijebu-Ode. Abiona never believed him.

Abiona himself was one of "those children". Baba Aafa's wife had died many years before without a child and the old man – then in his middle age and still as itinerant as ever – had simply had no time to settle down among his people, the Yoruba, and think about a second marriage. Some years later he met a beautiful Kanuri woman whose smiles always made him feel many years younger. After months of courtship, cleverly disguised under the cloak of trade from the woman's parents who were also goat merchants, the coming of Abiona into the world could no longer be concealed. The parents were enraged. It was simply unthinkable for their daughter (whose reputation was not exactly chaste) to be given into marriage to the man from the south, in spite of his religion which was like theirs, Islam. In the end, however, it was that same religion which saved the day. A child had been conceived; it had to be born. Hawa was allowed to mother her child until the time the father could take full custody. This came eight years later. He had given the child the name Abiona because he was born while he, the father, was sojourning in another land.

Baba Aafa cared for his son a lot, but he was always careful not to let it show lest he should betray one of the unwritten codes of manliness which men of his generation treasured dearly. It was only when, occasionally, the boy took ill that it became difficult to persist in this paternal game of dissimulation. Then the sweat he shed, the breath he drew and released would all be coloured by anxiety, and the whole house – wherever he was staying at that time – would be taken over by roots, herbs, concoctions and other items of traditional medicine. For this reason Baba Aafa refused to leave Abiona behind with his relations whenever he was going away on his trips. The boy was always by his side – through the dry, hot, scorching heat and the cold biting Harmattan of the north, to the sometimes wet, sometimes burning climate of the south.

Baba Aafa had another reason for being so possessive about his son, but he never let anyone know this – especially not Abiona himself. For reasons which the boy could not explain and had never bothered to find out, his father never allowed him to mix with his age-mates – male or female. Indeed, over the years Abiona had come to realise that this was the surest way of incurring his father's wrath. He grew in limb with the years, his eyes blind to most of the things which were commonplaces to his age-mates, and remained very much his father's son.

Baba Aafa inherited the role of diviner and general medicine-man from his own father, but unlike the late sheep-drover he had never practised it for money. He was content to see it as that vital but very much endangered link between the past, with all its imperfections and innocence, a world which never went beyond the merging of tree-tops with the sky-line, and the present, with its sophistication, moral corruption and young girls puffing away at cigarettes and gambolling frenziedly to meaningless beats. Of course he always delighted in those occasions – which were by no means rare, when a distraught mother would run screaming to his house with her child, trailed by sympathizers, and he would come out and in no time the case of convulsion or whatever ailment it was, would be gone. Sometimes however, the pain which drove people to Baba Aafa's threshold was not of a physical nature, so enquiries were first needed. On such occasions Baba Aafa would call his son . . .

Abiona was very handsome. He had somehow succeeded in a way that surprised many, to combine the rugged and masculine features of his father with the tallness and grace of movement of his mother. Whenever he laughed, Baba Aafa was always reminded of the beautiful Kanuri woman, with the perfect set of teeth, whom he could not marry. But the old man liked his son more when he had disobeyed him and the young boy stood timidly before him, quailing before his threats. At such moments the boy's eyes would be suffused with such intensity of unadulterated youth and a silent demonstration of innocence that the old man would find it difficult to continue scolding much longer. It was little wonder then, though Baba Aafa almost always threatened to "break every bone" in Abiona's body, that in practice he rarely ever raised his hand against his son.

Some weeks after Jimoh Saliu came to make enquiries, Baba Aafa did the unthinkable: he allowed Abiona to be taken to Lagos after much persuasion on a week's holiday by Baba Aafa's youngest sister. He agreed only after a promise that Abiona would not be allowed to play with "awon omo Eko" the Lagos street children. And so, the following day, Abiona was taken for the very first time in his life on a visit to Lagos, the city which he had heard so much about.

In Lagos Abiona was too overwhelmed to express his first impression of the capital city. They arrived around eight in the evening, and all around and above him, Abiona was amazed to find so many lights chasing the looming darkness into retreat. From cars, gigantic sky-crapers and sprawling mansions, street lamps on broad highways that reminded him of a foreign city he had seen on television in the north, the lights came and hit him with such an intensity that left him almost cowering. Not even Ibadan or Kano, which he had visited in the past could boast such an array of artificial lights.

His aunt lived on Victoria Island. Her husband, who was one of the big men (no one really knew what his position was) behind a big construction company, was away on transfer to Ibadan, from where he came over to Lagos to spend weekends. The house itself, a bungalow, looked so foreign. The gates were always locked as soon as Mama (as Abiona called his aunt) left for the private school where she taught, and Abiona would be left with his cousins – Tola, a boy of four, Bunmi, a girl of two, and the housemaid Aishatu, a girl of twenty who came from across the border.

The routine of taking his meals by the clock wasn't easy for him to cope with: he was either not hungry at all when it was time (like breakfast), or famished (like lunch, when they would have to wait for Mama to return). But more than this, he did not relish the feeling of being caged in, in a bungalow where the only sounds that broke the monotony of silence was the roaring of an occasional car, the chirping of birds on a guava tree, the cries of infants, or the scraping of crockery in the kitchen. He often dozed of, but these siestas were little better than short, intermittent cat-naps since he was not used to sleeping in the day-time.

Mama was an observant lady. Before leaving for work on the third day of Abiona's stay she instructed Aishatu to slot in some video cassettes to create some excitement for Abiona. This was a pastime which was reserved for those times when her husband was in, or for festive occasions. On her own part she did not care one bit for video films, but she did not want her nephew to hate his first impression of her home.

Video instantly opened the door to a new world for Abiona. He sat glued to the set as the world was brought to him in technicolour, by young ladies with exquisitely beautiful faces and reed-like bodies, who only waited for the slightest excuse to drop their garments, and smart, cocky handsome young heroes who never lost a fight. One cassette after the other took its turn, and Abiona sat enraptured through them all. Occasionally, Aishatu would dash away to the kitchen when the smell of burning food hit her. But she would always come back, for she was delighted by the world of video as much as she was with her ward.

He could never really tell how it all happened, except that he vividly remembered the second day of watching films when Aishatu told him about a "film" daddy and mummy liked to watch. Midway through the film Aishatu had volunteered to teach him "how", and before he knew what was happening she was taking off his clothes for him, before stripping down her own wrapper.

He was baffled by it all. But in addition to the blankness of his mind which made thinking impossible, Aishatu's cool and calm confidence mesmerised him and urged him on. His tall fifteen-year-old body covered hers well enough, but beyond that he was helpless as he felt a wave of paralysing feelings sweep over him. The maid guided him and worked the numbness out of his body. And suddenly he felt a new wave of alarm as a new being came into life between his loins and, in defiance of his will, strained and jerked in search of ancient pathways which did not take long to discover – with Aishatu's assistance. He did not know for how long it continued, but again the alarm bell rang as he felt himself carried away on ocean-waves and gradually sinking, drowning. This feeling, this sensation, was in his ears, in his nose and in his eyes, as he struggled desperately to come up, to break surface, but he felt himself slammed back into the dark pit by a greater force. He gave up the struggle when he found himself draining into the maid faster than he had ever done in his life . . .

In one of the rooms Bunmi who had just woken from sleep, started to cry.

Baba Aafa missed his son and was glad to have him back after his stay in Lagos, though he concealed his excitement in the usual manner. He was not particularly interested in Lagos life; but nevertheless he asked Abiona how things had gone, and what places he had visited.

It was mid October, barely two months to Christmas, so Baba Aafa set out again on one of his trips to the north. It was a year of drought, and now that the scant

50

rains had stopped coming, the sheep, rams, goats and cattle were dying daily in their tens. Where vegetation had been earlier, there were now dry, hard stretches of arid land, caused by the cruel winds blowing south from the Sahara. The prices of live-stock had gone sky-high and for some time Baba Aafa was in doubt whether to buy or not to buy. Finally he hurriedly gathered together a flock of about sixty gangling, under-nourished rams and sheep and prepared to head for the south before iska, the impending Harmattan, made matters worse.

On the eve of his departure he had a visitor, one of the few Yoruba residents in Maiduguri, who knew him as a man of reputation in traditional medicine. The man was young enough to be Baba Aafa's son, and the old man had always been particularly fond of him for his humility and the perseverance with which he faced the odds of working and living as a bicycle repairer. The man, Ojoge, had never come to Baba Aafa for that kind of favour before. He prostrated before the old man and, after the initial greetings and felicitations, implored him to help save his trade from folding up.

"What happened?" Baba Aafa asked. In reply the man told woeful stories about the escalating prices of spare parts, lubricants and other tools of his trade, and how he would rather die than return to the south with nothing to show for his many years of sojourn.

Baba Aafa sat for a while, his teeth almost mechanically crunching the kolanut in his mouth. Then he spoke:

"Your problem is a straight-forward one, Ojoge. Your trade is becoming too expensive to run, abi? Look here, no herb, no incision can bring the prices of goods down. That remedy does not belong with the babalawo. Only the government can cure that ailment. When you were entering didn't you see the miserable creatures I will be herding home? Should I tell you how much I paid for them?"

"It is not that, Baba. Things are expensive, but some people still manage to get customers. Look at Haroun, the young Kanuri man, who has his shop next to mine: people flock to him ..."

"Why shouldn't they do so? Tell me why? Do you blame him if he knows more people than you do, right in his hometown?"

"Enh, Isola nko, that young boy from Ado who came three years ago?"

"Irawo e ni. It is time for his star to shine."

Ojoge prostrated. "Baba, that is why I came. I don't want anyone to cover my own star for others to shine. A hole that is big enough for the needle should be no less so for the thread that trails it. A market is never too full. I too must make it – as they are doing."

Baba Aafa sat brooding for some time, and then he told his visitor to get up. "Enquiries will first have to be made."

"I think it is better that way, Baba".

"Good. Wait for Abiona to return. He went to buy tuwo."

"What does he know about it?" Ojoge asked. Then he had a flash of insight and he burst into laughter. "O-ho, you are already teaching him "how"!"

"O ti o. It is he who will make the enquiries for you."

"But Baba, don't you think ... a delicate matter like this and such a small boy who may not be able to keep secrets?"

"Stop troubling yourself. How many children have you seen him playing with? That matter aside, neither you nor I can do it. Only he can."

"Why?"

The old man weighed the question.

"The secrets which the eyes of innocence can see may not be visible to those which have answered the call of the flesh." He paused and bit another chunk of kolanut. "Before Abiona came it was always difficult to find a girl or boy who was old enough to understand what was being revealed to him and yet young enough to have remained untainted." He shrugged. "The children of these days ... only Allah knows from where He brought them. I too used to do it for my father before I knew a woman."

"So you mean someone who has slept with a woman can't divine?"

"With the method I practise, no. Rara."

Ojoge opened his mouth again to speak, but he kept quiet because at that moment Abiona walked in carrying a steaming bowl of tuwo. His father told him to put his meal aside for a while and brought out the wide, flat enamel plate of divination which he always carried with him on his journeys. Abiona sat.

In the usual way the son repeated the formula after his father. Then the old man sat back and waited with his customary self-assurance. To his left his visitor sat, expectant. But after three full minutes Abiona could still not come up with anything.

"What is the matter?", said the old man.

"They are not coming."

"They are not coming?"

Frantically Baba Aafa took another look at his son, and as the blood rushed to his head and heart and nearly choked him, he silently blamed himself for not having known before now. For the boy who sat baffled before him was now wise.

"When did it happen?" he managed to ask.

"What?" Abiona countered, his eyes still protesting the innocence of an error he did not realise he had committed, because no one had told him what the error was.

And so, in the darkened room, father and son looked at each other, each neither knowing when nor how.

ODON BALOGUN

THE EARLY RETURN

Tradition has to be respected on an occasion like this. Only on occasions like this, mind you, when you are in pursuit of something fundamental. Not this foolish fuss in search of cheap popularity with second burials, thirtythird birthdays, fifth marriage celebrations, return from overseas, holiday jubilations, purchase of sixth car parties and all the other "joyous occasions" financed with kickbacks, bank loans, mobilization fees and all of which celebrations are pre-announced with pre-paid, long-running advertisements such as this: "With a life well-spent and a sorrowful heart, we regret to announce the untimely death of our dearly beloved..." Wouldn't it have been better if we were announcing the timely termination of this unwieldy sentence? Our ancestors, forgive us. You, surely, did not intend it to go this absurd way...

Accuse me of envy, if you like, and say I am being holy only because I could never raise the loans or get the kickbacks or mobilization fees to celebrate these joyous occasions, however much I wanted. I should know better, however, than to argue because two parallel lines, my maths master used to say, never meet. But I would still insist that life were better simple and straight and that we would find this rule in the Book had our fathers thought it necessary to write it. In any case, we still remember and cannot argue the wisdom in their injunction, to always first consult Ifa priest before burying the dead.

This, surely, is an occasion when tradition must be respected. How else would you know what killed the dead? Who to blame or not to blame? Whether to rejoice or be sad? Which precautions to take? Which burial observances to follow to the letter, which to discard? How to know whether you are burying a human dead or a spirit dead? How else to "read" the will of the dead? How to know how soon the dead intends to return?

Even though I am only a poor middle-aged school headmaster, I know which traditions to observe; indeed, I can distinguish between authentic traditions and their pretentious absurd shadows. Hence, as soon as it was certain my father would not wake again having started on his journey to our ancestors, I put some naira in my pocket and went to consult my favourite Ifa priest.

I did not have long to wait in the reception before the customer who had engaged the priest at my arrival emerged from the dimly-lit inner-rom. I entered, and as always, I was instantly gripped by a feeling of mystery and awe as I surveyed the items at the shrine, exchanged customary greetings and paid consultation fees.

I have been in this shrine for consultation often enough and was more than familiar with the effigies, the skulls, the bones, the feathers congealed with old and new sacrificial blood, and the sacred instruments of Orunmila divination; yet I would be lying to you if I said my fears had nothing to do with the spiritual identification caused by these objects. The core of my fears however, emanated from the awareness of my total alienation and ignorance; when realising that a man, born of woman, who drank the same water, trod the same soil, and lived by the same beliefs and customs like myself, could make me small like a child as I watched him so physically near, yet soaring so far away in spirit, on the wings of Ifa divinatory poetry which moved so rapidly, so melodiously on his lips. This man, who outside in the streets was so ordinary, would here in the shrine be visibly transformed by his enlarged vision, until he ceased to be of this world, except as he remained the possessed physical channel to transmit and translate Ifa divine wisdom to ordinary mortals like us, who have come on consultation. At these sessions I was always more keenly aware than ever before of my blindness, my ignorance, my pitiful nothingness and vulnerability in this world to which I was now a double stranger – materialistically and spiritually; this world which for all its absurd "joyous occasions" was not so plain after all but was full of mysteries, spirits and men who were more than men. Men who knew the secrets of leaves, barks and herbs, men who could read you like a book and cure your physical and spiritual ailments, who could lead you deftly by the hand and reveal to you guided secrets of the beyond. Before such men of knowledge and power, I always felt insignificant, a non-entity, awed.

"Your father greets you," the Ifa priest said, his voice so near yet coming so mysteriously from far away; his right hand busy arranging and re-arranging the stringed pieces of his instrument of divination; his eyes fastened in strained concentration reading and re-reading these stringed pieces ... "He greets you, and said you have nothing to worry about." As the priest spoke, my eyes riveted inwards seeing my father where he lay in his bed, arranged accurately stiff and dignified; remembering how not too long ago, I had teased him, saying he would have himself to blame if he lived indecently too long and have me squander the money I had saved these many years for his burial; wondering if the old man had taken my joke ill, even though he had laughed and said he feared that the indecent impatience of our generation might drive us too hastily to the reunion with ancestors thus cheating ourselves of the pleasures of ripe old age... "He said you need not worry about anything," the priest-diviner repeated, noticing I was abstracted into a reverie. "That he died at the appointed time." It was reassuring the old man held nothing against me. "That all you need do to facilitate his smooth admission into the ancestral world was the usual burial rites, nothing extra." It was reassuring the old man had not blocked his journey with earthly atrocities demanding of his children expensive ritual expiations. "And one thing more," here the priest hesitated a little and remarked that the old man must have had a special affection for my wife. Yes, I confirmed, she was his favourite daughter-in-law. "He said you should treat her nicely."

Only a few days ago, both of them were still having their usual tête-a-tête and he had told her jokingly he feared he might find the other side too dull without her, and that even if it was sweet over there, he might soon be rushing back to her since she was honey, every inch of her. My wife had giggled and said dirty old man, that she would be glad if he returned soon for double smacking both for his present naughtiness and the future ones as well. To which he had replied he would not come if she was going to be a harsh mother, and my wife had said oh no, she would never lift even a finger against him, he should hurry up and come back.

I had always liked the way the two related even though it had meant his teaming up with her against me any time I quarrelled with her. But that too was the reason I had remained in his good books most of the time to the envy of my brothers. The old man was a good man, a faithful man. I liked him. "Treat her nicely." She would be happy when I told her this. It would compensate for her loss. I asked the priest of Orunmila, baba Ifa, if there was nothing he had omitted or was holding back. He said nothing. I then left the mystery of the dim shrine and emerged into the outside light of burial responsibilities.

The old man was buried the next day and I remember, as we carried and placed him into the coffin, nailed him in and lowered him into the pit, everybody, my wife most of all, started crying and wailing as if the old man had just died that instant, as if he was not over ninety and had not carried a frozen faint smile of happiness with his stiff dignity into the grave.

Late in the night, both wearied and tired, my wife insisted still on making love.

"You should be mourning," I reprimanded.

"We should rejoice," she said.

"Because I should treat you nicely?" I asked playfully.

"Treat me nicely," she demanded in earnest.

Late in the night nine moons later I was anxiously pacing up and down the corridor by the waiting room of the delivery ward of "Faith Hospital," fervently praying for my wife's labour not to be prolonged, that she should deliver quickly and safely. My prayers were answered. She was delivered of a baby boy in the early hours of the morning. After mother and child had been dressed and taken to their room, I went in to share the joy. My wife was radiant in spite of after-labour pains.

"Come and see, come and see!" she called, jubilating.

"Who do you think he resembles?" she asked. I saw the features of my father standing out prominently and I smiled happily, saying nothing.

"You mean you cannot recognize your father?" she asked disappointed.

"It's too early to tell," I said, bending to the bed to kiss her, and then turning to smile welcome to my boy as I solicitiously touched his tiny soft right hand, intrigued by this early return and its prospects.

MBUKENI HERBERT MNGUNI

GOOD-BYE NTOMBENHLE

Ntombenhle had told me what time she would come. I waited all day and she did not come. I was very disappointed. But finally she came. It was early evening by then. I did not see her arrival. I was playing with my sister Mamazi in our living room. It was my mother who saw her first.

"Ntombenhle is here," my mother said to me.

I hurried to the kitchen. Ntombenhle was already sitting on a chair.

"Hallo! How are you?" I asked her.

"Fine! Just fine," she replied. Her face was radiant. Mamazi was standing next to me sucking her thumb.

"How old are you Mamazi?" Ntombenhle enquired.

"Four!"

"Come nearer!" called Ntombenhle.

As Mamazi went to her, she smiled. It was a smile of a child who never knew what it was to suffer or what life was all about. A little cry, my mother would demand to know that was wrong. She was cared for. Ntombenhle stroked Mamazi's face and head.

"You are a beautiful child," she said smiling.

My mother appeared not to be interested in what was going on. But every now and then she looked at me with a broad smile on her face. I knew that deep down in her heart she was extremely happy. She was proud of me. Among the AmaZulu, when young people are in love, the whole family and the extended family rejoice. As soon as the news comes into the open people start celebrating. All over the village one can hear people singing and ululating. Young women dress in beautiful beaded leather skirts. Young men too dress beautifully for the occasion. My mother was imagining all these happening to her son. She then broke our conversation by asking:

"Ntombenhle, are you going to eat with us?"

"No, mama, I can't eat with you because I have to be home soon. My brother Themba is leaving tomorrow morning for KwaMashu," she replied.

We then went to my room leaving my mother and Mamazi behind. We sat for a short time talking and laughing. We didn't dare to kiss each other. What if my mother would come in? AmaZulu regarded it as impolite for young lovers to kiss in front of older people. Later I went to the kitchen to tell my mother that I was taking Ntombenhle half way to her home.

"Alright son! It is late now and the young woman should not walk alone at night. Please visit us again my daughter."

So we left my home with Mamazi standing in the middle of the kitchen doorway. She waved her little hand as a sign of good-bye. Ntombenhle waved back. We walked, one behind the other, along the pathway to the main road. It was not very dark – we could see people some few kilometers away. The sky looked clear and blue. It was a beautiful summer night. We could hear the birds singing, even though it was difficult to see them. When we reached the road, we walked side by side. The grass was green and the trees were standing in full splendour. Forgotten was the winter's dryness and the lack of rain. We could feel the wind making the grass wave to and fro like a boat swinging on the sea. Fields of mealies, sweet potatoes and madumbes, the high mountains and small beautiful green hills, peppered with tiny trees, stood firm and strong. Frogs sang as though they were enjoying summer's beauty too.

But it was the grass I remember above all – from which we made our houses, where we encounterd snakes, where we played hide-and-seek; it was a constant back-cloth to our lives.

We reached the bridge. The water was bubbling. We looked into it, it was like a mirror, we recognised our own shadows. Here we spent some time, talking about the river and our love. We looked at each other and sat down. Put our feet in the water, saw the refracted image of our toes under the water, quite thrilled by the coolness round our feet.

"Do you love me?" Ntombenhle asked. As she smiled I could see the dimples on her cheeks. I nodded my head without answering her question. Few minutes later I said:

"Yes, Ntombenhle, I love you," and squeezed her hand to transfer my dizzying floods of emotions.

"What are you thinking now?" she enquired.

"Nothing!"

"But you look sad. What is wrong?"

"I'm not sad. Perhaps I just cannot express my happiness to be with you here."

At that particular moment my hands were trembling, and I don't know why, because it was not our first time to be together in the evening. Suddenly, I closed my eyes and kissed her. My hands this time became stable and tender. I stroked her face. It was like going over an infant's face. When my eyes opened I realized that hers too were closed. She breathed deeply and looked at me with her intense wide brown eyes. I remember that particular moment because she looked extremely gorgeous. I just did not want her to go home. We lay there on our backs watching the small silver clouds sailing in the breeze across the blue sky.

"I must go home now," she said standing up.

She cleaned her dress, in case some grass might have stuck to it. We kissed each other and parted.

When I came home, my mother was plaiting her basket.

"I like your girlfriend, she has respect," my mother commented happily.

She reminded me of that night when she gave birth to our only sister Mamazi. There was no joy greater than that of bearing a baby girl after four boys. Above all, she had some good news to tell her friends in the village – that her son had a girlfriend. The village excitement could now centre on "when is he going to get married?"

My father worked in Durban, and we did not see him often. He used to send us money to buy our books and pay school fees. There was no doubt that when he got the news he would be very happy too. I could imagine him reciting some of our praise names and talking to our ancestors to express his joy.

My parents were Christians, who were still also able to enjoy African customs, such as African traditional weddings where there was much Zulu dancing, much eating of meat and drinking of Zulu beer. They lived in two different worlds.

It was after lunch-time on Saturday. Today was quite different from previous Saturdays. Usually, on Saturday afternoons, the clouds sailed from the South to the North of our village. This particular afternoon there were no clouds and it was very hot. The sun looked as if it was standing still, refusing to go down behind the Ongoye mountains. Its heat was only interrupted by few showers.

"Ki. .ki. .li. .ki. .gi!" The cock crowed somewhere in the village. Perhaps warning the people that, though hot it was, the night was definitely coming.

"Ke. .ke. .ke. .ke. .ee!" The hen in the background. The birds too sang their afternoon songs.

Women sat under the trees plaiting each other's hair. Others taught their off-springs how to walk. Young women carried water with their calabashes and giggled about their boyfriends. The young men drove cattle back home and sang love songs. These were some of the cultural activities that kept the people of my village together.

I sat leaning against the orange tree. This tree was in the middle of our yard. I was finalizing my radio play, "Sipho Come Home". I still remember one line I wrote sitting under the orange tree. It read "life is indeed a force that brings movement and change". Two women passed me. They had covered their heads with blankets. A sign of mourning among the AmaZulu. A thought came to me that someone may have died, but I quickly dismissed it. I told myself that people nowadays do what they like, depending on how they feel like at a particular time. Later my mother came to me and she was sad. Speaking breathlessly and in half broken syllables she said:

"Ntombenhle has gone!"

"Gone, where to?" I asked anxiously.

"These few women you saw passing here brought this dreadful news," my mother said crying.

"That is impossible mother! She cannot die just like that! No!"

"I also can-not-be-lieve-'!"

I broke her off by saying:

"I was with Ntombenhle two days ago! She did not show any sign of being sick. Not at all! She is not dead! No!" I walked up and down imagining how such a thing can happen.

My mother stood there and cried. The two women came out from the kitchen. One touched me on the shoulder and said in a low voice:

"It is true my son, Ntombenhle is not living anymore. She died this morning."

"Let us go," said my mother.

I left everything under the orange tree.

As we entered the yard at Ntombenhle's home we could hear women crying. A middle aged man greeted us, his face was covered with shock and sadness. We entered the house. I was still fighting against the idea that Ntombenhle was dead. As we entered the house I saw her body covered with a white cloth. An old woman unveiled Ntombenhle's face. She was lying on her back. "Yes, she is dead," I told myself. I shouted: "But why? Why did you die?" Tears came streaming down my cheeks. Her face was laced with dignity. Her eyelids were shut and remained so over her beautiful eyes. I wished she could smile at me in order to see her dimples. I stroked her cold face and called her:

"Ntombenhle! Ntombenhle! Do you hear me? Please say one word to me. Do you remember that first day we met at Eshowe Teachers' Training College?"

All this seemed to mean nothing. She was dead.

People came from all directions of our village. It was part of our culture that when death occured the whole community rally around the bereaved. They help with food, and all household chores. This period was seen as both a sombre and a highly sacred occasion.

Ntombenhle's mother sat next to her corpse. She tried to explain how her daughter had died all of a sudden, but the shock gripped her. She cried aloud. Other women comforted her.

"My daughter complained of something stabbing her in the chest like a spear. She then vomitted blood, collapsed and died," she sobbed. "Everything happened so quickly that there was no time for anyone to take her to the hospital. As you all know we have no hospital and no clinic in our village. There ist also no public transport. Empangeni hospital is very far from here."

There was a short silence. And then people started chanting and humming their eternal songs. Ntombenhle's grandfather said:

"Great Spirits of our forefathers, go ahead of our child! Accept her young and tender spirit. She was our flower which was starting to open its petals to our village. We have lost one of our dearest daughters."

"Yes", said one woman, "this is not our last home."

There was sadness, only sadness.

And then silence interceded.

The small lantern burnt dimly in the middle of the room. Singing started again. It was low and harmonious. I fought against the thought that nagged me, it wanted to know whether she could say one word to me. Just one word, I kept thinking. Silently, I asked: "Why couldn't I have discussed with her more intimately?" The silence again returned. It was a stubborn silence, hanging over our heads like a hungry guillotine. It was violently broken when an old man coughed harshly.

The round thatched mud house we were in remained cool. The night dragged on and on slowly. We were happy to see the sun slowly casting its first rays into our eyes. The woman spoke with a soft voice:

"The sun is coming out! The sun is coming out!"

It gently moved up and its flames warmed the whole village.

Early in the morning a number of men went to the graveyard to prepare Ntombenhle's last home. I joined them. I was carrying a spade and other men held picks. Four men remained at home to slaughter two goats so that after the burial we all could wash our hands with blood. Washing one's hands with blood of a slaughtered animal after the funeral is thought to protect from bad luck. Women had to cook the meat of the slaughtered goats and everybody had to eat it.

We dug the grave. It gave me a terrible feeling. Here I was preparing my girlfriend's last home. Tears came rolling down my cheeks but I continued digging, until we finished. We went home. People were waiting for us. The corpse had been washed and put in a dark brown coffin which the men had made. The procession started, the men carried the coffin. Women were weeping and trying to walk straight. As we approached the cemetery the church bell tolled – "Dong! Dong! Dong! The local orator conducted the services. The coffin was opened for the last time before it was lowered into the grave. Ntombenhle was once again lying on her back. Her mother collapsed and was carried away. When the coffin was lowered, I threw a symbolic handful of sand before the soil covered her forever. People left, I stood there for a while, and then followed them, leaving Ntombenhle alone. We all went home to wash our hands with blood. Later I left for my home. In my room I looked at the necklace Ntombenhle had given me and said: "this necklace now stands for the past love and courtship." I put it around my neck. It was the only thing that Ntombenhle had given me. It is part of Zulu tradition that a young woman gives her boyfriend a nicely decorated necklace made by her. This was an expression of her deep love.

I missed being close to Ntombenhle. But these feelings I can live with them. I tell myself again and again that I must live with them. Sitting alone in my room, I have so many memories – the closing of the eyes – lying on the backs – heavy breathing. Her smile at Mamazi. These memories break me, because all I remember about our last day doesn't matter anymore. Except that we met and Ntombenhle never showed a sign of being ill. She had looked very happy and beautiful.

Before I left home I visited Ntombenhle's grave. People were cleaning the graves of their beloved ones. I too weeded the grave. The silence again was there but this time graceful. As it was my last day to visit her grave, I scribbled on the tombstone these words: "GOOD-BYE NTOMBENHLE!" I kissed the tombstone and left.

CHRISTIAN ISAAC

PA MUSA'S LAST STORY

It was close to Christmas and the pangs of nostalgia were once more giving my thoughts those gentle but effective nudges that had characterized the last decade. It was hard to believe that I had not been to the village for the last eleven Christmas celebrations. Eleven years had done nothing to dim the memories of Christmas Day in the village. Infact my idea of a good Christmas Day had grown out of the early impressions I had of the great day.

There were the new toys, fire-crackers, distant rumbling of celebrating drums far in the distance and the night and the cosy family dinner. As much as these were very essential parts of my Christmas, they were by no means the most enduring and endearing. The midnight service at the little village church, the shimmering moonlight shining through the fogs of the cold misty morning and Pa Musa's fire-side stories were the most lasting memories of Christmas in Baiima.

Dad had died, the family had moved to a bigger town, we had grown bigger and gone our different ways in life and for eleven years its had not been possible to return to Baiima for Christmas let alone re-create the past if only for once. Christmas services in the bigger towns were quite good and professional but I missed the familiar face of Grandma Mary for example. The town choirs were too professional and accurate for my taste. They had no Auntie Naomi to occasionally miss a note her or there. What about this idea of modernising the good old carols! The good old booming organ playing to the familiar old tunes was quite something. Then in the big towns, one would walk for miles without noticing that the moon was hanging there. In the village, the dominant light was the moon. You had to notice it. Its cool hazy light always gave one a strange affinity with those shepherds of long ago that saw the angelic host of the first Christmas morn. And of course Pa Musa's stories were nowhere else but in Baiima. After the midnight service, Pa Musa was always there sitting by his cosy fire, inviting the willing and eager children to story time. Dad and mum must have enjoyed the stories for they also became regulars at the fireside. Most times 3 a.m. came too soon and we were asked to go to bed. I also remember that as the only time in the year we the children were permitted to have late nights.

An avid desire to relive some of these memories must have taken me to Baiima for the twelfth Christmas Day since I left. I knew things were never going to be the same any longer. Dad could not be there. The little innocent children that were Pa Musa's faithful audience and gave credulity to his most impossible plots were all grown – too wise in the ways of the world. I looked around the yard that once constituted my entire world. Could it be the same yard that I had to take the whole day to explore? It seemed to have shrunk considerably. The distance between the large berry tree and the tall guava tree was now only a mere ten yards. In those days, my brother and I used to stand at either ends, kicking ball to each other and at our best, we could just make it. The mountains I used to scale had become mere mole-hills, the lakes only dirty puddles. With tears in my eyes, I turned to Pa Musa. I wanted to ask him why nature had played such a cruel trick. Then I noticed for the first time that he looked so frail and tired. This energetic man who never seemed to sleep day or night was suddenly looking weary and sleepy.

"Pa Musa, you must be tired. I think you . . . . . ."

"Oh no! I am not tired at all. Do not suggest anything like that. I get tired only once in this life – when I lie down for the last time," he interrupted me. I sensed that old defiant tone. Even as Dad's watchman for twenty years, he always vehemently objected to any insinuation that he got tired or sleepy on the job. I was happy that at least one thing from the past was still the same.

"How is Auntie Naomi?" I asked hopefully.

"She is also no more", Pa Musa said slowly. All the good old faces at the village church had passed away. The organ had broken down and the old building had cracked so dangerously that services were now held in an empty classroom. I had no appetite for the midnight service. I would miss the stern eyes of Pa King, the booming voice of Mr. Boima as he read the lesson in Mende. It seemed I had waited too long. I made one last desperate trial.

"Pa Musa, would you tell me a story?"

The old man's face lit up in a grin.

"What? Don't tell me you want to hear one of my stories after all these years".

"Why not?"

"Well, you've grown bigger. I mean you have gone to big schools, you read stories from books and watch the pictures. How can my stories be of any interest to you?"

"Because your stories are neither in the pictures nor in the books. Please, if you can, tell me a story and I will listen even more attentively than ever before".

This seemed to please the old man very much. Soon he was all over the place putting the stones in place for a fire.

"Pa Musa", I ventured to ask, "when did you last tell a story to the children?

"Not since you all left. The children that came after – well, they are just different. At nine, they are too young to understand the stories. At ten, they are too old."

As the night grew colder, the heat from the red embers of Pa Musa's fire was a source of comfort. The two cobs of corn that were turning into a rich gold colour by the fireside gave off an aroma that was very reminiscent of the days gone by. The moon was overhead like a faithful old friend. On the other hand, there were no distant rumblings of the native drums.

"You don't celebrate Christmas here anymore?"

"We do – in our hearts".

"What happened to the all night dances around town – the masked dancers?"

"The masks and the drums are still there, hanging by the roofs. They will stay there till they fall to pieces. All the old hands are gone. The younger ones have all gone to the big towns. When they return, if they ever do, they speak a different kind of language and dance the kind of dance the old District Commissioner and his wife used to dance – holding hands trying to lift each other from the floor."

He handed me one cob of the roast corn. We ate in silence for a while.

"Tomasi", he said suddenly. He had always called me Tomasi – his own version of Thomas. "Before I tell you a story, I want you to promise me something."

"What is it?"

"I want you to promise me that you will never put my stories in any book."

"But why?"

I was taken aback by the old man's aversion to books since he had particularly been a source of inspiration to me during my school days.

"If you put my stories in books, people will never bother to come to the fireside."

I saw his point but I wanted to ask how people would hear his stories after he was gone but of course I could not ask him that. He seemed to read my mind for he said, "when I'm gone, there'll be others like me. They must come to listen to them. Do you promise?"

"I do," I said hesitantly.

"Well, let me tell you my story then. This is my last story I will ever tell. I do not think anyone else will come after you anyway. My story is set in the present. Sometime not very long ago, the good Lord saw the sorry state of the African. He saw that He had let them have their way for too long. Look around you. What do you see? The black man seems to have developed no sense of direction. He is guilty of selfishness, greed and a thousand different sins."

"But the whiteman is equally sinful, Pa Musa", I suggested.

"My son, I don't know about the whiteman. I am talking about the blackman. And kindly refrain from interrupting me. God the Almighty gave the blackman everything to make him a respectable human being on earth. What did he do? He threw everything away and craved for what the whiteman had. The blackman did not know how to admire or appreciate without losing his identity. I may admire your good looks but I should not change myself into another Tomasi. Anyway, the good Lord decided to straighten this out. Long ago, He sent His son. This time, He decided to send just an ordinary blackman like you or me. He was an ordinary man. The only difference was that he thought straight, and saw things the way they were meant to be. He came and led the blackman to his true destiny. The first thing he did was to remove politics from its pedestal. The black people have given politics and politicians too high a place. Why should we put one man in a big building, stand around to protect him so that the would swindle and suppress us? Anyhow, when this messenger came, we all became equally important. Decisions were taken by a council of elders. Young people had their say but learnt to respect age. We are born in a particular order and this order must be respected. When struggle for power was no more for you cannot fight to be old, the blackman concentrated his attention on improving his society. A very flourishing society was soon built. The blackman learnt to admire things from outside. He could even afford to buy anything he wanted but he never forgot his own. He discovered that he could still wear his suit and take a turn in the village square. He found out that to be called "black" was a compliment. The whole society was re-organized. The council of elders lived with the people so they knew what problems they had. Everyone was a soldier and a civilian. Each man had his own gun and ammunition to defend his country in time of trouble. Because a bloody fight would ensure if one group tried to dominate the rest by force, no one thought of taking power by force. The elders themselves knew they were grandfathers to the citizens and could not possibly wish them any harm. If on the other hand the devil found a foothold and a tyrannical group of elders evolved, age did not permit them to stay around for long. Then blackmen developed their nations into strong economic and cultural powers. A country is politically powerful only if the society is a unit and is economically and culturally strong. So that is my unusual story son. It is about the great day Africa was reborn."

It was more like a historical fantasy. I knew the old man had good intentions and high hopes for the future of the blackman but I could not help thinking that his ideas were a bit too simplistic and his hopes far-fetched. I was however grateful to him that after eleven years, he had helped me relive the past even though the empty places around the fire left a larger emptiness in my heart.

"Well, thank you Pa Musa. I sincerely hope this dream will become a reality one day for the good of all blackmen."

"It is not a dream. It is a fact. Didn't you listen very well?"

It was just like the old man to give you a jolt.

"A fact? Aren't you going a bit too far?"

"I mean the sending of the messenger. I told you he had been sent."

"But I don't understand. If he had been sent and he is supposed to have done all that you said, why is Africa where it has been since . . . . . .?"

"Tomasi, those big Colleges must have ruined your understanding. You used to be quick at comprehending in those days. You see, the messenger was sent ever since but unfortunately he never arrived."

"I don't understand", I said slowly.

"Of course not. You see all these little tablets the young people take these days to stop pregnancy? Well, his mother that should have been took one and that was the end of the great black hope."

MESSERET CHEKOL

FETTERS GONE!

This is a story which took place in 1965.

It was just the close of rainy August on a rather hazy afternoon. The upper rugged section of Yedawratch where most of its eroded farmland lies, with St. George Church above, was heavily covered with grey clouds. The round huts, with mud-plastered walls and thatched roofs of grass, at the heart of the village, as well as the grazing meadow below were covered by the clouds, streaks of sunlight occasionally escaped through the clouds.

Hailu, and his young brother Lakew, crouching on a levelled piece of ground about ten yards away from his smoky hut, were skinning the second heifer he had lost that day. He was tired not only because of his task and deep grief, but also because of the boring questions all passing villagers asked about his losses. Shortly after, his father Meri-Geta Leul arrived from church whit his parchment book hanging at his right side. His nephew had just met him on the way home and told him about his son's catastrophe.

"What a plight has befallen us, my son?" Meri-Geta began in a low disturbed voice.

Hailu looked up: "I must only accept what God has sent upon me!" he replied in a bereaved tone.

"Why, God is not to blame for all evils. It is only the magical craft of those rascals, I am certain!" the old man said. He was alluding to his neighbours with whom he held a long-standing conflict.

Hailu remained silent, and continued with his work.

"These creatures of dung, who are they to settle here?" Meri-Geta went on after a few moments. "The whole of Gojjam knows that this is all my land and that of my fathers. Bastards, they once descended from the uplands like rolling stones, and now want to sit on our heads! Huh, I should not be called a man if I fail to drive away these pigs!"

Hailu still held his peace. After all, such boasts were too common for his ears.

"If he had only let me attend the askuala, the modern school, following my training at the church school", "Hailu would always sigh after such losses, "I would not have needed to bother about boundary disputes, cattle, sheep, dung, or other absurdities!"

Noticing his son's reluctance to converse, Meri-Geta headed towards his house, mumbling words of insult against his upland neighbours.

His wife, Emebet, is at home as usual. She hurried to set the mesob, a basket with food, as she saw him approach the door. Then she bustled out with a can of water and basin for his hands, for she knows too well the touchy and wrathful nature of her 62-year-old husband.

After his meal Meri-Geta ordered his wife to prepare coffee, to which Hailu was invited. His wife went to one of her friends' houses to grind beans. And Lakew left for the pasture to check with the cattle and sheep.

Hailu was in the same pensive mood at the coffee get-together. His desire to move into town, especially to Addis Ababa, reached its peak whenever such a desaster befell him. He had many a time implored his father to send him away in peace, but Meri-Geta would not for one moment consider such a request.

"It's a sheer waste of time to linger over this matter with my father," Hailu thought, but finally made up his mind to forward it for the very last time.

"Father," he started as he was handed the second cup of salted coffee, "why do you keep me in distress? Earlier, you denied me of the blessings of the askuala. When some of my friends made it to town, you kept me in chains here, and still I am here. I wish you could see what honourable positions Ayalew, Melese and others are holding in town today! But me, I lie on ashes! Now, Father, please send me away with your blessings!"

"Hush, do you dream of attending askuala at thirty? It is only to loiter here and there that you desire to be in town!" replied Meri-Geta sternly as he waved his white swish against a host of flies.

"Mark my words, father! I go there, ask around for a job, and then look for means of schooling!"

"No, do not tell me that-never!"

"But father, please think about my troubles: I have already lost four cattle and two sheep this year alone. Must I wait until I am utterly destitute or naked?"

"Why go naked?" replied Meri-Geta disdainfully, as he stroked his long black beard. "You shall not half face that. Son, take this into your heart: sorrows or joys, penury or wealth, have their beauty only at home!"

"But I was taught that God blessed Father Abraham because he left his country and all his kindred. . ."

"What a scholar you have grown, my son?" the old man interrupted angrily. "What do you then say about our first father Adam who was commanded by our Lord to till the ground and eat his bread in the sweat of his face?"

Heilu realized for the umpteenth time that his father would not give in. His desire to quit village life was now stronger in him than ever; he must resolve it. He cleared his throat as he was arranging the sheep-skin over the mud-seat, and declared in an oddly stiff voice:

"Father, I have no more guts to keep myself on this unyielding land. And I am tired of dragging along with those bony oxen. This is my last breath, father: I want to try my luck in Addis, please bless and send me away!"

Meri-Geta was startled by the desperate words of his son; he had never kown him that way before. He saw his determination and turned fearfully soft, much unlike his temperament, and implored: "Who would I be left with, dear son?" Who is going to see me and your mother off to the grave? Come to think of it, who is going to recite the psalms at our funerals? And you know well that I live honoured in my village because of your presence: otherwise, who would shield me against my neighbouring enemies? And most of all, who is going to keep the heritage of my noble forefathers to my children's children? Only you, my son!"

Hailu was in turn amazed by the gentle tone of his father's words, though the had little impact on his decision.

"Believe me, I shall take heed of all that you have said. But now, please bless me off to Addis!"

"Shoa is nothing but Shoa, and Addis is part of it, child of my river. But our part of the country – Gojjam – ever blossoms! That is even how the saying. . ." intervened Hailu's mother, as she was giving off forceful breath to re-kindle the fire.

"I say, stay in your position of womanhood, lady. You have grown into the habit of interfering in the affairs of men!" growled her husband.

"Why, isn't he my son also?" she murmured, and returned to her work.

Hailu disregarded his father's usual disrespect against his mother, and deliberately turned to her:

"Addis Ababa – the name speaks for itself: A new flower it is indeed! Mother, don't you remember how I came back born young after those two trips? I was shining like polished silver!"

But Emebet was not allowed to answer him.

"It is not without cause that our ancestors were saying, "I feel more pity for the belly-full than for the hungry," Meri-Geta tried to persuade his son, "We are honoured in the whole world, thanks to our noble pedigree and wealth! How can a man in his right senses choose to be the servant of a townsmaster, loathing his homebred fortune?"

"Why should I be a servant?" Hailu resisted. "Wasn't it last year, when I went to Asefa's wedding in Addis, that a certain captain asked me to join a singer's band under him?"

"By Saint George! The son of an honourable churchgoing man to a cheap bard? Enough with you, I curse mercilessly you!"

Hailu was shocked by the word "curse". "Well, I-I would manage to get another job, and later become your benefactor."

Meri-Geta remembered how regularly the sons of his friends sent money and clothes to their parents. But it would be a disgrace for the old man to expect petty charities from his son. So Hailu's honest promise did not ring well in his ears.

"Oh, just forget that, Addis should not mean so much to you. Don't you know that the sons of Balambaras Menkir have turned heathens there? They have utterly abandoned fasting on Wednesdays and Fridays, on Filsetas and Tsome-Yesus. They no longer observe holidays either-neither Saturdays nor Sundays. Worse, they refused to take wives from Gojjam and chose to live with townswomen. People of Addis are all mixed – who can tell if a woman has in her the blood of a weaver or of a tanner?

Nay, my son, town life profits you nothing but the condemnation of your soul into hell!"

Hailu assured his father that he would always pay great heed to the faith of his ancestors, yet Meri-Geta would not give his consent. Finally, Hailu decided to leave his father with soothing words "I cannot struggle with fate – I am predestined to die here where I was born" he concluded, and rose from his seat to go and give straw to his oxen.

That evening Hailu could hardly converse with his wife, as a matter of fact, she too felt downcast. He ate his supper-dough soup of peas, drank two mugs of tella, the local liquor and went to bed early. His wife worked at the fireplace in the alcove with the aid of a kerosene lamp until late in the evening.

"Oh my father," Hailu began to meditate in bed, "he is unwise – He takes pride in this worn-out land and diminishing cattle wealth. And what is the use of counting pedigree – I cannot tolerate him any longer. I shall hold my peace and slip away secretly! Nobody should know about it, lest my father hears about it and binds me by the divine words of his priesthood. Never mind, he will come to realize later that my escape was for his good."

"Ah, but I have no money for transport and provisions! If I sell off two or three heads of my cattle, Father will grab me by the neck, and be immediately aware of my plans!" Hailu thought and thought about a safe means of getting money. He finally decided to ask his Uncle Ato Teferra, a bee-keeper and farmer who would probably be kind enough to lend him some two hundred birr from the sale of his honey.

"I shall in no way share my secret with him," he decided. "I shall simply ask him to lend me the money. I shall also ask him if he could keep three of my cows for me, pretending that he has got abundant grass at his place. He can keep them when he learns that I am gone for good. In this way I will keep myself from being guilty of dishonesty."

Then his thoughts turned to his wife, whom he loved dearly: "I shall write her letters of assurance now and then. And when I get well onto my feet I shall arrange for her to come to me," he consoled himself. Finally he decided to carry on with his daily activities for the next four or five weeks, as though he had forgotten all about going to Addis. That would keep his father from watching over him closely.

Indeed, Hailu was not only a man of perfect bearing and honesty, but also of wits. Everything went as he had planned. He got the money from his uncle, and sent him three of his cows. Now he had to act quickly.

While he was planning his trip to Addis, he could not think where he could stay: if he went to Asefa or Asefa's father, he feared they might reveal his visit to some of the village relatives when happened to meet. "No, I must think of another relative or acquaintance who keeps little contact with my village people."

Finally he decided on Ato Mulat – a distant relation but more of a friend, that brought a smile to his slender face, "I hope he has not moved since we met last year. I cannot forget how he entertained me with a delicious chicken soup," Hailu recalled.

"And this time I trust I will not be much burden on him, especially now that I have got this money with me."

Two days later, Hailu got up at five o'clock in the morning while his wife was still asleep. He washed his hands and wiped his face. He dressed himself in his best clothes and secretly packed another set of clothes in the rather old bag he had bought in Addis last time.

His wife awoke with the noise he made.

"Where are you going so early?" she asked, straightening herself and yawning.

"To the market in Markos," replied Hailu curtly, putting his new gabi over his shoulders.

"Will you bring me some pepper, salt and spices?"

"Very well," he complied, "you don't need to get up! I have enough money with me for that."

He paused for a moment, and added: "In case I fail to return this evening, don't forget to tell Lakew to bring all the cattle back into the barn."

Then he set out on his journey wishing her a good day. She urged him to wait for breakfast, but he feared that the longer he stayed the more chance for further dialogue, so he preferred to go without food. That did not bother him at all, as he never had breakfast whenever he happened to go to faraway places on Wednesdays or Fridays. As he stepped out of his hut, his courage betrayed him and tears dripped down his cheeks – when he thought that he had to leave his wife without a fervent good-bye kiss. He felt equally guilty leaving dear Lakew and his mother, and, to a smaller degree, to his father. But he must forget what was behind him and stretch out to attain what lay ahead. "May you go with me, Holy Savior," he entreated, and proceeded in full swing.

In a short while he reached Boghena the river where he and his age-mates swam and washed their clothes, where their flocks drank, and where his wife and other women drew drinking water.

"Do that which is favorable to me, O Boghena, the river of my land" he prayed as he crossed it, thrusting himself forward energetically.

It is not the nature of men to look back. But when there is a little yeast of sin or uncertainty, they have to turn around now and then for safety's sake. This is how Hailu covered the first seven miles, accompanied by his songs and whistles. Most of all, he was escorted by the celestial sight of the endless fields graced with green grasses, yellow maskal flowers, and the scent of bean and pea foliages.

Once more, he felt he had to look back: behold, someone on a horse galloping toward him! His heart melted in him! Where to hide? It was all open meadow. Whichever direction he attempted to run away, he would certainly be noticed and overtaken. He remembered what the rabbis at the Quinae Academy had taught him: Pharaoh had too hard a heart to let Israel go.

Hailu stood numb, fixing his eyes involuntarily on the advancing figure, it drew nearer and nearer every moment. And when he learned that it was a red horse with a tall, stout man on it, he shuddered even more. "What am I going to answer to Uncle

Fenta? My father must have sent him to hunt for me!" His shaky legs could hardly hold him on the ground. "But who could have told my father about my plans? Would the devil do it? Because I kept my secret all to myself!" He could not help worrying about the curses that would await him at home, his father's irrevocable suspicion toward him till death, the boring life of tilling.

The horse was now only a few yards away, and the man stretched his right hand pulling up the reins. Hailu looked and looked at the man, unable to believe his eyes – behold, it was a stranger! He saluted Hailu in the way every such passer-by does, and continued his gallop. Hailu sighed a number of times in relief, his legs could not help swaying out of the path for joy. Nevertheless he composed himself a few minutes later and went on his journey with greater courage and speed.

At Markos Hailu kept out of sight: he took the best care not to be seen by any of his relatives in town. He decided to stay for the rest of the day and the night at the western end of the town, where his relatives were unlikely to appear.

Hailu got up early the next morning and headed towards the bus station. It was not difficult to get a bus.

It was shortly past three in the afternoon and the bus was just about to complete its 305 kilometer trip. Hailu shouted for a pull-up as they passed by St. John's, deciding it would be better for him to get off there than at Markato – the terminal post.

He had ample time to ask for the direction to Ato Mulat's house. From his last two trips he had learned that it is useless and foolish to ask for directions to individuals' residences in Addis because it is much bigger than Markos, and even more so than his village Yedawratch. "I know he used to live quite near Medhane-Alem Church," he remembered and started asking every person he came across. Some people responded in harsh tones, others with contempt, some politely. Every few yards he would ask people if he was on the right track.

At last, Hailu managed to get to the church. As his custom was, he bowed and kissed the outermost wall, uttering words of praise to the Holy Savior. Then he asked an old lady to show him Ato Mulat's house. She shook her head. But he insisted: "I have just come from Gojjam, and I do not know where to stay except with this man. Please, for Trinity's sake, show me the house!" He had to push hard because he knew from past experienc that townspeople do not feel at ease with such requests. The old lady examined him for a few seconds, and felt sympathetic: "Wait, let me ask those men on the lawn, if by any chance they know him."

She returned soon and told him that they did not know the man. She instructed him to keep to the left side of the street, go down the hill, go up another hill and past the bridge, and then ask for the exact direction. He bowed, thanked her and left.

Hailu followed the woman's instructions, praying on the way "O Holy Savior of my native land, help me find Ato Mulat!"

After many inquiries, Hailu managed to get to another church, to Miskaye-Hizunan Medhane-Alem's. He bowed and kissed the wall, half in praise and half in supplication. This time he met a man at the exit and asked for Ato Mulat. He realised Hailu's village innocence and asked: "Where do you come from?"

"From Gojjam," Hailu replied.

"But where in Gojjam?"

Hailu thought that his village Yedawratch would be too small to be known by people of Addis, and so chose to give the name of its neighboring village, Yabokla, since it once was the home of the princes of Gojjam.

"I do know Ato Mulat," the man confessed, "but he is not here at the moment."

Hailu felt relieved at the mans first words, and drew nearer to him with a smile on his face. He begged to take him to Ato Mulat's house, but the townsman would not welcome such a request! After more pleading, the man conceded to first go and see whether Ato Mulat was at home. Hailu was now worried that the man might not come back! It was six o'clock, and night was coming. He waited.

Ten minutes later, he saw two men advancing toward him. He leapt for joy as he recognized his host's face, and ran forward to meet him. They fell on each other's necks, on each other's cheeks – so many hugs, so many kisses, so many "how-do-you-do's". Then Hailu kissed the other man on his knees a couple of times, expressing his gratitude, and, finally, kissed the outer wall of Medhane-Alem church a number of times, uttering words of praise.

That evening Hailu told his story to Ato Mulat and his idea was heartily welcomed by his middle-aged host as he, too, had moved into town because he detested village life. "They have the land, cattle, water, grass, diligence, but what else? They have little knowledge of handling their possessions and themselves!" Ato Mulat complained.

"Only find me a job where I can earn my daily bread – be it chopping wood, keeping a compound, or anything of that sort. I hope I will get a better job as I proceed with my evening classes as some of my relatives did here in town," Hailu explained. "And I do not wish to be a burden on you. I can take care of my belly out of doors only allow me into one of your rooms!" he pleaded. He was relying on the hundred-and-eighty birr left in his pocket. It was his nature (and that of his mother) not to stay long on the shoulders of other people, no matter how friendly they may be. His host assured him that he would appreciate his company in his lonely life until things got settled. But Hailu would not listen – he would stay out of the house during meal hours.

Only four days after his arrival, Ato Mulat got a job for Hailu at a private garage on Jimma Road. It was far from his friend's house at the other end of the city, and so Hailu used it as an excuse for moving into a simple house nearby at a monthly rent of three birr. He thanked Ato Mulat for all his kindness and promised to visit him frequently, determined to repay his gratitude to his faithful friend.

The garage owner liked Hailu very much for his diligence, obedience and honesty: "He's worth two people," he often remarked, and wanted to promote him to a better job if he continued.

Hailu was catching up fast with Addis life-style: he put away his village gabi to use it only as a nightgown, covered his feet with a pair of canvas shoes, bought himself shirts and sweaters for a good part of the money left from his trip. When he was off duty, he would go around residences, chop wood and get paid. All was perfectly well except that he missed home when he sat down for his rather small meal, and at night when he found himself alone in bed!

Meanwhile, there was growing concern about Hailu back at Yedawratch. The whole family had learned from his wife about his trip to Markos. They waited for his return for three long days. Then they started asking villagers who had gone to the market at Markos that week if they had by any chance seen Hailu there. Not one person had, and that made them more worried. They did not know what to do. They couldn't imagine a river accident, as the rainy season had gone away for over a month now, besides, Hailu was a good swimmer like other village youths. His peaceful nature did not give them any room to think that he was involved in a fight. But his wife looked at the other side of the coin: He might have fallen victim in trying to stop a fight between townsmen," she cried.

"It might well be, daughter, it might well be!" his mother wailed.

But Meri-Geta had a different view: "I know my son well – he is firm with his intentions, although slow. He has deserted to Addis. Ay, ay, ay, he left us all in the open for beasts!"

Soon Meri-Geta ordered both his wife and daughter-in-law to prepare him provisions in abundance. "I shall set out to Markos, search for him there, and in case of failure, I shall cross over to Addis and fetch that rascal back!" he boasted.

"You in this old age to go to Addis where cars flow ceaselessly like a herd of goats released from their folds?" resisted his wife, recalling her trip there three years ago to visit her cousin.

"Shut up and mind my orders, gomer! I have always told you not to act above your position!" growled Meri-Geta.

"Oh, I better leave it all to you," Emebet murmured, and went on with her business.

"I shall go with Fetene. He is a master on Addis, thanks to his aunt there. And he is the most faithful of my sons-in-law," he explained, by way of taking back his wrath.

While the two ladies were busy with the preparations, Meri-Geta sent for Fetene at Tamba village, about two hours' walk to the east. Fetene came to Yadawratch with the messenger the following day. The two men discussed the matter through and decided to carry out their mission as soon as possible.

Fetene at his age of a little over forty had never inclined his heart to city life, despite his frequent visits: "Nothing like Gojjam, fellow, where you find sweet tella and plenty of Injerra bread more than your belly can hold!" he would remark at times. "Townsmen are only outward smiles. They keep neat and dress well, but roam around with empty bellies! All our grain flows to their markets and we see them buying and buying: but this custom of theirs – eating clean and little –. I detest that. Nothing like Gojjam, old chap!"

Ten days after Hailu's flight, Meri-Geta Leul and Fetene set out on their journey with Lakew to accompany them, to Markos. The young boy was put in charge of a donkey loaded with provisions – teff flour and two sizeable baskets full of roasted wheat bread, which would last for several days.

At Boghena river Lakew first helped the donkey cross over. Fetene followed. The old man held down the stirrups with the utmost strength of his toes, gripped the mane of the mule and gave it a whip. The beast would not move an inch! A couple more lashes followed, it would not stir! How about a few more lashes together with words of insult? The mule now turned impatienty and nearly threw her master into the river.

"Devil! What sort of demon is in you today?" shouted Meri-Geta.

It was an old belief that whenever a transport animal refused to move, this was a bad omen to the master.

Foreseeing the danger Fetene dismounted from his horse, and came to the help of his father-in-law. He asked the old man to get off the mule, and with the assistance of passersby he finally got the beast over to the other side.

Lakew marched ahead of them driving the donkey. The two men turned their faces back to the river, bowed and made supplications for a happy return! Nevertheless the mule continued to be a big nuisance until they were halfway through their journey.

At Markos Meri-Geta and Fetene searched and searched for Hailu with the help of their relatives in town. But no corner hid the young men! Therefore they made up their minds to cross over to Addis on the third day, and sent Lakew back home with the animals.

In Addis Fetene was a great help. They stayed with Abberra, Emebet's cousin, just a little above Menelik School. In the company of their host, the two village men searched for Hailu three long days. But Addis is so large that a man could hide in any one of her bosoms!

Meri-Geta and Fetene were very disappointed. Somehow they wanted to stay longer in town, hoping that time might betray him, yet they could not stand the dull countenance of their host.

"I mean, they are really unbearable – they think I have nothing to do all day long. Because of them my recovering daughter is missing my attention!" Aberra complained.

They wanted to move to the house of Fetene's aunt, but they had already delivered all of their teff flour to their host. Their dabo quolo bread, too, was nearly gone as they had shared it with people here and there. And their village custom strictly forbade them to got to a friend's house empty-handed. So they decided to return home. But it was already Saturday! Meri-Geta, as a church man above sixty, had to observe the weekend sabbaths during which he could not go on a long trip in which the bus covers so many miles and crosses so many rivers. So only against their will they chose to stay with Aberra until Monday.

"I am a lord back in my village, but here I am regarded no better than a flea!" Meri-Geta regretfully complained into the ears of his son-in-law.

Early on Sunday morning the two men were shown to the nearest church, Saint Mary's, which, in fact, their hearts desired most. Meri-Geta was permitted to render service together with the large group of priests. He felt so proud that he did not notice the witty contempt the other priests held over his village eccentricities.

At the other side of Addis, Hailu was coming to like town life more and more. Despite his quick adjustments, he stuck firmly to his religious obligations. So this Sunday he too went to a neighbouring church. He entreated his favourite saints and angels for continual guidance and happy life, just as his "hunters" did on the other side of town.

Back home he ate his breakfast, washed himself and changed his clothes. After lunch he made up his mind to visit Aberra's sick daughter, of whom he learned a week ago. He was informed about her in an unexpected encounter with their uncle who was driving to the provinces on a fortnights working tour.

Now that Hailu was well on his feet, his fear of meeting relatives in town had calmed down. He knew well the residence of his mother's cousin as he had stayed there during his last two trips to Addis.

So he walked to the bus station and caught the number 3. bus. He got off just opposite St. George's, and walked toward Menelik School.

His destination was a rather large compound with a green iron gate. He knocked. A teen-age boy opened it for him. Hailu recognized him and kissed him. But the boy looked and looked at Hailu, trying to identify him. He was sure that he had seen him before somewhere, and so let him in. Hailu asked the boy if his father was present. He pointed to the service quarter, and went back to his duty in the main house.

Aberra hat just eaten his lunch in the company of Meri-Geta, Fetene, and the rest of his family. They were now dragging on with the day chatting and drinking coffee.

Hailu crossed the lawn and approached the house. It was full of people – men and women, young and old, some city-style – talking and laughing softly, others village-style – speaking aloud and laughing hoarsely – but all confined in the mud-plastered room! The door was slightly open, Aberra was sitting on a stool behind it. Meri-Geta and Fetene were on a bench opposite their host. And the rest, mostly women, were farther inside looking after the coffee pot.

Meri-Geta was talking to his wife's cousin. Fetene gazed here and there, sometimes turning to the women and at other times outside through the slightly open door.

Hailu's gentle steps were heard distinctly as he drew closer to the house. At a distance of nine feet, he called out: "People!"

It was yet another time for Fetene to gaze out. He told his host that somebody was calling out. There was a moment of silence, before Aberra got up from his stool. Fetene looked more intently at the man standing outside. Hailu in turn looked at Fetene as Aberra flung the door open to meet him. He recognized Fetene, turned around immediately and scampered toward the gate. The next moment Fetene recognized him and cried: "Hailu!" Meri-Geta's knees strengthened in disbelief and he sprang up from the bench. Fetene pushed Aberra aside and ran after Hailu. Meri-Geta also dashed out to grab his son. There were now three pairs of legs racing after one another with utmost speed and anxiety. Aberra called after Hailu.

Meri-Geta called out at the top of his voice for his son to stop, entreating him in the names of the most honourable saints. So did Fetene. Hailu was determined not to listen. He ran out of the compound gate, so did Fetene, and Meri-Geta. Aberra was still in his compound, walking towards them rather indifferently.

In a moment the trio was on the pavement. Hailu glanced at the busy street and jumped into it. Fetene stood rooted, examining the street. Meri-Geta had neither the mind nor the time to consider the street, and threw himself into it desperately.

Seconds later Hailu found himself safe on the other side; Meri-Geta was in the middle of the street. Fetene saw the traffic lights turning green and cars rushing down. He screamed at Meri-Geta in the street. Several other people screamed at Meri-Geta in the street. It was too late. Brakes screeched ceaselessly! Horns! horns! horns!

Footnotes

1   Yedawratch (Yedewratch): a small village about thirty kilometers to the east of Debre-Markos, the capital of Gojjam Region.
2   Meri-Geta: an important title in the Coptic Church system bearing the responsibility of directing a group of priests in their melody recitations.
3   Gojjam: One of the fourteen regional divisions of Ethiopia mostly in the northwestern part of the country, and almost entirely encircled by the Blue Nile.
4   Upland: refers to cold areas often rugged and uncomfortable to live in.
5   Askuala: a derivation from the Italian word scuola "school"; commonly used by villagers in Northern Ethiopia to refer to the modern school system vis-a-vis the traditional church school system.
6   Quinae academy: a training centre within the traditional church educational system (peculiar to Northern Ethiopia) where one specializes in the art of allegory.
7   Fasting on Wednesdays and Fridays: followers of the Coptic Church fast on Wednesdays and Fridays; probably borrowed from the Jewish sect of Pharisees according to Luke chapter 19.
8   Filseta: a Coptic fasting season held between August 7 and 21 in honor of St. Mary. (It is actually believed that she held fasting during this time of the year.)
9   Tsome-Iyesus: literally translated "the fasting period of Jesus". Although variable, it is generally held between February and April every year for fifty-five consecutive days.
10   Holidays: there are many kinds of holidays observed by followers of the Ethiopian Coptic Church with variable restrictions. Some are weekly holidays (Saturdays and Sundays), others monthly (St. Michael's, St. Mary's, St. Gabriel's, St. George's, etc).
11   ... On these holidays one is not allowed to travel too far, pick firewood, or do any kind of serious work like the Jews.
12   Weaver/tanner: regarded as outcastes by traditional societies.
13   Wancha: cup-like mugs of horns of oxen beautifully shaped by village artificers.
14   Tella: local liquor accompanying meals among villagers.
15   Dabo-quolo: food prepared from a large dough of wheat by way of cutting it into the size of maize seeds and then roasting them. Preferred for their capacity to last for days and weeks without spoil.

CHRISTIAN ISAAC

AS THE DUST SETTLED

Gone were the days when Flomo used to wonder how he could be a 'success' in life. Those days he used to wonder what job to do in order to be able to build a house, buy a car and wear the neatly pressed suits some other people wore. It could take a year or two after finishing school. What really did it matter whether it was one or five years as long as one did not have to wait forever.

"I'll buy myself a small car first then I'll sell it and buy a bigger one after a few months", he used to tell himself.

He dragged his toes in the dust and thought about those days when everyone told him that school was the key to success. He had believed them. At least until he started noticing that the mathematics lessons were becoming a little too complex and that the village 'tycoon' who owned the large store had not even attained grade nine in school.

When his mother had therefore talked about the difficulty she was facing in raising his school fees, he needed little persuasion to play the part of the understanding son.

"Ma, I know how difficult it is for you to pay my fees each semester. I think you should let me stop here and look for a job right away so that I can help you. After all, grade nine is not so bad. Look at Mr. Pasawe ...."

"Flomo, you should not talk like that. Different people have different fortunes in life. You may be like him or you may not. If your Pa were interested in you, he could at least have sent part of the fees but I guess he is too busy with his new wife and baby".

His father and mother had separated while he was still too young to remember. Flomo had grown up without a father in the house and he did not know any differently. His actual father had married another woman und never came to their house. As far as Flomo was concerned, he might as well have germinated spontaneously. He did not know a father and he did not care. The only times infact when his mother mentioned his father was when problems of supporting Flomo became too much for her.

So Flomo had dropped out of school in the ninth grade. He had refused to stay in the village to work on the farm.

"I am going to Monrovia to look for a job. When I get a job, you can then come and see me every month. You won't need to kill yourself on this farm anymore", he had told his mother.

When Flomo said those words two years ago, he sincerely meant every word of it. Today, he dragged his naked toes in the dust of Monrovia city and wondered where his next meal would come from.

Things had not worked out exactly as Flomo had expected. On the day of his arrival in Monrovia, he had found out that Blamo was not living in exactly the kind of house Flomo had envisaged. Blamo, his friend in the city, had often gone back to the village in grand style. He always arrived in a taxi and gave everyone the impression that he was doing quite well for himself.

Blamo occupied a little square area in the basement of an ominous looking building. Above lived a couple of elderly ladies who never failed to shout down abuses and threats if they heard any noise from the basement. The structure of the house made it impossible for the sunlight and fresh air to flow in freely. So to see ones way around, a one hundred watt bulb had to be kept on constantly. Of course this made the room unbearably hot.The mosquitoes that bred in the illsmelling self-made moat around the house always found their way into the little room.

As if the accomodation was not disappointing enough, Flomo discovered that Blamo really had no permanent job. He was a regular car-washer by the stream where the taxis parked to be washed at the end of the day.

"Blamo, how then did you afford those taxi rides to the village?" he had asked.

"Can't you see that I'm well known here? Well, sometimes a friendly taxi driver does me a little favour and I throw in a fortnight of free cleaning".

Then Flomo started to look for a job. It seemed as if no one wanted even an sweeper. Public and private places could not offer him any job. The offices could not even consider anything below Senior High School level. In the homes and shops, the people could not trust him. As one woman clearly put it, "Son, no one is going to employ you to work in his house if you are not recommended by a known and trusted person. How do we know you are not going to make off with our furniture and things while we are at work?"

So Flomo had decided to pair up with Blamo in the car-washing business until he could get something of his own. That was about a year ago. Six months after working with Blamo, he had discovered that his income was too small and uncertain. Sometimes the drivers did not bring their cars at all. Many new service stations with cleaning facilities were springing up and most drivers preferred the quicker and more efficient service even though it cost a few cents extra.

Flomo had then decided to go into money-changing. He could see little boys offering fast money-changing service to taxi drivers at the rate of five cents per dollar. This in effect meant that a driver would be offered ninety-five cents in quarters, dimes and nickels in exchange for a piece of silver dollar. "So", Flomo thought, "if I can do this exchange a hundred times a day, I can earn five dollars a day which is twice as much as I used to get on my best day in the car washing business."

The other children laughed at him because he was bigger than any money-changer they had seen in the business. Flomo was above twelve and they were all much younger. Although this had irritated him at first, he found out that he could punch them into silence. He however encountered another problem he could not easily overcome.

One day, a taxi driver had hurriedly squeezed a coin into his hand and pulled off. It had turned out to be a British Fifty pence piece. The money was quite useless to

Flomo and he realised he did not have much of a capital to start 'throwing' dollars about.

Although he had always tried to be honest, he decided he had to be crooked even if only once to save his stomach. He thought if someone could pass on a useless coin to him, he could also pass that coin on to someone else.

He waited until dusk and after some hesitation, pulled himself together and confidently walked into a little store.

"I want a loaf of bread and a tin of sardines madam," he told the middle-aged woman behind the counter.

"Sixty-five cents", said the woman as she wrapped up the sardines and the bread. Then she held out her hand for the money. Experience had taught her to keep at least a finger on the parcel until she got the money. Flomo placed the money in her hand. Maybe it was the way Flomo placed the money in her hand or maybe her vast experience did not lack intuition but she decided to take a good look at the coin. Flomo did not wait for the result. He left the parcel on the counter and hurried out. He had hardly gone out of ear-shot when the volley started.

"Common irresponsible rogue ... you think you can get away with this kind of thing ... wait till I call the police ... you damned sonofabitch ...", Flomo did not wait to hear the end. He felt hurt. He felt hurt not because he had been unable to fool someone the way the taxi-driver had fooled him. He felt hurt because he had been forced to stoop to cheating.

That was when Flomo decided to give up the money-changing trade and become a newspaper seller. He had found it easy to join the group of boys who sold the DAILY OBSERVER on the streets of Monrovia. As times had grown harder, he had become more resourceful. He had concluded he would get more income if he polished shoes as well. So to kill two birds with one stone, he had chosen a spot under the Ministry of Education building. He put his papers on a box beside him where he sat ready to shine a pair of shoes for a quarter. Gentlemen who came to shine their shoes invariably bought the papers and vice-versa.

This had worked very well until yesterday. As Flomo aimlessly dragged his feet in the dust, he reflected on the unfortunate series of incidents that had brought him to this state of frustration and dejection.

****

As usual, he took his place under the roof of this building that gave shelter and location to so many shoe-shine boys. Business went on as usual until about mid-day. The lunch period started at about mid-day so it was a busy period. As the stream of workers poured out of the buildings around, a man in a blue suit walked towards Flomo. Flomo could not tell whether he wanted to shine his shoes or buy a paper. He probably wanted both because when he got to Flomo, he put his left foot on the shoeshine box and took a copy of the paper to read.

"The paper is thirty-five cents sir", said Flomo as a reminder that the paper was not for free reading. He had been in the newspaper business long enough to know that people who could afford to buy the papers preferred to shamelessly skim through the papers while the sellers waited on them.

If the man heard Flomo, he did not make any comment. He kept on reading. When Flomo had finished shining the left shoe, he put the right shoe on the box. It took at most three minutes to do a good job. At mid-day, one had to be fast to earn more. He gave his box a knock with his brush. This is an understood signal that the work is over and one should be paying and leaving.

The man in the blue suit decided to leave alright. He neatly folded the paper, put it back on the box and started to walk off.

"I say sir, er – em – you've forgotten my pay", said Flomo with a smile. Of course he was convinced the gentleman had forgotten. How could a man in suit and tie and all that cheat a shoe-shine out of a quarter! But to Flomo's surprise, the man retorted, "I didn't ask you to shine my shoes so get lost".

"But sir," protested Flomo, "you put them on the box yourself and ... and ...". He was at a loss for words.

"I am not paying a single cent and that's that." He started to walk away. It was then that Flomo decided he was not going to take any more. He lunged at the man. Hours afterwards, Flomo himself wondered why he had lunged at him. At that moment, he could have done anything to act as an outlet for compressed indignation. As he clawed at the man's coat, he heard him shout "Rogue! Rogue!"

In another minute, two policemen were dragging Flomo off the man. A large crowd had gathered and were jeering at Flomo.

Someone in the crowd threw a rock and it hit Flomo on the side of the head. As the pain surged through him, he felt another kind of pain swelling inside him, "He is the rogue ... not me", he pointed at the man in the suit.

The policemen laughed and the crowd roared with laughter. The man in the blue suit was vigorously trying to wipe the smudges Flomo's hands had left on his suit. "Imagine it Officers! Right in the middle of the day! The rogues in this city are becoming too daring."

****

The gentleman in the blue suit had preferred not to press charges so Flomo had been released. Of course his shoe-shine kit had disappeared and his future as a newspaper boy was at the end. As he dragged his toes in the roadside dust, he observed that the dry season was really back in Liberia. A large dump truck roared by raising a big cloud of dry brown dust. The driver stuck out an angry face and shouted something obscene at Flomo. He could not hear the exact words as they were drowned by the roar of the powerful engines. Flomo however noticed he was too close to the road and moved further to the edge. As the dirty brown dust settled on his head and on the roadside plants, Flomo dwelt for the first time on the difficult life the roadside vegetation was living.

RICHARD ABEKHE MASAGBOR

DENDI

There she sat, with her wrapper packed between her legs, like a spent lone straggler after a tedious country race. The fragile fingers kept weaving the shreds of raffia leaves, crossing and criss-crossing them with an agility that could only derive from unspent youth. She stretched herself and looked around, the beads of sweat forming a ring on her thin forehead.

"But a year ago, my son Gambo left for Kaduna. What an indifference to my aging limbs! Well, perhaps, he is happy there, which is all I care about. Perhaps he is not, but who is to blame? They only come home for the farming season. Let me see now, he left home this time last year, only a year ago. No it is not, but yes, just a year ago. He ought to have come back."

"But Iyaka, don't you understand that our yearly rhythm of life wears out the spirit. See how it happens. The rains come, we work on the farms. The crops grow, we harvest them. Then comes the problem what to do with our time. Some of us sit and drink and drink, travelling from one tunga or wine market to the other. For some, like you, Iyaka, time is killed only by such pastimes as weaving."

"Yes Ishaku, my son, the rains have always come and gone and yet I'm still living. Dendi is a new coinage of your age whereby you escape your ancestral responsibilities."

"But Iyaka, those were your days. The world is changing fast."

"My days indeed, son. The family remains, the tribe isn't dead yet and our tradition is alive. It is the duty of children to look after their parents in the dusk of their lives."

"It is so granny. We neither doubt nor wish to shirk our responsibilities. The problem does not lie there at all. It's all right for the woman to stay and weave mats and brew drinks for the tungas. For the men it's a tempting spell for laziness and sometimes heavy drinking. We all agree that when the season of harvest is over, it is better to go to the city to seek odd jobs and come back with a little money, rather than hang around stuck with the problem of killing time."

"Well, ominous clouds have been forming and yet my son hasn't come back. Each day that passes chops off a huge chunk of my time on this side of eternity. I always deem it proper for young ones to stay not too far off from their aging ones. Look at Ishaku. The other day the one wish he cherished was for his son to be around when the final call came. Alas, when the hour struck he left with an unfulfilled yearning. But look son, I'm frightened of that word Dendi. But although we lose to the city every year, I pray to God it won't happen to me."

"God forbid, Iyaka. Gambo is not of that breed."

"But look, young men have been returning. Is it not yet time for him to be back? Perhaps there is news already."

"Yes, Iyaka! Ali's son arrived yesterday."

"What news do they bring of him, tell me ..."

"They say he is living well and that he's coming back soon."

"That's encouraging isn't it?"

"Yes Iyaka."

"Is there any news as to when we should expect him? He must come home quickly. It's time to prepare the land for maize and groundnut cultivation. Besides, my little debts have piled up, all in the hope that my son will pay them off on his return. Allah, the Almighty, send him, send him back to me."

"But here granny, here is a message for you. It's from your son," said Isa gushingly.

"O welcome, welcome my son, what message have you for an aging mother? Is it true it is from my son? God be praised for it."

"I saw him. He is well. He says he'll be around tomorrow."

"Thanks be to God. Yet I must not be quick at rejoicing" Iyaka mused; "my hopes have been raised over and again only to be shattered. The emptiness of such unfulfilled expectation could make this vacant longing more serious. Are you sure, my son, that he is coming tomorrow?"

"Madam, that is what it looked like yesterday, we went shopping together. I should be surprised if I don't see him tomorrow."

"Thank you my son", said Iyaka, "whose child are you?"

"Yakubu", he replied.

"Yakubu, my cousin? Come nearer, are you the one that was gone some two years ago? You look so well fed. You went with my son. You are back so he must be back too."

Early the next day the house was swept clean in great expectation. Gambo would be around. Iyaka had strolled twice down the Kamuru road. She looked agitated. She had just come back when she heard one of those heralding shouts of "maraba", welcome. She went to the outhouse to see who had arrived and to her surprise and great joy it was Gambo, tall and plump, with a small suit case at his side. He rushed towards the old woman and embraced her. She heaved a sigh of relief and tears of joy ran down her cheeks. He was back at last.

They went to the sitting room and as they do when a retired civil servant comes home, they flocked round him to hear what wonders he had to tell about the city. Of course he had a lot to tell. The sheer marvel of city life. Its bustling, the rush, the traffic and the immense variety of all sorts. Like an experienced story teller, he unfolded his tale living up to his audience's expectations. To the gallivanting young he told of his many escapades, justified by only one fact – to release the pent up feelings of these many months away from home. Well, it did seem quite an adventure and Gambo had come back from "Dendi" the better for it materially. As the evening wore on, the number of visitors began to trickle out till only the family was left.

"And now my son, why did you keep me waiting so long for your return? Had I died without seeing you would you have been happy? Anyway, I decided to wait. I can now take my leave in peace."

"Well mother", retorted Gambo, "we've got to rejoice with the God above that you are still alive. This is no time to talk of departing. The ancestors can bear your absence for some more time yet. I bought you a wrapper, a new "atampa". I also got you a bag of salt." And he began sharing what he had brought.

"This babban riga is for maman; this piece for Shetu."

"Shetu!, Shetu" shouted someone nearby, "come along, your prayers are answered. Only this morning you were thinking how to replace your shreds of loin rags. It's the work of Providence."

Usman's only son had a jumper, and sweets and biscuits were shared among the other children. Everybody seemed to have benefitted somehow.

The rain clouds were beginning to gather. Gambo thought to himself, "I'm a bit late. I have got to start early. My bush has got to be cleared and a house built. What matters now is that the walls are raised to ceiling level."

Early the following morning, girls went down to the stream to fetch water. Breakfast was late – some gruel or porridge in a calabash bowl.

It was Sunday and time to greet old friends. It was also Tunga day at Gidan Bako. In these parts, Sunday was really a resting day. A lot of drinks had been brewed the previous day so that there was a drinking spree for all. The first house Gambo went to was his friend Daudu's.

"Hello and welcome" said Daudu, "you are welcome back home." "Maraba" said an elderly man, "I must congratulate you, for many a young man goes and never returns".

"Thank you" said Gambo.

"Maryarmu, these are my guests, serve them some drinks." With a grin on her face she retorted, "Don't forget that this liquor is the product of my toils and for sale", replied Maryarmu.

"Hi woman, take it easy – here is one naira. Let's have some brukutu. But hold on, let's taste ist first. There's a lot of brewed wine around, we must be selective." She handed him a little brukutu to taste.

"Youwa, it's good drink. Now go on and serve them in that big calabash." And so they drank – the young men seated around the calabash full of brukutu honourably referred to as BKT.

At last someone from the group stood up to speak. It was Sumaila.

"Silence everyone, I want to say a word or two – you my friend, shut up, I wish to speak." There was silence at last.

"Our kind host, we must relax over this bowl of BKT for where poverty is rife men split hairs over little issues. Give me a sip of BKT before I continue ...

"Sit down my friend", said Yusuf, "If you have nothing to say, sit down and take your drink."

"Oga, you are my Oga" said Sumaila, "so I reserve my respect, I just wanted to thank our host and introduce my good friend Gambo who has just come back from the city."

They sang and drank. It was a kind of Communal drinking from the same calabash. When noone was looking Gambo sneaked into one of the rooms where a young lady in her early twenties was sitting. Her name was Hanatu.

"Hello Hanatu!" said Gambo.

"Welcome Gambo. Who told you my name?" asked Hanatu.

"I cared to know and I found out", he replied.

"How was your stay in Kaduna?" asked Hanatu.

"O fine" replied Gambo, "It's a place one needs to visit once in a while. It can be rough and tough but some do make it easily and refuse to come back – sun bi dendi' we say of them."

"And what did you come with" Hanatu added.

Like the gallant one he was: "A lot of things, you've got to see them to believe my story."

Hanatu coyishly added, "I needn't see before I believe."

"To be frank with you, Hanatu" said Gambo, "I came with practically nothing – only a little cash and my worthless self."

"Oh don't say that. You look quite a man when all is considered", said Hanatu.

"And now to other matters," said Gambo, "What are you doing here and what are you to your host?"

"That's quite a mouthful", said Hanatu; "but I'll try to answer them to satisfy a curious man like you. My host is my uncle. I am the type of young lady our people refer to as "Swali". I couldn't cope with my husband so I came back home. Heaven save us from such men."

"It's good meeting, indeed. I'm single and need a partner but, to begin from the beginning, when you said you couldn't cope with your husband, what did you mean?"

"I mean everything you might read into it, even the dogs have times. The pleasant can lose its savour of pleasantness with surfeiting." Patting her on the knee Gambo said, "But you look a handful and by my father, juicy ..."

"Please leave me alone", retorted Hanatu; "I've just been through a sad experience of your masculine behaviour."

"Yes, I believe you, Hanatu" said Gambo, "but remember the swali state is a disrespectful one. All types of suitors come to you. You are neither protected by a husband nor a father, who sees a suitor in every corner."

"You are right" said Hanatu, "that's why you are here sitting with me, I've had enough scorching from men. I need some respite."

"You do indeed, Hanatu" replied Gambo. "Tell me could I come again this evening for candid discussion?"

Hanatu feeling quite excited about it all added, "You may come later in the day, I'll be here waiting."

"But tell me" asked Gambo, "How long ago did you part with your husband?"

"About two months" replied Hanatu.

"And you've been here ever since?" said Gambo. "Come to me. I think I'm in love with you."

"We've only just met" observed Hanatu; "I think lasting relationships are not often based on chance meetings."

"I'll be back" said Gambo, "but give it serious thought." So saying Gambo left to join the others who had been wondering where he had gone. Much money was spent that day in a facade of ostentatious display. The week that followed seemed of the same pattern moving from one village market day to the other. One of the hottest spots was Anza where Gambo got into a scrape.

"Fellow, keep off that Hanatu of a woman. She is my wife" said the young man.

"Hey man" retorted Gambo, "that's no business of mine. If the young lady wishes to attract the attention and admiration of other men, who am I to decline such alluring passes."

"Better be warned my friend" said the young man.

"You'd better be warned", Gambo retorted, "a hundred shilling bride price does not make a lady your chattel. It can never buy her liberty, man."

"Thank you big man, I learn you've just come from the city with a few pounds in your pocket to paint the place red with. I dare say that in the next one or two weeks you will have spent all you came with. Then, only then you will join us. In fact poorer than us."

"Gaskiya", added Yohanna who like a dog on a leash had been itching for a fight. A friend of Gambo's literally dragged him off the scene and he was saved a fight. But they went on drinking in more peaceloving company till late at night when they had to get back home.

Meanwhile the affair between Gambo and Hanatu grew into a serious one. They had accepted to be married. Gambo had sent some of his friends to prepare the way for the bride price discussions. It was not elaborate.

As the lady was a swali, he paid only seventy five shillings. Later that evening, Gambo came home with his wife. It was a quiet affair – there were no ceremonies. It was a simple home coming. The next morning Gambo and Hanatu went to the Tunga – Madauchi it was. They bought a basket of cocoyams, some measures of millet and guinea corn and a few other odd things. Their meals were simple – gruel in the mornings and occasionally gruel or "pete" in the afternoons and tuwo in the evenings. They were a loving couple, at least so it seemed. Considering the circumstances of their meeting, there was much to commend in the harmony and love shown by them. Gambo had a keen sense of humour that would tide him over the difficult times ahead.

The rains had started in earnest. It was hard work all day. This was no time for contracting marriages. He just had to have a wife at the time lest he had no money left later. He had a confidant in the village headmaster.

"Good evening teacher Marcus."

"Good evening Gambo! What's the matter with you? You look so worried."

"O teacher Marcus, my savings are quite depleted now. My wife is beginning to demand too much. She saps the energy out of me each night. This, indeed, is not time to lie late in bed with a woman when the ease of life in the following year hangs on the season's work in the farms. Somehow these women never try to understand."

"Take it easy, Gambo. When you take a wife, you must be prepared for the bitter and the sweet. I think they are quite reasonable if at the onset, a suitor has not given a bloated image of himself."

"But ... but teacher you don't seem to understand me."

"I get you alright. Some other woman had just been complaining that these days her husband comes home so dog tired that at night he cannot fulfil part of his marital obligations. So you see, yours is not a peculiar case."

"Well teacher, I hope you do not make up for the failure of the husbands. In any case, thank you. I must hurry back now."

"Damn it Gamo, all teachers are not the same."

Gambo set out for his house. He was now in a state of abject poverty. This virtually meant that he was now like his predecessors who had gone to town. One thing with this sojourning in the cities was that on their return, these men assumed a new standard of living. When their fortune was on the wane they resorted to desperate measures to plume up that false status of theirs. Gambo moved as if he had the cares of the world on his shoulders. Though his store of food had diminished, his house was just being thatched and, he now had a wife, and as an only son his mother to care for. Somehow, he felt that there was always a way out of these dire straits. He got home resolved on nothing. His meal of tuwo was reday. He ate but not with such relish as he was used to. The wife took note of this and tried to soothe him out of it with encouraging words. Later that evening, Gambo went to bed rather early. He had a sleepless night. He turned over same plans in his mind again and again. He saw no way out of his problems but to set out again. Even in this he was beset with more problems. He needed fares for himself and his wife. He thought of his old mother whose heart would be broken. Gambo just had to stay.

He was up early at the break of day. Gambo went for a walk in the fields. It was a beautiful sight. The lush green in orderly patches, shooting upwards and ever upwards and swaying in the early morning breeze. These were the nursery beds of millet. In a day or two the transplanting would start. Gambo was overjoyed looking at his beds but it seemed that every joy had a dark spot. How would he get his ridges ready for the transplanting of the beautiful millet shoots before him. He needed to call a "gaya", the traditional form of collective labour. For this he needed food and a lot of brukutu.

Returning from his morning walk he talked matters over with his wife and Iyaka. They decided to brew some native liquor – burukutu. Iyaka would provide the millet for it as well as for the food. That arranged, Gambo went round that morning to invite the youths around to his "gaya". He equally sent word to nearby villages like Kan Dutse and Anza. It was early on Friday that the young men arrived on his farm. It was a great occasion. Work began without much ado. It was a sight indeed the way heads and trunks lowered in unison at intervals when ploughing the hoe blades into the earth and flinging the earth onto the ridges. There was much talking initially, but when work started in earnest, all that could be heard was the rhythmic movement of the long hoes and the knocking of the long hoe rods with the cleansing ring. It was so orderly that it portrayed a beauty even in labour. Before noon, one could see an expanse of farmed land. It was now the turn of the women – a trail of carriers bringing loads of uprooted millet shoots for transplanting and others stooping and doing the planting. And so it continued all day long with only a little break for food and drink. At about 4 o'clock that afternoon, they began to disperse after a good day's job. Gambo had every reason to rejoice, for his guest workers had really done their best for him. They had done in one day what most groups would have taken some three or four days to accomplish. He could now relax. The yam ridges came much later. The ground nuts and cotton ridges he could handle in a much more leisurely pace. Millet was the staple food and it was the hub of their farming system.

At this time of the year goats and sheep are usually tethered so that they cause no destruction to the sprouting crops.

Saturday was market day in Zonkwa, some ten miles away. Gambo had a brainwave – a very evil one indeed. He contemplated stealing some of the tethered goats to sell them in Zonkwa. He had observed and taken note that these animals were usually tied up at a little before noon and taken home at sun set. Towards midday on Saturday, he set out with a piece of rope. The time seemed auspicious for his plan because there had just been an unexpected shower so most people were in their houses. There were no overhanging clouds so that everyone seemed taken unawares. He sneaked into that part of the bush, untied the animals and set out with them across Kan Dutse for Zonkwa. The hill was wet and slippery and Gambo couldn't go as fast as he would have liked. The goats seemed stubborn. They bleated and were reluctant to move. He pulled and pulled, yet progress was little. What would he do to avoid being caught red handed. Perhaps no one had seen him yet, but Kan Dutse is a sister village on the route he had chosen, and reports from there spread quickly to his village, Kamuru Dutse. Just at the brow of the hill, he gave a tug at the ropes and this sent the animals running after him, but this was short lived.

A man emerged from a footpath nearby. It was Daudu, a good friend of Iyaka.

"My son, Gambo, where are you going with these animals?" he asked. Gambo, who was now fidgetty tried to turn over in his mind a quick reply but before he could say anything, Daudu had cut it again.

"Don't you hear me, big rascal? Better take a wiser step and go back."

"No, Daudu" said Gambo, "I was sent by the owner. I must get payment of the money he owes me."

"You tell that to the marines! It cannot be, Gambo. It is better you tell credulous lies. You are saying this to a friend of your family. Your mother is old. She awaits a happy death. Will you begrudge her even that? No Gambo! Let it not be said that though he couldn't feed the old woman in her old age, he helped to hurry her to her grave. Posterity will not forgive you, my son."

"Leave me alone, old man!" retorted Gambo; "Whoever told you these animals are stolen?"

"Nobody my son", replied Daudu, "but common sense tells me that people do not normally sell such animals at this time of the year. Look at that goat, for example, it should be giving birth within the next few days. No Gambo, the owner won't forgive you."

"Clear out of here!" said Gambo, "an old man who will not respect his age risks shabby treatment. I say, get out of my way."

"Well goodbye and goodluck, Gambo. A young man who will not heed good counsel risks disgraceful living. All the best in your nefarious enterprise."

He was hardly gone ten yards from the scene when Gambo began to suffer the smarting of his conscience. Yet he decided to go ahead and sell the stolen goats. He had gone just too far to turn back. The market was only a mile and a half away. Some traders who had come in their over-zealousness to rush these things from sellers could be seen about a hundred yards away. Gambo was happy at this because it meant he could dispose of the stolen animals without the ordeal of going into the market. Standing on the sellers ground could expose him to many dangers. There was the danger that the owner of the goats would be around. There was the danger, too, that villagers who knew he'd just come home from Dendi would infer immediately what had happened and cast disdainful glances at him.

Some buyers ran towards him and took hold of the ropes. The bargaining was fast. He made some thirty naira for the lot. What a sigh of relief he heaved. Here was cash at last. He went into the market, bought some provisions and then set out for home. He was happy that only Daudu had seen him, but how was he to be sure?

He came back late in the night. He had stopped in one of the villages along the road to have some drinks. In the meantime, a lot of talking had been going on at Kamuru, about Gambo's behaviour. He had been seen by someone else as he untied the animals from where they were tethered. The owner of the animals had been contacted promptly. Daudu who had been around when the theft was reported, had gone to see for himself hence he had gone straight for Gambo.

"Alas the day, who would have thought that a strong young man should so tarnish the reputation of his family by such infamy as theft. It is the corruption of these times. Men have lost their sense of shame. No one would have expected a son of Iyaka to be capable of such a disgraceful act." Such were the thoughts of Daudu as he thought over the matter, how to break it to Iyaka and what to do to mitigate the penalty and disgrace.

It was now day break. Gambo woke up late. He had no foreboding what lay in store for him. After his breakfast he prepared to go to the farm; somehow there was something peculiar in his looks today. He never seemed to be able to look people straight in the face. This was quite unlike Gambo.

However, things were moving fast. The chief had sent word round to the other elders. By 9 a.m. they were beginning to assemble in the square by the school compound. When they were all assembled, Gambo was sent for. Ishaku, the aggrieved owner of the goats was equally sent for.

"Good morning, Gambo", said the messenger; "You are wanted by the elders in the public square." In a flash it dawned on him that he was wanted for the theft. He felt like following the messenger but on second thoughts he rejected the elders invitation.

"Tell them", said Gambo, "I'm off to my farm ... No, I'm not well."

"Well Gambo", said the messenger, "It's the chief that has sent for you. You may not really know what's all about."

"All right, you go ahead and I'll follow."

When they got to the square, Gambo could see from the men's faces that it was a gathering meant to try him and mete out justice for the theft committed.

"Yes Ishaku", said Adamu, "lay your complaints before the elders."

Ishaku stood up, confident, expecting nothing but instant justice.

"Our most respected elders. I am very grateful that you've handled this case promptly: Yesterday my goats went missing and till this moment of speaking, I have not found them. They were tethered in the Eastern lawn of the village and could not, therefore, have wandered and got lost. Yesterday, coincidentally, Gambo was seen leading what looked like my goats to Zonkwa. For this, our respected elders, I would like something done to retrieve my missing animals. I want them back."

To this address, Gambo, not waiting to be called upon retorted with utmost despatch, "It's a most blatant lie."

"Keep quiet Gambo, wait till you are called upon," said Adamu; "you shall have your turn." Turning to Ishaku, he said "my son, you've made your case very well and in the politest manner as if you were a lawyer. You have not come out directly to accuse anyone. Can you substantiate what you've said with evidence from witnesses?"

"Yes, of course!" he replied; "Peter son of Baran, can bear me out. Besides, there was an old man who asked me to keep calm and promised to get them restored to me immediately. It seems that his entreaties fell on deaf ears."

With this, it seemed that Gambo was completely disarmed. Here were witnesses whose integrity in the community were beyond any doubt. They were known to condone no injustice or dishonesty. They always spoke the truth, regardless of whose horse was gored.

An elder called out in a rather stentorian voice "Call one of the witnesses please, rather than promote an atmosphere of argument and denial. We must show openness and impartiality!" The gathering seemed to be in favour of this. So Daudu was called in. Without mincing his words, he narrated what had chanced the previous day – how on Ishaku's report he had chased Gambo through the paths till he had caught up with him at Kan Dutse, leading the goats to the market. He narrated his exchanges with Gambo and what he had heard so far – that Gambo had returned from the market without the goats. He remarked that the guilt was not difficult to establish and that in the interest of the village harmony he had this plea to make:

"Fellow elders, I know this is a grevious offence, but let's consider that this man has just come back home, married one of our daughters and set up a house of his own. Besides, our elderly woman Iyaka, will be broken hearted if she hears anything about it. It's already bad enough the way it is. When we come to think about it the fault does not lie with Gambo alone. It is in our system. It is in our government. Our system keeps driving our youths to the cities where they learn bad habits and practices and false living. Our traditional system seems to be out of touch with the needs of the times. Let us therefore be mild with Gambo and temper justice with leniency. Before I take my seat may I ask Gambo one question, only one question? Now my son Gambo, I hope the old man is now a self respecting one. What do you have to tell us?" He seemed tongue tied looking like a sheep sent before its shearers.

"I am sorry!" he murmured indistinctly, "I was tempted and the evil aspect got the better of me. It is my fault not to have resisted the urge."

"Well," said the chief, "it's a simple case. He does admit. Let us bemild with him. I know your responsibilites and therefore, your predicament. You shall restore those beasts or the cash – whichever is more acceptable to him. As for you, you've got to bear some degree of loss. We sympathise with you. View it this way that in similar straits we might be tempted to take desperate measures."

"My respectable elders, I am content with your judgement. Knowing his lot, I forgive him. Thank you immensely. He may not know it, his late father was a friend of my father and in respect of the dead, I choose not to treat him as shabbily as he has treated med. The problem with our young men is that they never seek advice. I shall be as lenient as ever. Gambo shall pay back during the grain harvest, four bags of millet."

Gambo raised his eyes in astonishment. It was like being let off the hook.

Ishaku then went on to explain that all he had asked for was the refund of the money for which the goats were sold for he had got his goats back. Alhaji Maduki of Anza had brought them on recognising them as his.

Hearing this Gambo knelt down and thanked him and pleaded to be forgiven. He was disgraced. His problems were solved for the moment, but at what cost indeed!

ODUN BALOGUN

MOTHER AND SON

"No Sweetness Here" – (Ama Atta Aidoo)

The closer the end of school year, the broader the smile the mother perceived on the face of life. Life rarely smiled at her. In fact, she had known only hardships all her days.

It all began when her loving parents forced her into an early marriage with a man she didn't love. To make matters worse, her husband wielded sufficient local influence to thwart her two successive attempts to divorce him. There was nothing else she could do. Some people in her situation attempted suicide, but life was too precious for her to try that. She resigned and started bearing him children. Just like his four other wives.

Thirty-five years have passed. And now for the first time life was a bosom friend, all smiles, patting her lovingly on the shoulder and warming her heart with the good news. In three months her eldest son would be completing his studies in a university in some strange, distant land and would be returning home.

Six years he had been away. And six years she had waited anxiously, praying day and night to her ancestors, the household gods, and the Almighty above, to watch over him. And now he was due to come home to her! How good life is! One only needs to know how to be patient when it is hard.

The mother certainly knew how to be patient. And her patience was tried a great deal. When both her parents died in their mid-forties, she was left alone in the world. No brothers, no sisters. Her husband was just her husband. Nothing more. If he had loved her, if he had made her his favourite wife, perhaps she might have overcome her initial objections. But she gave birth to a daughter with her heart still revolting against him. She was actually contemplating a third attempt to divorce when her first son arrived. She resigned completely.

In a polygamous family where your husband, even when he wished, did not possess the means to provide for you and your children, a son was the greatest blessing you could expect. He was your future protection, your bread winner and the consolation of your old age.

But a son was not only a blessing. At least not now anymore. When she was young, it was all so simple. You were born to a farmer to be a farmer. The more children there were, the more hands to help on the farm. You could marry as many wives as you wished, and have as many children as survived childhood. Today it is all different. You have to educate your children. Education is now the only sure way to economic and social survival. And she was determined to survive. So she sent her son to school.

She spared nothing. But it soon reached the stage when she could no longer change the children's clothes at Chirstmas, much less her own. She went into debts. All the same, failure was imminent. The husband could bear it no longer. He called his elderly sons, and said to them:

"Look, this woman has tried enough. Her son too is bright. We must help them. After all, if they make it, they'll remember us."

But all their help amounted to little, and the boy would still have dropped out of secondary school, had not the local Catholic Teachers' Association offered a helping hand.

The mother smiled for the first time in many years that day when her son completed his secondary education. Eight months later, when she was thinking her son was only eighty miles away at his teaching post, she suddenly received a telegram from the capital. It was her son informing her that he was leaving that day on a government scholarship for some strange, distant land.

The news spread like wild fire. The local people rejoiced with her, were proud of her, and showered her with compliments. She was happy but embarrassed by all the welldeserved praises. Life was suddenly smiling on her. Really broadly. They say scholarships were not easy to get, and the foreign ones less so.

Her only worry was for his protection in that unknown and unheard of land. She also feared the evil eye on her other children, and on herself.

And now it has all come too true. Some malicious person has secretly left an evil medicine in some place for her unsuspecting foot. A dull persistent pain began to torment her in her right foot. She ran up and down for a cure. It would not go away. She had a letter written to her son about it. As she had known beforehand, her sceptical son denied it had anything to do with witchcraft. He suggested a natural cause, advised a practical step, and sent some means. The pain persisted.

Four yours had passed since he had left home. His former classmates who attended the local Universities had obtained their first degrees and had all settled down and started providing for their next of kin. That, of course, was the purpose of education: to yield financial returns. What good was it otherwise?

The mother became restless for her son. If he were home, he would know a way to cure her foot. The permanent pain was sapping her energy. She tired very easily, and she could no longer work as much as she used to do. Suddenly she realized that she was already older than when her parents died. A certain kind of fear gripped her. If only her son would come home as soon as possible.

To make matters worse, people began to ask embarrassing questions as to when her son was expected back. She hated to answer such questions. Who could tell? People might begin to say about that she was boasting that her son was doing something more serious than their sons. If only her son would come home soon.

But he did not. It did not depend on him. So he had written. That was the order of things in that strange land. One has to spend six years. It was not for nothing that the thought of him going so far away had worried her in the beginning.

But she would wait two more years. She had waited four already. Waiting for a better life had always been her lot. She was patient. She would be patient some more. What were two years to the fifty and more years she had waited already?

Now didn't she say that six years would finally come to an end? Just look, only three months are left. Everything says there are only three months to wait.

The burning midday sun pleads gently with her: "Tolerate me a little bit more," it says. "Your son will soon be protecting you from my heat."

The moon, smiling broadly, teases her good-naturedly: "Sharpen your imagination, mother, for soon you'll have all the time to stay out late and dream under my caressing light. There'll no longer be any need to hurry early to your hard mud bed for fear of waking late in the morning for work."

Young twigs bend mischieviously across her paths to the plots and plead with childish simplicity: "Let's caress your legs, mother, a little more lingeringly, for your son will soon be claiming you from us."

Everything was kind and sweet to her. Even her foot didn't hurt her as much. The days swiftly went by. She hid her tumultously radiant inner life from outsiders while she secretly and intricately planned a welcome for her son. In the middle of the last month she left the farm for town. Some twenty miles away.

At the end of the month, instead of her son, a letter arrived. Perhaps he was regretting he had to delay a week. No, not a week, not a month, not even a year, but three years! Would they kindly reread the letter to her? No, there was no mistake. Another three years! No, it couldn't be. The family council agreed that it couldn't possibly be. He was to be immediately written to and told to come home at once.

The mother was still walking about dazed when two days later another letter arrived. Especially for her. Unlike the aerogramme letter to the whole family, this was in an envelope. Pages and pages. They had been written a whole week earlier than the family aerogramme, yet the aerogramme had arrived faster. How could she have failed to realize that the other letter was not meant for her? How could she have allowed herself to be persuaded even for a moment that her son would ever behave selfishly? Some had even gone so far as to suggest that it was some woman holding him prisoner. How little they knew of her son!

She had the letter reread to her. This was him for sure. Her son. Full of love and consideration. Detailed explanations of everything, with the pros and cons clearly stated. He was going to write the family in a week or so, but that would be merely a formality. His decision would depend solely on what she thought. He knew exactly what he was asking for, and would she honestly let him know whether or not she could stand another three years?

Of course, she could. Let them write and tell him she definitely could. After all, what did she want for herself? She even felt ashamed of her former impatience. Wasn't her real concern for her children and grandchildren, and were not his plans in the best interest of these? Surely, she could wait.

Again the local people were inquisitive to the point of embarrassment. Then suddenly, as if by general agreement, they stopped mentioning his name in their conversations any time she joined their company. She knew they were being delicate in their concern for her. But what right had they to treat her son that way? As if he was some queer disease, as if he was some person to be ashamed of. And what was most disturbing, they were treating him with that silent scorn reserved for only those who die young.

Dying young, God forbid, is of course awfully shameful. What right has anyone to die young? Giving birth to you was a responsibility your parents fulfilled both to their own parents and to you. In turn you are duty bound to live to old age, and to give birth to others. That is how life is meant to be. Dying young is shirking one's responsibilities, it's cheating. Cheats are to be scorned. To even mention their names in conversations is to do them honour. But her son was not a cheat.

The mother did not at all like what was happening. Yet she dared not protest. She wanted to assert that her son had done nothing wrong, but how dare she bring up her own son in a conversation of this type when she had not been asked? Who would stand such a breach of propriety? When she could no longer bear it, she left town and went to the farm. Twenty miles away.

A year passed. Two more to wait. The mother was again on the farm. This time as a necessity, rather than due to shame. She was weeding. She looked up at the sky to see if it was time to eat lunch. It was yet early. The sun was only just approaching the center of the sky. She bent down and resumed her work.

Her stomach kept arguing with her, but one must not trust it. The sun was more reliable. After a while she raised herself up again to check the position of the sun. Suddenly, everything went blank. She staggered, struggling to maintain her balance. She made it to a tree and leaned on its trunk. The dizziness following her fainting spell lasted a little while more, and then was replaced by fear.

She was not afraid for herself. She wanted nothing, and was in absolute peace with herself. She could die now happily, knowing her children and grandchildren would be provided for when her son returned. Her fear was for him. In his last letter he had pleaded: "Mother, please take care of yourself. You know there is nothing that would give me more happiness, than to be able to show my appreciation for all you suffered on my account ..."

Even in this she wished not to fail him. But the uncertainty of it all made her feel helpless. She gripped the trunk of the tree she was leaning on in desperation, wishing painfully she could dictate her own terms to nature. But the hard bark of the tree scratched her brutally, as if purposely pushing her away. The mother recoiled in anger. As she did so, she cast a suspicious glance upwards to make sure a treacherous dry branch was not at that moment threatening to crash down on her. The branches of that tree, and those of all other trees around, were motionless. Nature looked on as if unconcerned. As if she was not there. She poignantly wished she could hug her son just then.

II

"Ah, no! The thought I cannot bear,
And if God please my life to spare
I hope I shall reward they care,
My mother." (Ann Taylor).

After reading the letter, the son lost desire for everything. Extremely disturbed, he climbed into his bed in order to give reign to his thoughts. In case he fell asleep, he took the precaution to set the alarm clock.

Two hours later the son jumped into a half sitting position at the sudden ringing of the alarm. Throwing his weight on his right elbow, he leaned sideways, his left hand mechanically reaching for the clock on a chest drawer. At the same time, he tried to wake.

But a frightening awareness suddenly crashed into his consciousness. He was neither asleep nor awake. Worse still, he felt he existed in two separate parts, with no knowledge of where his real self was located.

Nothing at all was real except for a vague, vast spaciousness where he seemed to be timelessly hanging. He felt an unbearable incompleteness. He wanted desperately to be complete. He struggled for his own unity, fearing and wondering where he was, what was happening, if he was dreaming, if he would ever wake again. An eternity of incompleteness, of uncertainty, of fear ...

Suddenly he felt that he was there again, united, complete. His weight was resting on his right elbow, his left index finger was still pressing down the knob of the clock. It was hardly sixteen seconds since hearing the first alarm signals. He was in a half sitting position, with the sheets covering half his body. He jumped quickly out of bed, afraid of a repetition of this frightening experience. Now awake, he sank into an armchair. He was perspiring, and his heart was beating rapidly.

He tried to understand what had just happened, but comprehended nothing. Still afraid, he muttered: "Oh God, I hope nothing happens to me."

That precisely was the thing. Nothing must happen to him. How could it? When he did not belong to himself? When he was only his own keeper?

Many times before he had wished he were his own master, that he could live and die as it pleased him. But that was wishful thinking. He knew too that for the foreseeable future he would have to watch carefully over his charge, taking no risks, exposing it to no danger. He would have to avoid all adventures in a country where only the adventurous foreigner could be happy. All adventures involved some risks. Every child knew that. And he dared not take any risk.

He was strict over his charge. No going out alone late at night. No visiting noisy pubs where fights could break out. Always swallow insults to avoid a brawl. These and many more. And, of course, the heart too must be tamed. Whoever heard that a keeper married off his charge against the expressed wishes of the owners?

Only the other day he had met a girl. What a girl! All day long his heart had pumped and thumped. It seemed to him that his happiness was smiling on him. All he had to do to find out was to take the phone and arrange a date. If he was not rejected outright, then an involved relationship might develop. The latter was even worse than the former, being doomed from the very beginning. The experience was always most painful. No, he remained a good keeper and did not take even that risk.

And that was exactly what anybody in his position would do. The opposite could be possible only if he were not his mother's son, only if the memory of twenty-eight years of mutual selfless love between mother and son were erased off his consciousness.

And that was impossible. Nothing could ever remove the impressions of that December afternoon twenty-two years ago, when he suddenly woke up from the slumber of a careless childhood and grew up all in a day.

Then he was sitting in the shade under a tree, taking care of his nine-month-old sister. His mother was weeding a yam plot, the merciless midday sun piercing her back with millions of hazy arrows.

She had been singing for quite a while. At first her voice easily scaled the undulations of the road. Then the undulations gave way to little hillocks, which were in turn replaced by massive hills that were followed by insurmountable, slippery, rocky mountains. The son trailed along, observing the painful climb. Then it reached a point when it seemed his six-year-old heart would break seeing the agony of the effort. He cried out in a compassionate, mournful entreaty:
"Please, mother, do not cry anymore."

And he himself started crying.

Until then it never occurred to the mother that she was crying. She rubbed her cheeks and was surprised to find her bare arms wet with tears. She immediately abandoned her hoe, wiped her face clean of tears, and hurried to her crying son, when it was she herself who needed consoling.

"You see, I'm not crying. Who tells you I'm crying? I was only singing," she said, caressing his head and pressing him close to her high thigh.

No more words passed between them, but similar thoughts revolved in their minds.

He had failed the year-end school examination that December. His father concluded he was a dullard and decided not to waste any money on him. Until then the boy had not known what school meant. He had taken it for a place to play and be merry. And indeed he was sent there when he was only approaching his fifth year, partly because he was a fast growing child, but more because he was an unbearably stubborn, mischievious imp at home. Since the average age of his class was seven, some instinct told the child that school was only a way of getting rid of him. So he got zero on every sum and failed all examinations, and was not the least bothered. But now his father had proved to him that his instinct was all wrong. The mother didn't think so. She believed the child ought to be given another chance.

The mother and father had quarrelled over something shortly after that. Perhaps it was also because of this that the father had detained his older sister at home when their mother needed her help on the farm.

The son knew that his mother was his only hope of returning to school.

95

"Mother, please say you'll send me back to school," he pleaded later when they were in their way to the hut.

He looked up at her with an expression of pain. "I will, I will my son, my own heart. Only promise me you'll never fail again."

Both sides kept their promises. A miracle happened in the case of the boy. Not only did he never fail afterwards, but was always one of the best two in class. The mother lived only for her promise. She went half naked, she went half starved; she sacrificed her health fulfilling this promise.

All along the son watched the mother climb the undulations, the hillocks, the massive hills, and the insurmountable, slippery, rocky mountains on the path of her promise. And all unknown to himself his heart grew larger and larger until a bottomless well of love for her, his brothers and sisters was sunk forever deep in his heart. He burned with the steady fire of this boundless love, and lived with a single purpose before him: to make it in life, comfort his mother's old age, and do for his brothers and sisters what their mother had done for him.

This was a heavy responsibility, the details of which had the effect of stripping him clean of his individual freedom, of making him, a twenty-eight-year-old man, not his own master, but only his own keeper. And as a good keeper he was always in constant fear and anxiety lest he should fail in his duties both to his charge and to the owners.

He could, of course, deny his charge, liberate himself and be the sole master of his life. But then would he be able to erase the memory of a dedicated mother? Would he be able to ...

What's the use of enumerating the impossible? Besides, he was only too well aware that life had meaning for him only because these responsibilities existed. His goal, his constant striving constituted his happiness. Thus, however difficult it was, however much he complained, he was always vaguely aware of some basic happiness.

Now it was all different. He had known what it meant to be in dire need for money, what it meant to be hungry, to be lonely. But all these were nothing compared to the feelings that now dominated him.

He reached for the letter from under the alarm clock and once more read his youngest brother's girlish handwriting:

"Mother is sick. The worst may happen any moment. You had better come home, although she said ..."

Each word struck terror into his heart. As if he was hearing the deliberate voice of the judge pronounce:

"You are a murderer. Your guilt has been proved beyond reasonable doubts. You are condemned to ..."

"But I had not meant to," he defended. He did not believe himself.

"She said she could wait," he tried to reassure himself.

"But you knew better," someone countered. That was the truth but he still waved his last argument, hoping for a miracle.

"I knew all right, but I was counting on her psychological preparedness to do the trick. Besides, it was in the best interest of all the family that I got my higher degree."

"The psychology worked all right, and it is surely in her best interest," someone mocked.

As if to counter this mocking he grabbed the letter again and began to read.

"Mother is sick ..."

"She is only sick," he emphasized as if trying to convince someone. It didn't work.

He remembered fifteen years ago in his last year in Primary School when a letter of this type had been dictated to him. Then the son of the woman concerned, an apprentice to a watch repairer, was only about two hundred miles away.

Villagers are wise. Why cause an unnecessary pain, anyway, when the worst has already happened? A little hope left in the doom might to the trick. Mother is only sick.

The room could no longer contain him. He started walking up and down the sidewalk on his street. The neighbours saw him once, twice, thrice ... An unusual exercise. They grew suspicious. One fellow came out to check if the doors of his car were properly locked. Night fell. Neighbours' dogs barked at regular intervals all through the night. When they were driving to work in the morning the neighbours saw him dressed exactly as yesterday and walking in the same way. He said not a word. He did not answer greetings either. When the dogs began to bark the second night, the neighbour with the car called the police.

FUNSO AIYEJINA

HIS EXCELLENCY'S VISIT

The final year class of Uzoto Grammar School, Uzoto, rose as Mr. Akim, the History teacher and Vice-Principal, entered the classroom.

"Good morning, Sir," the class chorused.

"Good morning. You may sit down."

They sat down and Mr. Akim drew his belted pair of trousers up his bulging stomach, fell into the teacher's chair behind the big oak table and relaxed his body muscles. He always enjoyed sitting on that platform before the students who looked, to him, like subjects with him as their ruler. They were the other parts of the sentence and he the verb. "What is a sentence without a verb? Verbiage," he always joked. He cleared his Sunday-school-pastor's voice and the students poised their writing hands in readiness for the words of wisdom which would soon issue forth from Mr. Akim, "the Doctor". That was their own little joke behind Mr. Akim's back. They called him "the Doctor", among themselves, because of his love of flowery language and "jaw-breaking" words which often sent them scampering for their Michael West dictionaries. They had to master such words for reproduction in their examinations since he always gave the highest marks to those who reproduced his exact words, phrases and sentences. At the bottom of such answer scripts he would scream an "Excellent!" in bold red letters.

"Where did we stop last week?"

"The first ten years of the Republic of ..."

"Yes, yes," Mr. Akim agreed before Tinu could finish her sentence.

"Today," he continued after locating that point in his neatly written lecture notes, "we shall take a look at the collapse of the First Republic. During our last lesson, we discussed the corrupt and decadent oligarchy which had the singular misfortune of ruling the First Republic. They plundered right, left and centre. They reaped where they did not sow. They ran the affairs of the nation like a band of executive thieves ..."

"Did you hear that?" whispered John, the class bully, to Tinu.

"Hear what?" howled Tinu, angered by the fact that John had distracted her and made her miss Mr. Akim's next words.

"Executive Thieves – E. T.," answered John as if he did not hear the anger in Tinu's voice.

"Idiot, stand up!"

Tinu froze in her seat as Mr. Akim's electrifying command crashed through her ears. Her heart missed a beat, regained its function and doubled its normal tempo. She feared that the water gathering in her bladder would let go the moment she attempted to stand up. She brought her thighs together and prayed that her bladder would not disgrace her before the many boys in the class whose amorous advances she had sunned.

"Did ou hear me?" shouted Mr. Akim. "I asked you to stand up, John."

"Me Sir?" asked John with his most innocent voice inflection, pretending to have been unfairly picked upon.

"Yes, you sir," mimicked Mr. Akim.

John got up fast, knowing that it was no use arguing with Mr. Akim, except, of course, if he wanted to spend the rest of the week cutting grass under the scorching sun.

"I have told you times without number not to cause any disturbance whenever I am in this class. Some of you forget that I have children who are older and more intelligent than you." The last bit being for the benefit of the whole class.

And so what? thought John.

Tinu was still breathing heavily, wondering how Mr. Akim had known that it was John and not herself who was the actual culprit. She breathed a sigh of relief as the heat between her thighs started to peter cut.

"Where was I?" asked Mr. Akim. "Let someone read out the last sentence".

"... they ran the country like a bang of executive thieves ..."

"Alright," interrupted Mr. Akim before the eager voice could finish the sentence, "I said band, not bang."

The class laughed. Mr. Akim looked through his lecture notes and found the point where he had broken off.

"The result," he continued, "was eventual bankruptcy – financial and moral bankruptcy."

"Tinu did you hear that big word? Bankruptcy! I hope you can spell it." John was bent on distracting his mates since he could not write standing up. But this time, he had again chosen the wrong moment to cause a distraction, for at that very moment Mr. Akim paused for breath and the silence which followed amplified the tail end of John's whisper.

"Excuse me, Sir," shouted John, shooting up his left hand, trying to act to cover up his crime.

"I have told you not to ask questions until I have finished teaching. Have I finished? Have I said 'any questions'?"

"No, Sir." But I can't wait till you finish, I need a legitimate interruption to save me from your rage, thought John as he put on an apologetic demeanour.

"Okay, John, what is the matter?"

John grinned and suppressed the self-congratulatory smile he so badly wanted to flash to his friends.

"Oligarchy, Sir," announced John.

"What about it," asked Mr. Akim.

"The meaning, Sir."

"My friend," shoutet Mr. Akim, "this is not an English language class. This is a history class. Use your dictionary. Do you understand me?"

"Yes, Sir." John sat down acting as if he had only got up to ask the question.

"Anyway, obligarchy means a government by a few," Mr. Akim volunteered.

"But Sir, you told us that there were party officials, ministers representing all the ..."

"Yes, but crucial decisions were taken by only a handful of people who belonged to the party caucus – the party's inner-circle."

A few glances were exchanged across the classroom between those students who belonged to the circle of friends which had formed around the Senior Prefect of the school. They had styled themselves the Inner-Circle or IC for short.

"Excuse me, Sir," a hand went up from the back row.

"That's enough. Reserve your questions for the revision week." Mr. Akim resumed his dictation poise and proceeded with his lecture. "I was talking about the decadence of the First Republic. The list of the leaders' crimes became endless, their inequities piled up and threatened to knock off the sky and the stench of the debris of their sins and malpractices spread like a plague all over the land. The few public spirited social critics who dared to call a spade a spade were clamped into preventive custody, 'in their own interest'."

"One fateful morning, God, after his customary long wait, decreed that enough was enough. And as he had delivered the Israelites from the hands of Herod, he delivered the oppressed and silent majority from the evil clutches of our political tormentors. We woke up to hear sweet new songs and the sweet voices of new leaders. Members of the armed forces, seeing that things had gone from bad to worse, seized power in a coup. That singular act by men who had the love of this nation at heart, had altered the course of our history; it ushered in a new dawn: the era of the benevolent men in uniform. It was on a ..."

There was an interrupting knock on the open class-room door and the school messenger, fourth cousin to the Principal of the school, stood there fidgeting, waiting for Mr. Akim's permission to enter and deliver the message from the Principal. Mr. Akim beckoned him inside.

"Oga say make you come for office quick quick, sah"

"Tell him that I am coming directly."

"Yes, sah."

"Sorry, class," he apologised as he started for the door, "we shall continue with the saga of the Military in Politics in our next class."

As Mr. Akim left to go, John followed behind him at a safe distance and his classmates knew what he was up to. It was another one of his favourite pastimes: he would go and hide behind one of the windows in the Principal's office and eavesdrop on his conversations which he would promptly relay to the class soon after. As they waited for John, the class broke into smaller units and gossiped about various issues and events and, in no time, the noise in the room was loud enough to rival that of Oyingbo market.

"Will you keep quiet and stop speaking Pidgin!" shoutet the Class Prefect at no particular group. "Don't you known that vernacular speaking is forbidden in class?".

"Pidgin is not vernacular," retorted Tinu. "You no dey see Pidgin for Chinua Achebe novel? Abi you never read "Man of the People" self?"

"Because Chinua Achebe writes Pidgin in his novel does not mean that Pidgin is not a vernacular, my dear clever lady. You want to tell me say because Wole Soyinka used some Yoruba words in "The Lion and the Jewel", Yoruba is not a vernacular?"

"Look at you saying ,say because' instead of ,that because'. You are speaking Pidgin too!" Tinu was bent, as usual, on deflating the Class Prefect.

The class roared with laughter, gleefully jubilating at the fact that the Class Prefect had been saught violating the very law he wanted to enforce.

"Will you all sharrup!"

The class froze. They could recognize that voice from any distance and in any crowd. They glued their eyes on the doorway in trepidation, expecting the huge frame of their Principal to materialize with a cane in one hand and a lighted cigarette in the other. But instead of the Principal, John walked in with a mischievious smile stamped on his face. The class sighed and, though angry at his antics, laughed at having been successfully fooled by John again. It was yet another one of his pastimes: mimicry. He had tried it on the class a number of times. He would slip out of the class whenever there was a commotion and return to the door mimicking one teacher or the other. After a few instances of this, the class stopped obeying hushing voices since they were sure that they would invariably turn out to belong to John's arsenal of voices. But they had neglected a hushing voice two weeks before and it had turned out to be the Principal's. They spent the rest of that day cutting the bush in the area behind the Principal's house which his wife had earmarked for the planting of late maize. John had escaped that punishment, of course. He had claimed that he had left the class to study in the school's reading room when his mates' noise had become a source of distraction to him. John knew the Principal would not bother to cross-check with the reading room attendant.

"John, but you promised not to frighten us again," remonstrated Tinu as soon as the noise had died down.

"I am sorry," pleaded John. "I needed your attention and that was the easiest way of getting it. Can you guess why the Principal wanted to see the Vice-Principal?"

"Why?" asked several voices.

"Guess."

"Tell us."

"Please."

"H.E. is coming to visit us, here in this village."

"Who is H.E.?"

"If E.T. is Executive Thieves, H.E. will be Higher Executive Thieves."

"Kalu, you are a dunce. If it meant Higher Executive Thieves the abbreviations would have been H.E.T."

"Your are the ninicompoop, Jadi. Don't you realise that people call them H.E. instead of H.E.T. so that they would not know that they are being called thieves?"

"Kalu, you are wrong. Do you think that you can just take the Doctor's use of

Executive Thieves to describe the First Republic and apply it to the governments which came after?"

"John, na you sabi. But as far as I, Kalu, is concerned, what is good for the goose should be good for the gander."

"Stop wasting time John. It will soon be time for our Maths class. Tell us what H.E. means."

John proceeded to unfold the poster he had been holding behind his back and held it up to reveal the picture of the region's Military Prefect. Everybody in the region knew that picture like they knew their names. It hung on all public buildings, parks, stadia and offices. You could hardly cover a hundred yards through any part of any town, no matter how small, without seeing one of these pictures. It had become the regional symbol of the spirit of the revolution. One even hung in the boys' latrine; thanks to John.

"He is H.E.," volunteered John. "His Excellency".

The rays of light which came through the window nearest to John fell on the picture of His Excellency, the Military Prefect. The glow on the medals and brass buttons dazzled the admiring eyes of the students.

Mr. Akim took full charge of the preparations for welcoming His Excellency. He was worried at the short notice but he was determined to make His Excellency's visit something that would go down in the villagers' memory as a huge success.

"Today is Thursday and H.E. comes on Monday." Mr. Akim wondered how best to utilize the days between Thursday und Monday and grumbled at the fact that they had not been informed earlier so that they could plan an unprecedented reception for His Excellency.

"What do we need to do by way of preparation?" asked the Principal who always left Mr. Akim to handle such logistical aspects of projects.

"Let's cancel classes for the rest of the week so that the students can start on a massive clean up of the school premises," suggested Mr. Akim. "Between today and Sunday, they should be able to cut the grass on the lawns, line the paths with flags and white-washed stones and have their uniforms washed and ironed."

"We could spend Sunday rehearsing them for His Excellency's reception," added the Principal who already began to see himself at the centre of Mr. Akim's plans. "I shall cancel the Sunday worship so that they can practice throughout the day. You know, we just must make an impression on him. You can never tell what that man has up his sleeves; he might be shopping around for another Commissioner of Education or a Chairman for a prospective Local Government area."

"Very true," agreed Mr. Akim, his eyes full of excitement.

Mr. Akim paused to reflect on the significance of his being named the Chairman of a Local Government Council. He would automatically become the most powerful son-of-the-soil in the village. Was he not already very powerful as the Chairman of the local Uzoto Descendants' Union? Second only to the village Head, who, thank God, could neither read nor write. If only he could be appointed to head a local council, he would definitely become more important than the village head. He imagined himself, standing, erect and regal in the regalia of a chief, before the council members, drowning them in words of wisdom from ancient books of knowledge. A welcome speech for H.E.! He must go at once to inform the village head of the visit and to volunteer to write a welcome speech to be read and presented to H.E. He would put all those oratory tricks he had accumulated from the numerous "How to ..." books into use and make an everlasting impression on both those who could understand English, as well as those illiterates who did not know the difference between "go" and "come". He would gesticulate to stress points and whisper to make his audience listen in silence: silence, the weapon for arresting and carrying an audience along with the speaker.

"Why are you so quiet, Mr. Akim?" asked the Principal, startling him out of his day-dream.

"I was thinking of other possible plans for the reception of H.E.," answered Mr. Akim.

Mr. Akim announced that he would go and inform the village Head of the impending visit of H.E. so that the villagers might complement the school's welcoming activities.

"That is very thoughtful of you," commended the Principal. "Give my regards to him and tell him I will call on him as soon as I have a minute to spare."

"I shall."

"By the way, remember also, to summon a staff meeting for this afternoon so that we can inform the other members of staff of His Excellency's visit."

Once out of the school compound and on the major road leading into the village, Mr. Akim stepped on the accelerator of his battered 304. The car responded, surprisingly gathering speed as it headed for the palace. It was as if the good news of H.E.'s visit had pepped up the car as much as it had its owner.

"You definitely will not die young," exclaimed the village Head as Mr. Akim walked into his reception room. "I was just about to send the Court Messenger to go and call you."

"Long live Your Highness; may your shoes last long under your soles, may your crown sit long on your head."

"Sit down Mr. Akim, ,the Teecher'."

Mr. Akim, popularly known to the villagers as ,the Teecher' sat on the indicated stool, facing the village Head.

"A letter has just been brought to me from the District Officer and I wanted you to come and read it in case it needed urgent attention. You know that since my children went back to their boarding schools, there has been nobody in the palace to read my letters for me."

Striking an all-knowing pose, the Teecher suggested that he could guess what was in the letter.

"You mean you already know what is inside this letter even before you open it? You book-people never cease to amaze me. Is it good news?"

"His Excellency, the Military Prefect of this region is coming to visit us this Monday coming," the Teacher announced as he took the letter from the village head. In order to be absolutely sure, he opened the letter. It was exactly the same as the one the school had received.

"The Military Prefect is coming to visit us? Here in this village!"

"Yes, your highness."

"This is too good to be true. Wait until I tell my chiefs. And all those who said my reign will not be successful, ask them for me, if a recruit visited this village during the reign of their fathers, let alone a whole Prefect. Our gods don't sleep. Do you hear me, ,Teecher'? They may be a while in acting. But they don't sleep."

"Yes, Your Highness. The Prefect is long overdue to visit us. Our village is one of the few villages in the region which he has not visited. Even this time, he is only stooping over to see us on his way to go and declare open the well which the people of Okumagbe have dug through communal labour."

"That is still good enough. There is always a beginning. It is the mouth which accepts a small piece of meat today that will get a bigger piece tomorrow. It is enough that he is passing through here. After all, there are better routes to Okumagbe. If we impress him enough, he might even change his mind and stay the night here."

"I hope Your Highness is not already thinking of bed-time comfort for the Prefect?" Mr. Akim teased. "There is nowhere good enough for the Prefect to sleep in this village, your highness."

"Okay, Teecher. But whether he is passing through or staying the night, we must still make preparations for receiving him. You know of the necessary plans to be made."

"That's why I am here, Your Highness."

"I give you total control. Tell the town crier to announce your plans to the people this evening. If there is anything I can do to help, my doors are always open to you."

Assured of a total control over the reception plans for both the school and the village, Mr. Akim left the village head to go and put his plans into action.

The day's activities spread out before Mr. Akim's inner eye as he sat down to a heavy breakfast. He had instructed his wife the previous day, before they turned in for the night, that she should prepare an early and sumptuous breakfast for today as he would be out most of the day making sure that everything was ready before the arrival of His Excellency. The sound of the special gong as the town crier relayed his message the previous evening had assured him that the day's gathering would be the largest in the history of the village. The special gong which was normally used to call out adult males during the annual night of the ancestors. However, because of the significance the village Head attached to His Excellency's visit, he had instructed that it should be used to call out all the villagers to the square to welcome His Excellency. To disobey the gong was tantamount to disobeying the voices of both the elders and the ancestors of the village. Nobody had been known to do this. Mr. Akim knew, therefore, that no reminder was necessary to ensure a remarkable turn out, especially since he had demonstrated on the previous day that he would stop at nothing to ensure that everybody toed his line.

The previous day, he had driven into the village to inspect the clean up process when he was attracted to an argument between some of the men who were involved in the cleaning process and Mama Odun, the woman who sold provisions in a stall opposite the village square.

"You will not touch my stall. You think that because your excellency is coming to visit you, that you have the right to pull down the stall I have built with my hard earned money?"

"But it is only for two days – today and tomorrow," pleaded one of the young men who had been charged with the task of pulling down all the wayside stalls along the major road of the village. "You can put it back up as soon as he is gone," he further suggested, hoping to placate her.

"You forget that it will cost me money to put it back up."

"We will come and do it for you, Mama Odun," another man offered.

"But that will mean that I cannot do any selling between now and when your excellency has come and gone." She was adamant.

"What is the trouble, Mama Odun?" asked the Teecher as he stepped out of his car.

"These young men say that they have been asked to pull down all stalls by the roadside," explained the woman, hoping that the Teecher would contradict their position.

"Yes, they are right," confirmed the Teecher.

"But why?" asket the baffled woman.

"Because His Excellency is going to pass through this road and we want all obstructions on it cleared."

"Don't people buy and sell where your excellency comes from?" asked the woman indignantly.

"Woman, don't lawyer me; I have no time for unnecessary arguments," snapped the Teecher. "We are doing all this for your own good."

"Pulling down my stall for my own good!" exclaimed Mama Odun. "Wonders will never cease."

"Gentlemen," said the Teecher, turning to the men, "pull down the stall."

The men set to it instantly and proceeded to pull it apart. Mama Odun rushed to grab the Teecher but she was seconds too late. He had got into his car and headed for the palace. She was engulfed in the trail of smoke and dust left behind by Mr. Akim's car.

"We are doing all this for your own good" kept ringing in her ears until she broke down and cried like a baby.

Mr. Akim could not have asked for a better day for His Excellency's visit. It was a bright morning and the sun seemed to have risen even before the cocks crowed the day alive. The sun shone brightly as if it was already noon.

Two hours before the scheduled arrival of His Excellency, the boys and girls of

Uzoto Grammar School, in their white-over-blue uniforms, had been lined up on both sides of the approach road. Their classrooms and dormitories had been put under lock and key so that the students would have no alternative but to go out.

Mr. Akim inspected the lines and ticked off each student's name on the school register so as to make sure that none was missing. He reminded them not to forget to wave the miniature flags which he had distributed to them when His Excellency drove through. He had personally supervised the lines, measuring all the students and placing the tall ones at the two ends and the short ones in the middle. The two lines, therefore, looked like streched out Vs.

V for Victory, Mr. Akim thought to himself as he took a final look at the lines before going to join the Principal in his office. The Principal and Mr. Akim joined the other members of staff and, together, they left to join the village head and elders under the shed which had been erected in the square. Drummers and dancers were out in front of the shed performing vigorously to the applause of an appreciative audience. The members of staff of the grammar school took their seats among other notables in the second row while the first row, except those seats occupied by the village Head, his High Chiefs, the Principal and Mr. Akim, was reserved for His Excellency and his entourage.

Mr. Akim was soon engrossed in a mental rehearsal of the welcome address which he was going to read and present to His Excellency on behalf of the community. It had been duly signed by all the important members of the community. Those who could not write, and that meant almost all those who were not directly connected with the school, had their thumb prints against their names. Now and again, Mr. Akim took time off from his rehearsal to scan the actual speech and he smiled a self-congratulatory smile each time he got to those sections where he had showered praises on His Excellency. The other notables of the village killed time by discussing the latest feuds and gossip in the village. The drummers drummed, the singers sang, the dancers danced and, together, they charged the atmosphere with their gaiety.

Time flew by and as His Excellency's scheduled time of arrival approached, those few who had wrist-watches started to cast furtive glances at them, wondering whether or not he would be on time. One hour after the scheduled time, there was still no sign of His Excellency. It did not surprise the villagers, especially the elderly ones, who had grown used to waiting for their leaders, many of whom never arrived.

All was quiet as the entertainers took a break, when all of a sudden the students cheered and waved their flags frantically. Those sitting, with the exception of the village head, sprang to their feet, craning their necks to catch glimpses of their visitor. The drummers rushed to their drums and struck the welcoming tune, singers followed with the lyrics and the dancers threw up dust as the intensity of their movements increased. Not having heard the traditional siren blasts which usually heralded the arrival of leaders, Mr. Akim wondered whether His Excellency had decided to walk into the village so as to demonstrate his humility and meet as many people as possible. Such a move was not beyond such a hard working, dynamic and original Military Prefect. Didn't Jesus Christ ride on a donkey to make his triumphant entry into

Jerusalem? Wasn't it this same man who had disguised himself as a beggar in order to spot the perpetual late comers to one of the big big government offices in the regional headquarters? Nothing is beyond him, concluded Mr. Akim.

People whose houses bordered the square and who had stayed indoors, listening out for His Excellency's arrival, rushed out of their houses to join the expectant crowd.

When the people were able to discern the reason for the students' cheering, they discovered that it was the figure of a man on a bicycle, riding towards the square. As soon as the cyclist got close enough, the crowd realised that it was the village palmwine tapper who was being hailed as His Excellency by the students. The entertainers stopped their performance as soon as they realised that the students were cheering the palmwine tapper and not His Excellency. As the dust which the dancers had raised began to settle back to earth, the waiting crowd realised that the overcast which they had attributed to the dust was a genuine one. The weather which had promised to be bright and dry had started to change.

Many were still busy contemplating the change in the weather when approaching siren blasts filled the air. Almost simultaneously, the heavens opened. The students and the rest of the crowd scampered for every available shelter from where they hoped to catch a glimpse of His Excellency. The village Head looked back in the direction of his rain-maker who had collected his traditional fees and promised to hold the rains at bay for the day. He had disappeared from his seat.

The rain poured harder as the siren blasts drew nearer. The shed under which the notables were seated swayed and crashed. As its occupants started to run for the safety of the surrounding houses, His Excellency and his entourage came to a screeching stop in front of the collapsed shed. From the safety of his airconditioned Mercedes, His Excellency surveyed the drenched welcoming team. Suddenly, Mr. Akim sprinted into the nearest house and rushed back out with an old and tattered umbrella. In a flash, he was beside His Excellency's car with the umbrella at the ready.

His Excellency looked at the soaked Mr. Akim, the large pools which had formed between the car and the debris of what used to be the shed and at the large holes in the umbrella which let water through like a discarded basket. He looked at his immaculate uniform, his glistering black shoes and again at the pools of water. He ordered his driver to drive on.

Oblivious of the muddy water which the cars were splashing on him, the perplexed villagers and the jeering eyes of his students, Mr. Akim ran after His Excellency's car, carrying the tattered umbrella high with his right hand and waving the welcome address with the left. He shouted, "Your Excellency, Sir; the Address; Sir ... the Welcome Address ... Sir ... I wrote it myself, Sir ..., the Welcome Address ... Sir ..."

CHRISTIAN ISAAC

BENEFIT OF KNOWLEDGE

"Alright Class. That's it. You write it down now – step by step – as clearly as you can". Mr. Jones put down the piece of chalk and started washing his hands at the laboratory sink. It was like the Biblical Pilate washing his hands off the matter.

"Please Sir", came a deep voice from the back of the class, "what is the purpose of the experiment?".

Mr. Jones smiled to himself. He knew exactly what Amara was up to. Mr. Jones had recently made it a habit to ask Amara one or two searching questions at the end of each experiment. This was because Amara was not doing very well and he hardly asked questions in class. Well, until recently because Amara had also learnt that if he asked Mr. Jones a question first he would be at the asking end. Unfortunately, he invariable asked questions that Mr. Jones said "lacked intellectual depth".

"Amara, you tell me the purpose of this experiment." There was silence. Amara had not expected this turning of the tables. Earlier in the term, Mr. Jones had humoured him wishing to bring him out of his shell but Amara was turning the lessons into regular cross-examination sessions. Amara remained silent and the smaller boys began to chuckle. One in particular had already turned a transfixing grin on the over-sized Amara. "Now he's not going to answer with grinning Ngombu staring at him," Mr. Jones bellowed at the little boy. "Come on Amara. Why do you think we brought out all these beakers and test tubes?"

"To do an experiment", said Amara triumphantly.

"Obviously, yes – I know – but which experiment?"

There was silence again. The chuckles grew louder and Ngombu's widening grin could have put the Chesire cat to shame.

"Alright Amara. Now look here. Let's put it this way. A purpose for doing something is the reason for doing it. For example, I am trying to go over this experiment because I want you to know it. Silly Ngombu is grinning at you because he does not want to know it. Now let me ask you this. Why for instance did you leave your home and walk all the way to school this morning?"

"Well, because – er – Sir, my father is too poor to buy me a bicycle Sir."

The class roared with laughter.

"Be quiet!" roared Mr. Jones. He tried again. "Amara, I don't mean that. I mean for instance, why didn't you just stay in your house? Why did you have to leave your house this morning?"

"I did not leave my house this morning Sir", said Amara confidently.

"What do you mean? Where did you sleep last night?"

"My uncle's house. My own house is in the village Sir". The puzzled look on

108

Mr. Jones' face gave way to alarm and then pity. He could not believe that it was happening.

"Look here Amara – and that goes for the rest of you also", he glowered at Ngombu. "The purpose of the experiment is to find out the effect of carbondioxide on limewater. Is that clear Amara? Is that clear class?"

Mr. Jones hurriedly went into the small adjoining store-room apparently to collect more chemicals but actually to recover from the shock.

"Phew! Heavens! How can any-one be so stupid?" he muttered to himself. He did not want to discourage the boy especially when he had started showing some interest in the gas experiments lately. He wanted Amara to develop some selfconfidence and actively participate in class discussions. So far, he had only succeeded in creating a comedy show for the rest of the class. He remembered the day he had introduced the topic 'CARBONDIOXIDE'. The problem had started when the class had attempted to define the gas by giving two characteristics. Amara had said: one, it possessed the sickening odour characteristic of rotten eggs; two, it originated from the bowels of people suffering from indigestion. Where he got his Chemistry from, Mr. Jones could not tell.

Amara was visibly the largest and oldest boy in the class and he quite easily proved the class dunce. He hardly showed any mark of interest in his lessons except of course quite recently. He always sat at the back of the class and invariably smelt of tobacco and mampama, strong native palm-wine.

At the end of the chemistry lesson, Mr. Jones called Amara into the little store which was actually his sanctuary. When one was teaching students like Amara, one needed a sanctuary.

"Amara, you must stay after school and go over the experiment with me. Is that clear?"

"Yes Sir." He said it without any trace of distaste in his tone. Mr. Jones was puzzled. He was even more puzzled when he found the boy patiently waiting for him by the laboratory door at the end of the school day. Normally, Amara would have conveniently forgotten the appointment.

An hour and seven or eight filtering sessions later, Amara was able to properly filter a saturated solution of lime. He enjoyed blowing into the colourless liquid until it turned cloudy and milky.

"See how easy the whole thing is?" asked Mr. Jones looking very pleased with himself. It was his second year as a contract teacher in the country. He had five years teaching experience in Britain but few had been the occasions in his entire teaching life to equal this triumph. To be able to teach a boy like Amara to do an experiment like that all on his own was indeed a victory.

"I guess the teaching world would go insane if there weren't occasional challenges like Amara – but only occasionally," Mr. Jones thought to himself. He was so pleased with himself that he relaxed his usual hawk-like guard, otherwise he would have missed a little packer of lime, some test tubes and some straw when they decided to call it a day.

Amara trudged along the last mile of the path that led to his village. He felt just a little hungry and wondered whether his parents would be on the farm or at home.

"Of course they'll be at home," he remembered. "Today is Friday. Farmers stay at home on Fridays because that is when all the evil spirits roam the forests and bushes."

He wondered what Mr. Jones would say about that. "Yes, Mr. Jones. He's quite a good chemistry teacher. He knows the stuff but he does not have what the Mendeman calls sense," Amara chuckled to himself. "Oh boy! I can't wait to get to the village. I'll show them I've been learning book – plenty of book".

His mind went back to the awkward questions the villagers always asked him.

What are you learning at school? Doctor? Lawyer? When are you going to start? Haven't you had enough learning? Or, how many books have you read now?

"I'm going to teach them I've been learning book and plenty of it".

The village of Kalu was only five miles from Sengu where both the famous mission hospital and one Methodist Secondary School were situated. Few villagers around came to the hospital. Most had lost interest in the hospital when the white doctor started his campaign against rats. He said the people should have nothing to do with rats let alone eat them. He said the rats were the cause of the latest epidemic, the terrible lassa fever. Although the missionary doctor had gone to pains to specify the kind of rat he meant, it had come down to the people as rats in general. That had done it. The villages around Sengu did not have much reason to communicate with either the hospital or the School and Kalu was no exception. Amara had been forcibly taken by his uncle to be enrolled in school much against the wishes of his parents. His parents complained less when the uncle sent Amara every Friday to spend the weekend in the village. This arrangement had started since his elementary school days and it seemed to suit all parties concerned. Amara even grew to be a celebrity in his village. He was the only schoolboy in the village, he could dance the Reggae and Cavacha and he could speak and read English. To the villagers, these assets served more of a cosmetic rather than a utilitarian purpose.

When Amara arrived, he was glad to find that there was a plate of rice set aside for him. His mother always did that on Fridays. That was one of the best things about coming back to the village.

"Father, I have something important to tell you," he said as he licked the plate clean.

"What?" asked the old man with a slight touch of alarm in his voice. He sat up in his hammock he had been lazily swinging. He took another puff at his pipe and an even thicker ring of smoke wriggled its way up the mud-plastered wall.

He waited. It was not often his son had something important to say.

"I mean something important – something for the benefit of the whole village."

"What are you talking about?" The old man looked worried.

"Let's go into my room. I'll show you".

Amara led the way into his bedroom that was illuminated by an old hurricane lamp with a broken globe. The voices dropped to whispers as behind the closed door, Amara unfolded the mystery.

"You often ask me what I am learning at school," said Amara as he looked down at the impressive array of test tubes and beakers on his bed. "Well, I never told you because I wanted to make it a surprise. As you can see for yourself, I've been learning to be a doctor."

The old man looked from test tubes to his son and back and forth again. His eyes misted.

"Son, I don't know quite how to tell your mother about this but rat or no rat business, I am proud of you".

"Well, have no fear father. This has nothing to do with rats. I mean as far as I am concerned, people can eat whatever they like. My business is to cure, I can cure about twenty different ailments."

That evening, the word got around that Maada Mdulu's son was as good, if not better, than the white doctor who cut people open und sewed them up again.

"The difference here is," one elderly man was explaining to a little group of eager listeners, "in Amara's case, you can really see the sickness in the water. Did the white doctor ever do that?"

By the time the news was ten mouths old, far greater things short of only Jesus were attributed to Amara.

Amara spent Saturday and Sunday morning attending to simple villagers who blew into clear water und saw the water turn milky before their own eyes. On the table lay the school supply of Vitamin pills which were going down the throats of the villagers at the rate of one Leone each. Amara had charged a higher price for the tablets but the timely intervention of Maada Ndulu had been to the advantage of the villagers. Anyway, Amara soon learnt that he could easily prescribe two tablets for adults and increase his earning power. He also knew which villagers could afford more he found a way of making them take double treatment.

The potency of the tablets was exhibited when 'treated' patients came back to see if they had been cured. Some were given ordinary water to blow into. Those who could afford a second treatment were given filtered lime-solution to blow into again. The mere milkyness had a devastating effect on the victims who willingly opted for a second treatment.

"You see, some of you have the disease for quite a long time. It takes two treatments to cure the stronger cases," Amara explained. By Sunday afternoon, all the villagers were declared cured by Amara.

****

Monday morning at school do not always endow students with the vitality and alert attitude one would expect. Teachers sadly realise it is only the beginning of another week and students are anything but fresh and ready for work. Yet Monday morning is the one morning teachers from time immemorial choose to say "But you had all the weekend to do it." Mr. Jones was no exception. When he entered the Chemistry class, he almost sang "Go–od mor–r–rning class. How many people did the assignment?" All hands shot up except Amara's.

"Amara, have you done the work?" Mr. Jones asked, half pleading, half threatening. After that fruitful Friday afternoon, he expected at least some effort.

"No Sir".

"And why not?" snapped Mr. Jones. He could have killed Amara. He stood with arms akimbo and stared with red unbelieving eyes at the boy. "You had the whole weekend to do the work but no! You decided you had better things to do".

The grinning Ngombu, true to his duty had already turned a chesire-cat grin on the bigger boy.

"I went – to my – my – village Sir and – and – – – –".

"Oh shaddup! Your village indeed! I know that story too well. You do that work right now!" Mr. Jones rushed into his little sanctuary to cool off and wash his hands off the matter. "And it was only on Friday I went over it ten times with him. How he in particular will ever benefit from school, I wonder."

SOONDERLALL RAMLOUL

CONVERTS

The ghost of Mr René Ramsamy was destined to haunt our household because of my unfortunate father.

"Who was Mr René Ramsamy?" I used to inquire from various quarters; I obtained many versions of his life as the villagers were eager to gossip about him.

Therefore, before I go ahead with my rather rambling family reminiscences, I should, perhaps, give a composite version of Mr René Ramsamy's life and activities.

Mr. René Ramsamy, a convert who had eventually degenerated into bigotry, held cynical views on Hinduism. Rum was the stimulant. Often, carried away by his bout of drunkeness in the restaurant, he would vociferate, now carping or slandering Indians; now claiming with vehemence to be of European stock.

In the din of a restaurant drunkards may be guilty of countless blunders. They normally recover in sober moments. That was not the case with Mr. René Ramsamy: even in periods of sobriety he moved about, chin propped up in contempt and hoad inflated, with the vanity of putative distinguished parentage.

To all and sundry he blurted out his wretched French, sometimes jarring the ears of his wiser colleagues; but nevertheless, keeping in awe the credulous village folk.

What an impact Mr. René Ramsamy must have had on those simple souls, victims of subtle and organised oppression of colonial days! They were led to believe in the superiority of a certain culture with Mr. René Ramsamy as a protagonist of.

Nature must have been unfair to him. Pro-French, pro-white yet so miserably dark and puny, so much like a Tamil, how that mousy faced creature must have despised his own self! However, one might concede one fact; his French, picked up while his mother and himself had been serving a Mulatto family, was better than the Tamil of his orthodox kin.

His loquacity, engendered by daubts and a gnawing conscience, had reduced him to a terrible bore. A fanatic about French culture, whatever that might have meant to him, he waded through the books of Alexandre Dumas, Victor Hugo and what not. His desultory reading was never aimed at augmenting his knowledge but rather at supplementing his fund of fashionable gossip.

With the passing of years his passion never abated; he became, on the contrary, even more enthusiastic and effusive. Nobody knew of many futile attempts at poetry. Everybody acknowledged his dedication to culture.

One fine day Mr. René Ramsamy suddenly discovered in himself an ardent promotor of French culture. That happened after the publication of a meagre book of verses, a fruit of years of his spasmodic and laborious efforts. Mr. René Ramsamy had solicited some comments in the press. The reviewer, who had privately confessed he could not make head or tail of poetry, wrote favourably to please Mr. René Ramsamy and lovers of French. Invited to cultural parties, he came across journalists and teachers with some inclination for writing. Most of them were Creoles and many were yet to produce their first work. Their discussion invariably revolved around the popularity of French in the island and the place that it should ultimately occupy in the world. French should live even at the expense of other languages! That was their motto; they aimed at attaining their goal by drinking as copiously as they talked.

Mr. René Ramsamy and his friends had been deprived of their own culture. Not surprising though that, when an attempt was made by a group on the coast to revive their heritage, the sega dances, Mr. René Ramsamy and his friends immediately frowned upon it and dismissed it as vulgar and plebian. Mr. René Ramsamy disparanged it: a skirt lifting, violent hip swinging and body writhing dance of obscure origin; a dance that does not conform to any rule or pattern, usually reaching its climax in spasms of wild pleasure, often in a pool of dust, to be ultimately followed by a general fatigue.

With all his intellectual looks, enhanced by a pair of dark glasses resting on that dark mousy face, it might have been beyond Mr. René Ramsamy to realise where he stood in this world, a world where one, born dark, remains miserably dark until one's death, whether one likes it or not.

Certain preposterous people, unable to face the realities of life, their colour and creed for instance, allow themselves to be caught up slowly and steadily in the web of their own fantasies and follies. Mr. René Ramsamy was such a person.

He looked down on Creoles. "Their laziness, utter lack of realism and initiative depress me," he would say to Indians as if to make up for the hatred he harboured for Indians in general. "Give a black fellow hundred rupees now, soon afterwards, you'll see him drunk, inveighing against people; next day, you'll see his children in the same rags. You Indians should never trust them, never give them anything."

Yet most of his friends and colleagues were Creoles. The best part of his life was spent among them, feasting, dancing or talking about culture. But he never could identify himself with them nor with any other group for that matter.

For Indians, he had an inexhaustible fund of erractic criticism, "Indians are hopeless; they quarrel among themselves over the hard earned wealth of their parents. Hygiene is unknown to them; they eat with their fingers and spit almost anywhere. Their ill-manners and atrocious behaviour infuriate me. In India they sleep and defocate in the streets. How shameful!"

Whenever Indian mothers went to inquire about the progress of their children at school, he would greet them with contempt and lecture them on the misdeeds of their broods. On certain occasions he adopted a patronising attitude, actuated by a seething resentment, a positive manifestation of a deep rooted weakness.

Women clad in saris put him off as they reminded him in a flash of his own mother.

He disclaimed his Indian origin; his features betrayed him. European in outlook, in dress, in comportment, Mr. René Ramsamy was adrift in a strange world, a world of make-believe where he was clinging in desperation of his own illusion; a world where he was groping about, his role reduced to minicry. For him reconciliation was impossible.

Deep within he was aware of his appalling failure. He was sandwiched between the world at large and his domestic life. On the one hand the necessity to put up a daily show was quite a strain and on the other to suffer in silence was heart-rending. He cringed before the truth; illusion was his only refuge. Cast out by his own people, bullied by his flashy Mulatte wife, he bore his miseries quietly. Afraid of being made an object of derision he never confided in anybody. Before the overpowering presence of his wife, he stammered. He took the aggresive lashings of her tongue passively. Threats and hysterical scenes, particularly on payday, had reduced his speech to the minimum at home. He was stamped as mean, black and incompetent. He had practically no say in domestic matters. Under such strain, his actions became inconsequential.

At school, freed from constraint and fears, he gave vent to all his spleen. His pupils wetted their pants; late-comers were severely punished. Mr. René Ramsamy's reputation as a great beater was approved by most parents. They agreed that regular doses of flogging helped to keep their children on their toes. The little fellows were therefore abandoned to the whims and fancies of Mr. René Ramsamy. He entered the class half-drunk and manhandled them on the slightiest provocation.

"Your father? Come on now, who in this village didn't know that father of yours?" Lall would bubble with sombre insinuation while chatting.

He was one of our distant relatives and, in spite of his advanced years, a fast friend of mine. Whenever I dropped in, he would gossip endlessly on village life, always managing to direct the topic on to the nefarious activities of father.

"Basoo was a hell of a man, a real specimen", Lall would say cynically in a yap of laughter, throwing up his arms and slapping his thighs in delight.

Age was no barrier between us. He would talk freely. "Basoo was a debauchee at your age. Lazy, reckless and rowdy, yet not in the least lacking in joviality and mischief. He was compassionate too."

Lall had his own way of tolling a story, narrating the incidents incoherently, covering up lapses with sprouts of laughter or confusing dates, sometimes bringing in a new fact on which I would request him to elaborate.

Thus, through the tortuous reminiscences of Lall I gathered much on the early life of father and his environment.

Father appeared to be of another breed. There was little affinity between him and his brothers who, since the death of Parsad, their father, had established themselves as the main pillars of the house.

The fame of the deceased Parsad as a social worker and well-wisher of the Hindu community had spread far and wide.

At the very outset, then, my uncles Sewduth and Sounoun followed suit and proved themselves worthy of the illustrious Parsad. Getting up in the raw morning long before the sun peeped from behind the mountain, they went away shivering and whistling with sickles and bundles of rope to fetch forage for the family's cows and goats.

They hastened back just in time to cloan the cowpen, tidy themselves a little, gulp their tea and hurry down the grassy lane towards school, cloth bags bouncing on their backs.

The School was a stone building of haphazard architecture. It recalled to them not without misgiving the sturdy and sinister aspect of the local prison, where malefactors like José, Madhoo and Vel had been hanged.

In fact, school was some sort of prison for them. Punishment always awaited them there as they were confirmed late-comers. This sheer lack of discipline never failed to exasperate their teacher, Mr. René Ramsamy.

"I appreciate cleanliness and discipline; you bloody Indians are helplessly lacking in both," he would mutter with sarcasm and a glow of triumph in his wine-swollen eyes.

My uncles were his regular victims. Mr. René Ramsamy neither would listen to their stale excuse that they lived very far from school nor could he stand their cow-piss smell. That rarely failed to rouse his abhorrence and disdain. He would shout in a tremulous voice, sometimes with tears in his eyes, "Stupid swine, don't you have the decency to wash your bottoms before entering this class? Bastards! It's my business to impose discipline here. I'll see that it is scrupulously observed. Brood of a backward race!"

He would order the boys to bend over the desk; stretching their pants across their buttocks, he would apply his rod with gusto muttering "discipline and cleanliness" between alternate blows. Then he would rub his hands briskly together and laugh while spittle dribbled at the sides of his mouth.

Mr. René Ramsamy was constrained to be secretive about his domestic life; his wife, on the contrary, criticised him overtly to all and sundry behind his back. So unknown to Mr. René Ramsamy some inquisitive villagers patched up a suitable version of his life.

That tragic-comic story was given much publicity in the village: the ill-treatment meted out to him by his wife, his patronising attitude towards both Hindus and Creoles, his imprisonment for sodomy and his untimely death.

He was much resented by Indians. Each and every fault of his was attributed to his being a convert.

No Hindu worthy of the name would stoop so low as to embrace another faith. They knew too much about the systematic and powerful organisations, which they believe, throve at their expense. They, the underdogs, knew too much about those shameful campaigns to convert Hindus: threats, coercion, criticism, suppression, lofty promises, ruthless boycotting and what not.

Father never knew Mr. René Ramsamy's caprices for he absolutely refused to enter his class, the sixth standard.

Grandmother threatened, cajoled, and wept. At last, she surrendered to father's obstinacy.

Father, the last of three children, was orphaned at two. Grandmother, before leaving for work, left him in the care of a neighbour who did baby-sitting for a few cents.

In the fields she over fretted the dangers to which he was constantly exposed – fire, water, and the pit latrine. She was genuinely happy only when she was back home fondling the baby.

Uncle Sewduth and uncle Sounoun were big enough to look after themselves. They received less attention.

Father, the darling of everybody, was cuddled, tickled and fed on cheap sugar sweets, bought by the brothers; he was given rides on their back. They pampered him so much that he was spoilt.

In later years he displayed neither fear nor respect for my uncles.

Nobody could persuade him to go to school again once he had set his mind against it. Uncle Sewduth and uncle Sounoun beat him. He cried and grandmother chid my uncles. It had been their coveted ambition to make of him a teacher, a far better teacher than Mr. René Ramsamy. Alas, that ambition for ever was shattered!

Lall had this to say: "Basoo, with his uncouth behaviour could never have become a teacher. It's no joke to be a teacher, mind you. Basoo was wild and rough. You'll agree with me those are not the stuff teachers are usually made of. To be frank, your father's behaviour was simply atrocious. Once, I remember, your grandmother's brother, Panray, tried to lick him into shape. It was over a question of money if I'm not mistaken. Yes, yes, I'm right. Money. Always Money. Your grandmother categorically refused to give Basoo a certain sum of money. In her absence he rummaged the cupboard. He broke the only pieces of China you people had in those days; he tore a mattress. In the afternoon Sounoun tried to reason with him. He failed. They had a fight in front of your house. Sounoun belaboured him. There was a bottle of consecrated water near the Mahabirsamy. Basoo got hold of that bottle, broke it on a stone and lacerated Sounoun's arm with its jagged edge. It was then that Panray was called for. He gave Basoo a sound thrashing with his walking stick. Later Basoo appeared with a pocket knife. He raged and puffed and tried to stab Panray. Your grandmother slapped Basoo. He left home for three days. Oh, what an impetuous fellow that father of yours was!"

Uncles Sewduth and Sounoun, like many poor boys, started their careers in a conventional manner. At twelve, after leaving school, uncle Sewduth joined Mohun's garage as an apprentice mechanic; at eleven, uncle Sounoun was employed as a shop assistant in town.

Uncle Sewduth developed into a healthy man with a swarthy face, a squat nose, a wide jaw and tiny brown eyes, overarched by bushy brows that crossed each other. His hands were large and supple and he was very good at his work.

He kept those working around him bubbling and tittoring with raw jokes, suitable for his milieu. Through the years the assiduous efforts he put into his work were justly rewarded when one fine day Mohun sold him the garage together with its machinery at a reasonable price.

Uncle Sewduth was always to be seen in an overall of coarse dark-blue material, stained all over with grease.

He smoked and ate with greasy hands.

I had completed my own apprenticeship under him. Kind, strict and practical, he used to cut in my complaints with sheer logic, "Work hard and talk less, and you'll be rewarded. Your're aware that I'll leave you in charge of this garage, and as owner you'll find out pretty fast it's always wrong to make much of the conditions of work. Don't allow yourself to fall in the same rut as your father. A sensible man should stick to a decent job. I advise you to work sincerely; you'll get your due and you'll have your place in society".

Uncle Sounoun was even more fortunate in life. He grew into a handsome man with an oval face and a fine nose. His hair was sleek black und well groomed. He used to take great care in combing it. It was fascinating to watch him in front of his dressing-table. He would dress the hair downward to the forehead then with a flick of the comb draw a neat line from the middle of the head lengthwise on the left and brush the hair on either side. With a slight touch of the comb, he would arrange a pompon on the forehead.

His work required him to be clean and neat. Neatness became a habit with him.

Two years after the wedding of father, my uncles got married. Uncle Sewduth brought a plump fair-complexioned girl from a village in the north.

The image of the beautiful girl was no longer discernible. She had grown fat, phlegmatic and sterile.

Uncle Sounoun's wife was one of the ugliest persons I had ever come across. Her voice was coarse and throaty, her eyes were black und heavy-lidded, goatlike; her skin was grainy and rough. But she came from a well-to-do family, bringing in enough money to free uncle from worries for the rest of his life. They were blessed with seven children.

"I'm lucky," uncle Sounoun would reminisce.

He was lucky, indeed, for during the war he was lured into the cigarette business that prospered at a fantastic rate. And to add to his fortune, he bagged a first-prize in the lottery.

Eventually he amassed enough wealth; as owner of three textile shops and two wholesale foodstuff shops in the cities, he could look upon his good fortune with satisfaction.

Three of uncle Sounoun's children had gone abroad for higher studies; two were busy in the shops, the last two were attending school.

There was much incompatibility between my uncles and father. Father, the most unfortunate of the lot, had no gift for anything. He lacked the necessary enthusiasm and will-power to make his way successfully in life.

After leaving school father roamed listlessly in the streets. He came home often in a morbid state of mind to consume his meals, then again he was in the streets till very late in the night.

Soon he was swept away by the influence of hooligans; he took to smoking, at first secretly in the latrine or near the Chinese shop, then openly, flouting even the elders of the village.

After sniffing the pockets of his jacket, grandmother tried to corner him one day. "You smoke?" she asked.

Father did know how to wring the love of a mother to his advantage. "No, Ma, your son doesn't smoke; I swear on my head I don't. Come on now, cheer up. I want you to trust me, you should, dear ma."

Grandmother with tears in her eyes believed him.

In the company of hooligans he turned out a nuisance, stealing fruits, livestock, anything they could lay hands on. They exchanged their loot for cigarettes and wine with the Chinaman in the vicinity.

One day, it happened, they sold the Chinaman's own goose to the Chinaman himself!

Their notoriety spread like wild fire. Many vowed to beat them and hand them over to the police. There were threats and menaces. People talked to my grandmother with an edge of anger in their rough peasant voices.

Grandmother tried to bring father round. She did everything in her capacity – affection, menace, tears. Nothing worked with that embittered son; it was plain that grandmother bored him. When uncles intervened, father, accusing them of high handedness, left the house in disgust. Then grandmother searched for him everywhere.

Everybody at home gave up father as a difficult subject. He was put to various jobs; he was equally unsuccessful at each and every one of them. Grandmother lost hope. She implored her elder sons to look after their small brother after her death.

Then suddenly at the age of seventeen, father was married. He had turned out to be the rooster of the village, and he was hatching illegal affairs with three or four married women at a time. Husbands were biding their time to murder him. They convened in secret; furious at their misfortunes, they vowed to slice him and feed to the fish in the river. Others thought it better to scald him alive.

Through the reverence of grandfather, grandmother enjoyed a good reputation in the village. In the beginning the husbands talked to her about the blasphemous and immoral behaviour of her son politely and even with a slight fear. Gradually they grew pugnacious. They muttered with rage and asperity.

Matters took a decisive turn, when a strange woman made a dramatic appearance at grandmother's door, a pregnant girl at her heels.

"See what your useless son has done to my innocent child. See for yourself. I think you're satisfied. Who will take care of her baby? Come on tell me, who'll marry her? Tell me," she bleated.

Grandmother emerged out of the kitchen and tried to pacify the woman whose name was Sabit. She requested Sabit to talk slowly.

Sabit explained that father was in love with her daughter. She had not been aware of their love affair until her daughter got pregnant.

A small crowd had gathered and they were craning their necks inquisitively. Women, children, and even the carter with his bull. Grandmother shooed them away.

The girl was standing shyly with bowed head, fussing with the edge of her dress. She smiled coyly when grandmother stroked her cheeks.

Grandmother assured Sabit that she would talk the matter over with her elder sons and her brother.

Consequently adequate inquiries were made and it was established that the girl was immoral. She had had relations with almost all the bad guys in the village.

Next time Sabit turned up with her daughter, grandmother flailed her broom-stick and ordered her to leave her door-step at once.

Sabit flared up and became so abusive that she did not fail to attract a large crowd.

Her daughter, apparently innocent, turned out to be a real latrine when she opened her mouth.

When they satisfied themselves that they had delivered enough obscenities, they walked away with the skirts billowing.

The crowd dispersed.

Then a long period of quiet followed. Grandmother and my uncles were uneasy and nervous. They smelt imminent danger. Father was as stubborn as ever. He stayed out till late in the night and never bothered about the warnings of grandmother.

One night, after heavy rains, everything was calm as usual except for the honkings of frogs. Grandmother was awake waiting for father, while my uncles were snoring snugly in bed. Suddenly somebody banged on the door.

"Who is it?" she asked with anxiety.

"It's me, Madun. Open the door please."

She sprang to her feet and unlatched the door. Madun was soaked to the bone; he was shaking all over.

"What happened?" she asked.

Madun swallowed his saliva and passed the tip of his tongue rapidly on his upper lip before answering, "Basoo has been badly beaten. He's bleeding heavily. I think we should take him to hospital."

Grandmother's face lost colour. A tremor went through her limbs and she felt dizzy.

"Where is he?" she asked hoarsely.

"In the cane-field."

Grandmother immediately woke up uncles.

The lane was squelchy. Uncle Sewduth flashed his electric torch.

Father was sprawled in a pool of blood. Blood had stained blades of grass.

He was hospitalised for five weeks.

As grandmother had made the necessary arrangements for a quick and an inexpensive wedding, father was married to a respectable girl in the adjoining village within a week of his recovery.

He was still jobless. Three children were born in three successive years. I, the last of the lot, was born in the tenth year.

Father of four, he still evinced no interest in life and he just did odd jobs. Mother pleased with him to look for permanent employment. He was flippant. Uncle Sounoun offered him a light job in his shop. Father pompously declined it, "I'll look for a job myself und I don't want anybody's help."

Years afterwards, thanks to my uncles' good fortune, we moved to a more spacious concrete house in town.

It was the uncles who looked after the expenses of the whole household. Uncle Sewduth provided food, and uncle Sounoun supplied boots and clothes.

My mother was embarassed by the generosity and leniency of her brothers-in-law. She felt father was taking undue advantage. She plucked up enough courage to talk to him about it. Father shouted her down, but she did not give up. She aired her grievances so often that it ultimately stirred him to listen to her with a vague expression on his face.

"Our children are growing fast. We must see that they get everything, food, clothes and education. For how long will we prey on the goodness of others? After all they have their own family. If you're not prepared to work, I'll find a job for myself."

"Ah ... don't bother me. I'll try to find a job, all right, pretty soon too," he told her in a brusque manner.

The whole family was surprised when father went on duty on the following Monday. He had joined the staff of "Bernard et Fils" as clerk.

Grandmother lived a moment of pure joy, but that was too sweet to last. Soon it came to her knowledge that father was no more a Hindu but a Christian; his Godfather was Mr. Bernard; his new name was Gaston.

Given that terrible blow in the evening of her life, grandmother wept profusely and cursed her fate. She swore never to talk to such an ungrateful son again.

"If one has no respect for one's own religion, one shall be burnt in hell fire," she said.

My Uncles were outraged at this transgression. Their lives were so much scarred by the tyrannies of Mr. René Ramsamy that they actually loathed the very idea of conversion. They never expected to have a Ramsamy in their own family. But quite a different mechanism seemed to have operated in father who had embraced Christianity so easily. Why had he taken such a rash decision? Was it because he could not follow his brothers' pace, and in an attempt to compensate for his shortcomings, had accepted the very faith to which they were so vehemently opposed? Or was it simply because he had come to know it was the easiest way to get a job that suited him?

Father was apparently not affected by the family's new attitude. He joked and talked to everybody as usual. He potted and spoiled the children with sweets, sometimes he was affronted by cold stares from aunt Sounoun, but he pretended not to notice.

The pain of mother was even greater. She had to put up with the unpleasant remarks of her sisters-in-law; following the tradition of the Hindu wife, she remained by father's side.

There was a perceptible change in the manners and habits of father. He bought two new suits, a felt hat and a leather bag.

Father refused to eat off brass-plates. He was given a porcelain plate, a steel fork and a spoon.

He smoked a pipe after dinner, while he pored over the Bible. Sometimes he related stories from the Holy book, Jesus as a child, Jesus as a man, working miracles and preaching; he also told us about the crucifixion of Jesus by wicked people.

The children would cluster around father avidly, sometimes aunts and mother would join us. We all agreed that he was a wonderful story-teller. At his request a picture of Jesus and the virgin Mary, framed in passepartout, was hung in the God-room, side by side with Ram, Vishnu and Krishna.

Father made new friends, Marc and André. Both wore hats like him. On Sundays they frequently dropped in, midly drunk. They offered us sweets and patted our cheeks. They were never annoyed when we pulled their hats on our heads and hopped about in the yard. They were nice people.

Mother disapproved of these new acquaintances. She asked father not to bring them home often. But Marc and André visited us so regularly that mother found herself providing them with lunch.

Two plates were reserved for them. Nobody else at home was allowed to use them because they were beef and porkeaters.

Grandmother and my aunts viewed them with suspicion.

The changes father was undergoing were much discussed at home, sometimes with disgust or disapproval in hushed tones, sometimes with subdued admiration.

Incidentally, it was one of the changes in father's habit that caused the row which ultimately prompted his departure. It was the children who first noticed that father had discontinued taking water to the latrine. Instead he was using old newspapers. When this information was imparted to my aunts, they laughed wholeheartedly and volunteered all sorts of comments.

Even mother could not help laughing.

From then on, he had a group of children spying after him every time he was seen going towards the backyard. They would immediately report to their mother, "No water today also."

Within a short time my uncles came to know about it all; they made some deprecating comments.

Everybody was kept amused at the expense of father, until he overheard a remark which aunt Sounoun was inadvertently passing to her child, "It's in your blood. Go and clean yourself before I flay your back. Can't you take water to the latrine? You're following the good example of your Christian uncle, that swine."

That piqued father. Furious, he bolted to the backyard where aunt Sounoun was standing, arms akimbo.

"What you call me, a swine?" he asked querulously.

"Yes, I did. It's a shame a grown up man like you is giving innocent children dirty manners."

"Shut up, you bitch!"

Aunt Sounoun was stunned. She gasped. Her mouth opened and shut like a fish's: no word came out.

She stared at father with bewildered eyes as he moved away hastily.

Grandmother witnessed the scene from her room without comment. She bewailed the impious language of father. She asked her elder sons to request father to reform his manners and mince his words at home.

The intervention of the uncles displeased father. He labelled every member of the family as savage.

Uncle Sewduth could not stand it anymore. He lost his temper and slapped father.

Father announced that he would not stay any longer in the house. Grandmother sent word that he was free to move away.

Father tried to drag mother and his children with him.

"Come along. I'll get all the children and you too converted. Christians are rich and powerful. They live close together, backing up each other. Our children will be provided with a healthy education. I don't want to stay a single minute more with a pack of dirty pagans," father said.

Mother threatened to commit suicide if father ever again talked of converting the children.

Disappointed, father left alone.

What an experience mother must have had with father.

My own experiences with him are varied. As I write now I can recall a few.

Foremost in my mind is the incident of the jackfruit. Early one Sunday morning we left home, father and I. He met Marc and André and left me at the barber's. There I waited interminably. People coming after me had their hair cut and disappeared. I waited and waited, my heart heavy with boredom.

Suddenly father dashed in. He left a jack-fruit on the bench beside me.

"Keep an eye on this," he said and followed out Marc and André.

At long last the barber beckoned me. I was perched on a tall chair, facing a tall mirror. On the table before me were displayed the barber's paraphernalia:
combs with dirt at the roots of the teeth, bottles of lotion with faded labels, scissors, a half-full pot of cream – a finger hole in the cream. There was an overpowering odour: lotion mingled with the soil of a nearby latrine.

The barber, lanky and hollow-cheeked, turned my head this way and that briskly. He combed my hair jerking back my head; he rang his scissors in my ears and cut my hair with alacrity.

My hair fluttered down and settled on the floor among other mossy bits of hair.

All the while the barber was conducting an animated political discussion with five or six men seated on the long bench behind me. I had glimpses of them in the mirror. When they had come in they had invariably asked, "Whose jack-fruit it is?" The barber had answered for me, "His."

"Who is he?" one of them had asked.

"Gaston's son".

"Gaston, that women-eater!"

The discussion suddenly turned on my father's private life and it was a friendly one no doubt, but sometimes the barber shouted; the others shouted too. He challenged them jerking his comb; he agreed or disagreed with them. At one moment two or three sided with him; at the other he had the whole lot against him; again at another moment he found himself grappling with those who had backed him up earlier.

The barber settled the discussion, saying "Whatever you may say, he is a gentleman and a friend indeed!"

At ten o'clock I found myself following father, Marc and André with the jack-fruit under my arm.

They went into one restaurant. They ordered rum and drank one glass after another. I moped about, burdened by the jack-fruit.

I sighed with relief once we were outside, but they again went in and consumed more rum.

I was exhausted.

They swaggered out. "It's my round of drinks," said André. They argued. Then they agreed they would serve a round each. And we visited three more restaurants.

At one p.m. Marc and André bid farewell to us. Father stumbled along the grassy lane. I trudged after him until we reached his place.

There, a woman emerged out of her house and said, "Oh, what a beautiful fruit. It's nice for curry."

Father considered her and said, "You like it? Take it."

The woman protested. Father pressed her; she accepted the gift.

At home uncle Sounoun asked "Where is the jack-fruit?"

"Which jack-fruit?"

"The one I gave to your father for you to bring home."

"Oh that, he has given it to a woman."

"A woman? Your father is crazy after women."

Uncle was right. Father was crazy. This incident would demonstrate it. Several times I had seen him talking to a woman next door. She was slim and graceful. Her hair was thick and long. A few days later while I was going by her house, I saw her crying.

"Your father is fighting with my husband. Go and call the police."

"Where are they?"

"Behind the house."

The husband had father under him. He was pounding father wildly with his fists. I jumped on him and pulled his hair. He brushed me away. I pounced on him again and scratched his eyes. He growled in pain. The woman was watching on. I hit the husband with a stone. Blood oozed away. The woman got scared and wailed, "Help, help!"

Neighbours came and stopped the fight.

The whole village came to know that father had slept with that woman. The scandal was given several twists.

My uncles could not talk the matter over with father; he was nearly always drunk, during the rest of the time he stayed with us. Several times I had helped to carry him home unconscious, his mouth reeking of liquor. He blabbered and raved. I remember the time when he wetted his trousers. The news spread like wild fire adding to the gossip of the village.

He took a room some distance away and retired there. Mother dispatched me to his house with food every evening. Sometimes I saw father alone, sometimes with Marc and André, drinking.

He degenerated into an instant drinker, his body debilitated. For two or three days on end, he would not touch his food.

When I reported that to grandmother, she mumbled with resignation, "let him die in his own dirt and vices."

Three months away from home had caused a great change in father. He had become seriously ill und he grew weaker and weaker every day.

We carried him home. My uncles called for doctors who prescribed all sorts of medicines.

Father's condition aggravated. He survived a heart attack but his left limb and arm were paralysed and he could not talk distinctly.

Mother prayed ardently for his recovery.

Grandmother wept heavily and cursed her fate.

"God should have taken me away, and left my poor son alone."

My uncle tried to console her.

"Don't worry, Ma, he'll be all right."

To cheer her up they would talk of their childhood. Grandmother would brighten up, but soon her smile would vanish and tears would well up in her eyes again.

She forgave father and forgot all the wrongs he had done to her. Often she would be seen in father's room rubbing him with liniment or massaging his head with coconut oil.

Gradually father recovered. He stumbled and collapsed many times before he could stump around his room with a walking stick. Sometimes he insisted that we put him in an armchair in the back verandah where he would sit for hours feeding his eyes on green leaves.

Once I caught him in tears. As soon as he spotted me he turned his head in shame and humiliation.

I told mother about it and she hugged me and wept as if her heart were breaking to pieces.

The tears of the elders depressed me.

Father started moving about the yard.

He lost his job, his friends wilted away and disappeared one by one.

When he recovered enough strength he absented himself from the house most of the time. He was happy in the company of his old cronies.

Father paid Mr. Bernard regular visits. He was granted a modest pension that he spent on his cigarettes and wine.

In spite of the repeated protests of mother, father brought old clothes home. "They are good for the children; I got them free." Mother was embarassed: father went on his begging rounds everyday.

He dressed himself in second-hand clothes he got free. They were two or three sizes too large for him. He took after Charlie Chaplin with his baggy clothes, cane and battered hat from which he did not part till his death.

Normally father would come back home at about seven the latest. On that inauspicious day father did not turn up in time.We set about looking for him, near the Chinese shop, at Marc's and André's. Finally he was found lying in a gutter in the yard of Mr. Bernard. Probably he had gone there for his small pension and had fallen down while nobody was around.

On the following day I watched father die. The house was crowded and stifling. Father was stretched on his cot, his face drawn and very pale, his lips blistered. He lay still and inarticulate; only his eyes were mobile, eerie with fears.

Mother, grandmother and aunts were weeping silently at his sides.

Now and then grandmother dabbed his forehead with the edge of her sari. We looked at father helplessly.

Somebody had gone to calling uncles.

Gradually father's breathing sounded hard and noisy. He opened his mouth slightly.

His children were edged closer to him.

"This is Anand, your oldest son," grandmother said with a choking voice. "This is Vijay."

Father stared blankly at us. Then a slight twitch was noticed at the sides of his eyes.

Somebody had tulsi water ready in a brass lota. "Take this, my son," said grandmother, pouring some water between his parched lips; mother did the same. After that every member of the family was requested to serve father a drop of consecrated water.

He was taking a long time to die. At one moment, we thought he was dead. At the signal of grandmother, everybody gave a wail in unison, but father reopened his eyes again.

At last the uncles came in, they sat on the edges of the bed. Father, as if knowing they were there, opened his eyes and two big tears rolled down his cheeks.

They also gave him the holy water.

Presently father's face assumed a devilish lock. His eyes dilated, only the white was visible. His body convulsed. His legs twitched in sudden jerks.

We watched petrified and there was total silence.

Father's tongue shot out and I noticed it was very long. Grandmother tried to push it in with her dirty fingers, but it glided through and stayed out.

Grandmother was trembling; she collapsed. Aunts and mother took her on one side. Aunt Sounoun engaged herself in fanning her.

Uncle Sewduth held father's tongue inside his mouth.

Suddenly father stiffened his body and his life left him.

Father died with his eyes wide open. Mother closed them with her fingers.

Now with her head on his stomach, she was weeping hysterically.

My uncles had forgotten that they were adults; they wept like school boys.

In the afternoon, Mr. Bernard appeared with a wreath. With much gusto, he announced that father should be buried according to the Christian rites. Many relatives present tried to oppose this. They maintained that father should be cremated. A short discussion ensued over father's dead body. Then uncle Sewduth said that Mr. Bernard was right and father was buried.

When we came back from the cemetery, uncle Sounoun said: "I wonder whether Basoo was really one of us!"

DEV VIRAHSAWMY

THE WALLS

The early summer morning sun is already bright. Joshua Abraham as usual is in his garden looking proudly after his flowers. He loves them all. But he knows that some of them give him a special pride and satisfaction. They are those successful grafts. The new blooms, he calls them. New in shape, new in beauty, new in brightness.

He turns round to look at his house. It needs some repairs and a fresh coat of paint. It is old but still in good condition as he never allowed age to weaken it. But now he too is old. Moreover the costs of repairs have gone up. His pension is insufficient for all his needs. He does whatever he can do by himself. As for the rest, he knows that he cannot force time back. Soon he will have to go and the house will go after him.

Shakti, like all those of her generation, will surely have it pulled down and have a new concrete one built. He looks sadly at his open veranda, the wooden shutters, the carved freize, the variety of plants beautifully arranged in it by his wife. He wishes that the new house which will stand in this place one day will not just be a huge ugly concrete box like those which are mass-produced. He only hopes that Shakti will be able to afford a marriage of the new and the old.

The noise in the kitchen wakes him from his reverie. Kunti, his wife appears on the doorstep carrying a mug of tea, his usual morning tea which he always takes in his little flower garden except when the weather is bad. She is draped in her saree. She never goes outside the house dressed otherwise. They have been married for over thirty years and on this issue she has remained adamant. A smile appears on Joshua's lips. He knows why and he respects her for it.

"I don't think Shakti is well. She doesn't want any breakfast, she says."

"Don't mind her. She knows what she wants."

"I told her she was killing herself with work. Speak to her. She can't go to work on an empty stomach."

"Do you think that will change anything? If she's not hungry, she's not hungry. Kunti! I've been working on an empty stomach as well. You don't seem to care!"

She prefers not to insist. When he is in such a mood he pretends to take everything lightly. He pretends. She knows that he is of the worrying kind, but he does not like people to know.

"Can't I have a slice of bread?", he asks.

"Soon is late again. I bet he got drunk last night. When he comes I know that he'll invent all sorts of stories ... the baker's gone on strike, his bicycle broke down ... There's yesterday's farata.* Would you like some?"

"No! I'll wait for Soon's fresh bread."

128

She goes back to her kitchen. He quickly swallows his mug of tea, places the mug on the veranda's balustrade and goes back to his new flower bed. With dedication his fingers run through the soft soil mixed up with manure. A front door opens. It is the one which opens from Shakti's room onto the veranda. Without raising his head.

"Shakti! Your mother says you're hunger striking!"

His words hit a wall of silence. This is not her normal behaviour. He raises his head. She is there on the threshold of the veranda, beautiful but not in her usual self. Joshua's heart throbs. Something is wrong!

"You're not well, coco?"

"I'm o.k., papa!"

"No, you're not."

He goes to her. He finds her face pale, and her forced smile cannot fool him. He knows his daughter well. She quickly kisses him and leaves him standing there. Reaching the end of the short paved alley, she stops at the gate, waves to him and disappears behind the high wall which surrounds his neighbour's yard.

Joshua stands there, very ill at ease. Shakti, he knows, has avoided any conversation. This is unusual. He senses that something has gone amiss, but what, he has not the faintest idea. He looks around himself as if the answer was written on the trees, the flowers, the bamboo hedge, the stone bench, the facade of the wooden house. Nothing has changed. They all look the same ... And yet ...! He no longer feels like going back to what he was doing. He stands there, his eyes fixed on the brick wall behind which she disappeared. He has always hated this wall. He remembers well the day when his neighbour proposed to him to share the expenses to have the bamboo hedge of that side of the yard removed and replaced by a brick wall. He refused not through meanness but because the bamboo hedge had a history and a personality of its own. It was old, the roots were rising to the surface, there were holes through which dogs and chickens crossed over to mess up his garden. And yet he refused something clearly to his advantage. He made a counter proposal: leave the bamboo hedge standing but line it with wire-netting all along to keep off stray animals. His neighbour rejected his suggestion and had the hedge replaced by that ugly brick wall. Over a period of ten years all the bamboo, feuille rouge and other hedges in his street have been replaced by brick walls. Box-like concrete houses stand where "cases créoles" used to be. Burglar-proof windows lock up people inside their cells. People no longer seem able to enjoy life in the open. Walls are growing up all over the place. There's now one around Shakti. This thought makes him miserable.

****

The bus is packed mostly with office workers and students. It is the peak hour. Shakti wanted a place in front but had finally to take one in the rear. Next to her on the two-sitter seat a man in his fifties is smoking while reading his newspaper. The smoke makes her more and more uneasy. She feels dizzy. She starts to cough. He looks over his newspaper at her.

"Something's wrong, miss?"

"No ... It's the smoke."

"Sorry!"

He puts off his cigarette. The bus is now on the fly-over bridge. Signal Mountain like a lion scrutinizes the horizon. The long period of drought has left visible traces on the back of the old lion. The tawny grass is lacerated by blackened patches here and there. Fires on Signal Mountain are a fairly common event during the hot dry season.

At Victoria Square there is the usual traffic jam and stampede. Shakti knows all the short cuts and soon she is in her office.

Five minutes later, Lall, the Office Attendant, goes into the Director's office with Marc Samson's attaché case. She knows that Marc will go straight to his office and then call her through the interphone. The phone rings. She does not feel like picking it up as if the moment she does it, her life will start changing. It's him all right calling her in his usual suave voice. She puts down the receiver, takes her notes-book and spiritless goes to the door, knocks, opens it and enters.

Marc Samson greets her with his usual genuine smile.

"Good morning my love! The night was long without you. ... Eh! You're moody ... Anything the matter? Come on love, give me a kiss. Bless me to face a most boring day."

"Marc, I'm in no mood for your lovey-dovey stuff. Just tell me what you want."

"Shakti! It is really my Shakti talking in this way to me. Surely not! Call Shakti. I need Shakti."

"Shakti is pregnant!"

"Say that again ... Come off it! ... You're serious? My God!"

"God has nothing to do with this."

"You're sure?"

"I've missed two periods. The test is positive."

"Why did'nt you tell me before?"

"That's beside the point ... I was not sure myself."

"What do you intend to do?"

"Don't you think you too are involved?"

"Yes, but ..."

"But what?"

"I mean ... You've taken me by surprise."

"Doesn't it occur to you that I too was taken by surprise?"

"What do you mean?"

"Forget it!"

He stands up, goes round his table, comes to her, puts his hands on her shoulders, asks her to sit down. She sits down on the chair, without raising her head. She finds it hard to keep her tears, but she knows that she must. She feels small and if she breaks down it will make her situation worse. Two adults on equal footing have to face a complex problem squarely. Any sign of weakness on her part will give him the beau rôle. She must not allow him to don the paternalistic garb. If she lets herself

130

go, she knows that she'll just hold him tight and weep and this is just what she feels like doing. But she controls herself.

"Why do you dramatize the situation?" he asks. "These things happen. Don't worry I'll look after everything."

"What do you mean?"

"It's simple, darling. Unwanted pregnancy."

"Unwanted pregnancy perhaps, but not an unwanted child."

"What do you mean?"

"This baby in my womb is the finest fruit of the most intense moment of love I've ever felt."

"You mean ... the first time?"

She remains silent. Quick but clear images flash in her mind.

The interview. Her first day in the office. She could not help being attracted by his charm, manners and efficiency. Was it the non-white girl's fancy for a white man? Was it the traditional secretary's helplessness vis-a-vis the powerful boss? Was it an infatuation, a crush? She was sure of the contrary. It was love. They started going out together and one evening at Piton du Milieu, in the wood, near the lake she gave herself completely. She was still a virgin.

Two weeks later she got a little worried when she missed her first period. As she had gone on the pill after that evening she attributed it to a change in her metabolism due to the pill. She got very worried when she missed her second one and had a test done. She was pregnant.

"I must leave this office," she murmurs between her teeth.

"Why leave? No harm has been done. I'll send you abroad on "study leave". Come back when you're fit again!"

"Marc, I need no charity ... Can't you understand?"

"It's not charity, Shakti! We've got a problem. I am proposing solutions. I'm a married man! Separated with my wife, but not divorced!"

"I don't want you to marry me! I'm not after your name or your fortune."

"Please don't take it this way! We are adults, let's look at our predicament as adults!"

"But you will not kill my baby!"

"Nobody wants to kill your baby. Who's been talking of killing anything? Don't get hysterical!"

This time his tone is harsh. She looks up with anger and pain. Is he finally like the rest of them? Class-conscious, caste-conscious, race-conscious and clique-conscious? The moment he finds himself off-balance, he adopts the big boss' tone, and starts to speak from his pedestal. He suddenly appears to her as an old medieval moat house with its bridge raised. Will the bridge ever be lowered? She now strongly feels that her place is elsewhere. The man she has known has become a stranger. There's no point staying. There's now a giant wall between them. What's the point of talking? Words will only rebound reinforcing silence. She stands up to leave. He gets angrier.

131

"What do you think you're doing? Sit down and listen! Don't behave like a baby!"

"Don't baby me! You hear, don't baby me! Look for another secretary. I wish her good luck."

She slams the door behind her, picks up her things and leaves.

****

Kunti is tidying up the kitchen. Joshua is silently smoking his pipe. He watches the laces of smoke rising gently, meandering its way up, gracefully changing shapes. Kunti knows that when he is in such a mood, he must not be disturbed. She leaves him alone to his thoughts knowing well that he will talk about them only when his ideas are clear.

In the back yard she puts her washings on the line and then goes to look after all the animals of her ark. Snow-white, her black mongrel, lays its front paws on her for the usual tender pat. Mimi, the cat, standing on a stone, stretches its body, licks its paws and delicately treads the ground towards the steps leading to the kitchen. The naked-neck rooster with its shiny velvety fiery feathers runs after a randy hen while another white hen watches over its new hatch. They all look normal and happy but her own heart is heavy. She hears her husband calling her. She leaves the empty bucket by the tap near the stone on which she does her linen and goes in. Joshua looks agitated.

"Mother, do you think our Shakti is pregnant?"

****

In the market place, Shakti has to elbow her way through. Since the fire which destroyed one wing of the market, it is always crowded as all the activities of the past are now carried out on less than half the space. Why has she come here? She cannot explain. But all she knows is that she always comes here whenever she has experienced great emotions, pleasant or painful. The Central Market in Port Louis bubbles with life. The stalls swelling with goods of all colours, shapes and scents, people of all races and status mingling together, foods from Asia, Europe and Africa make of "bazar central" a very special place. Here more than anywhere else she can feel and hear the heart and pulses of a young nation beating. But this morning, Shakti's vision is blurred and her feelings numbed. The movement around her is inchoate, the noise inarticulate. She sees the world through the confusion in her mind. Somebody calls her name in a familiar voice. She makes a vague effort to situate the voice. A soft hand tenderly touches her left arm. She turns round. It is Azad.

"Shakti! It's you, alright! Aren't you working today?"

She does not reply but just holds his hand tightly. Azad, her good old friend, always there at the right moment, always running to her rescue. He knows by the pressure of her slender fingers on his palm that she needs help. He allows himself to be dragged into a café nearby. He orders two coffees and a sandwich for himself as she refused one. For a few minutes she remains silent. Azad feels that he has to say something to break the wall of silence.

"Sure, you don't want a sandwich, a samoosa or something?"

"No thanks!"

"You don't want to lose your waist line?", jokingly.

"I have already lost it!"

"Come on Shakti! How am I supposed to know what to say if you don't help me."

"I'm looking for a job!"

"You've got a job. A very good one in the most flourishing firm. Your boss is perhaps the most dynamic entrepreneur of this land. What are you talking about?"

"I've just packed up."

Now she breaks down. She sobs aloud. At first Azad feels embarassed. He recovers rapidly, moves to her, holds her by both shoulders.

"Come on Shakti! Control yourself. Let's go outside ..."

They walk silently to the water front. There, sitting on a bench facing the sea they look blankly at the ships loading and unloading without saying a word. She takes out a handkerchief, blows her nose, then looks at him with a timid smile.

"Sorry Azad! I made you look like a fool."

"Don't worry about me girl! What's your problem? You're getting me worried, you know!"

She does not want to upset him. She puts on a light mood but he is no dupe.

"To cut a long story short, my dear Azad, your idiotic friend needs a job, a house and a ... a father for her baby!

"Your wish is my command, Madam."

"That would be incestuous! I love you as a brother."

"I have always loved you more than a brother."

"I'm serious, Azad. I'm up to my neck in muck."

"You're pregnant? ... And your white and rich paramour has dropped you as rotten fish. The bastard!"

"Look Azad, this has nothing to do with his money or the colour of his skin. I loved him ... I think I still love him."

"O.K., O.K., you still love him! What next?"

"I understand his reaction. The walls of traditions, the walls of taboos and prejudices are still strong."

"Were they strong when he drove you to the wall?"

"Don't be so crude!"

She doesn't know whether she meant crude or cruel. But it does not matter. She feels good to be with him. They talk and they talk under the hot summer sun. He speaks of his work, of his plans and then, out of the blue:

"Shakti why don't you accept to be my wife. I'll be so happy to be your child's father."

"No, Azad! I love you too much to get you into this. You know your parents are highly religious people. This will upset them too much. Anyway I can't pretend to be your wife when it's him I love."

"I'm ready to face anything. My parents, the Imam, even your fake love. Please Shakti! I mean what I say."

"Azad, your parents want you to marry a Muslim girl ..."

"You can become one ... It's a simple ceremony."

"I'll then hurt my parents. My father is a fervent Catholic, my mother a Hindu. They've been married for over thirty years without anyone trying to impose his faith on the other. I believe in this freedom, I want my child to enjoy it ... There's so much people can share without imposing ... Azard please take me home. I don't think I can make it alone."

They walk along the new trunk road to Victoria Square. Azad is silent. He knows there are many walls between him and Shakti. There is a narrow passage but it leads to a maze. It's perhaps too early to try to bring the walls down and in the meantime it's equally pointless hitting one's head against them.

****

Marc Samson catches himself lighting another cigarette. His ashtray is already full of half burnt cigarettes. There's no point getting worked up, he thinks to himself. There must be a civilised way out, acceptable to both. The phone rings. He picks up the receiver. It's his wife on the phone. She wants to know whether he's coming to take the children out as he does every Wednesday. He replies that he cannot, being taken up by an unexpected, urgent matter. A note of disappointment on the other side of the line. He puts the receiver down, presses on the buzzer of his interphone. An unfamiliar voice answers which irritates him still more. He tells the voice that he will receive no phone call.

Shakti Abraham, twenty-four, a fully qualified secretary with experience. Three months ago she was for him only a file number, a name on a list of persons to be interviewed. When her turn came, he could not believe his eyes. She looked so much like Kamla Devi, a young medical student, he was very much in love with. All their friends at the university thought that they would get married. But they didn't. He chose to break off fearing the hostility of his relatives and friends back home. He didn't want to be an outcast on his prejudice-ridden sugar island. After his studies he returned home from England, married a second cousin, had three children with her. Appearance was saved but the lively black eyes, long black hair, the sunny brown face and the slim but firm body of Kamla Devi kept haunting him. Then Shakti appeared. Almost a living reproduction of a memory. Slightly taller but with the same shiny eyes, bright smile and cheeky face at times. He felt as if God was giving him a second chance. But now? He is powerful, rich, respected, awed, feared. Can't he impose his will? Can't he ignore the pettiness, intolerance, hypocrisy and stupid prejudices? He knows he can, but will she fit in. Will she not be miserable in his circle? He is fortyfour. Is he not too old for her? Can he, should he leap over the wall.

Questions without answers flow into his mind and he cannot decide. He no longer recognises himself. As the Managing Director of the biggest and most prosperous firm in his country making decisions has become with time a natural habit. But now his mind and his will are paralysed. He tries to think again of Kamla Devi but the image fades out and Shakti comes in instead. He becomes positive about one thing: his fancy for Shakti is not just an attempt to recapture memories dead and gone, to reincarnate a passion lost for ever. No it is not fancy. It is love. Of this he is sure. But the walls of taboos and prejudices keep rising. He is no longer a young romantic lover ready to take the leap and start afresh. He is paralysed and immobilised by generations of suspicion and fears, misunderstanding and misgivings which have sunk in deeply into the collective unconscious.

****

Shakti and Azad do not go straight to the Abraham's. He takes her to a snack bar where, to please him, she eats a pair of dalpuri pancakes and drinks a glass of coconut water. Then he takes her to the pictures. The film is lousy. They finally decide to leave. For the past three hours they have practically said nothing to each other. When they reach the gate to her house, he turns round to go but she asks him to come in. Joshua is in the open veranda reading his afternoon paper.

"Good afternoon uncle Joshua!"

"How are you my boy? Shakti, you've had a good day?"

"Fine papa! Where's mama?"

"She's gone to the market. She won't be long ... Do you two want some tea?"

"No thanks Tonton," says Azad. "I must push off. I've got a few things to look after for tomorrow."

"Azad, please stay ... Stay for dinner. The pot's luck!"

"Yes, Azad. Why don't you stay? I challenge you to a game of chess."

"Tonton, how can I resist such temptation."

"I leave you to your game of chess. I'll go and make the tea."

She goes in and Joshua sets the table for the game of chess. For some time they pretend to concentrate on the game. But the comedy does not last. Joshua, lighting his pipe, speaks first.

"Azad, is Shakti all right?"

"Why do you ask?"

"I fear she is in trouble. Did she not tell you anything?"

"She told me plenty of things but nothing to worry about."

"Azad you're not telling me the truth!"

"Why should I lie to you ... Checkmate! See I've got you this time!"

Shakti returns with a tray full of tea things. She pours the tea and gives each one a cup.

"Aren't you having any?" Joshua asks her.

"No. I've just had a glass of coconut water."

"Who's won?" She asks.

"He took me unawares."

She bows towards her father, kisses him on his forehead. His heart glows. This is how he likes her. Thoughtful, considerate and loving. Maybe he is really worried for nothing. Maybe she just has a slight indisposition. But he still finds that she looks pale. Maybe its only his imagination.

Kunti appears at the gate. Azad goes to meet her to help her with her heavy bag. He kisses her. They exchange a few words. Azad chuckles, shakes his head. Joshua looks at them. What are they talking about? Azad is surely hiding something. Maybe he is the responsible one. They used to go out a lot together, though since three months he has not seen much of him. Azad takes the bag to the kitchen, followed by Kunti and Shakti. He heard vaguely the murmurs of a conversation. He thinks he has heard something like "We must tell your father". But he is not sure. Azad comes back.

"Tonton, another game?"

"You're now too good for me. What was tantine saying?"

"Nothing special! ... Tonton, may I ask you a question? When you and tantine decided to get married, did you get a lot of problems from your parents, relatives and acquaintances?"

"What do you mean?"

"You know! A Catholic marrying a Hindu."

"Yes! But attitudes have changed. Now I suppose that these things are found less objectionable. People are more open-minded."

Joshua looks at the young man with sympathy. He is persuaded that Azad will, at any moment, inform him of his intention to marry Shakti. He is now convinced that Shakti is pregnant and that Azad is the father.

He feels that he must do something or say something to make him feel at ease so that he may feel free to say what he has in mind.

"You know, Azad, the times have changed. The past was full of towers of Babel, of fortresses and citadels. They are tumbling down one after the other. Each generation has brought in its contribution. Your generation will not have to experience what we went through. There is more tolerance, more mutual respect and understanding nowadays."

Once he has started on this theme, Joshua cannot stop. He explains the prejudices of the past, describes how things have changed, expresses his optimism which he qualifies with his fears of a certain excess he notices at times when young people behave rashly and impatiently. Azad is struck by this old man's lucidity. If only the whole human race could display such wisdom! Their tête-a-tête is interrupted by Kunti's voice telling them that dinner is served.

After dinner they all go onto the veranda, the only cool place in the house in summer. Joshua lights his pipe, Kunti picks up her sewing things.

"Mother, what are you sewing?", Joshua asks.

"I must get things ready for the baby!"

"Which baby?"

"Our baby."

"Our baby?"

"Papa, I've got something to tell you. Please, let me finish with what I've got to say first. Papa, I'm pregnant. The father, a man you don't know, cannot marry me, nor do I think I want to marry him."

Joshua remains silent. So it's not Azad. He feels as if he is spinning in a maelstrom. He does not know what to say. His tongue is parched, his throat dry. He feels nausea. Why should this happen to his daughter, his flesh and blood? He looks straight in front of him into the darkness of the sky.

"Papa, the towers, fortresses, citadels and walls you always talk about are still very strong. As we destroy some here, more grow up there."

Her mother intervenes.

"Shakti, we'll talk about it again tomorrow morning. Your father is upset. Let's all sleep on it."

"Mama, I won't be able to sleep if I don't say what I have to say."

Joshua walks up and down the veranda.

"Who is the bastard who did this to you?"

"Don't misjudge him. I don't think he's to be blamed. I love him, I still love him papa, but we belong to two different worlds."

"But Shakti, what are you going to do?"

"Sit down papa."

He sits down. She moves towards him, squats near him, puts her head on his lap. He pats her gently on her back and strokes her hair.

"Why should this happen to you, my baby? What will happen to you now?", he murmurs.

"Don't worry papa, don't worry. I'll be all right. I want to have this baby. It is the fruit of the most intense moment of love I have ever experienced. This cannot be destroyed. What has to be destroyed are those walls which are denying my child a normal life. Papa, you and mama defied the world to have me. For this I love you. My son will be born in love, will grow in love ... Yes papa. I know it's going to be a son. I'll call him Joshua after you. My Joshua will fight his battle of Jericho. All the Joshuas of this land will one day shout all at the same time with one and the same voice ... And papa, the walls will come tumbling down."

She cannot continue. She sobs. Joshua's eyes are filled with tears. He cannot speak. He holds his daughter firmly by her shoulders for a moment.

"They will, coco! They will! They will because people must live and living beings must love. We need love."

A cool breeze sweeps across the trees and all the branches gently nod in the dark.

On the veranda of an old wooden house in a badly lit street four persons are listening to their hopes.

---

* Savoury Indian pancake

DEDE KAMKONDO

A SCENE FROM THE PAST

The court, packed as if it was a morning bus to town, was still – very still as everybody waited for the Judge to reappear and pronounce judgement. But this was no small case. It was a murder case – not only that – it involved a young whiteman called Continho.

In his chamber – just behind the courtroom – the judge looked at his notes again. He had to handle this case with care for his future depended on it. It was his first murder case since he was appointed High Court Judge a month ago.

The Judge was as sure as the Zambezi flows into the ocean that the Africans in Maputo wanted a guilty verdict. Understandably so. Gone were the days when the whites could get away with the murder of a blackman. Those days were gone. These were now the days of an independent Mozambique; the days when the sons of the land were in power.

The evidence against the whiteman was purely circumstantial and hearsay as far as the judge was concerned. The man was being accused of having poisoned his houseboy who died writhing and gnashing his teeth like a live grasshopper dropped straight onto the fire.

The Lower Courts had found the man guilty but he had appealed against the judgement. So the case was now in the lap of the newly appointed judge in the young country; a country which was still trying to get over the nightmares of four hundred years of colonial rule.

The people wanted this trial to be used as a reminder to the whites about who was in power (lest they forget) and – to an extent – a reminder that the people hadn't forgotten the horrid days of colonial legacy.

If the Judge declared the whiteman "Not guilty", he was for sure going to be branded as an impostor, as a sell-out, as a stooge. If he said, "Guilty", he was for sure going to be tormented with the thought that he had sent a innocent man to face the firing squad for a man is a man – black, khaki, yellow or white.

At 40, the judge could recall vividly an episode which happened when he was very young. What happened was that the District Commissioner for Nyanza Province came into the village one day at dawn. The Commissioner's name was Continho. That episode, that scene, happened years ago but now here was another Continho standing trial for murder. Were these two Continhos related?

The Judge knew that his decision was bound to be influenced by that incident which happened years ago. A scene from the past. As he sat behind the desk, stroking his pen, he found himself recalling that bizarre incident from the past ...

Just as the cocks were flapping their wings in readiness for the final crow, Senor

Continho the District Commissioner arrived in the village, accompanied by nine barefooted African soldiers and one mulatto sergeant.

Eyes bloodshot, either as a result of too much alcohol or too little sleep, he pressed a megaphone to his lips and snorted, "Everybody out! Hurry up! Children and women too!" Then taking out his revolver, he fired at a tree three times.

Within minutes, the entire village was in front of the District Commissioner. The villagers were just a pool of frightened faces and whimpering minds. The children, still half-asleep, clung to their mothers like little crocodiles, their expression puzzled, although they could sense danger in the air.

"Sit down!" bellowed the DC and the mulatto sergeant edged closer to him to act as an interpreter.

"Where's the headman?" demanded Senor Continho. The aging headman rose to his feet as if the joints were on fire. He looked up at the sky and his lips moved in a short, silent prayer.

"Now, mister headman," began the DC, "reports have reached me that you're harbouring terrorists in this village. Is that true?"

"No sir." The headman, the hair all white, shook his head vigorously.

"You lie!" thundered the DC, "Why is your village full only of children, old men and women? Where are the young men? Where are they? Tell me!"

"Gone to work in the mines in South Africa, sir."

"You expect me to believe that?" roared the DC, "Where are the young men, the youth?"

Without waiting for an answer, the DC strode over to a woman whose twin daughters were sitting by her side like a pair of watchdogs. Grabbing one of the daughters by the ears, Senor Continho dragged her away from the mother.

Turning to the headman, the DC said, "If you don't tell me where your able young men are, I'll blow the top of this girl's head off. I mean it."

The headman, his eyes blinking rapidly, turned again to look at the sky. He muttered another prayer.

"I've told you, sir, that they've gone to the mines," he said slowly, the veins in his neck standing out like a bundle of twigs.

"Try a better lie!" snorted the DC, and the next moment he pulled the trigger, blowing the brains out of the little girl. Just like that. Her mother fell in a faint.

"Where are they?" yelled the DC, his eyes flashing with anger. Receiving no answer, the DC looked at his gun and then aimed it at a little boy who was sitting in his mother's lap sucking his thumb. The Senor was about to pull the trigger when the old headman, as if with strength borrowed from another world, rushed forward, hurling himself at the Senor, a knife in his hand.

God knows how many bullets were pumped into that frail old body that morning ...

The Judge shook his head, trying to get rid of that horrible day from his mind.

"Lucky I'm still alive," he muttered softly. "If it hadn't been for the headman ... well, that was years, years ago. We don't live in the past, do we?"

Slowly, he stood up the way the headman had stood up on that fateful day years ago. It was time to pass judgement.

Minutes later, the courtroom was still noiseless. Nobody could believe what they had heard. Was the Judge in his right frame of mind? Really, "Not guilty"?

ERNEST SIDNEY FELLOWES

SERPENTS IN THE SUNSHINE

Edson Thuli stood up from behind a desk that seemed to make him look even smaller than the bare five feet and one inch that he actually was; born and raised on an inadequate diet of maize meal in the Eastern Highlands of Zimbabwe, like many of the Manyika people, he was proportionately small in stature. His small body was clothed in a sober dark suit, white shirt and a tie with a sober pattern that befitted his legal calling, and his secret ambition to one serve his people as a Minister of Justice. He was now a shrewd and able advocat though denied the opportunity of ever being called to The Bar. The closed ranks of the fascist white legal fraternity ensured the minimum of black faces deriving any of the legal cream to be skimmed from more expensive litigants. He derived a small but steady income from giving inexpensive but accurate legal advice and providing a secretarial and typing service, to the steady stream of country peasants, urban workers and the occasional "poor whites" of whom Seren was one.

Seren Wolleff had come that morning to meet Edson Thuli expecting to meet a political fire-brand who looked over his shoulder before he spoke. It had not been like that at all; after leaving instructions with his young assistant and his faithful, discreet typist Marylyn, they strolled the length of Queen's Boulevard discussing the matter which had brought Seren to The Capital. They wended their way through the bustling jostle of sophisticated townies, families of bewildered country folk laden with masses of goods, older children holding the hands of their flocks of brothers and sisters, mothers burdened with the latest arrival on her back, the slightly obvious swelling in her belly of yet another mouth to feed in the months to come, women juggling, the main load of family bedding, pots and pans plus sleeping mats, carried on their leads with the ease, dignity and grace that these wonderful women, the mothers of Continent Africa, daily and yearly through all their working lives preserve.

Edson had been right in deciding that they should walk. The permanent lounger perusing the semi-porno magazine at the entrance to the block of offices, was there for that special purpose – to report on his movements. Seren's arrival would also have been carefully noted. Edson reasoned that an open walk along the Boulevard would tend to place Seren in the innocuous category of yet another naive "White Liberal", bent on showing he didn't mind being seen with a black! In the safety of the open street they talked of the day that the capital itself would erupt in the war of attrition which the Bush Fighters had carried right to the outskirts of the capital. Once only did Edson permit himself to deviate from the subject for which Seren had been summoned from his distant place of residence in the Low Veldt; they were about to cross a busy intersection when Edson restrained him saying "It's much safer if we cross the crowd, some keen young S.P.U. recruit might try for promotion by running you down, just being with me makes you a fair target!" He said this with just a faint wry smile as Seren looked and felt aggrieved; "You are forgetting that we are together Edson, he would get you at the same time". As they waited to cross, Edson answered "Yes Seren, but being with me, you are clearly a "Kaffir buttie" and the White Front can do without you – whereas I, Edson Thuli, am a constant suspect presently out of P.D. for a while at least and in the hope they can get some lead from those who contact me, so for your sake, let's hope they think of you as just a Kaffir lover"!

They proceeded without a further word until they reached The King James Hotel; Seren stood aside to let Edson in ahead of him when a very blonde and florid complectioned white was about to leave. Seren guessed that her vrow type and manner almost certainly identified her as a farming wife. Edson led Seren to the Beer Garden telling him that it was the only multiracial section where they could drink and have a snack together. The waiter who came to them looked disapproving, he had his own standards of what correct social behaviour was, serving Seren and Edson made him feel embarassed. He continued to show his feelings for the whole hour they spent over a sandwich lunch and a few beers – he looked hurt when Seren failed to give him a tip. They left and emerged into the hot early afternoon sunshine, the Boulevarde which stretched ahead of them was less hurried and crowded. The temperature had climed to nineties Farenheit and there was the annual oppressiveness in the air like the Mistral or Khamsin winds of the Mediterranean or North Africa. The cloying perfume of the avenues of jacaranda tree hung around, parked motorists cursed loudly as the heat denied them easy starting. They reached the block of offices where Edson worked. Outside a Mazda pick-up of an indeterminate hand-painted shade of green was parked. In it sat two whites, one dark and swarthy aged in his late forties and deeply suntanned, the other, Seren suddenly realised as a slight prickle of alarm raced across his scalp, was a gangling, long-haired "hippie" type with an oval face and full wet lips. He was the one who had shared the two-bearth railway compartment with him the previous night on his journey to the capital! The two in the cab of the Mazda sat immobile staring straight ahead. Without appearing to notice the two Special Police Unit operators, Seren and Edson entered the office block and spent a few minutes cross-checking their arrangements. There was nothing written. Then, as they shook hands to say farewell Edson warned: "It looks fairly certain now Seren that the S.P.U. have tied us together. That's no coincidence. These people are often miss-fits from recruit ranks and are given a very free hand to act as they please, almost freelance and not much for the routine stuff. All I can say is, for all our sakes and our work watch-out!! and good-luck – go well and take care." Seren thanked him and put an arm round the shoulders of this little man who hourly walked a tightrope.

"Thanks to you I shall be on my guard now, and I hope that at my age I may not let you or our brothers in the Bush down – good-bye and YOU take care!"

As he walked out into the heat that bounced off the sidewalk, past the watching occupants of the Mazda and sought a cab – Seren felt suddenly all his sixty years of age, lonely as only a widower can be. He saw his reflection in a shop window the image of a rather round-shouldered, slightly more than middle-aged man, with hair, once blonde and straight from his Saxon forefathers, now slightly balding and turning a mousy colour, a darkly tanned face with prominent cheek-bones and not much flesh, stocky in build but not weighing more than 140-150 pounds. Not very impressive he felt, to deal with a serious show-down, but for the certain toughness still left, he felt grateful to the commando-type training of thirty years before. He took a cab to a second class multiracial hotel.

Seren spent the afternoon asleep until it was time for his night-train back to Southdorp – the Mazda and it's occupants were at the station as he left. After the normal, rather slow and uncomfortable night journey, Seren arrived at Southdorp before the shattering heat of the day ahead had a chance to sully the tranquillity of a typical colonial Sunday morning. Seren stepped out of the Station entrance, gave a casual glance around and was not sure whether to be relieved or anxious when there appeared to be no one watching for his arrival. He decided to make sure by walking down through town to Pioneer Avenue and his destination.

Like any other Sunday morning Southdorp was no exception in the then colonial Africa, it's street cleaners being the only signs of activity on empty avenues, a faintly nostalgic sound of distant church bells that stirred Seren's memories of schoolage years in a frost-bound landscape, an age when Spartan parents insisted on cold water washing of hands and face and of course, all round your neck and ears. Steaming and stodgy oatmeal porridge to prepare reluctant children for that "brisk walk, that will do you good", through snow-bound lanes and country roads to an ever cold Anglican Church. The fullsome, bland, even smug face of the incumbent Vicar, heartily bellowing through hymns, droning his way over the sermon he felt his congregation was in need of, but with a wary eye on the Local Squire and his entourage to be sure it was them he pleased, because if not his very comfortable and subsidised living could be in danger – it only needed a faintly disapproving report to his Bishop!!

Seren pulled himself back to the ominous present; the sun was climbing rapidly down the rows of office blocks and was starting to burn the dew off the red corrugated iron roofs of the single storey Colonial Era houses. He walked past the notorious "Great Western Hotel", illfamed haunt of "short-time" novice whores, black gangsters with their body-guards and big-hipped full-busted prostitutes, the ever present S.P.U. agents, the white dregs of human wreckage from the Southdorp doss-houses. Even at eight-thirty in this Sunday morning they were there, these pathetic remnants of what had once been European men and women, squatting there on the kerb; their burning alcoholic and gaunt bodies screaming silently for more drinks. It took Seren half an hour to stroll gently down through the town, he needed the time to quieten an unease like snakes slithering around in his guts.

His destination, The Villa Roma, was almost the largest, and indeed, the oldest Italian eating-house in Southdorp; in addition to being the place where the clients, or rather "Patrons", could get the best Italian meal in the whole of Southern Africa and at a price unrivalled anywhere, the proprietor baked and sold Continental breads and pastries of every description. In fact it was more a community meeting place for all middle-class local Italians – but not openly popular or talked of by the prestigious and wealthy members of that fine old race, due to it's connection with an organisation known for its ability to wield considerable and persuasive influence, "The Family" – frequently referred to as The Cosa Nostra! Seren once got involved with The Scalloni brothers, Vittorio and Nico, and with the business and hidden influence they wielded. But that was another story.

Seren chose to visit The Villa Roma on this hot and sleepy Sunday morning because they were the "fixers", whose influence covered not only Southdorp, but had tentacles that reached to all but the eastern part of the country, and that included a hold on many apparently spotless citizens of the capital! The result of Seren's discussions with Edson Thuli the previous day meant that he would have to be required to transfer his present scene of operations in Three Rivers, a God-forsaken rail terminus situated in the deep Bush at the junction of a trio of rivers and within a matter of yards from the border with the Portuguese colony Mocambique. It was a means of earning sufficient to maintain a modest livelihood, and had served as a low-key "cover" for operations over the last year and a half. Seren was employed by The Railway as a low clerk and assistant to the resident Station Master, a neurotic hyperchondriac who lived on a massive diet of pills, to either quieten his nerves or boost his energy. This product of an English northern slum tolerated Seren only because he had no choice, the "Powers That Be" in Railway H.Q. Southdorp had ordained that it should be so – and at least some of them had been influenced by the pressure of outright blackmail. The greatest psychological weakness of the most dedicated fascists in the White Front was that they all shared the same enjoyment of the flesh of African women in bed, and though it was tacitly accepted as the right of every red-blooded white male, such was the veneer of Victorian hypocrasy with which the whole colonial social structure was covered. Neither Vittorio nor Nico were arround when Seren arrived at The Villa Roma. The old waiter greeted him with a smile of pleasure.

"Morning to you Boss Seren – good to see you again", the greeting was genuine. Both, as older men, liked and respected each other, Seren smiled and replied;

"Good to see you again Baba – is your family well and yourself?"

"A little well Boss Seren – but with my youngest wife I have problems, she complains that I do not sleep with her only and she is not yet pregnant!" He looked aggrieved.

"Baba, you must go home just a little drunk one night after work – then you will be strong and she will become pregnant".

Seren lazed over a breakfast of two fried eggs, rashers of bacon well done, with fried tomatoes, mushrooms and a couple of kidneys, and of course as the remnant of a Saxon English upper-class family, the traditional pot of tea. He chewed slowly, while also digesting with a high degree of disbelief and cynicism, the contents of "The Southdorp Sunday Chronicle" – he smiled a quiet smile when he read that in the opinion of the Minister of Defence, "the white life-style of the country was safe for at least the rest of HIS lifetime"!

Nico arrived at about eleven. Like his brother Vittorio he was originally a Sicillian peasant, who like hundreds of his kind had been contracted to build the largest dam in Africa, a monument to Italian engineering and daily courage that quietly surprised the British and Afrikaanse members of the White Front, to whom most Italians were regarded as beaten ex-enemy and designated as Wops and Dagoes. The tough dark-haired man with huge shoulders held out a hand that was like a miniature shovel, the smile of perfect teeth in the unlined and well-fed face was spontaneous, but the dark brown eyes showed an inner caution.

"Buon giorno Seren my friend – is this visit business or pleasure – you have eaten?"

"Yes thanks Nico, and the reason is business and after – some pleasure I hope". Seren got to business right away as Nico sat down opposite in the curtained booth that was the late 19th century style of The Villa Roma, and allowed it's patrons a measure of privacy for their often discreet assignments. Seren said "Nico, you must get me transferred to the capital – and soon, because only inside the capital there are no road-blocks – I am also not sure how much longer I can operate or hold the fort!". Seren reported about the meeting with Edson and his anxiety caused by the watchful S.P.U. agents.

Nico listened without showing any emotion, he hardly seemed interested, but Seren knew from experience that Nico had taken it in, and weighed every aspect of his report. This was evident a few moments later when Nico replied;

"The transfer – that will be no problem, Seren, it will take a few days only – maybe a week – but not more. But the others, those who watch – did you see them today, or any of their kind?" Seren shook his head.

"Not a sign Nico, but even so I have a feeling I cannot explain —".

Nico broke in – "I think I can. From their records supplied to them by Railway Security, they know your base is Three Rivers. I think it is there they will wait. You must watch out for them on your journey. Now, what else do you need from me?"

Seren was blunt and to the point;

"Nico, do you mind if I take Sally out for the day? Now, this is not business, but as a girl-friend for today"

Nico looked with a flash of sympathy at Seren; it seemed, he understood the loneliness with which Seren was forced to cope with.

"Sure Seren; it is her day off anyway, you telephone her eh?"

He said this almost as if Seren had observed a currently very out of date costum, – and had requested permission to take out his sister for the day – instead of one of at least forty or fifty "call-girls" and prostitutes who were the main source of Nico's and Vittorio's income, and the power of coercion that the two brothers exercised over male whites of many positions of influence in the White Front.

"You like Sally – she is a good girl, she was mine for a little time. But you know I and my brother, we like our girls to be big, but Sally is the one that men like you prefer. She will make some man a very good wife one day when she has saved enough money to open her own bottle-store".

Seren phoned Sally; she had been washing her underwear und tidying her bedroom in the single storey house she shared with four other Scalloni girls, each with their own room but a shared lounge with a well stocked bar. She would be pleased to see him. Half an hour later, Nico's own chauffeur Pasta MacDonald, an African in spite of his name, whose driving skills would have qualified him more suitably for either Monte Carlo or the Nuremburg track, dropped Seren at Sally's place.

Without make-up and in a tight white linen frock it was hard to believe her trade.

Sally came down the steps of the verandah with a backdrop of hibiscus bushes and bouganvillia creepers which grew against this house in Regents Park. She greetet him easily with a quick soft kiss on the lips. There was a bond between them immediately, like old friends, yet he was sixty – she was barely nineteen! She handed Seren the flasks and sandwiches and cold chicken for their picnic lunch and gave a little laugh as she said;

"Do you know Seren; this is the very first time a man has actually taken me out in daylight, even my clients pretend they have never seen me when I meet them in town; so I hope we are going somewhere quiet!"

Seren climbed into the little Renault taxi-cab and gave her a hug, and told Pasta;

"Head for a bottle-store to pick up some cold drinks and a few beers for yourself. Then head for Khami Dam – that should give them something to talk over – you will wait a couple of hours for us, will you?"

Pasta gave a huge smile; "Sure Boss Seren – I can always sleep while you keep paying my waiting time".

The Dam: the traditional site for the white family picnics complete with Nanny, taken along for a treat whether it was her choice of free afternoon or not.

As usual, there were some hundreds of couples, holding hands as they walked, seeking a little privacy and even the hope of uninterrupted intimacy; Seren and Sally headed for the shade of trees overlooking the sparkling blue waters of The Dam. They could not have attracted more attention if they had both been stark naked; as the only couple of mixed race. They attracted cat-calls, whistles from many young African males, and shouts of "Kaffir lover" from both male and female whites. An elderly white man and a young attractive black girl had their picnic in full view of hundreds of voyeurs and ill-whishers – ignoring them all!

With no attempt to do more than occasionally hold each others hand they talked. Sally asked Seren about his former life in England, English customs and habits, and if race division and prejudice was the same as in the land of the Zimbabwean people? Seren was ashamed to admit, that except for some parts of Europa, Britain still was mainly race and colour conscious, saw little wrong with the policy of apartheid, and cared little for the plight of Blacks in a distant colony.

Sally on her part, sensed the hidden question in Seren's mind; of why she had come to town, what her reasons were for becoming a prostitute?

Her story was simple and similar to that of thousands of other peasant girls who were literally forced to sell their bodies during the fascist regime of the White Front. Her two elder brothers acted as runners and information carriers to the Freedom Fighters, who operated in the hills near their family home. One day, each carrying only a threadbare blanked, an old enamel plate and a drinking cup, some home-made snares and a dema, a traditional small axe, the boys left home to join the other young men and women who were streaming across the country's borders for training in neighbouring countries as fighters for the freedom of their people. On the word of a local informer, the whisper reached a nearby unit of mercenary commando-mounted forces under the control of an ex-American Green Beret Major. They took Sally's father while he was working on his fields alongside his wife. After bludgeoning him until he urinated blood, they tied him with wire to an old spring mattress and lit a fire below to make him tell what he did not know. To destroy the evidence, these psychopathic sadists "from the advanced World", shot what was left of Sally's father, and told the distraught woman to bury the body before nightfall. Sally and two younger children watched in silent horror from the cover of the bush where they had been to collect firewood. Since their father was no more the next harvest was meagre and it was obvious the family would starve unless Sally took a job in Southdorp.

Barely seventeen, Sally got her first, and as it turned out her last, position as house-girl to a white family. She was expected to wash and iron the family laundry, do simple cooking, act as nursemaid to two small children – for a monthly wage of ten Dollars!

In the colonial era, an extra duty of all house-girl was to act as unpaid whore for the head of the house when the wife was absent. The first time Sally's Madam went to visit her parents in the capital, Sally was ordered to provide this service. Fearing she would lose her job, she complied and three months later she was "visibly" pregnant. She was fired and returned to her village to bear her child. With her natural stubborn determination Sally went to the district herbalist to drink an infusion that would render her sterile.

She then returned to Southdorp, and, because of the protection they offered, became one of The Scalloni Girls, paid well for the professional services she supplied.

Sally finished her story and gave a small shrug of her shoulders.

"So you see Seren; it was all the will of God, it was as The Mlimo directed me. My mother looks after my son, the family now eat well, my younger sister and brother and later my own son will get a better schooling than I did. I save each week so one day I can open a bottle- and general store in my district and with money, I may even get married – who knows?".

The sun was slanting to the horizon. They walked in silence back to the taxi and roused Pasta from his snores. The interior of the car was like an oven.

"You and your family really had a lousy deal didn't you?" She shook her head;

"No, I am more fortunate than you are Seren. Now will you do something for me and also for you? Eat with me at my place tonight – please do?"

"I am so glad that you asked me Sally. After this afternoon together, I don't fell like going back to The Roma to eat before I go to catch my train. I will."

In about an hour Sally produced a simple meal of stewed steak, boiled vegetables, mixed with a relish of sauce from onions, tomatoes, a dash of chilli and served with the traditional African dish of thick maize meal. She brought the customery bowl of water, presented it to Seren on her knees, and after him, she also washed her hands.

147

The food placed between them on the floor, they ate in the traditional way – with their hands. When they had finished she said;

"Please Seren; so that you may travel safely with my Spirit to protect you, can we wash our bodies together? Please do not ask what this is for."

Seren understood her request, he felt lonely at the thought of tonight's journey; "Yes, let's finish our day together as we have spent it – for each other."

She led Seren to the shower in a corner of her bedroom. They stripped the clothes from each other and stepped under a lukewarm shower; she washed his body from head to foot as if it was the most natural action, then her own, and when she had finished she turned and pressed her supple dark body against his, her arms crept round his neck and with the shower drenching both their bodies, she kissed him.

"Take me this time Seren, as a man takes his new wife after she has washed his body."

Seren lifted her wet body and without a word, carried her to the bed. With the hunger of a peasant girl for her man, Sally pulled his face to hers and kissed him passionately; she drew his body between her legs. In the unison of their love, Seren murmured in her ear; "Sally, we need each other always, not just now but for the future."

She smiled and her eyes were warm and loving, but shook her head.

"No Seren, take what we have now – love me for a little while as you would if I were your wife. Later in their quiet tranquillity in body and mind, they lay contented in each others arms; Sally get up and showered again;

"Come please Seren;" He did as she asked, she again washed him from head to foot and after thoroughly rinsing them both with cold fresh water, Sally sprinkled some herbs into a bowl of tepid water and it seemed as if she spoke what may have been a prayer. She bathed him and finally poured the rest of the herb treated water over them. Sally insisted that they both kneel down while she murmered a prayer to her own Spirit, asking to protect Seren on his journey. She made Seren put his clothes on his still wet body.

By the time Pasta came to collect him to catch the night train to The Low Veldt, Seren had a sense of inner tranquillity and happiness he had not felt for many weeks. The fealing of crawling snakes in every nerve of his body – had vanished!.

Sally refused his offer of a personal gift of money with quiet and firm dignity. They said good-bye in her room, Seren held her tightly to him, they kissed with affection. He searched for the right words, "Sally, thank-you for spending the day with me, you made the day a loving and happy one for me – and I hope it has been be same for you."

She drew away and said "Seren, other men use my body. I am a prostitute, a "bitch" as they call us. It is my work and my choice, but you today, you have given me respect, friendship and I have felt it in my heart – love. Go well and with care. Have no fear in your mind, my Spirit will take care of you – you will come to no harm! Good-bye my dearest Seren – go now."

As the slow rocking train rolled through the night Seren slept like an infant at the breast of it's mother – in perfect peace!

Seren awoke soon after sunrise and idly watched the seemingly endless miles of sugar-cane and citrus plantations. The "LowVeldt Express" which this night train was ironically called, was a non-corridor train, usually with only one coach attached of second-class status, specifically for those odd whites who might either choose or be forced as Seren was, to travel by this highly uncomfortable mode. Assured that he had not been observed by any other passenger, in addition to his own canvass valise Seren took an item down from the luggage rack, which had been in the taxi already when Pasta arrived to take him to Southdorp Station. According to Pasta it was a bundle of unassembled fishing-rods, given to him, as he said "by Boss Nico for Boss Seren". Fresh from his idyllic day with Sally and it's love sequal Seren gave little thought to this unusual gift. He suddenly wondered why either Nico or Vittorio should imagine that he had developed a hobby for which he had never shown the slightest interest? He started unwrapping the package, it struck him that the fishing rods seemed unusually heavy. This was hardly surprising when on a closer inspection, Seren discovered it contained an automatic rifle with a magazine attached, and a loaded submachine-gun! So Nico felt that this need was as serious as that. It was a depressing thought!

Around nine, with the daily heat gathering in strength, to turn the average human into a bundle of streaming sweat and sodden rags, "The Express" eventually rattled and clanked to a shuddering halt. They had arrived at Mubuzi Junction, where the single branch line eventually commenced it's two hundred or so kilometers lonely crawl to Three Rivers.

Unwashed and unshaven, Seren called a station-orderly to carry his luggage. After the customary greeting neither of them spoke as they trudged across the tracks through ankle-deep red dust to where his Citroen C.V. 2 was parked. The orderly threw the bags on the rear seat and Seren gave him 20 cents to buy a Coke.

Sophia was waiting for him at the door of the pre-fabricated Railway House, set slightly apart under the tall gum trees – Sophia and her husband Carlos, the shunter, were Coloureds. Sophia put her hands on Seren's shoulders and kissed him warmly on the lips, then led him into their dining sitting room. Carlos was just finishing his breakfast. He granted his wife's affectionate greeting for Seren and greeted Seren.

"Hi! Seren, good to see you again, good to see any different face around here, have some "scoff" – sit your arse down!" Seren gratefully accepted his greeting and invitation. He enquired "How's it going Carlos? You've been waiting for us to start the Shunt for our Bush Metropolis?"

"Yes Seren; thank Christ you're early for a change, so I can get done and get to Villa early." He spoke of the nearby border town, to which he and others crossed regularly to visit their Portuguese/African girl-friends on the other side, and drink "vinho verde" in large amounts as it was cheap – as were the numerous bar-girls! Sophia called from the kitchen for Seren to "wash-up for food", he did as she asked and the food was on the table when he returned from the bathroom.

A piece of steak with two fried eggs sitting on top, freshly baked bread and black coffee. Seren was ready for it. His meal-break finished, Carlos got up and went back to work with a casual wave of the hand – it was by now mid-morning heat, only slightly less than a normal furnace. Seren asked Sophia if he might have a shower and shave, she came close and said "of course you can my dear – but for anything else – you'r out of luck, that's why Carlos is going to Villa this week!". Sophia was a light Coloured, she had a superb figure, and even after five kids, her sexual appetite was impossible for the normal man to satisfy; they had been lovers twice before while Carlos was at work and Seren had asked to use their shower, and once on the Night Train to Southdorp, when she had come to his coupé. Sophia was a very determined woman!

After a little chat with Sophia, Seren went out to check fuel and oil on the C.V. 2. In order to make the journey ahead to Three Rivers a little more bearable, he asked the house gardener to cut some light and leafy branches, with which to cover the car roof, a device he had found effective for deflecting the beat of the sun.

He was waiting for the gardener to cut the branches. Seren reached for his binoculars in the front of the car. His eyes caught sight of a dark patch under the gumtrees – it was the Mazda! Seren focussed the lens – it was the same pickup and the same occupants. Nico had anticipated correctly, they were waiting for him and the whole operation was balanced on a knife's edge. His stomach churned, he had nowhere else to go – he had to start the journey to Three Rives, he had no choice. Suddenly his stomache ceased to churn, his mind became clear and calm! Seren thought he heard Sally's words inside his head "have no fear in your mind, my Spirit will take care of you, you will come to no harm!" – It helped Seren to think clearly, he could evaluate the situation and plan ahead.

Seren chose a branch with the least leaves, tied a long length of line to it and hung it over his rear window, taking the line the length of the car in through the open windscreen, and with five or six feet to spare, secured it to the front bumper.

Seren gave the gardener money for a bottle of beer, and went inside to thank Sophia for her hospitality. He knew that this might be the last time, but did not say so.

"Thanks a lot Sophie for all you've done – you've been like a mother to me".

"I very much hope not my love, I haven't felt like a mother, and you have never treated me like one, still, I know what you mean; we must arrange a week-end together in Southdorp when I go there to see my family some time. Then you can really show me how you feel – you can screw me until you're knackered!" She laughed and pressed tight against him. They kissed, Seren hoped it would come true.

The Citroen waddled over the tracks. The automatic rifle and submachine gun were within easy reach on the back seat of his grasp and loosely covered with an old blanket. In his mirror, Seren saw blue smoke emerge from the back of the parked Mazda pick-up – they were following him.

He drove at a quiet steady pace on the first few miles of gravel road. It gave him time to think and evaluate the whole situation. Besides, the heavy corrugations and deep pot-holes necessitated constant concentration and violent swerves to keep even his Citroen C.V. 2 on the road.

The first and inescapable factor was, that even if the two S.P.U.agents allowed him to reach Three Rivers – he could not afford to let them do so. He was the only person who could prevent that – he had to try to kill his pursuers!

The second glaring factor was, that his old Citroen C.V. 2 did not stand a "cat's chance in hell" of putting any great distance between himself and the Mazda Diesel pick-up. If it was their intention to ambush him instead of just tailing him to his base, they could do so at any time they chose.

A third factor was Seren's own choice of terrain where an elderly man, even as desperate as he was, would stand a chance against two trained agents many years younger than him.

Given the right conditions – thick bush, rocky outcrops, or even a small kopje – there was just a chance the scales could tip in his favour. The two agents behind him might just be a little more at home in the slums, in the high-density townships, – and hopefully not so used to the harsh terrain of the Low Veldt – he might just swing it in his favour!!

Trying to trick out the two human jackals behind him, Seren figured out that he had another eight to ten miles before he could reach the valley before Mtilikwe River with the kind of cover arround that would reduce his two-to-one handicap. But that was also too near a main tarred road to the Low Veldt capital. At that stage, neither could attack the other without the chance of other road users being witness – it had to be sooner, he could not wait much longer!

His options were reduced to one! Seren was forced to consider the vague idea that had flickered through his mind when he had arranged the branch to hang over his rear window. As his pursuers continued to maintain a steady gap of just under half a mile, Seren reasoned that they would continue as long as the dust cloud he raised enabled them to pin-point his position. If they once had reason to doubt how far ahead he was, they would most certainly increase their speed to get closer.

Seren knew from experience, that less than a mile ahead the corrugated gravel surface finished and gave way to a sandy riverine soil, now ground to a fine dust by daily traffic. For a distance of two miles or so, the sandy road was bordered by scattered grassy hillocks, similar to sanddunes, on each side of the one-time river bed. An area, as he had discovered once before when he had stopped to urinate, inundated with burrows inhabited by nests of puff-adders!

Seren reached the sandy track doing forty m.p.h., swerving wildly in the fine soft sand. He released the cord that held the branch over his rear window, letting it slide through his fingers until he could see in his mirror that the branch was now trailing in the sand at the rear of the car. Fighting the steering he pushed his speed to fifty. If the dust cloud behind him could be followed with ease before, the thick and blinding fog of dust that was now thrown up, was almost impenatrable. Seren hoped it would slow down the Mazda and give him the few precious minutes extra, that he needed.

Reaching out behind him, he dragged over the automatic rifle with it's attached magazine, cursing to himself as the machine-pistol dropped to the floor out of his reach. Round the next right-hand bend, he chose a point where the riverbed inclined to a wide and shallow bottom, then deliberately steered the little Citroen C.V. 2 down the slope, the four independant springs of the car kept the vehicle upright as he turned it in line with the direction of the ditch, hitting his brakes hard and coming to a violent halt, killing his engine as he did so.

Seren opened his door and jumped out the rifle in his hand. He placed his weekend bag on the steering wheel, draping the blanket over it, hoping that at first it might look as if he had an accident – giving him just enough time for an initial advantage.

Slamming the drivers door shut, Seren raced for a sandy hillock about fifty yards from the ditch to his right. It had a ledge about six feet from the top that would give him a good range of fire, and was the nearest place with minimum cover. He suddenly changed his mind and though his heart was pounding wildly and he was gasping for breath, he changed direction and ran towards another hillock higher up and more to his right, giving him extra cover. He reached his cover and threw himself down in the short grass, rifle in front. He peered round the hillock and waited.

Barely three minutes later, before Seren even heard the sound of the Mazda, he saw it making it's way slowly out of the dense cloud of red dust, it was on full acceleration when it turned the corner and came in sight of the Citroen sitting in the five foot deep ditch. The driver slammed on his brakes – it was the blonde "hippie". As they came to a halt, his partner threw himself out of the door furthest away from Seren – from his cover. Seren opened fire. His first burst hit the radiator of the Mazda which immediately gushed out clouds of steam. An immediate response came frome the older man with the beard. From the cover of the nearside front wheel he let loose with a sub-machine gun and blow out the windscreen and windows of the Citroen, aiming at what appeared to be a driver behind the steering wheel.

The blonde "hippie" did not make the same mistake. He screamed to his partner; "On the hill – the bastard's on the hill – get round him!"

His door flew open and he slid out, spraying the hillock behind him with bullets. The blonde hit the ground, and before he could get off another burst, Seren poured fire into him. The boy's gun kept firing into the ground as he collapsed and lay still. Out of the vast blue bowl of a cloudless sky, the noon sun roasted the air into a palpitating stillness. Flickering heat-waves distorted the vision like mirages, not the slightest sound filled the empty stillness of the arena of destruction, the "hippie" lay quite still, the dust was clearing and there was no sign of the bearded partner, he had simply vanished!

Seren put his ear to the ground beneath him, it was vibrating with the running footsteps of the other hunter but he was out of sight, keeping the first hillock chosen by Seren between them and using it for cover. Agile now as any rabbit, Seren ran for his life towards the cover of the other hillocks, he turned for a snap shot from the hip at the man as he reached the ledge of the first hillock. After a few shots his rifle went silent – he threw it away and ran, zig-zaging for the Citroen and to reach his submachine gun.

The bearded man now realised that Seren was unarmed. He could be more deliberate. Seren reached the riverbed, and ran bent double towards his car. He reached it, and from below opened the door. A burst of fire thudded through the vehicle as Seren grabbed his gun from the floor. Then he turned and sprayed the hill. His shots were wild, Seren risked a careful look to see where his adversary was hiding and just in time to see the man throw himself flat on the same sandy ledge of the first hillock rejected by Seren. As the first shots cracked out from the man's gun, he suddenly sprang to his feet with a scream, high-pitched and terrified; the speed at which the first puff-adder struck at the intruder's legs had been too fast for Seren to either see or understand, only when the bearded man sprang up screaming, did Seren see the second snake propel itself in the peculiar backward flip of it's kind, across an intervening space of several feet to strike with deadly accurace at the man's bare arm!

The S.P.U. agent turned and poured fire into the two adders at his feet; Seren did not hesitate, he stood up and started firing, even as the man on the hillock remembered Seren's presence and turned the fear on his face showed wild and twisted, the front of his body and open shirt turned into a sudden mass of dark red blood. As the man crumpled to his knees then toppled face down, Seren stopped firing – then nothing, only the silent and merciless heat-waves, beating down like electric needles on Seren's back.

With his nerves numbed, his brain seemed to act like that of an independant being, Seren made the necessary checks. The bearded man was dead, near him was the bloodied pulp of the two snakes that had played such a vital role in saving Seren's life. For a brief moment he wondered what had made him change his mind when he first ran towards the hillock where the pair of puff-adders had been peacefully enjoying a noon-day doze.

The blonde "hippie" was laying face down in a pool of his own blood; even now the flies were gathering round his mouth and nostrils, feasting greedily on the blood that was dripping slowly into the sand beneath him. Seren went back to the rifle he had discarded; he carefully rubbed it with sand to wipe out his fingerprints, then dropped it again. He did the same with his submachine-gun and threw it as far as he could from the Citroen.

He reversed the little car out of the ditch and back onto the road. Parked deep in the river bed, not a shot had hit the engine, but it's canvass seats and roof were in shreds and the body riddled with bullet holes.

Seren drove as fast as road conditions allowed until he reached the tarmac road to Chidzaka, the only town of any size in the Low Veldt; a car was approaching, so he pulled to the centre of the road, got out and flagged them down; it was a white family heading for Mubuzi Junction, they gaped at the shattered windows of his car. He told them:

"Don't go any further – there's a bunch of "Terrs" five miles down the road – I was lucky to get out alive!" They believed him and turned their car round. Seren headed for the nearest Police Post at Hippo Camp. When he arrived, a white officer and several African police officers gathered to inspect the Citroen. Covered in dust, his slacks and bush jacket fit only for the rubbish tip, he turned down a warm beer, but gratefully accepted a large mug of sweet tea brewed by one of the officers. Then followed the Official Police Report; "he had been fired on from somewhere to his right – ditched the car to gain cover – then the Mazda arrived". Seren related the whole incident as he had supposedly seen it from the safety of the storm ditch, "the killing of the two men in the Mazda by unidentified "Terrs" ...!" Seren reflected a less than heroic figure; but the officer in charge agreed that without a weapon, Seren had been wise to lay doggo and then get the hell out of it!

Leaving Hippo Camp behind he turned onto the bush road. It was nearly three hours before he reached Three Rivers, Harvey Grielson came out of the Station Office. The news had arrived before Seren. Grielson stared and said: "Jesus! What the blazes did you get into, how come you weren't cut to pieces?"

"Because I didn't wait to be a blood hero – I dived into a ditch – and stayed there!" Seren was exhausted, all he wanted was to flop down on his bed and sleep. He turned his back on Grielson and entered the Railway cottage that was both his home, and without the knowledge of his Railway superiors, his base of operations – the sole reason why he had been sent to Three Rivers – by courtesy of the Scalloni Brothers!

The cottage was nearly derelict when he obtained authority to take it over. With the sole help of Donaz, who was not only his houseservant but also local Party Cell Leader, they had made the four roomed building fit to live in – and over months of work they had dug out a cellar! The daily piles of earth extracted were turned into the flourishing garden that gave Seren the privacy he needed.

This, and many other events, intrigues, subversion and seductions, mayhem and murders into which Seren had been drawn, were but the long trail which led to this last event – "Serpents in the Sun".

Tired as he was, with nerves stretched to snapping point, he had one more duty to perform – to ensure for all those thousands of young black Zimbabweans, so many no more than school children, who daily, monthly, who over years, sacrificed their lives, their education, careers and futures, for Freedom, Justice and Self Rule!

Walking over to a section of wall between his lounge and the passage at the rear that led to his bathroom, Seren turned a key in a lock, set flush in the side of a full length mirror mounted on a strong wooden frame. It swung open silently on its well-oiled hinges. He reached inside and switched on a light, it revealed a set of a dozen cement steps and stack upon stack of wooden boxes, containing hand grenades, land mines, A. K. rifles, submachine guns.

They had been carried at the dark of night, and left in his care for the day – the day when the capital itself finally exploded into The Revolution of The Zimbabwean People!

CHIEDZA MSENGEZI

STARLIGHT

Maria sat on the rock, cold and goose-fleshed, desperate for a ray of sunlight. It was one of those days; cloudy and windy, the dry leaves flying past and the sun struggling to filter through. They could have stayed indoors by the fire, but she and her aunt were at the river.

"Mainini Maria!" her aunt called out, tightening her head scarf with a fresh knot.

"Sitting with your cheek in palm – are you still thinking about it?"

"No, not at all," Maria said, her voice unnaturally cheerful.
Her aunt resumed her washing, work hardened hands scrubbing the blouse harder against the rock.

"Forget about it, "she continued." Put it behind you. Start a new life."

Maria could sense the questions that remained unasked:
Why couldn't you scream for help?
Couldn't you lift your foot and kick him between the legs?
For goodness sake couldn't you run away? A girl your age?

Her aunt held the blouse by its collar, feeling the current tug it downstream. She rung the water from it violently.

"You have torn it," said Maria.

"It can be mended."

There was a silence, an awful one, heavy with suppressed feelings. Maria could still hear the man's voice – cold an errie. His smell was still with her. Even her skin was crawling with his touch – a multiple caress of lice, ticks and fleas. Bravely she resisted the urge to scratch.

"You were wise to keep the police out of it," said her aunt, selecting another item from the small mound of dirty clothes.

"Was I?"

"Of course! It's not a nice story, you know."

"And Tobias?"

Maria's aunt gazed at her in disbelief.

"I suppose you want to tell him and then expect him to marry you!"
Maria lowered her head to hide the tears.

"You're just a child," continued her aunt. "You know nothing about men. Nothing. Take it from me, your Tobias must suspect nothing."

Maria nodded. Wasn't her aunt her traditional mentor in matters like these? As custom dictated she had introduced Tobias as the man who was going to marry her. He was a young man from the same village, Maria's childhood friend. Now he was working at Blue Star Bakery. From his meagre wages he had saved enough to start the lobola payments. In his latest letter he informed her he was all set for marriage. Maria decided to heed her aunt's advice and say nothing to upset the marriage plans.

A few weeks later she joined her new husband in Harare. When Tobias was at the bakery, Maria busied herself with the housework. The small room they rented was always shining clean and she never left the kitchen sink choking with bits of burned sadza and grease. Mending the holes in the pockets of Tobias' trousers, replacing buttons on his shirts, she had never felt happier.

The afternoon she was nosing the point of the iron between the pleats of her skirt when she noticed it was four o'clock. Time to start supper. Soon the beef was sizzling in fat to an appetizing brown. She was cutting tomatoes in the palm of her hand when Tobias appeared in the doorway.

"Smells good," he sniffed. He walked over and peered into the pot. Maria playfully pushed him aside.

"You'll be dipping your hand in next!" she laughed.

"No man can resist such cooking," he replied, hanging his coat on the chair. That night they clung to each other in bed. Their love-making was voluptious. Next morning Tobias woke up feeling relaxed and self-confident. He dressed hurriedly, fumbled in his jacket and pulled out a $ 5 note.

"Supper money," he said, throwing it onto the table, as he rushed to work.

Later Maria sat on the edge of the bed, knitting. She put down her needles to untangle the yarn and suddenly thought how well she was coping with what happened. That night when. . . .
"No! Don't allow yourself to think about it!" she whispered. "Concentrate on the happy things in your life. Then you'll be fine."
That was when she smelled smoke from the pot on the stove.
"Maiwe!"
She rushed to the stove and tipped the meat onto the dish to see what she could salvage. But it was inedible. The rest, charcoal black and smouldering, stuck to the bottom of the pot. She rummaged in her handbag for some coins. Not enough for meat.

That evening Tobias looked angrily at his bowl of sadza and boiled cabbage.

"What's this? You know I don't like cabbage!" he said.

"Burned the meat." Maria was embarrassed.

Tobias shot her a cold look.

"What's wrong with you?" he demanded.

"It's not as if you have a houseful of children to occupy you all day. And another thing. I noticed you scorched the collar of my white shirt."

"Sorry I. . ."

"Next you'll forget to switch off the iron. You'll burn down the house!"

They ate in silence. In bed they slept back to back, resentful of each other.

In the days that followed Tobias no longer rushed home from work. What was there to burry for? The novelty had worn off and Maria was no real company anymore. It was better to be with his frends at the beergarden. Worst of all was bedtime. Tobias didn't want to think about it.
"What with her so stiff, it's like a fight. Me trying to coax her into it and her struggling to free herself," he thought. "Leaves me with a hell of a conscience, too. It's like I am. . . like attacking her."

Soon a pattern emerged. Tobias was never home before 10 pm. Maria began to be jumpy, unsettled. Darkness was beginning to bother her. Whenever she switched off the light she heard the shuffle of footsteps. Sometimes she saw the shadowy outline of a male figure. Could it be all in her mind?
One night, unable to sleep, she got up and flicked the light switch. The harsh glare of the single lightbulb flooded the room. She was alone, apart from the immense silence. A wall of silence. She turned up the volume of the radio, loudly. Anything to banish the silence.

Then Tobias staggered in. He stood at the foot of the bed, swaying unsteadily. He slumped onto the matress, groping for Maria. Something deep down in her recoiled. That terrible breath reeking of the spoilt yeast of Chibuku. That smell of unrefined tobacco. It all evoked a memory of someone else. Someone she had been trying hard to forget. She flinched and pulled the blankets over her head.

"Get up an warm up my sadza." He ripped off the blankets, moved towards her. "And let me tell you one thing: you'll sleep with me tonight whether you like it or not. You are my wife not my sister, I paid lobola." Maria jumped up as if ready to run. But she stood still, staring at Tobias, trying to establish his identity.
"Why do you look at me like that?" snapped Tobias. "Don't you know me?"

Maria took a few steps back, distancing herself.
"Yes that's him." she thought. "Smells like him, talks like him."
It was that man she had met that evening, three months ago. That evening she was walking to her aunt's house.

"Jesus, Maria! What's wrong with you?" Tobias' voice was uneasy now. She moved closer to the table, to the cardboard box where she kept her kitchen utensils. She drew out a knife and stood erect, feet together. Like a soldier waiting for the signal to attack.

"My fathers in the ground!" shouted Tobias, panic flooding his eyes, as she turned towards him. "Would you knife your own husband?"

The words thundered through her head. Horrified, she dropped the knife. But it was too late. She could't stop the inwash of memory. She was reliving that evening three months ago. Reliving every detail.

She felt the rage in the man's fingers as he ripped down the line of buttons on her blouse. Saw him tear away her hands from her exposed breasts. The glint of polished metal in the moonlight made her close her eyes. The point of the knife blade was cold against her flesh.
"Lie down on your back," she heard him say.
"Please, don't", she implored but the man was beyond hearing.
She was thrown to the ground. With a brute force he flung her thighs apart, keeping her pinned on the ground with the pincer-like grip of his left hand. Beneath the dry leaves crunched. The dried blades of grass speared through her skin. Numbness spread throughout her body.
She looked up at the great open sky, sequinned with stars. A line from a geography textbook, studied years ago, flashed through her mind.
"Stars so vastly distant that their light takes millions of years to reach the earth."

The thought shifted something in her being. She felt strange. Disembodied. Up and up she floated so that when she looked down she saw skeletons of trees silhouetted against the moonlight. It was September. The tips of the twigs were thickening, ready for a burst of new leaves. She found herself at vantage point on the top of a tall msasa tree from which she could watch the two figures below. She saw the man heaving up and down in feats of strength over the empty shell without a trace of enjoyment, until he finally rose to his feet and hitched up his trousers. With shaking hands he fastened his belt and was off like a shot. Afraid of the devil was he? Maria kept her gaze on him as he scurried away. A contemptible shadow dissolving into the night.

The scene had rerun itself to the end.

Now, huddled on her hospital bed she hears voices. The squeak of rubber shoes in the corridor.

"How is she?"

"Nervy, twitchy. Never comfortable."

"And what's she been on about all day? She's never quiet!"

"Don't know. But her husband came to visit and she didn't recognise him."

"More tranquilisers."

A trolley rattles along the corridor, a fat night nurse waddling behind it. Maria watches the nurse pick a tablet from each of the bottles on the tray; yellow, orange, white. She swallows them with difficulty. Looks past the grey walls with peeling paint and out through the window. Her eyes settle on a great galaxy of stars in the sky.
"Gwara raKurumbwi – the Milky Way."
From the cluster she singles out one. Faint and yellow, it glows feebly. Soon it will flicker out into everlasting night, black as pitch.

JOSEPH ENUENWEMBA OBI, JR.

A FIRE IN THE FOG

George Krilby sat staring through the doctor who was speaking to him. For all he cared, the man might not have been in the same room with him. He was thinking of the sequence of events that had landed him in this little hospital in a dusty black town far away from home.

Since Krilby's wife died five years earlier, this was his first trip accross the border on a vacation route that used to be a yearly pilgrimage for both of them. Although they had lived in a quiet suburban neighbourhood in the nation's capital, this small next-door country had provided the Krilbys with the kind of escape they so dearly needed after the hectic worklife they both led as magistrates in the city.

The little town of Cecilston was their favorite vacation spot. To them, it was the best of Africa. They were never tired of the pleasant country inn that overlooked a gently rolling grassland that was the scene of some of the most spectacular sunsets they had ever witnessed. To the left of the grassland was a wooded area that was as picturesque as a postcard. Here they would sit in the cool glades fishing in clear waters of silent streams that sparkled like emeralds from afar.

Ever since his wife died, Krilby had tried to resist the nostalgia of their little paradise, however, this time the impulse to recapture some of that magic had gotten the better of him. He had decided to undertake the journey alone. Moreover he had hoped to combine this particular vacation with the writing of a book he was preparing on law and society. It was a cruel twist of fate that resulted in the near fatal accident which put him in hospital for two months.

Having set off from home early on that fateful morning, he and Sana, his driver, had arrived at the border at about one o'clock in the hot afternoon. After customs and immigration formalities, they had set off for the inn at about two-thirty. Sana had said something about feeling ill but Krilby had made nothing of it. As things turned out, Sana was ill, for just as they had negotiated a bend on the road he apparently had a blackout. All Krilby knew was that one moment they were on the road and the next, they were hurtling down a grassy verge that ended abruptly in a pile of rocks. As they hit the rocks, Krilby remembered repeating "God" over and over as the hellish fugue of tearing metal, breaking glass and Sana's screams enveloped him.

Upon regaining consciousness, he found himself in a hospital. What struck him first was that everyone was black. In his country Krilby had never been inside a black hospital. He later learnt that their wreckage had been spotted by some peasants who immediately notified their local police post. The police had extracted them from the mangled car and brought them to the hospital.

The hospital itself was not big but it was surprisingly well equipped. This was because it had been built for the management of the nearby Strickland Mines – the largest copper mines in Africa. Before independence only management staff (who in any case were whites) enjoyed the facilities of the hospital, there was another one a few miles away for blacks. After independence, the colour bars were abolished and black personnel and patients arrived. It was here that Krilby was brought. As soon as the doctor had seen him, he had decided upon surgery for Krilby's left shoulder. Luckily, the hospital had a specialist orthopaedic surgeon stationed there to deal with the mostly physical mining injuries of the workers. That doctor, Doctor Tsotho, had operated successfully on Krilby, but Krilby had needed more time to recover from his other internal injuries.

Sana had been luckier than his master. In one of those curious quirks of life, he had been flung through the car door just before it hit the rocks. He escaped with a few cracked ribs and minor concussions. He had since returned home.

Now, as Krilby was about to be discharged, he was listening to the doctor's parting advice.

"... so if you are good to yourself, there will be no serious side effects", Dr. Tsotho was saying with a professional smile. "If I were you, I'd stay away from alcohol, tobacco and strain. Try to see your physician regularly because some conditions are only dormant, not absent. You want to spot the symptoms if and when they occur".

Krilby swung his attention to the dimunitive middle-aged black man who sat behind the massive table directly in front of him. He managed a condescending smile. There was something he found vaguely disconcerting about this scene. The doctor's confidence nettled him. Normally he was not used to anyone telling him now to carry on. Coming from a black man it was even more irritating. For all his life George Krilby had spoken to blacks not they to him. He was used to seeing them literally from his magisterial chair. When he spoke to them, it was in a manner that was curt, authoritative and final. To have this ebony black country-boy-made-good give him such a paternalistic lecture was a disturbing novelty. For the first time Krilby was in the presence of a black man to whom he owed something – his life. It wasn't a comfortable situation. Krilby could just not bring himself to the conviviality of the usual parting scene.

"Well, thanks for your advice" he said after the doctor had finished. "I shall see to it that my government remits all pertinent monies for your services".

"The pleasure is ours" Dr. Tsotho beamed. "I am informed that your replacement car is here and I am sure you are itching to leave for home. Remember your prescriptions". The doctor stretched out his hand as he gave his patient a friendly thump on his good shoulder.

Krilby flinched inwardly at this show of chumminess. He accepted the outstretched hand and promptly turned around and went out into the brilliant sunshine.

It was with relief that he settled himself into the coolness of the waiting Mercedes-Benz.

*****

Krilby stifled a yawn as he rose from the wicker chair on his shaded verandah.

He had been reading some correspondence since he woke up from his siesta. Seeing that the sun would soon set, he decided to take a little walk before supper.

He was now feeling as fit as he had ever felt in his fifty eight years. Since his return home he had grudgingly conceded to himself that Dr. Tsotho's prescriptions were wonderful for his health.

As he opened the gauze door of the verandah, Nene, his elderly house-help came out to clear up the tea things he had used during his reading. She bowed slightly as she passed her master and he in turn, gave her a faint fleeting smile. Krilby and Nene presented a curious couple. While he was short and impatient with other blacks he had contact with, he hardly ever raised his voice at Nene. For one thing, they had practically grown up together. Nene's mother had worked for Krilby's father. Krilby was then a young boy and Nene was just the maid's daughter with whom he hardly had any personal interaction. Indeed he only saw her when she came into the dining room to help her mother clear plates or clean something. He never really knew much about Nene's father apart from the fact that he was working on some government mine where he was required to stay in a hostel with other men. On one or two occasions Krilby's father had secured a pass for his maid to go and visit her husband for he and his likes were not allowed into the Krilby neighbourhood. One day the news came that Nene's father had died in a mining accident. Krilby remembered his father giving mother and daughter a day off to mourn in their little room ot the back of the house. Since then nobody ever spoke of the dead man.

When Krilby's father died some ten years later, he moved with Nene to his own house leaving her mother with his elder brother Kurt, who had elected to stay on at their faither's ranch and manage his livestock business.

In spite of the fact that Krilby had lived in the same household with Nene for practically all his life, there was still a marked chasm between them. Neither of them forgot who the other was.

Nene had finished with the tea things and was about to step into the house when Krilby called out to her.

"Nene, my pipe" he said.

"Yesseh".

In a minute, she was back with his pipe, some tobacco and a silver lighter. Krilby liked to smoke his pipe on his evening walks. It enhanced his contemplative mood. He took the items from her and walked towards his gate set in a perfectly trimmed ixora hedge that was about four feet high.

Nene watched his back for a second and made for the kitchen. It would soon be time for her master's supper. As she moved, it was plain to see that her size belied her agility. She had descended from a proud fighting people who were concentrated in the South-western part of the country. For ages her people had fought off trespassers until some foreigners with rifles and cannons – Krilby's ancestors – had arrived and subdued them in the nineteenth century. Since then Nene's people had always served Krilby's people.

In the kitchen Nene ran an expert hand over the potatoes. She frowned as she noticed some buds that had begun to sprout on them. She had been a beauty in her time. It was that beauty that had sent her late husband head over heels at first sight. He was one of the men who used to drive the garbage truck that served Krilby's street. His insistent pestering coupled with the stream of gifts to her mother (some of which he later confessed were "salvaged" from white people's trash) eventually wore her into submission. The marriage, like most marriages of Nene's people was a stay-apart affair, but it was nonetheless happy whenever they were allowed to see each other. The sole shadow over the union was its childlessness. As they were to discover later, her husband had become impotent due to some exposure he had undergone in the chemical waste factory in which he had worked before he was transferred to the Municipal Waste Disposal Services. It was a disease that later killed him and made Nene a childless widow.

Nene had many reasons to be bitter, but nobody could ever see beyond the wan half-smile that was fixed on her face. She had once dreamed of having a happy family and well clothed children who would have the benefit of a strong, loving, live – in father that she had missed in her own time. Now those dreams were cold ashes for her. In her society, that kind of life was meant for another type of people. Now and again she would remember her mother's bitter responses to her childish prattling about love, children and family life. "Ta!" she would say "you only dream like that because you think you are human, but you are not my dear, we are not!" Thereupon tears would well up in both their eyes, then her mother would gather her in her arms whispering words of solace.

That was years ago. Nene now understood the sphinx-like silence of many of her people. It was not the silence of resignation, rather, it was the rock-steady calm of knowing. She understood the abnormal chemistry of her society perfectly. She and her people had been denied all that man cherished. Their "education" was limited and anaemic, they could not vote, love, or move about according to their wishes. Their lands were eroded and overworked, and their hovels in the government built reservations were as disgusting as they were overpriced. It was a world that constantly challenged their humanity. Nene was however, also aware that her people were becoming increasingly militant, she knew that when the struggle arrived in her neighbourhood, she would do what she had to do – she would live free or die.

As Nene prepared his supper, Krilby was relishing the fresh evening air. The temperature was in the sixties and he loved it at this time of the year. The trees were shedding their leaves in a riot of colour which was most accentuated at that critical moment when the final blaze of the dying sunlight burst through the trees in heavenly shafts. It was a glory of nature. As he walked home he found himself whistling a jaunty little tune. The sedate houses on his street seemed so peaceful in their large manicured lawns. Some birds warbled in the high pines to his left and he whistled in response.

As Krilby was about to open his gate, he noticed the edge of an envelope in his mail box. He could have sworn that it was not there on his way out. He took the letter out and looked at the address. It simply read: George Krilby, no sender was indicated. With a slight grimace he put the letter in his pocket and unlatched the gate. He walked up to the house and stopped to smell his beautiful roses that grew alongside the verandah.

Little did he know that he was about to undergo an experience that would change him forever. *****

Krilby pushed his plate away and reached for the evening newspaper. He always scanned the papers before retiring to his study at night. This particular evening he had eaten mashed potatoes, prawns, breast of duck, green peas and an excellent salad. As usual Nene's cooking was superb.

"A very good meal, Nene" Krilby said as she entered to clear the dishes. "I'll skip coffee tonight".

"Yesseh".

As Krilby reached in his pocket for his glasses, his hand touched something. The letter. He had forgotten all about it. He brought it out and opened it. The handwriting was elegant and unhurried. He began to read:

Dear Mr. Krilby,

There is something that I think you should know. First of all let me introduce myself. I am a journalist – a black journalist and most of my stories are about things that you and your kind do in our country. I will not bore you with broadsides against your cherished policy of Independant Evolution. Our struggle, as you know, has gone beyond that. A more mundane matter has prompted this letter.

Do you remember your accident? (Of course you do!) I am sure you also remember the hospital where you were treated for about two months. Well, I was a regular visitor to the hospital during the period you were there. A cousin of mine was hospitalized on account of a back injury. Now listen to what concerns you:

The operation that you underwent required a lot of blood. You did receive the blood – five pints of it to be exakt – but get this: THE BLOOD THAT WAS TRANSFUSED INTO YOUR VEINS WAS BLOOD DONATED BY BLACKS. Believe it or not magistrate, You are, in a manner of speaking, one of us.

I wonder what your pure white community will say when they learn that their respected and principled legal luminary – the man who puts all the troublesome coloureds and blacks in their places – is himself loaded with negro blood? Think about it because they will know. In exactly a week from today, (i.e. on the 10th) our paper "The Voice", will carry details about your operation in my colomn on page 3. You are the magistrate. You know what it means, legally, to have one drop of coloured blood in your veins.

Watch out for "The Voice". I'll be seeing you – brother.

Subu Ngali.

Krilby's hands were shaking as he finished reading the letter. His eyes were transfixed to the sheet as the full import of the situation hit him ... You are one of us. The phrase branded itself on his mind with searing pain. His insides were hot. It was as if some poisonous lava were coursing through his body eating up every tissue in its way.

In his black haze, Krilby was remotely aware of a constriction around his chest. He abhorred any kind of racial miscegenation. Indeed some of his harshest sentences were on those who crossed racial lines illegally. To be so totally locked into the object of his abhorrence churned his stomach.

Had he been a liberal the shock might have been slightly easier to absorb. But here he was, a staunch, blue booded Right Wing Republican. An avid defender of Independent Evolution. God! He would never be pure white again! He felt as if his veins were on fire.

Having overcome the initial shock, but still badly shaken, Krilby's legal mind quickly sifted through the situation. For a moment, he thought of suing for blackmail, but he discarded the idea almost immediately. What would the charge be? Where was the criminal threat? What was being demanded? No, blackmail was totally inappropriate to the situation. He scratched the back of his neck as he always did when he felt nervous.

He wished he had someone to talk to. Just then Nene came into the room with his house slippers. He suddenly realized that Nene was perhaps closer to him than anyone else – even more than his own brother. But he could not talk to her about this. No, she was one of them. At this moment she was so near yet so far.

Having given Krilby his slippers Nene turned to go. As he watched her retreating figure his lips formed her name silently, then she was gone. A heavy feeling of loneliness descended upon him.

Krilby slept fitfully that night. He tossed and turned ceaselessly. He dreamt that he was a participant in a ritual black cannibal feast in which the main course was a big bloated white man. As the chief of the blacks uncovered the head of the white body, he saw that it bore his own face. He had woken violently from the nightmare.

The next morning he woke up temporarily forgetting the events of the previous day, but soon recollection flooded over him and he lost his appetite. He also noticed that he had begun to hurt all over his body especially around the shoulder that had been operated upon.

As he shaved he looked at his face closely. He wondered whether the transfusion had anything to do with the dull glaze that was over his eyes. He thought it looked like a negro glaze.

While Krilby was getting dressed he realized that he had not prepared for the day's sitting. The letter had cut through his evening like an evil knife. With a grim look on is face, he knotted his tie, checked his watch and picked up his briefcase. At his front door he met one of the two white security men detailed to ride to work with him daily. It was a precaution made necessary by the recent co-ordinated attacks on state officials by freedom fighters.

As he stepped onto the path leading up to his gate, he noticed a newspaper on his lawn. That was strange. All his morning papers were sent to him at the office. He motioned to the security man.

"Sergeant, bring me that paper over there."

"Yes Sir" the sergeant replied as he went for the paper.

When Krilby saw the paper, a chill crept up his spine. It was a copy of "The Voice." He threw it at the guard.

"Dispose of it!" he barked.

The guard nodded, surprised at the vehemence in Krilby's voice.

During the ride down town nobody said a word. The driver, white this time, handled the car adeptly. One security man sat beside him in front while the other sat with Krilby behind.

The drive to town went around a hill that overlooked a native reserve. From a point of the road, if one looked down, one could see the blacks tending their few raggedy sheep. There were also scattered patches of maize, millet and tobacco visible. However, the most striking features of the reserves were the dome shaped huts. The little windowless dwellings looked like boils on the land. In the mornings, the smoke that emanated from their backyards made them look like little brown hats with silvery plumes.

As Krilby looked at the Reserve below, his bile rose. His body ached badly. He felt lower than the three white youths in the car with him. How he envied them!

At the court, Krilby was grouchy with everybody. His assessments were cryptic and his decisions questionable. He spent most of the day mulling over his problem.

Over the next three days, he was docile and self pitying. It was as if all his esteem had run out of him. Indeed on one occasion, he actually bowed to Nene as he received a cup of coffee from her.

From the fourth day onwards, Krilby became edgy and irritable. All of a sudden Nene had begun to repel him. The faint smile she normally carried on her pudgy face now appeared to his hate filled mind like a leering grin. Her slightest action irritated him and on one occasion he slapped her over a trivial matter. But Nene bore his edginess with an equanimity that only made him boil the more.

To worsen matters, "The Voice" kept coming. Try as Krilby and his watchmen did, they could not catch the hidden vendor. That badly printed liberal newspaper was fast becoming a guillotine over his head.

Then came the tenth.

When Krilby woke up on this particular day, he bathed and dressed early, after which he went into his study. He walked slowly round the room staring at the old family pictures that hung from the walls. He stopped at a picture of his parents. Both of them stood rigidly upright in their period clothes. He was still looking at the picture when he heard Nene enter.

"Is the car here?" he asked curtly.

"Yesseh"

He turned around to face her.

"Nene, come here". There was an edge to his voice.

As she came up to him, he looked into her face with gun-metal grey eyes. "Nene," he jabbed a finger in her face. "I'm white!" His mouth was a tight vicious line.

"Yesseh". Nene's face was expressionless.

Krilby picked up his brief case and headed for the parlour.

"Let's go" he said to the waiting guard. As they walked towards the car he noted with satisfaction that his householp had already disposed of "The Voice". He would see to it that that newspaper ate its words after which everyone associated with it would pay the price.

*****

As fate would have it, there was only one case before Krilby that day and it was a case involving "illicit sexual relations" between two white males and two coloured females.

When he entered the courtroom, he had the sensation of being peeled by human eyes. Krilby was certain that by now, the majority of people in the room had read or heard of the story about him in "The Voice". He went up to his chair and sat down. Thereupon everyone else in the court resumed sitting.

As the first witness in the case was going through oath – taking ceremonies, Krilby looked at the accused. Both males were obviously in their early twenties. They looked somewhat bored with the proceedings. The accused girls sat to their left. One of them had long black hair and could have passed for white but for her tell tale Oriental eyes. She looked resilient and purposeful. The other girl was slight in build and was clearly Indian. She kept her face down. She was obviously distraught by the whole affair. The four of them had been caught in compromising circumstandes in the apartment of a well known white liberal physician.

The prosecuting counsel stepped forward to question the first witness who was the policeman who had made the arrest.

"Officer, please tell the court how long you have been on the force". He began.

And so it went, Krilby could hardly concentrate on the proceedings. His mind kept wandering. Every now and again he would search the faces of those present in the court-room for some sign of sniggering towards him. He was not sure of what lurked in the minds of the faces he saw.

"... I then told them that it was an unnatural act against the law of the land" the officer was saying.

Krilby snapped out of his reverie. If that was unnatural, what about a transfusion? How would the officer feel if he had black blood in his veins? How would any self respecting white man or woman feel about it? How long would this charade last anyway? Krilby wondered. Of course the people knew about him. Sooner or later someone would jump up and shout "Hey, the magistrate here is a freak! He shouldn't hear this case!"

"I am sure you understand what the legal definitions of the races are, even a drop of coloured blood makes you coloured". The counsel was now addressing the accused girls. His words cut ruthlessly into Krilby. So this was it, they had known all along and were now making snide remarks about him.

Krilby was hot. His eyes were swimming, his temples bursting, and his breath came in short gasps. When he looked up at the two accused white boys, they were facing him. They now appeared much taller, indeed to his fevered imagination they seemed to be growing and arching menacingly over him. He looked around. In his opaque vision, the whole courtroom seemed to be staring at him. Suddenly it looked as if they were all converging upon him. He saw hands groping for him. Something snapped in his head.

"I'm white!" he screamed "I'm white! I'm white! I'm white!" he kept shouting. He was still screaming when the white jacketed medical attendants arrived to carry him away.

*****

The day after Krilby's breakdown, his closest office acquaintance, State Counsel Jan Veindigger was striding down the main corridor of the court building. He was a tall handsome blue-eyed with man in his thirties. He was known as one of the most ambitious characters in the Ministry of Justice. This morning he was wearing a pale blue summer suit and looking every inch a go-getter.

As Veindigger turned left at the end of the corridor he found himself face to face with Hans Gore, the Court Clerk.

"How goes it" Gore asked genially.

"Fair" Veindigger replied accepting Gore's outstretched hand.

"Any news about Krilby?" Gore asked.

"The doctor says he is in bad shape. From the look of things, they think he'll be in the sanatorium for a long time", Veindigger answered.

"I hear he was muttering something about a newspaper article?" Gore went on.

"Oh that, yes". Veindigger bit on his lower lip thoughtfully. "It was the strangest thing. In the hospital he kept saying something about a character called Sobun – something who is supposed to be a columnist with "The Voice". He said the story on page three of yesterday's edition is false".

"What's the story about?" Gore asked.

"That's the funny angle to it" Veindigger replied with a laugh. "I checked up on the paper and there's no columnist like that on their staff. Moreover, the only thing on page three was a full-page ad for some brand of eye-wash."

Both men laughed.

"Well your Krilby had it coming to him. Being cooped up with a black nanny in a quiet house in a quiet suburb can do that to anyone", Gore said still chuckling.

"You can say that again", Veindigger replied. There was a sudden awkward silence as both men stopped laughing. Veindigger was the first to speak.

"Well let's go dispense justice" he said brightly.

"In the service of the people" Gore replied in mock humility.

With that, both men shook hands and strode off briskly in different directions.

SAMUEL KAHIGA

THE PARKING BOY

Rosa had arrived in the valley during the floods of 1972 with a tiny baby boy in her arms. The floods had swept away many of the houses in that grim valley in which the poorest of the poor sought shelter; property and lives had been lost. At the best of times few in the valley would have paid any attention to a young girl and her sick child as everybody had troubles of their own. Wayward girls like Rosa had to pay for their mistakes like everyone else. What they had failed to learn at school the valley quickly taught them.

Yet, there are kind angels everywhere and an old woman who was just repairing her damaged shack, took one good look at Rosa and her crying baby and knew she was alone and needed urgent help. Rosa was weeping as she tried to soothe her baby from her bruised lips and closed eye, it was clear that some brute in the valley had beaten her up badly.

Esta, the old woman, walked up to her and talked to her softly.

"Why are you crying? Whose baby is this?"

"It's my baby."

"God have mercy," said Esta, "You are just a baby yourself. Do you live here in Mathare valley?"

"No," said Rosa, "I came in today. My child is hungry. I don't know what to do. I don't know any people here."

"Well, don't cry now. Give me the baby. And here is some money. Up there, near the road you'll find the shops. Buy some milk and bread for your baby. I'll hold him for you while you do that. Now go on."

And from that day Esta and Rosa were great friends. Esta helped Rosa settle down in the valley. She let Rosa stay under her roof for a week or so and later on, as the shack was very tiny, she showed Rosa how to construct her own shack with bits of sticks, cartons and polythene discarded from city ware-houses. And when Esta lay in her shack complaining of aching bones or a bad stomach, Rosa nursed her back to health and those who saw them thought they were like mother and daughter.

The valley was just a few bus stops from the city centre, and in the city the old woman had established a precarious business of buying and selling old clothes. When fruits and vegetables were in season she would sell those instead, buying from the main city market and selling in small handfuls at the street corners. It was a risky business as she had no hawkers' licence. In their bid to keep the city clean the city council police were always chasing away such women, confiscating their goods and sometimes arresting and fining the offenders. Rosa became Esta's business partner. While one sold clothes, the other would sell vegetables and they shared the profits. Rosa always carried the baby on her back, even when fleeing from the police when they made a swoop. It was a very hard life but they made enough money for some food to keep soul and body together.

Three years later, the old woman was knocked down by a car. Over the years, she had taken to drinking changaa, the potent, illegal drink of the slum dwellers, saying that it helped her sleep and forget the pain in her bones. As she grew older she seemed to become more and more despondent and was drunk at very odd times of the day. It landed her in trouble for she couldn't think or run fast enough when the police swooped down upon the street women selling vegetables. A lot of the money she made went into bribing the police. Finally she paid the ultimate price, under the wheels of a car. They buried her at the old grave-yard at Kariokor. A few of her friends put some money together for a wooden coffin and one of them said a prayer for her soul because there was no preacher at the grave-yard. Rosa wept bitterly. Esta had been like a mother to her and her only good friend.

Three more years passed and Rosa was now a woman of the valley, coming every day to the street corners to sell her vegetables. She had been arrested and fined many times but had to keep up the trade in order to support herself and her six year old son, Mwangi. One day as she was selling vegetables in the street her heart missed a beat as it always did whenever she saw a blue Mercedes. Could it be Peter's? But by this time she had seen so many cars of that make – and been disappointed because none of them had Peter's registration number. As a smartly dressed city girl came up and asked for five shillings worth of tomatoes, Rosa's eyes were on the car. Of course it wasn't Peter's car – it couldn't be. Peter had disappeared forever and was just a memory that ached deep inside her heart. She sold the girl a handful of tomatoes and the girl went her way.

Rosa looked up again and this time the blue Mercedes had stopped at the red lights. She stared with shock at the registration number – KVM 876 – Peter's number! Rosa sprung to her feet. Without thinking she clambered over the iron railing that lay between the pavement and the road, something she often had to do, when the policemen made a raid. At a run she waved her way through the traffic, calling out, "Peter, Peter!"

******

The lights turned amber, then green. Peter Tombo released the clutch and the Mercedes began to move. But that same instant a hand slapped the glass of his window, on the passengers's side and a girl's shrill voice cried out his name. He stopped the car. While cars speeded past others began to hoot impatiently behind him. Peter had no idea who the crazy girl was who had stopped him so vehemently but he opened the door for her, all the same, to avoid a traffic jam. As she jumped with her crinkled clothes he wondered what on earth was going on. Rosa hadn't changed her dress for a week. She lived a hard life, sleeping on a sack on the floor of her shack and sitting on the dusty pavement, selling vegetables. Peter Tombo stared at her, through eye lenses that made his eyes look larger, exaggerating his bewilderment. What kind of a mad girl was this – and who was she? And then he recognised her.

"Rosa!"

"Yes, Peter. It's me. You didn't expect to ever see me again, did you?"

The cars behind him were still honking. Too stunned to say any more, he drove away. As soon as he could he left the main street and entered a side alley. He stopped the car and with a deep sigh turned off the engine. He looked at the girl again. Rosa stared back at him, accusingly, as if she could never forget or forgive him for the wrong he had done to her. At last they both looked away, Rosa staring at the fingers on her lap and Peter Tombo at the milling midday crowd heading for butcheries to look for roasted meat.

He was the first to break the silence. "Well, Rosa, I don't know what to say. I – I have been wondering about you."

"Have you?" she asked.

"Yes. Yes, of course. You know I left Thika town. I work here now."

Rosa said, "I also left Thika." Her voice sounded flat and thick, coming from a soul re-living unbearable pain.

Peter Tombo was thirty-six years old. But at that moment he was feeling a lot older, weighed down by guilt and remorse. He knew he had ruined this girl's life. He could see from her face that she accused him of it. When he glanced at her again she was silently crying.

"Rosa ... please don't cry," he said, "I have been worried about you all these years. I heard that you had left home. I tried to look for you but didn't know where to start. No one knew where you had gone."

"That's a lie," Rosa said, "You didn't look for me."

"I didn't know where to look. Do you ever go home?"

"No."

"Now you see. Nobody knows where you live. What happened to you?"

From a pocket in her dress Rosa took out a handkerchief. But try as she may to stop the tears, they kept on coming – as if a dam inside her had burst. Through her tears her voice came, full of pain and bitterness.

"I waited for you that day at the Thika petrol station and you didn't come. After three hours I went home and never saw you again. I hardly knew anything about you; I didn't know where you worked and so when you disappeared I felt so lost. A few weeks later my step-mother discovered that I was pregnant. I bet she was happy, for she had always hated me. She told my father and I was beaten up badly. He wanted to know who had done that to me. I said it was Peter. "Peter who?" he asked. And I couldn't tell. I didn't know your other name. My father asked where he could get you. I didn't know. I was so ignorant. I was kicked out of school. After my baby was born my father couldn't stand the sight of me. Influenced by my step-mother, he told me to pack und take the child to its father. So I packed. I came here to Nairobi. As I didn't know anybody here I went to Mathare valley. That's where everybody goes when they don't have a home."

"Then what happened?", Peter asked.

Rosa told the whole story of how Esta took care of her and the baby. "She's dead now, poor woman, and I have no other friend."

"Where do you live now, Rosa?" Peter Tombo asked.

"I still live in the valley. I sell vegetables. I buy them from the municipal market and sell them in the streets. I was doing that when I saw your car. I couldn't believe my eyes, Peter. And then I looked at the number again KVM ... I ran fast towards you. I could have been hit by a car. Is this a dream, Peter? Are you really here? Is this the same car in which ... in which so many things happened?"

Peter Tombo sighed again heavily. He wished it was a dream. But there she was – looking rugged and haggard, the little hands he used to hold all calloused and covered with grimy sweat. She wore plastic shoes and smelt of cheap, heavily-scented soap, the kind that is popular with poor people.

She was an attractive fourteen-year old school girl when he had picked her up at a bus stop near Thika town. From her small, battered imitation leather box and crinkled blouse he could tell she came from one of those poor rural families that eked out a living from growing coffee on small plots. Peter's father was still alive then and was a rich trader with one hotel in Thika town, another in Nairobi and a third way up in Eldoret. Peter liked to borrow his Mercedes and drive around looking for fun and excitement and especially for girls to pick up.

The girl his father wanted him to marry came from an even richer family than his. For this was the way things were done now. Those who made it wanted their sons and daughters to inter-marry and keep all the wealth in the family. Although Peter didn't really love the girl his father had chosen, the prospects of marrying her were attractive and he had inherited his father's love for money.

And so he married Wanja, his first wife. This girl here in the car was one of the many foolish ones from poor homes who were attracted by a flashy car like moths to a flame. In a way it was her fault that she had been so badly burned. But, on the other hand he should have known better than to toy with the heart of a school girl who was only fourteen.

Around that time Peter's father died. He moved to Nairobi permanently to manage the hotel there, leaving the one in Thika to his younger brother. He and his brother had, like most other Africans, been brought up in poverty, but then his father (who once had been a waiter in an English hotel) had quickly made money after independence. At eighteen Peter was driving his own car. Although he had some feelings for this girl, her look of abject poverty alienated and distressed him now. He was divorced from Wanja, living now with a wife of his own choice. The new wife had a rich father too who owned a chain of stores. He was on his way to pick her outside her office and go home for lunch. But here were all these strings from the past, tying ugly knots around his soul.

"Look, Rosa," he said, "We can't talk much now. I have people waiting for me; business associates. Tell me how I can get you. We have so much to talk about. So much, Rosa."

Rosa looked at him suspiciously. "You want to run away from me again. You need not worry! I know you don't love me. I don't want anything from you. But you have a son, Peter. Shall he never know his father?"

"A son ..." Peter mumbled, "How is he?"

"He's fine. I take care of him. But it is not easy where I live. I couldn't get him into a school. Something is wrong with him."

"Something wrong? What?"

Rosa said, "I started to notice it about a year ago. We were having supper in the shack, my son and I when he suddenly fell. I picked him up but he was rigid in my arms. His muscles were twitching. I screamed and the neighbours came. They told me that my son had epilepsy."

"Epilepsy!" cried Peter.

"Yes. I took him to a clinic in the valley which is run by the Christian Council of Kenya. I was told that he could not be cured but there were drugs to control his condition. I was told that he must take them regularly. So about once a month I take him to the clinic. They look at him and give me drugs he needs. Oh, Peter. I wish you could see him."

Peter Tombo did not know what to say. He had never seen the child and it was hard to think of it as his own. After so many years this woman had become a stranger, just a poor, dirty slum girl, and Peter Tombo would have liked to be far away and not here hearing about her epileptic child.

"So the child stays at home?" he forced himself to ask.

"Yes. I couldn't get him into a school. Not just because of his illness – they didn't mind very much about that – but also because they wanted a lot of money which I didn't have. Primary education may be free but the schools always ask for fees for their buildings funds. And he did badly in the nursery school ... Few schools would take him."

She went on and on. Peter's mind wondered away to his other children, the ones with Wanja, his former wife. He and Wanja shared the school fees and the two boys were doing very well at one of the best schools in Nairobi. He didn't really want to hear about this strange epileptic child.

"So he's at home all day"? he asked lamely.

"How can he stay at home all day? Peter, do you have any idea where I live? Right in the heart of the slum. What kind of home do you think I have? Can a child really stay there all day, with no one to look after him? I can't lock him up in the shack when I come into the city to sell vegetables. He stays with the neighbours' children and they are all very rough. They have taught Mwangi very bad habits. Would you believe it? At his age he smokes cigarettes! Many of these children have mothers who encourage them to come into the city and beg for money from tourists. They spend the day in the streets showing motorists empty parking spaces, thereafter pestering the car owners for money. I was in the street selling vegetables one day last year when I first saw Mwangi in the city with a large gang of boys from the valley. They were passing through the street checking every dust-bin. When he saw me he ran away. I beat him very hard that evening and I told him that I don't want him to be a parking boy or a beggar. But how can I keep an eye on him, when I have to come to the city everyday to sell vegetables? He could be here now. I have almost given up trying to control him. He could get a seizure inside there and fall in the fire. He is safer with the others."

Peter Tombo looked at his watch. "Really I have to go now. Tell me how I can find you."

"I'm always at Kilimo Street," Rosa said, "Near the Standard Bank. But Peter, don't lie to me, like you did. I can't forget that day – 18th March 1972. Six years ago. I was pregnant and you had told me that you would take me to a doctor who would help me to get rid of it."

"I was scared, Rosa," Peter said. "You were very young. You didn't know what was involved. It wasn't just a matter of the doctor giving you some pills. It could have been very dangerous."

"So you abandoned me? There is no need to abandon me again. I want nothing from you. I only want you to see your son. I want him to know you. One day he said to me. 'All the other children have a father. Don't I have a father, Mummy?' I didn't know what to say. I would like him to see you and know he has a father too."

"I would like to see him too," Peter Tombo said, "I can come and see you where you sell your vegetables."

She looked at him pleadingly. "Can you?"

"Yes."

"When will you come to see me?" she asked.

"Will you be there tomorrow?"

"Yes. I'm always there."

Peter Tombo promised to come there the following day after work. Rosa got out of the car and went back to her vegetables. Only after he had driven away did it occur to him that he should have given her some money from the large bundle of cash he had. But oh, well, he would be seeing her tomorrow. He drove on thoughtfully to Moi Avenue, where his wife was waiting.They drove to their home in Lavington Green for lunch.

*****

He did try to see her again. But not the following day as he had promised: That was a bad day. What really happened? Yes – the flowers.

Besides the hotel, he and his new wife Njeri were partners in a horticultural business. They exported all kinds of flowers, fruits and vegetables to London. Some of those flowers they grew themselves in their three acre garden at Lavington Green. On the day he was supposed to see Rosa he learnt that there was a problem at the airport and he had to drive there. There was a difficulty in obtaining space for the flowers on the flights bound for London, and after spending two hours at the airport trying to cajole and bribe the officials he realised that there was nothing that could be done. All the roses and the carnations would wilt – and what a great loss! He spent the rest of the day at a golf-course, trying to recover his composure and it was late in the night that he woke up with a start, as if from a bad dream. Rosa! He remembered their meeting. She must have spent the whole day waiting for him, only to realise that he had failed her again. Cursing himself for his forgetfulness he tried to go back to sleep. He would see Rosa tomorrow and apologise. After all, she was always there in the street, she had said.

But he couldn't make it the following day either, for some other urgent matter came up. His diary seemed cluttered with activity that week and it was several days before he found some time to drive to Rosa's street.

But as he neared the Standard bank he saw the police' "Black Maria" drive up. He saw a group of women surrounded by police and being hustled into the van. As some of the women resisted arrest, they were hit with police batons on the elbows and knees. One of the women spun round during the struggle and Peter saw her face. It was Rosa. She saw him too as he walked up.

"Peter!" she cried, "Wait," she implored the policemen. "There is Peter. Peter will help me!"

"No one can help you now, woman," a policeman said roughly, "Get in."

Her frail hands seemed to be reaching out for him. Her eyes were wide terror, mingled with the excitement of seeing him – and there was a plea in her eyes, a message. Her last word was "Peter," just before she vanished into the dark interior of the Black Maria. The van drove off, sounding a loud siren.

What was that last message in her eyes? What was it she would have said, had the policemen given her a second? That look on her face would return time and time again to haunt him und he would bury his face in his wife's breast, trying to forget. Did she want him to follow her to the police station and bail her out? Or was it their son she was concerned about, the boy who would suffer if she was imprisoned? "Peter, you betrayed me again," she would whisper in his dreams, for he had turned on his heels and hurried back to his office, instead of following the black Maria and paying her fine. His father had left him with a clean silver spoon in his hand and he was never able to cope with dirt, squalor and vulgarity. That day he decided to wipe out Rosa from his mind. The whine of the siren reminded him that she belonged to a different world, a world in perpetual moaning – and he hurried across the street towards light and laughter. That afternoon, which was Saturday, he went swimming with his boys from the first marriage, who he was allowed to take out on Saturday and Sundays.

*****

Rosa could not pay her fine and was imprisoned for three months. Two of the women came to see her in prison and assured her that her son was well and in good hands.

But when Rosa came out of prison her son was nowhere to be seen and it took her over a week to trace his whereabouts. He had befriended some other boys from Ngomongo, another slum area and had gone to live there. When Rosa went there she found three boys in a little shack they had made for themselves with sticks and cartons. One of them was her son Mwangi. He was in a terrible state, with bruises and scars all over his body. With no one to take care of his medication, he had gone back to regular seizures and had injured himself. A patch of his head was bold, where his hair had caught fire. His clothes were in tatters while lice and jiggers seemed have found a paradise on his person. Rosa cried so much when she saw him.

But the boy said, "I don't know why you are crying over me, Mummy. You should look at yourself. Haven't you been eating?"

"Prison is a bad place," Rosa told him. "I pray that you never find yourself there. Oh, I'm so afraid for you, my son."

When they got home to the valley Rosa had to build a new shack. In her absence the old one had been destroyed piece by piece by desperate people looking for scraps. That was one of the reason why her son had left.

After her lesson in jail, Rosa never sold vegetables again on the main streets. She took her business to the back-streets which few tourists visited, and therefore the city council askaris did not think it imperative to keep those parts of the city sparkling clean. One could break the cleanliness law there with comparative impunity. But business was slow as the back-street people had little money to spend.

Another three years passed and Mwangi was a big boy, nearly ten years old – big enough to take care of himself in the streets. His mother did not worry so much now about him, as long as he took his medicine regularly. And she was proud of him when he came home with ten or fifteen shillings every day, which he got from showing motorists where to park. Her one big worry was that, like many other boys of the street, he had learnt to inhale petrol fumes from car tanks. Whenever they found a loose cap the boys would open the tank and dip in a piece of cloth. They would inhale the fumes and stagger around in a daze – their own kind of high.

A slum woman has to let her son roam free quite early in life. Only that way will he learn the tricks of survival. Rosa did not fret too much when sometimes her son did not appear for a whole night. Sometimes when some strange "uncle" appeared, intending to spend the night with his mother, Mwangi would take in the situation and stay out of sight.

He was not at home during the great fire that swept through the slums when, according to rumours, a cat upset a kerosine lamp in one of the shacks and it caught fire. A large section of the valley was razed to the ground before the firemen arrived. Rosa, who had in her early days sworn never to touch alcohol had succumbed to regular temptation and drunk a little every night to woo sleep and also combat the repulsiveness of some of her own wooers. The man in her shack that night was a coward who fled through the smoke and the flames to save his own life, leaving that lovely body he had professed to love, scarcely two hours earlier, to perish in the flames. Rosa had drunk heavily and was like a person in a coma. She was very badly burnt by the time one of the neighbours sounded the alarm and a strong fearless fellow rushed in through the smoke and carried her out. But it was too late and perhaps he only prolonged Rosa's agony.

She was taken to hospital where her son wept bitterly when he saw her charred body. All her hair had been burnt and her limbs and body were a mass of suppurating wounds. She recognised her son and tried to tell him something. He was too distraught to catch the message but the nurse wrote something on the paper.

Later she said to the boy "Does KVM 876 mean anything to you?"

The boy said, "It's a car number."

"Whose car?" the nurse asked.

"I don't know whose car. But it's a car number."

"Are you one of those parking boys?"

The boy stared at the floor. Parking boys, like vegetable sellers were considered a great nuisance in the city and were also harrassed by city council policemen. The nurse in uniform could be leading him into a trap and the boy was quiet.

"Please answer me," the nurse told him, "A little while ago your mother kept whispering this number. It means something to her. It is perhaps the number of a person she wanted to see. Do you know anything about it? KVM 876?"

"No," the boy said, "Will my mother get better?"

The nurse stared at the boy. She was wondering how to tell him that his mother was already dead.

"Who takes care of you, boy, apart from your mother?" the nurse asked the boy.

"No one," he said, "There's only my mother."

*****

Friends from the slum came and took Rosa's body for burial. As they had no money for a coffin, Rosa's charred remains were wrapped in a new blanket and buried at the cemetry at Kariokor. A handful of women said prayers and went back to the valley. One of them pledged to take care of Mwangi.

But as the shack she had built after the fire was very small and there was nothing to eat there, Mwangi ran away and found his own place to stay, among his mischievious friends.

Several months passed during which he moaned the passing away of his mother and experienced terrible hardship. Every day he pestered motorists, begging them for coins after directing them to empty parking spaces the motorists could have easily found on their own. The motorists bitterly resented the presence of the boys in the streets because some of them deflated their tyres when they were not given some coins, while others connived with hardened criminals to steal things from people's cars. The criminals would try opening the doors while the boys watched out for cops.

One day, as he was walking through the streets alone he suddenly saw the number – KVM 876. Although he had never gone to school he had learnt from older boys to read car numbers and it was an interesting way to pass the time.

He drew close to the blue Mercedes and looked at it carefully. He remembered how his mother had whispered the number before she had died and wondered, with mounting excitement what the number had meant to her.

He was peering inside the blue Mercedes when a powerful hand grabbed him by the collar of his buttonless shirt.

"You little thief. Trying to rob me, are you?" a voice asked. An angry man was towering over him. But Mwangi had learnt the tricks of survival and before the man could kick him or call the police he quickly slipped out of his shirt and escaped, leaving the tattered garment in the man's hand. The man cursed in a low voice full of disgust and threw the shirt into an alley. The blue Mercedes drove off. Mwangi ran into the alley and retrieved his shirt.

His neck was sore where the man had grabbed him.

The next time he came upon the blue Mercedes was about a month later in a quiet side street. A lady was driving and Mwangi beckoned her towards an empty parking. With an angry snort the lady opened her handbag and threw him a fifty cents piece.

Again he went closer to the blue Mercedes and looked inside, trying to find a clue as to what it had meant to his mother. But on the back seat he only saw a bunch of flowers. Something about the flowers agitated him, for he could remember the slum women laying some flowers on his mother's grave.

He heard a step behind him and he turned quickly, thinking that the lady had come back. Just then a hand grabbed him by the neck and, with shock, he recognised the same gentleman who had grabbed him the other time. Father and son stared at each other, neither knowing who the other was.

"Why, you little thief? Whatever do you want with my car?" Peter asked.

He was about to kick the boy when something odd happened. The boy's eyes rolled and his muscles grew rigid. Alarmed, Peter Tombo let go of him and the boy collapsed on the pavement. His wife rushed up. "What have you done to the boy, Peter?"

"Nothing. Nothing at all. I think he's having ..." Peter Tombo did not finish. Suddenly his mouth was dry as he stared at the boy on his pavement.

His wife Njeri, who had the keys of the car, went to the driver side quickly and opened the door. "Peter, let's go. We don't want any trouble."

"But ... We can't leave him here!" Peter said.

"Oh, yes, we can. What is he to you? He's just a street boy."

"He's Rosa's son," Peter muttered.

"I beg your pardon?"

"Nothing," Peter said. Still staring at the boy he opened the car door and got in. Quickly he closed it behind him, as if shutting himself from the ugliness in the street and the past that kept following him. As Njeri reversed the car and drove away his eyes were still on the boy as his muscles jerked in the epileptic spasms.

*****

About ten minutes later Mwangi opened his eyes and saw a crowd watching him. He sat up weakly trying to remember where he was. He remembered the blue Mercedes, the beautiful lady, the fingers of that man around his throut. While the crowd murmured he stood up weakly and backed away.

When he came upon a fallen dust-bin in the alley he sat down to recover his strength and calm his nerves. He thought about the blue Mercedes and again wondered what it had meant to his mother Rosa. After a while he conducted that it had brought him nothing but pain and that he must never go near it again.

OMONDI MAK'OLOO

MATATU MENACE

Hi, my name is "Take Me Home". I'm one among several thousands of pirate taxis – better known as matatus – that operate on the Kenyian roads. Me, I'm based in Nairobi, the capital city of the country. Before I go any further, let me tell you briefly what I was before I turned matatu.

When I was brand new, I was bought by a touring company that used me to ferry tourists betweenNairobi and the national parks or game reserves to view wild animals. Those were happy days for me, though I was driven on worse roads compared to the ones here in Nairobi.

In those days I was serviced regularly, never overloaded and almost always driven within the authorised speed limits. I was in tip top shape. In return, as you may imagine, I readily gave good service. Why not, when my owner kept me healthy and happy?

All that, alas, is now past history.

Four years after buying me, my first owner sold me. This was in accordance to company policy that vehicles that had done a certain mileage had to go.

My second owner immediately converted me into a matatu. My life has been constant misery since.

The first thing he did was to increase my seating capacity, thus drastically reducing passenger comfort. Officially I'm licensed to carry thirteen comfortably seated people, including the driver. By shifting the seats and adding some of his own, my owner doubled my seating capacity such that at any given time, as many as twenty-four people could travel in me. This caused much stress and strain on my working parts and I aged considerably within the first year of being converted to a matatu.

As if that is not enough, I'm driven at incredible speeds. This is a job entrusted by my owner to a young rogue, who has so many business interests to look after that he can't confine himself to only driving me. As I was saying, I'm driven at dangerous speeds. I have a daily average of eight to ten close shaves with death. It's only due to luck, and nothing else, on the part of my driver that has so far kept me from getting involved in a fatal accident. I doubt if he has ever been to a driving school. He has a driving license alright, but I wouldn't be surprised if it is either forged or stolen.

When waiting, for example, at a bus stop or a traffic light, my driver unnecessarily revs up my engine; causing much noise, polluting the air, not to mention the wasted fuel this country spends well over half its annual revenue on to buy, and can ill afford to waste.

He also hoots for no good reason. The sign H for Hospital is just another erected structure by the roadside, as far as he is concerned. He flashes my headlights and blinkers indiscriminately, confusing other motorists and road users.

His driving technique leaves a lot to be desired. My driver likes overtaking even when it's totally senseless. You will see him changing lanes to overtake, not bothering to check the traffic condition behind him, sometimes forcing following vehicles to brake hard. Or, you can see me dangerously overtaking another vehicle only to come to a screeching halt ten metres ahead to pick up or let out a passanger.

Road signs and the Highway Code mean nothing to him. Once I heard him innocently remark that in all his driving years he had never seen zebra crossing the road. This was in reply to a warning from a passenger after he had nearly ran over on old man crossing the street.

He stops at the traffic lights only if there are other vehicles already stopped in front of him, otherwise it's full steam ahead! He has involved me in many near collisions. In spite of these incidents, he repeats the same mistakes again and again. My fear is, that I will one day end up a mangled wreck like "King Of The Road" and "Time Is Money" did.

"King Of The Road" was cruising towards the city centre at a speed approaching that of sound. It was in the process of blindly overtaking a tractor when an oncoming heavy commercial lorry appeared over the brow of a hill. It was too late then. They collided head on, killing all aboard "King Of The Road". The fire brigade had to use acetylene torches to cut through the mangled wreck to reach the trapped bodies inside. Looking at what remained of "King Of The Road", you'd think it had been through a rolling mill.

"Time Is Money" came to an almost similar end. It jumped the lights and was rammed by a speeding city bus, reducing it and its passengers to nothingness.

My driver behaves as if the road is his personal property. He wants his way to be clear when he's moving and that's that. Woe to the motorist who happens to be on his path when he's overspeeding. He'll be agressively honked out of the way with the horn. Many times vehicles have to swerve into ditches or into pavements to avoid accidents with me. My driver curses them for being careless!!

In the matatu world it's the rules of the jungle that prevail. Caught in a traffic jam, we won't queue like other vehicles. Oh no! Why should we, when there's the pavement to drive on? Or we simply cross the yellow line and drive on the wrong side of the road! A mere yellow line won't stop us. It is, after all, only a line drawn on the road. To stop a matatu you need something solid, like high kerbs or traffic islands along the dividing line but not just mere yellow line. That can be easily driven over!

But there's no hurry in Africa.

Ha! Whoever said that made the understatement of the century. I invite you to take a ride in me or any other matatu and you will come out convinced otherwise. I for one, do the stretch between city centre and a suburb estate in twenty minutes flat, regardless of traffic or weather condition.

Policemen?

Of course, there are policement but there is no danger from them. They get regular handsome tips from my driver and have learnt to look the other way when I pass, overspeeding with my overload of human cargo. Once in a while my driver encouters a difficult cop, usually these are new ones, but he soon puts them in line. All he has to do is inform the cop who my owner is and the cop makes no more trouble for fear he himself might get into trouble. You see, my owner is somebody big in this city and no cop, no matter how ambitious, would like to cross his path.

In this way my driver is able to drive in whatever way he pleases. He can stop anywhere, make U turns or reverse wherever he wants.

Apart from the driver, my owner also employs a conductor, locally known as manamba, whose job is to see to it that as many passengers as possible board me. He's left to his own designs on how best to achieve this.

Say I'm approaching a bus stop where a crowd ist waiting. My driver blasts the horn, while the manamba releases continous ear splitting whistles. This is supposed to draw the attention of the crowd – as if it were asleep – to the fact that I've arrived. The manamba jumps to the ground before I'm even properly stopped, and starts shouting my destination to the crowd. Meanwhile my driver revs up my engine to create the impression that we're leaving immediately and anybody who wants to travel in me should board quickly. Every time he presses the accelerator, the manamba slaps and thumps my body, screaming to the driver to wait.

This can go on for a good five minutes before the manamba decides that no more passengers are to be got from that bus stop and we move on to the next.

You can imagine what happens when several matatus meet at a bus stop. The ensuing din and pollution from the exhaust fumes make the sorrounding area a health hazard.

My manamba will use all kinds of sweet words to seduce a potential passenger to board me, but once inside, the passenger is at his mercy. All the niceness from the manamba is gone. The passenger may be even ordered to assume some very uncomfortable position in order to create space so that more people can enter. It's not uncommon to see people packed in me like sardines in a tin, especially during the rush hour when they hurry to and from work. It's at this time you find me carrying well over twice my authorised capacity with some people even hanging onto the door.

My manamba does not confine himself to persuasion alone as a way of getting passengers. Many a time I've seen him exchange blows with other manambas over a passenger. This happens when another matatu going to the same place as I reaches a bus stop simultaneously. There may be only one or two people, and the manamba tries to persuade them to board his vehicle instead of the other. The other manamba does likewise, resulting in an argument between them and an eventual exchange of blows.

If a passenger seems undecided, my manamba can actually pull or push him towards me. He has got so much guts.

My owner does not give a damn about my well-being, provided he gets out of me what he wants. A real capitalist he is. He is responsible to a great extent for the reckless and dangerous way I'm driven. He issued a permanent order to my driver to make at least twelve trips a day. This is very difficult, to say the least, and to meet this required number of trips, my driver has to resort to uncouth methods like driving on the pavement.

The regular inspection and services I used to be taken to, when I belonged to the touring company, are now things of the past. My engine is falling apart. The only time it gets attention is when oil is being poured into it. My owner does not know that such things like engine tuning and engine overhauling exists. It runs non stop from 5 in the morning till 10 at night because if it's stopped it's difficult to start again since my battery ran down two months ago. It no longer purrs contentedly like it used to do, but growls hoarsely like a dying lion.

My second gear cannot engage. The teeth were broken by the rogue driver.

My wheels are not aligned. They wobble as if they wish to part company. This may yet happen one day. The tyres are the same ones I left the touring company with. The treads are so worn-out you need a magnifying glass to see them. I skid when it's wet.

When you see me from a distance at night you think I'm a motor cycle. Only one of my headlamps is working. The other got smashed ages ago and has not been replaced.

Even my side mirrors are gone. My driver relies on the manamba to tell him when the way is clear to join a lane. When he wants to check on his side, he leans out of the window. Sometimes he has to use one hand for steering while doing this.

Passengers get wet rides in me when it rains because a side window got broken and allows the rain in. I wonder if it will ever be replaced.

I look haggard and dishevelled. The beautiful lustre and elegance my body had are long since gone. They've been replaced by dents and scratches, as a result of constant bangings and thumpings by my manamba.

My owner is aware of all these defects but won't do anything about them. He says as long as my wheels can roll, I can always transport people. He reaps huge profits from me daily but grudgingly pays for my petrol and oil, the only things he pays for. He prefers to top my radiator with tap water from his house rather than by distilled water. He says tap water is just as good: My radiator is getting clogged up and can no longer cool efficiently but my owner does not know this. The temperature gauge needle on the dashboard got stuck and now permanently reads "cold". One day my engine will simply burst into flames.

If my owner cared about my well-being he would have employed a more responsible "crew" to man me. He never even bothered to find out if my driver had any past experience in driving. He just picked somebody in the streets who could hold the steering wheel and press the pedals. I think he did this knowing that my driver led a devil-may-care life with no responsibilities to speak of, and wouldn't demand a high wage from him. He pays him very little. It's the same with my manamba. He lives only for the today.

My story is not unique. In fact it can be retold as many times as you see matatus in this country. Daily reports from different parts of the country telling of matatu accidents similar to those of "King Of The Road" and "Time Is Money" can be read in the newspapers.

The public is crying for something to be done. Letters complaining of matatu menace are published everyday on the reader's page of the newspapers, but the cries fall on deaf ears as the people who are in a position to do something are the ones who own matatus and prefer things to remain as they are. That is, for them to make easy money from unroadworthy vehicles at the expense of human lives. Many more lives will be lost if nothing is done about us, and by the look of things nothing is going to be done for a long time to come.

Kenya has its place in the world as the number one country in population growth. No country can rival her when it comes to that. Many a politician and professional have voiced their concern over this. Me, I wouldn't worry. The answer to the problem is already here in the form of us – matatus. There won't be any population boom in Kenya as long as we matatus are around to kill thousands every year.

Ironically, the country can't do without us. Everyone realises this. The few buses that are there can't cope with the high demand for transport. Kick us from the road and the country will grind to a halt; we matatus are a necessary menace.

DEDE KAMKONDO

REMEMBER, MAMA

The scorching sun seemed to have declared war on the land, for the entire earth was a basin of cracked, hard soil. There was no sign of vegetation. The area was like an extinct anthill.

Haifa woke up with a start behind the sand dune. I was dreaming, he thought grimly wondering what the significance of that dream was. He had dreamt he was a medical doctor and had come back to the village to cure every sick person – young or old. In his dream he had seen himself wearing a white coat as he gave out tablets and capsules to the sick. The whole village was there, singing for him, praising Allah for having educated the son of the village...

Well, that was just a dream, thought Haifa. He felt weak and his limbs ached. The saliva in his mouth was hot, his theeth coarse; his throat was parched like the back of a crocodile. And he was sure that the intestines were digesting themselves, the way a hungry cat eats its young.

Haifa's one objective was to get his family to the United Nations Distribution Point. Once there, the family would queue up and get a bowl of food to eat.

They hadn't eaten for two days now...

In a matter of hours, the sun would be directly overhead and that would spell trouble. They wouldn't withstand the heat. So they had better go on the move then.

Mama

Mama

Mama

"Mama", he called feebly, getting to his feet.

There was no response.

"Mama, where are you; Where is Ali; ... still asleep?"

"Mama", he called again, the effort draining the energy out of him.

Then he saw her. She was lying on the other side of the sand dune, the child at her back.

At twelve, Haifa could tell a dead person from a living one. And he didn't need a second glance to tell him that his mama had reached the end of the road.

The mother lay on her belly, her mouth full of dry, baked clay.

"I'm sorry, you tried so hard, mama, to get us to the food centre. Remember, mama, that night when we sneaked out of the village convoy? Remember, mama, that you took me aside and whispered in my ear that we had to go our way for you suspected that papa's eldest wife was living on the kids; that you suspected that she was devouring the little children, remember? You suspected that she was a cannibal – no wonder she was fat, remember, mama? We sneaked out, didn't we, mama – you

184

and me and little Ali? We sneaked out with just a gourd of water. We used to drink a few drops – little Ali and me, but not you, mama."

"You wouldn't want me to cry, mama, would you? You always wanted me to be strong and try to get the white man's education so that I'd be a doctor in Addis. So, I'm not going to cry, mama. I'm not going to.

When the rains come again, mama, I'll go to Addis and work and read at night... Then I'll come back und bury you properly. I promise, mama."

Haifa stood up slowly, the sleeping child in his arms. He looked at the lifeless figure on the ground, his eyes wet.

Then, pressing little Ali close to him, Haifa started walking away. He didn't glance back.

He couldn't. He had promised not to cry. He kept on walking. For a moment he stopped when he thought he heard the sound of an aircraft engine somewhere ahead of him.

He smiled as he summoned the reserved stamina in him.

Allah, he was almost there!

Haifa had been close to his mama. He had been born at the time she had given up hope. He had been born the day his papa took on a fourth wife.

For years there had been Mama and Haifa until little Ali came along.

Mama, muttered Haifa, as he staggered on towards the direction he believed was the source of salvation. Mama, maybe you were right. I do remember how that wife of papa used to look at our little Ali. She was like a hawk at the sight of a lonely young chick. She was like a hyena in the night waiting in the dark corners for a puppy to make a wrong move.

You were right, mama. You were always right. And to prove you right, I'll be a medical doctor with a smile for everybody. For sure, mama, I promise.

Two days later, a jeep carrying cartons and cartons of medicine, food and blankets, jerry cans of water and petrol to a United Nations Food Distribution Point came to a stop when the driver caught sight of two figures lying on the dry sand.

"Kids, just kids", he muttered softly, jumping out of the vehicle.

The little one was alive but the twelve year old lad who was wearing a wide smile was lifeless like a felled palm tree.

In the beginning there had been Mama and Haifa. So too in the end.

MEGDELAWIT DEDJENE

IT HAD A DESTINY

It was all around her. It has been around her for a very long time. It has been with her for such a long time that she had begun to think of it as part of herself.

Lifeless, hopeless, protruding eyes scanned the barren land around and rested on a mother with what seemed like twins in her laps. They were three of the many, three of the many under the cruel glare of the sun. They were examples of the wasted, struggling skeletons that were walking hand-in-hand with death. A stroll with death was common. Some came back from the outing, others went for good. But at such a time when death is not a rare thing, and it happens every second, minute, and hour of the day, there was not the traditional, "old" hair tearing and wailing. Only a numb sense of loss, and sometimes even relief.

The girl stood up with visible effort and went to the mother and children and sat down with them. They sat quietly, their sad lost gazes seeing, yet not taking in anything. The two children with thin legs and swollen stomachs were now both crouched near their mother, sucking at the sagging breasts that were no more breasts but old leather pouches, wrinkled from discomfort.

One of the twins started to moan, while the other began to scream. No, ... not to scream, although it was intended to be that, but small whimpering sounds. But no-one looked their way. It was nothing new, nothing considered bigger, sadder, than a child today, a mother tomorrow, dying daily. So what? One instance was worse than the other, but people had their hands full without bothering about other people's troubles. The mother shook her head tiredly. Her eyes seemed to say "what can I do for you, my babies?"

The flies were terrible. They came and settled in the corners of a boy's eyes, and on his upper lips that were covered with dried up mucous, but he did not shoo them away, and neither did his father. Both were too tired and careless about their cleanliness. Perhaps if his mother had been there she would have tried to make him cleaner than he was at present. But she was not there, ... they had lost her on their way here to Werebabou.

What mattered now was food and water.

The father's throat ached, from dryness as much as from the lump that was caused by his tears. Now even the God of his ancestors was cruel to him. His eyes did not blur. He had no tears. All the tears that he had to shed had been shed when they had buried his wife and his eldest son, a boy of fourteen. Ironically it was his younger son who had survived the famine.

He watched his eight year old son, who looked as if he were four. Slowly he run his eyes to the other side of the field, where he saw what looked like a family of five ... or was it six?

Yes, six. One unborn, unlucky embryo. For how long will he be unlucky ... or lucky? At least he was protected from the harsh rays of the sun, and the unpleasant sight that could be seen in that area.

The parents were carrying a bundle each, and looked as if they had come from very far. The girl swayed and dropped down dizzily to the ground. Her brothers had more stamina. They eased themselves slowly, each small movement taking two three seconds. From his position the man saw the mother take a small cloth sack from the bundle and give a hundful of "Kolo" of roasted cereals they had taken on their long journey, to each member of her family. Then, as quickly as she had got out the sack, she put it back in the bundle.

Without thinking, the man stood up and went to this newly arrived family. He stretched out his hand, indicating that he wanted something to eat. His son observed this from far away, sudden wisdom in his mind. He saw the woman shake her head in refusal and look away. Then his father came back, dragging his feet on the dusty ground.

There were more than two hundred souls in that area. All in bad condition. Some were worse now than they had been when they arrived, some were more or less the same, but none were better. They had one thing in common, they all wanted food and water ... they were all hungry people.

A boy sat alone bundled in his dirty "gabi", staring at his "kil", that was hanging at the end of his travelling stick.

It looked the same as ever and yet it was different. It was his favourite kil. The one that he used to take with him when he went shepherding. It seemed such a long time ago ... the laughter and the songs, the words and the sentences that had double meanings, thought of by his fellow shepherds to tease some of their friends. The difference, the main difference was the fact that today his kil was almost empty, whereas in the old days it was anything but that.

He had come from Chiffra and was only resting before he could continue his tiresome journey to Bati. He was determined to reach Bati whatever the cost.

There was nothing for him in this land. No more family, no more relatives. No ties. No land to cultivate, and no herd to look after. He had seen them drop one by one. Wanting to help but being unable to do anything about it, he had left his home town, the place where many of his ancestors had lived and died, the place where his umbilical cord was buried, the place where he had grown up and married, to lose his wife after a short year, defeated.

The animals were no good. They dropped dead before anyone could kill them and use their meat. If their owners were lucky one or two of their cattle might survive. But when they were slaughtered and their meat eaten, instant dysentery set in which weakened and killed many.

All sorts of diseases spread quickly, and because of their lack of resistance, people died like flies. Those who stayed alive suffered from different kinds of skin diseases, as well as internal disturbances. The lucky ones died and those who stayed alive became maniacs, eating their remains and dust and whatever else came their way.

187

There was no such thing as self-respect any longer, the only thing that mattered was survival, by any means. Those who were too tired to do anything but continue existing watched what went on dispassionately.

All in all things went from bad to worse as the days went by and many wondered what their future would be. What their destinies would be. Was the famine going to stop? Would it follow them from here to Bati as it had followed them to this place ... this place where everyone was selfish, everyone intent on saving his own skin?

The boy gathered his dust covered gabi close around him and dozed off, while the family of five-six left Werebabou behind heading for Bati. There was a small flicker of hope in their hearts as they set out.

Suddenly a woman who had been standing dropped down to her knees and stretched her two thin arms heavenwards. Those who saw her from afar were inclined to believe that she was a young girl rather than the thirty-two year old woman she was.

One could see her lips moving but nothing could be heard. As suddenly as she had begun the woman let her arms drop to her sides. Then she swayed in her kneeling position and tumbled face-down on the dusty ground, and lay there inertly, not the slightest movement visible in her bony body.

Two men who had seen her came from the nearby group and carried her to the far side of the field. The fact that they had to carry a person in their tired condition was laborious, but at the same time this person was not much of a load. The woman did not weigh more than thirty kilograms.

At the far side of the field a somewhat tedious job was being done. People with heads hanging were standing around a mass grave, if it could be called that. Father and son were holding hands, having seen that mother was buried. An old woman who had lost her grand-daughter, a half-blind mother and a crippled father saw their four year old hope being lowered among the heaps of corpses.

The mass grave was dug by tired, hungry and thirsty people, who following the old tradition, wanted to dispose of their dead. But being too weak to dig an appropriately deep grave, they had only dug a grave about a meter deep.

Two or three days later the dry earth would lift off the soil and expose the corpses. Soon the smell would diffuse throughout the whole area and call the hungry hyenas and vultures who would have a feast.

Trying to shoo them away was impossible, because both the hyenas and the vultures would turn on their enemies and tear them to pieces instead. So, unable to do anything they stood helplessly, seeing their beloved ones being torn to pieces by the animals.

The family of five had come from a small village about twenty kilometers north of Werebabou. Now they had had ample rest and were heading to Bati, where many of their kinsmen had gone to. Some had gone to Addis Ababa.

Addis Ababa! The land of milk and honey. Oh, how they wished they lived there. The land of the rich, where no-one had to fear a famine. It had to be beautiful, just like its name, Addis Ababa!

But now was no time for dreaming. One had to be practical. Maybe once they reached Bati, they could afford to dream.

So with hope and renewed effort they started their journey. They had not gone for more than 15 kms. when one of the boys collapsed. And as if on cue the girl and the other son fell to the ground. But they were in a much better condition than their ill-fated brother. Or was he luckier perhaps?

He began to retch, and what he had eaten only a couple of hours ago, the palm-full of kolo, came out undigested. In a few minutes it was all over for him. He slumped back, his eyes staring fixedly at the sky. A cloudless sky, a cruel sun and a merciful God. He had given him peace. He had to be somewhere up there, the Almighty. Silently the father dug a grave and buried the small body. They filled in the grave together, made a crude cross from two dry sticks, placed it on top of the grave, and as suddenly as they had paused they resumed their journey.

No tears shed, no faces scratched, no hair torn out. Dig a grave, place the body in it, fill it up with either a heavy or light heart. This was simply routine work.

The 50 kms. from Werebabou to Bati were not as easy to walk as they had thought. With almost no food and no water, the sun beating down on them mercilessly they walked most of the way in a stupour.

There were not many people on the road. The rugged plain and the rocky hills were not very appealing. Everything had dried up and there was not one single green plant to be seen.

They walked for 5 days. The last time they had eaten was more than twenty-four hours ago. If a half handful of kolo can be called eating. When they reached an area that was somewhat shaded by dried up fallen trees, the father told them that he had to relieve his bowels, and told them to go ahead and that he would catch up with them.

So they went on without him, but when they had covered a condiserable distance and he had still not caught up with them and was nowhere to be seen, the girl suggested she go back and look for him. She found him a couple of metres away from the spot where they had left him.

At first she saw his legs and wondered if their father had found some wild fruits growing on the tree. She went forward and stood directly beneath the tree and looked up. What she saw made her scream. His belt around his neck her father was hanging and head breathed the last of the suffocating air. He had given up. Two people seeing her look up and laugh hysterically thought that the man up there had found some fruit and wanted to join in the picking. But when they saw the unpleasant sight they just turned their heads away and without bothering to help her they went on their way. Sobbing tiredly the girl followed them and when she saw her mother she conveyed the message without having to put it into words.

She did not feel the loss of her husband then. She had been expecting his death though not in such a drastic way. She looked at her daughter and then back at her stomach in which she was carrying an unborn baby, a baby that was going to grow up without a father. She stood up and with a tired motion of the hands told her children to follow her and soon they were on their way.

Ahead they could only see stretches and stretches of land that seemed to have no end. There was nothing inviting about the rocky hills and the grassless land. Here and there they could see the bones of some domestic animals. There were also a lot of places marked with crosses made of wood. The place looked like a graveyard without a watchman. Everybody was either dead or had taken refuge in another country. There were definite signs of devastation about that place. The famine had completely changed it. Werebabou had never felt like this before. It was a country of good crops, hospitable people and a very friendly, inviting countryside.

There were some small huts devoid of human beings. They looked sad and isolated. The open doors seemed to say come and live in me; but that was quite impossible because now these huts had new inhabitants that occupied them during the night. They went and found themselves something to eat, then came back to pass the night there. The place belonged to the animals now and that seemed to be something that was going to go on for quite some time.

The mother leant against one of the huts and looked tiredly at the sky. There was not one single sign of rain. There were no clouds and she wondered if she would live to see any. If only her unborn could live to see any. There was not a soul to be seen for many kilometers, and not a single sign of any sort of human occupation. Again she wondered if they had not taken the wrong road to Bati. "My life" she thought, "is going to be a roll of wonderings and doubts". Then she resumed her walk and the children followed her.

The sun became intolerably cruel and they all sighed inwardly, their hopes beginning to fade, as they passed yet another accumulation of skeletons that looked as if they belonged to cattle. She felt the child stir in her stomach and suddenly she felt frightened. What if the baby wanted to be born now? She took the hand of her son and squeezed it tightly in her own. She looked back and wanted to return to the hut they had passed but decided against it. Even a couple of kilometers counted.

At night it got really cold. Drawing the gabi close around him the boy from Chiffra wondered what was going to happen to him and to the many others. He thought of the days when people were not as selfish as they were nowadays. He thought of the days when they would offer a stranger whatever they had. Be it an elaborate meal or otherwise. Now one gathered for oneself and ate for oneself. It was no more considered impolite or selfish, or greedy. It was called an act of survival. But he understood. He did not bear any grudges against anyone.

He wondered what the people of Wollo had done to deserve such a punishment. Could it be that they had thrown away too much good corn, and forgotten their God? That was what his mother had said when the famine struck them and they had to sell their home born cow to the slaughter house. He remembered how he had cried and he also recalled the words of his mother. She had said that there would come a day when he would cry for himself; she had said that he would cry so much for himself that there would be no tears left to cry for others.

The tears of God had dried. Now there will not be any rain. God had cried too much about his people and now there were no tears left for his people in Wollo. This time he was going to punish them.

He looked around. The faces had many things etched on them. Hopelessness, fatigue and of course hunger. Slowly staring at the faces around, his eyes closed and he slept.

As usual the hyenas came and digging at the graves they got out the corpses and had a feast. The people moved away and watched. They looked like disinterested spectators. No, not that ... but like some spectators who had grown tired of looking at the same scene over and over. There was no horror in their eyes now. They had got over that.

A father and his son who had been sitting close together saw a woman take some dried up "kita" from a tattered bag and munch at it slowly. She ate about a quarter of the thinly baked bread and then put it back again.

The man was too hungry, and the sight of food nearly drove him crazy. He had to get some food before the night was over. He had only one thing on his mind and though he was afraid he knew he had to do it or he and his son would die. For a moment he wondered if it was worth it. Perhaps he should join his wife and all the others, but that was too slow and the agony of the hunger might stay long. He looked at his son and told himself that it was for him. But deep down inside he knew it was for himself alone. His son was just an excuse to salvage his conscience. His son dozed away and slowly the man made his way to the woman.

She was sleeping with her bag clutched tightly to herself. Silently he took out his Adal-knife and brought it very near her throat. His hands began to shake and he was afraid that she would wake up and his plan go unfinished. Bringing the knife decisively close to her throat he made a small prayer asking God to forgive him. Then he covered her mouth with one rough hand and at the same time he slit her throat with one movement of the knife. Then he threw it away and grabbing the bag with one hand he crept away to his son who was still fast asleep.

Quickly he took out the kita and a small amount of kolo and got rid of the sack. He woke his son and silently gave him a small piece of kita. The boy at first did not seem to understand, but then he took it and sniffed at it. Then he stuffed it all in. But he could not munch it, because his teeth were too weak and his mouth too dry. It took him quite a while to finish eating and when he had finished he went back to sleep.

The father ate too, but after he had eaten and somewhat relieved his hunger he felt anguish in his heart. That was not the way he had been brought up. He had been an altar-boy as a child and a God fearing man after he had married. Now he had killed for a small piece of food and he wished he had not. As he dozed off he prayed that he would die in his sleep.

A mother and child were sitting together and the girl looked very frail. The mother looked better. She glanced around and wondered if any of these people would give her something to eat if she asked. She guessed not. When she looked at her daughter something told her to go and ask, despite the consequences. She got up quietly and went to beg for some food.

Some looked at her incredulously, while others just turned their heads away. At last an old woman handed her a handful of kolo and the woman went back to her daughter. But by that time her daughter was dead.

It was ironic the woman thought, those who found nothing to eat continued to exist, while those who found it died. Slowly she knelt beside her daughter and, the skeletal body in her arms, began rocking to and fro. The kolo was clutched in one hand. The picture they made seemed to say, "let me go with my child, but let me live-on".

The mother with her five children started to cry when she saw the small huts that looked as if they had been made of cloth. Tents! Many people were sitting outside and eating. Eating!

Two white men saw them from afar and came hurrying. She cried out then. She screamed with all her might. And in one of the tents she gave birth to a boy.

Upon entering this tent she left the famine behind and gave life to a small thing that had a bright future. Miraculously this small thing was alive, alive and strong enough to feed itself on the mother's breasts.

The sun outside did not seem to have a cruel glare anymore. In fact everybody looked forward to it.

And so the famine that had struck them seemed to have a destiny after all. It followed them and stopped right outside the shelter. There was no-one to nurse it and it died out there in the light and they enjoyed life to see it banished and forbidden to enter.

"Yes, there is a God up there", the mother thought as the child in her arms burped and closed its eyes contentedly.

Editorial note:

"Tooth of fire" was written as a stage play.
Since the play offers equally fascinating potential as a radio play, a few minor changes have been undertaken by the editor to make it suitable for radio.
Yet there is a fundamental difference between the author's second, revised stage-version and the radio version as printed here:

In the first version of the play, Khalid Al-Mubarak had separated "The Narrator" from characters like "The Old Sultan", "The Leader", "The Crier", "The Man, later Head of Security".

In a second version he extended the role of the narrator who, in addition, plays up to five additional roles:
"narrator as leader", "narrator as crier", "narrator as Muk", "narrator as Old Sultan", "narrator as Head of Security".

This dramaturgical principle is based both on traditions of the art of traditional story telling and the method of "alienation", "distancing effect" as developed by the German writer Bertolt Brecht in his plays.

Both methods are basically aimed at having the same effect on the side of the audience: the jumping of a narrator/actor in or out of a role breaks the continued flow of identification and dramatic suspense and calls for a critical reflection about the "characters".

Both methods, however, are based on theatrical effects, i.e. gestures, mimicking, quick change of costumes, light effects etc., in addition to different voice intonations.

The method will only work if such type of a narrator represents the most sophisticated, artistic skills of radio performance and the most brillant voice manipulation.
Such actors are rare, not only in most African radio stations. Based on my own experience with radio drama production, I feel that a narrator, playing apart from his own "role" up to another five, will cause confusion amongst the audience.

For this reason all the characters are separate as in the author's first version, leaving it up to radio drama producers which roles to add to the narrator, according to the "voice material" available.

WF.

KHALID AL-MUBARAK

TOOTH OF FIRE
A Play

Characters:

Narrator
Sheikh Farah
Muk
Sheikh Farah's Wife
Man (Later political officer, promoted to Head of Security)
The Leader
The Crier
The old Sultan
Maid (Suha)

Time: The 17th Century

Place: Sinnar, capital of The Sultanate of Sinnar (1505-1821) on the Blue
            Nile.

Based on the life and legend of the 17th Sudanese Sufi, Sheikh Farah Wad Taktuk.

Dedication: To Dr. L. Hodgkin, Ms Jan Shaw and Jamal Ben Omar of Amnesty
              International.

194

SCENE 1

SHEIKH FARAH'S HUT. A STACK OF BOOKS. HEAPS OF BOOKS ON TABLES. A SMALL MUD-BRICK OVEN IN THE FAR CORNER. A DRUM.

NARRATOR: Sheikh Farah. The Sufi of Sinnar. The anxious locking one in the corner is Muk.
(SHEIKH FARAH, STARTS TO BEAT HIS DRUM. THEN HE OPENS A BAG AND TAKES OUT A SHEET OF PAPER. HE SPREADS THE SHEET IN FRONT OF HIM AND BEGINS TO GAZE INTENTLY AT THE WORDS AND SHAPES IN IT. AFTER SOME MINUTES HIS CONCENTRATION BECOMES SO INTENSE THAT HE GOES INTO A TRANCE, UTTE-RING UNINTELLIGBLE WORDS, SPEAKS IN TONGUES. HE COOLS DOWN, MOVES VERY SLOWLY AND COMES OUT OT THE ECSTATIC STATE. HE LOOKS AT MUK AND SAYS)

SHEIKH FARAH: Now I can give you an answer.

MUK: Well. What is it?

SHEIKH FARAH: I accept. I'll do it!

MUK: Al Hamdulillah! Thank God for that. (HE HUGS SHEIKH FARAH). I'll go to spread the news. (MAKES FOR THE DOOR)

SHEIKH FARAH: Your coffee!

MUK: Some other time, Sheikh Farah. You've saved our lives. I must rush now. You were our last resort. I went to Sheikh Nadim — he said he was not feeling well and excused himself. As for Sheikh Salah, he refused even to open his door when he knew what I wanted to see him about. (EXITS)

WIFE (ENTERS): There's a man outside. He asks for protection. Says he's chased by a thug.

SHEIKH FARAH: Tell him to hide in the oven.

WIFE: In the oven?! It's very hot and it's too small for a man his size.

SHEIKH FARAH: I mean the remains of the old, disused school oven at the back of the hut.

WIFE: I doubt if that will hide him. There are more holes than bricks in the walls, and no door. (EXITS)
(KNOCKS ON THE DOOR. BEFORE SHEIKH FARAH MO-VES THE DOOR IS FLUNG OPEN. THUG APPEARS, ARMED WITH A KNIFE AND AN IRON HOOK.)

MAN: A man came here. I know that. Where is he? Where did you hide him?

SHEIKH FARAH: I didn't see a man.

MAN: His footsteps led to this direction. Where is he? Speak!! (PUSHES HIM)

SHEIKH FARAH: If you're loking for a fight come another day – you'll find one of my sons who's your age!

MAN: Where is he? Speak or I'll break your neck.

SHEIKH FARAH: He's in the oven!

MAN: Do you think I'm joking? (PAUSE) You don't seem to have realized who I am! I'm "Kamal Iron"

                 I'm well known all over the region (PAUSE)
                 I can break a chair with one finger, like this – (BREAKS CHAIR).
                 This hook of mine is more effective than all your books
                 (PUSHES STACK OF BOOKS. THE BOOKS FALL.)
                 I do what I like. (LOOKS AROUND)
                 I can take apart the wall of your hut with one hand ... Look ...

SHEIKH FARAH: Let me give you a hand. Huts and palaces fall apart anyway, with or without our intervention, in one year or in a thousand. Here, pull. Pull there! harder!

MAN: (STOPS, SURPRISED) Just who are you?

WIFE: (ENTERING) Sheikh Farah. Haven't you heard of him?

MAN: Sheikh Farah, Sheikh Farah – Aaaa! (LAUGHS) Are you the one who takes his students to the desert to watch he lizards and inspect the caves?

SHEIKH FARAH: I am, indeed.

MAN: Well, well. If that's the case, then you can do anything. You can well hide a man in an oven. (GOES TO IT, OPENS IT) It's empty, and hot. I won't waste more time with you. I'll find him (RUSHES OUT)

NARRATOR: The man came out of of the disused oven at the back of the hut and said to Sheikh Farah: "You accepted to protect me, then you betrayed me. I heard every word through your reed wall. You told him where I was." Sheikh Farah said: "My son. I told him and I didn't tell him. I told him the truth and the truth saved you. He went that way. You run in the opposite direction. Quick.

WIFE: What a beginning to the day! (PAUSE) Muk came earlier. I saw him leave. He never comes to visit you. What does he want? You

196

agreed to do something for him. What is it that made him leave so overjoyed?

SCENE 2

NARRATOR: For an answer to her question, one must go back several years in the history of this Sultanate of Sinnar, and turn some very interesting pages.

Sinnar had a leader. The "leader" had a camel. He rode it mercilessly and never gave it enough rest. Camels prefer the sand; but this camel was forced to run through mountainous areas. In the slopes of Jabal Al Barkal the camel slipped, stumbled on a rock and broke its leg. The obese leader had to walk all the way down to the plain where a horse took him to the palace. He was furious. The following day he went to the mountain and said:

"Jabal Al Barkal! Solid. Proud
like a bully, pushing round
it is time you were told
who is master of the fold
of the Nile White and Blue
of the grass and the dew
Jabal Al Barkal!
Are you ignorant of the fact
that the trees and the birds
and the undeciphered words
in the caves, are a few
of the things that can't exist
outside my control?
Jabal Al Barkal!
My command is over all:
High and mighty do not linger
If I just wag a finger!
Jabal Al Barkal!
when you hurt my camel "clever"
your own fate was sealed, forever!
Your're banished. Go to the Nubian desert.
Clear off. This minute. Do you hear?!"

There was no response from the offending mountain. The courtiers became uneasy. Tense. The leader might pour his scorn upon them.

MUK: Let me remove this smear from your sleeve, my leader. I wonder

197

where it came from. And this smudge on the shoes. (SHOUTS) Bring some cold drink for the Leader! And you umbrella bearers – don't you see the sun on the hem of the leader's gown? Move over here – quick!

LEADER: This impudent mountain doesn't know who I am, and doesn't obey my orders, which I'll never repeat.

I must teach this mountain a lesson. Now. (PAUSE) Crier! Go and call all young people of Sinnar to congregate in the main square. Immediately. I want every one of them.

(HE WALKS AWAY FOLLOWED BY UMBRELLA-BEARERS, FAN-BEARERS AND BODY-GUARDS)

THE CRIER: O ye o ye o ye!

All young men must stop work in the fields and everywhere and congregate in the main square. By order of the leader, all schools are closed. Parents will be punished if their sons and daughters do not show up. O ye O ye O ye.

Those present pass on the word to those who are not here. Ignorance of the leader's orders will not be accepted as an excuse. (REPEATS): All young men must ...

(ULULATION).

All the universe should beware
Our leader moulds us tough
See his portrait everywhere
held by people out of love
See his statues here and there
all of which is not enough
If he's slighted we declare
war on hawk, or on dove
In the movement of the sphere
we detect his name above.

NARRATOR: People pushed and hustled to get to the square (called leader's square) as quickly as possible. The "Leader's Disciples" organisation, with their distinctive green skull cap were active in street corners. They had lists in which they checked the names of residents who left for the square. These Disciples were not part of the regular army or security service. They had their headquarters in the Leader's palace and were as well-equipped as the regular army.

By evening the square was full. The Leader's Disciples (known as the LDs) distributed the Leader's portraits and small statues. Suspense was heightened several times when people thought that the Leader was on his way to the high platform, only to be

198

disappointed. In the end he did appear. His cortege moved slowly. The LDS led the rhythmical clapping. They were also watching to see those whose clapping was half-hearted.

One of the very few people who didn't go to the square was Sheikh Farah. The LDS knocked on his door. There was no reply. One of the neighbours explained that, on Mondays, Sheikh Farah fasted, refrained from speaking and spent the day in the desert studying and meditating.

MAID (SUHA):   (JUMPS IN) What about you, you were around, did you go?

NARRATOR: I had to. I'm not a rebel I'm a historian. (PAUSE) I'm like the writers, and learned men who witness events, analyse, record or retell but never comment ...

MAID (SUHA):   And live to the age of ninety, claiming absolute integrity!

NARRATOR: I'm not ninety yet, girl! Go away – no interruption!

MAID (SUHA):   Not before I introduce myself. A humble maid, one of Sheikh Farah's former pupils. I'll be back later. (EXITS)

NARRATOR: Where was I – ? A ... There was no response from the offending mountain.

When the LDS were satisfied with the build-up to the great occasion, the crier appeared on the platform and recited:

Today we shake the earth
and shape recorded history
The people face the elements
and will achieve a victory
the people if united
will counteract treachery
they now have got a Leader
whose perfection and mastery
Are unique in the world.

There was frenzy in the square. Then silence fell when the leader himself appeared. His words (which he had rehearsed several times in front of a mirror) were short and decisive. He raised his hand and said.

LEADER: Jabal Al Barkal has committed treason. By disobeying my orders it has defied you, the people. Your will must be reasserted. The mountain must be punished. It must pay the price of its villainy. Who is going to do it? We. Together. This mountain must be evicted. All efforts and resources must be channelled towards this end. We will move it to the Nubian desert. Work will start tomorrow.

SCENE 3

(A HALL IN THE LEADER'S PALACE)

NARRATOR: Hundreds of young men and women died in the attempt to move the mountain. The LDS saw to it that those who expressed any dissatisfaction or were suspected of lack of dedication to the "Historic Eviction" were forced to work until they dropped dead.

In the end some old women went to the Leader's mother. They explained the scale of disasters to her, and asked her to intervene, which she did. First she asked her son to pardon the mountain. He refused and said:

LEADER: If this matter is not resolved decisively who knows what will happen? Even the palace pigeons might try to defy me!

NARRATOR: His mother then came up with another idea. To give the mountain a period of grace in which it prepares to move out of its own free will or face the dire consequences. The Leader loved his mother so much that he reluctantly agreed. The period of grace was extended more than once. Then something very exciting happened. Some LDS reported hearing a strange noise from the direction of Jabal Al Barkal. The Leader sent Muk to investigate. He returned more excited than the LDS and told the Leader:
Oh great Leader. Something unbelievable is happening. (PAUSE) A part of the mountain has disappeard.

CRIER: Allahu Akbar!!

MUK: The mountain is obeying your command. It is moving, Leader!! Moving!

LEADER: It did take its time, didn't it.

MUK: It got a respite after your mother's appeal; but it toed the line in the end, as you expected. It is obedient now. (PAUSE) Your word is law.

NARRATOR: Reports kept coming in from shephards and travellers that Jabal Al Barkal was becoming smaller and smaller. The Leader was discouraged from going there himself to verify the reports.

MAN: Leader, why give the mountain the satisfaction of going there in person! Let it feel that it is nothing! Let it realize its insignificance!

NARRATOR: The Leader didn't go and the reports by the LDS multiplied.

200

In the meantime men returned to the fields. The schools reopened and the whole idea was quietly (but without any official declaration) dropped.

Life began to return to normal. Gold was discovered in a remote area of the country. The Leader put on more fat. On one occasion he was reclining on a sofa surrounded by maids. He beckoned to one of them:

LEADER: Hey. You. Come and scratch my back.

MAID (SUHA): (OBEYS) Here?

LEADER: Yes. ... No no. Lower you fool!
A little bit to the side ...
Ahh – That's it. (PAUSE) Enough!
(MAID RETURNS TO CORNER)
(PAUSE) Come here! (SHE OBEYS)
Wipe the perisperation from my eyebrows.
(SHE DOES) Sit down. (PAUSE)
I cannot finnish all this food by
myself, yet it is so well-cooked.
Eat for me! Take that red piece
of meat (OBEYS), no, no
the larger one! (PAUSE) with a piece
of bread. Now add some pepper.
Eat. Chew well. (PAUSE) Don't
swallow yet. Now swallow.

Take that banana. (SUDDENLY
LOSES INTEREST AND DISMISSES HER
WITH A GESTURE) Crier! sing me
something. Praise our mighty tribe!

CRIER: One
Sinnari man equals fifteen
Sinnari man equals fifteen
in time of war
Our girls are incense and jasmin
and a lot lot more

NARRATOR: The leader looked through the window and saw his camel, fully recovered now, moving its head to the rhythm of music. He was proud of the camel. He had no children and his wife ran away to a neighbouring country, where she got herself a job. So the camel meant everything for the Leader; rivalled only by his love for his mother who was still alive; but very frail.

201

	The Leader turned to the crier and said: My camel. Improvise something about my camel. The crier paused and recited:
CRIER:	"There is wisdom in its eyes There is feeling when it sighs Who among you, who denies, It can talk (if it tries)"
NARRATOR:	The obese Leader jumped nimbly to his feet and shouted:
LEADER:	By God, you are right. This camel has more sense than many people in my court. I'm almost certain that if it had better training it would have achieved more. (PAUSE) Go. Call all the Sheikhs here. This minute.
CRIER:	They're all outside requesting an audience with your highness. Today is their "pay day".
LEADER:	Did you say all were outside?
CRIER:	More or less. Sheikh Nadim and Sheikh Salah have mandated their sons to come on their behalf.
LEADER:	And Sheikh Farah?
CRIER:	He's off to the desert to study the Meroetic inscriptions in the caves! (LAUGHS)
LEADER:	Still. Let the LDS keep a close eye on him.
CRIER:	Some of his students report regularly to the LDS. He's only interested in his teaching. Words, books, paper. He's not a man of action. Actually Muk believes that he serves a good purpose. His irrelevant pursuits help divert potentially disruptive energies towards a harmless channel.
NARRATOR:	When the Sheiks were ushered in the Leader addressed them:
LEADER:	I want a volunteer for a teaching job.
MUK:	I'm the eldest, with most experience. I don't think any of my colleagues here will deny that.
LEADER:	So you are. You will be rewarded handsomely.
MUK:	Your generosity is without parallel, leader. I'll do my best to live up to your expectations. Will the pupil be your nephew?
LEADER:	No.
MUK:	Your niece?
LEADER:	No. My camel "clever". (PAUSE) You should teach it to read and write.

202

MUK:	But, my leader . . .
LEADER:	I brook no contradiction. You have three days to return with a detailed reply including a deadline for the completion of the teaching. And remember. If you fail, I'll have your hands and ears cut off before you are crucified. Your body will become food for the vultures. I'll see you in three days. Out! Out!
NARRATOR:	That's why Muk had every reason to be relieved by Sheikh Farah's undertaking.

SCENE 4　　(OLD SULTAN'S BANQUET HALL)

NARRATOR:	Now. A question which both Sheikh Omar and I faced with last year's group – and which might well be on your minds – is this: how could such a callous man be chosen as Leader in the first place?
	The answer lies in the fate of the old Sultan, Sinnar had an old and wise Sultan; but this Sultan had a problem.
SULTAN:	I welcome you all and thank you for coming. (PAUSE) You probably know that I'm not getting younger. Those who are my peers know that most of all (LAUGHTER). I feel that the responsibilities of government are becoming too much for me. Since my only son has tragically died in last year's floods, there's nobody to take some of the weight off my shoulders. (PAUSE) I've called you all here so that we select an heir to the throne. The short-list which some of you have helped me draw is now down to two names only, reached at by concensus.
	I have decided that you, as my advisers and as the respected elders of the land should spend the whole day and night with me here so that we, together, select the best candidate. To preserve the unity of our tribe, the runner up will be appointed crown prince. After we make our choice, I hand over the reins gradually and see to it that our armed forces and the neighbouring powers recognize the new Sultan. I'll then die in peace assured of stability and a smooth succession.
MUK:	It grieves me Great Sultan; that you talk now about succession. It was I who suggested last year that we call you Great Sultan and not just Sultan. To talk about succession while you're still alive and active is to talk about the end of the greatest period of prosperity which this country has known in its long history. God gave our land this prosperity because of the kind of country you

developed. In other words, your love of God, and of the fatherland and your even-handedness in rule is the bedrock of our prosperity. That's why we should never part with it. Your grandfather ruled until he was ninety years old. Why do you want us to talk about a successor while you are only 70?

NARRATOR: The Sultan insisted and began a discussion on the personal qualities of the two candidates. Suddenly, they heard a loud bang. The door of the large banquet hall was thrown open and the Leader stood there, armed to the teeth!

SULTAN: What is this? You're interrupting our meeting.

LEADER: Your meeting is over! There is no need to choose a successor. From this moment on, I'm the ruler. The palace is surrounded. We control all strategic points. All the senior army officers are already under arrest.

SULTAN: You're talking nonsense! This is treason. Get out of here! Guard – guard!

LEADER: Your guards! Ha! They've either joined our ranks, or are dead. Don't make things difficult for me. I don't want any bloodshed; but – don't move.

NARRATOR: He then made them stand with their faces to the wall. The moment they did that, he stepped forward and chopped off the Sultan's head. His followers, the LDS, had by now filled the hall. The leader then stated:

LEADER: The Sultan is dead. You the elders and dignitaries have two choices. The wise one, to swear allegiance to me and walk through the door in one piece; and the stupid one of being carried away with the corpse of the Sultan to be buried.

NARRATOR: All men-except one – chose safety. The two dead bodies were carried for burial in unmarked graves.
The first to swear allegiance to the Leader was Muk. As for Sheik Farah, he took out his crumbled sheet of paper and began to gaze at the shapes and symbols in it. By the time his turn came he was already in a trance and speaking in tongues. He was guided away oblivious of what was happening.

MAID (SUHA): Weren't you the one who protested openly?

NARRATOR: (THROWS A BRANCH AT HER) Out, out! You impudent girl. (PAUSE) Our proverb says: "Swimming seems easy for those standing on the shore." If this girl had a weapon pointed at her head she would have understood the situation of those who were in the banquet hall that night. Of course people swore allegiance;

but they did so under duress. Would they have changed anything if they chose death with the Sultan? (PAUSE) Remember, we were not faced with a debate or an argument but with brute force which had already controlled the country. (PAUSE) Besides, she'd never have got the job at the palace without my discreet help! (PAUSE)

In his moment of triumph, the Leader boasted

LEADER: (MILITARY MUSIC)
I take over as saviour
to save you from the spell
of yearning and behaviour
that lead you down to hell
Your women's dresses shine
but underneath the glitter
their hearts are grimy, rotten.
The aims of men seam fine
Their actions misbegotten
I have come as a saivour
to make the tribe pure
No envy or venality
I amputate to cure

NARRATOR: A list of orders was the drawn and read aloud all over the Sultanate of Sinnar. It included:

1– Dusk to dawn curfew. Indefinite. No meetings are allowed. That includes tribal councils, benevolent societies, sports clubs and school cadets.

2– Women's place to be strictly in the home to bring up good healthy citizens. No woman should work in any capacity outside the home. They should not go out without a male companion and should never wear perfume in public places like "souks" or zoos.

3– Business with neighbouring countries shall only be carried out by pious and reliable LDS.

4– All prisons should be demolished. They are useless hotels, costly and inefficient.

Deterrence should be the best guarantee of stability and peace. According to the severity of the crime, the judge should order the cutting off of a criminal's right ear, left ear, nose, upper lip, lower lip, fingers, private parts, or neck.

205

In the case of the cutting off of private parts, absolute privacy and self-respect should be observed. Nobody apart from the judge and the pious physician should attend.

5– Arguments are strictly forbidden. They, in all their forms, are a waste of time and energy. All books likely to provoke arguments shall be burnt in public. Possession of any such books will be a crime, punishable by the cutting off of the tongue.

The ultimate truth about everything is not to be sought through arguments or effete discussions; but should be deduced from our commandments which are foolproof, based as they are on sacred directives.

LEADER:
We only need one line
of thought and of truth
It's all in this, divine
an outcome of both
the wisdom that is mine
and God's commands and oath
No mortal has a right
to contradict or shout
questioning my motives
or casting any doubt.
Dissent is worse than syphilis
It is a sinful deed
It means a man is cursed
and has infectious seed

NARRATOR:
The crier held up "The little Yellow book" which – it was claimed – was revealed to the Leader in flashes of divine inspiration and as such had religious authority. All the LDS – some of whom didn't have a copy of the Koran – carried their "Little Yellow books" with them everywhere.

SUHA:
(ENTERS) That was when my elder brother, Nadir was killed. He tried to organise a protest.

NARRATOR:
I warned him, didn't I? I tried to deter him. That was my duty as a friend of your late father. I said: you're right; but don't stick your neck out. He didn't listen. He and several of his friends died – all under 25. Inadvertently, they helped the Leader. People saw the fate of dissedents and were scared. They became more submissive.

The Leader's grip on power tightened with every passing day. He shrewdly heaped privilege after privilege upon the LDS. This cemented their blind loyalty to him and persuaded more to join

206

the ranks. He gradually become more and more convinced of his almost superhuman status. This resulted in the wish to see his dreams and whims materialize.

SCENE 5

A HALL IN THE LEADER'S PALACE

NARRATOR: The whim regarding the teaching of the camel was taken very seriously by the Leader.

He sent for Sheikh Farah. The Sheikh went to the Palace.

LEADER: (IN A MOCKING TONE) Sheikh Farah, is it true that you collect snakes and scorpions from the desert?

SHEIKH FARAH: No. I examine them and release them unharmed.

LEADER: And what do you do in the caves? Some people are worried about the sanity of their children who accompany you sometimes.

SHEIKH FARAH: We just study the inscriptions and copy the fading ones in order to preserve them.

LEADER: (LAUGHS) Why?

SHEIKH FARAH: We should never underestimate the power of words, Leader. There was once a sufi sect called the "Hurufis". They saw the essence of truth and of God himself in the letters of the alphabet, the Huruf.

LEADER: But nobody knows anything about Meroetic alphabets or language.

SHEIKH FARAH: That, if anything, enhances the value of the search. (PAUSE) Consider also the name of our Sultanate – SinNar, Tooth of Fire. What does it mean? What is its significance? We know the meaning of the words but we also don't know it. I am working on that too.

LEADER: Well – good luck; but I'm more interested in my camel "clever".

SHEIKH FARAH: It is a noble animal. Camels are endued with baraka blessing; because they are used for the payment of blood money and for brides' dowry. They're animals of peace because their caravans forge links between different far away regions. The camels, Leader, are animals of mystery...

LEADER: (IMPATIENTLY) Stop. Come to the point. How long will it take you to teach it?

SHEIKH FARAH: Six months. But there are conditions.

207

LEADER: Conditions?

SHEIKH FARAH: I can only succed if the camel is fed what human beings eat, and in large quantities. A store next door to my hut must be filled with flour, fresh and dried fruits, potatoes and all sorts of vegetables. The camel must have continuous supply of mangoes, water melons and oranges. Apple and Guava juices are very important.

LEADER: Is that all?

SHEIKH FARAH: Yes.

LEADER: Agreed. I'll give orders today. But I also want you to know exactly what the consequences of failure will be.

SHEIKH FARAH: Death? (LAUGHS) I haven't got many years left anyway! But I won't fail.

LEADER: You'll suffer a great deal.

SHEIKH FARAH: And my reward if I succeed, or rather when I succeed?

LEADER: Let me think (LAUGHS) You marry the most beautiful maid in my palace. (LAUGHS)

SHEIKH FARAH: (LAUGHS) They're young enough to be my daughters or my students. If I succeed, you give me access to the library which is locked in the castle adjoining your palace.

LEADER: It's a deal! The idea of locking up the library came as a precaution against corrupting influences on our citizens. But since you already consort with reptiles and gaze at undeciphered tongues – What else can books do to harm or corrupt you? You're beyond redemption. (LAUGHS)

NARRATOR: Sheikh Farah left the palace in high spirits, repeating:

"Come, have-nots of Sinnar
to take your share of bread
The Leader erects castles
for all his senseless battles
but doesn't seek an end
to homelessness and hunger
that tear people asunder."

SCENE 6

SHEIKH FARAH'S HUT

WIFE: You seem so care-free; but the town is buzzing with gossip about our predicament. People ask me; but I have no answer because you don't discuss these things with me.

SHEIKH FARAH: You've had your fair share of troubles lately. I try not to burden you with more.

WIFE: I know I go out a lot; but you are aware of the reason. Our daughters seem to make trouble in turn – one week our oldest quarrels with her husband, the next week our second daughter quarrels with her mother-in-law.

The week after that our youngest, Rabiha, comes home and vows never to return to her husband. I daresay they inherited this quarrelsomeness from you –

SHEIKH FARAH: Girls take after their mother,
boys after their father.

WIFE: Well, on the last occasion at least, I was secretly pleased with what rabiha did to her husband.

SHEIKH FARAH: You were? You never said so.

WIFE: You didn't have time for a long story. (PAUSE) Of course I did the socially accepted thing, I went to his mother and said that my daughter was under great pressure at the time because you were ill.

I had to come up with an excuse! I said it would be a pity for Muna to be deprived of her father at such a formative age. I also apologized on behalf of my daughter to his mother and later to him. I quoted the Proverb: "A curse upon those who dismantle a house of matrimony".

But deep inside I was very pleased that she behaved the way she did.

Everything is settled now; but what happened is this. Their cow went astray, so Rabiha had to go and look for it. When she found and returned it, it was almost lunch time. She wanted to make an easy and quick meal; but he insisted on her cooking something "proper". She began to do so. He interrupted her asking for tea. You know how slow the charcoal cooker is – she took the lunch pan down and put the water to boil. When she took the tea to him, he complained that it was too hot, and asked for some milk to cool it down. So she went to the cow, came back with milk. Of course

209

the tea had become too cold by then. Both tea and milk had to be warmed up. The pan was taken off again. When he at last enjoyed the cup of tea, he called her and said: "Why is lunch taking so long?". "His highness" had his feet on the stool. Rabiha, blind with anger, got hold of his big toe and bit it as hard as she could. (LAUGHS) Although she was tired, she didn't know where she got the strength from. (LAUGHS) The poor man couldn't wear a shoe for a week! Worse than that, he couldn't tell anybody what really happened.

SHEIKH FARAH: I don't think anybody would have believed him.

WIFE: Well. He told people that he hurt his toe while repairing a door.

SHEIKH FARAH: She looks so gentle. I didn't know she was capable of such violence.

WIFE: Given the circumstances – I think she was restrained.

SHEIKH FARAH: What happened to the lunch?

WIFE: It was burnt! I took some food with me during my peace-making mediation; and a new cooking pan. (SMILING)
For fifty-something years
I never asked for more
than some real affection;
but now my daughters bare
their teeth, looking for action.
As for granddaughter Muna
She will – maybe – aspire
to rule a whole empire!

SHEIKH FARAH: You should thank God that I'm not interested in food.

WIFE: You should thank God that I'm not interested in toes (PAUSE) You never have time for anything except books. You have no time for your children's problems; because you're always in the thick of something which is not necessarily impressive or noble. For example, is it true what people say about the Leader's camel? I hope you know what you are doing!

SHEIKH FARAH: I think I do.

WIFE: Ah. Why don't you look at Muk. Look at the grand house he built for himself and his family. He didn't inherit any money. He's not a better sufi or scholar than you are. (PAUSE) Look at the clothes his daughters and his daughters-in-law wear — not to mention his wife.

SHEIKH FARAH: He made a choice. I made another.

WIFE:	You forget that your choice is not always for you only. Nobody is asking you to forget your principles; but to go out of your way to court trouble and disaster just beats me. You know as well as I do that neither you nor anybody else can teach a camel to read and write. Yet you accept the challenge – maybe just to spite me (WEAPS). I suppose you realize that at the time of reckoning your immediate family and in-laws will not be spared either.
SHEIKH FARAH:	Come, come. You've supported me for more than fifty years. Are you going to let me down now? I can promise you one thing. I'll do my best to make sure that – in the case of any complications – nobody apart from me will bear the responsibility.
WIFE:	But even for you. Why risk being killed over something so – so – trivial? There are many grave causes worth the effort and the martyrdom if need be. I haven't read as many books as you; but one doesn't need a great deal of learning to see this.
SHEIKH FARAH:	We don't seek our causes, dear wife. Our causes seek, identify and attract us.

(AT THIS POINT A KNOCK CAN BE HEARD ON THE DOOR. THEN MUK ENTERS WITH A BROAD SMILE.)

MUK:	My dear friend and his honourable wife. Sorry to drop in like this; but there's no barrier between us.
WIFE:	Shall I make some coffee before I go?
MUK:	Go where? To your son-in-law's? Have they kissed and made up?
WIFE:	They're alright now.
MUK:	Well. I never say no to a cup of coffe. (PAUSE) Well – Sheikh Farah. Can't you guess what I'm here for? (WIFE EXITS)
SHEIKH FARAH:	The camel.
MUK:	Exactly. The leader wants a progress report. It's already three months since this – "project" started. Half-way through the allotted time. He's anxious to hear that everything is on course. (PAUSE) That there are some positive developments. (PAUSE) Can I see the camel in order to report?
SHEIKH FARAH:	Absolutely not. Tell the Leader that I'm engaged in a very difficult task. It has reached a delicate and critical phase. Any exposure to inspection will probably wreck the whole exercise – and that's something we don't want to risk, do we?
MUK:	Of course not.

SHEIKH FARAH: Now. Let me confess something to you. When I undertook this –
"project" I had some lingering doubt at the back of my mind about
the basic intelligence of a camel or any animal; but right from the
beginning this camel showed such remarkable progress that all
my doubts were dispelled.

MUK: Really?

SHEIKH FARAH: The daily routine is not a secret. I wake him up at six. He's given
an early breakfast at seven. At seven-thirty the first lesson begins –
usually classical Arabic. It continues until nine-thirty. After a short
break writing exercises begin. He (I no longer say it) holds the
pen with his teeth, and manages very well. At twelve noon we
have another break for coffee. He prefers the black Abyssinyan
brew, with a snack of chips and biscuits. Then follows the last
lesson of the day: numbers. I do believe that this camel has a head
for maths.

MUK: Really?

SHEIKH FARAH: Then follows the lunch break; after which he takes his afternoon
siesta. In the evening we revise and devote an hour to exercises
and questions. Believe you me Muk – this camel can ask very
weird questions. They're usually most critical on Mondays.

MUK: How come?

SHEIKH FARAH: Because that's his day of fasting. His mind becomes very incisive
and clear. For example, last Monday he mused in verse:
If a lion eats a man
It is hunted and slain
If a human tells his clan
He has used his deadly skill
in the flaying of a calf
He is seen as "just a butcher"
in a species born to kill.

MUK: Well ... well ... What logic!

SHEIKH FARAH: I couldn't answer back – in all honesty. How is one to respond to
such an embarassing argument.

MUK: I suppose ... err, Well. That's the way of the world.

SHEIKH FARAH: Our world. If animals are included our values barely hold water.
Listen to this other point which he made last month, again on a
Monday:

If a person burned a forest
for a clear plot of land
he is just a robust farmer

all of us should understand
his desire for expansion;
and forget the homeless rabbit
and the bird that lost a nest
and the soil now defenceless
in the face of heavy sand.

I can't answer back this sort of argument. Can you?

MUK: If you're not sentimental or squeamish, you could of course say bluntly that trees and animals are not our equals. They are not like us. Errr ... They have no brains. They were created for man's benefit ...

SHEIKH FARAH: Hang on. He says they have brains and are often more reasonable than human beings. For example – animals compete for territory and fight as individuals; but they haven't got armies and they do not engage in mass slaughter in wars. They also haven't got institutionalized torture. (PAUSE) I tell you these things in order to see the difficulties of teaching this camel. I am doing my best; but teaching is like opening a window in a room. What happens when you open it is this:
You cannot control the sort of air that comes in. You can't choose what to let in. So, I teach this camel how to use its mind; but the moment I do so I also lose control over the process. It can get out of hand. This was driven home to me by his latest outrage.

MUK: What was that?

SHEIKH FARAH: One moment. (GOES TO WINDOW AND RETURNS)
These reed walls keep no secret. Just wanted to make sure that nobody will overhear.

MUK: (CONSPIRATORIALLY) What is it? Something immoral? Is the camel a depraved sex-maniac? That wouldn't surprise me. Camels fight to the death over females, you know. They'd mate with anything in sight – not excluding panthers! The giraffe, for example is the result of the mating of a camel and a panther! Imagine the sort of desperate drive that makes them mate with the dangerous panthers. They're turned on by danger!

SHEIKH FARAH: I doubt it!

MUK: I'll bring you the book. They're obsessed with mating. Have you seen camels mating?

SHEIKH FARAH: No, I haven't!

MUK: They face opposite directions, and raise hell – and a pall of dust. (PAUSE) My advice is: if it has anything to do with this aspect of camel behaviour – don't upset the Leader by revealing it.

SHEIKH FARAH: It has nothing to do with that at all.

MUK: What is it then?

SHEIKH FARAH: It's inflamable stuff, believe me. Let me make sure again that there's nobody outside. (WALKS TO THE WINDOW AND BACK)

MUK: You have increased my curiosity!

SHEIKH FARAH: Come closer. I can only whisper this. He said:
"If a ruler is in power
just because he wields a sword
What will happen if somebody
in a day of no accord
Lifted high another weapon
and clambered up aboard?"

MUK: I haven't heard this! I'm not listening to this. Goodbye. (RUSHES OUT)

SHEIKH FARAH: The coffee Muk. Your coffee.

MUK: Some other time (EXITS)

SCENE 7

SHEIKH FARAH'S HUT

NARRATOR: One day before the end of the six-month period, a man came to Sheikh Farah's hut. He was one of the LDS. Upon seeing him, Sheikh Farah said: Come tomorrow. We have another day to go.

MAN: I know. The Leader sent me.

SHEIKH FARAH: I'll see him tomorrow with my student "clever", the camel.

MAN: (LAUGHS) HA HA HA ... HA. You're as phoney as I saw you last time.

SHEIKH FARAH: Last time? Do I know you?

MAN: Try to remember (PAUSE) The oven is still in its place (PAUSE) I still can't work out how that man eluded me. You played some trick; but I can't put my finger on it.

SHEIKH FARAH: Ahaa! Were you an LD then?

214

MAN: I was recruited a week after I made your acquaintance; I'm now an officer, responsible for the political campaign.

SHEIKH FARAH: An officer, in six months? You must be very efficient.

MAN: I'm what is known as a high-flyer. Haven't you got high-flyers in sufism? A low-flyer like you wouldn't know! (LOOKS ROUND) More books. The more books a man owns, the more foolish he becomes; because books remove you from everyday life; and life is the best book of all. (PUSHES THE PILE OF BOOKS. PICKS ONE UP) "The Animals" by Al Gahiz. (THROWS IT DOWN. PICKS UP ANOTHER) "Animals' grievances" – (THROWS IT AWAY)

You know what. We were very disappointed the other day when one of our instructors at the "LD Orientation Course" suggested some, well distant similarities between the LDS and the sufis. His idea was that our organisation (in order to wipe out and replace all aspects of your decadent structure) must take over some features, reshape them, remould them and thus strengthen our new and rising forces which are historically earmarked for inevitable dominance.

SHEIKH FARAH: That's interesing.

MAN: For example; your sufis have a period of initiation before admitting a new member.

SHEIKH FARAH: That's true.

MAN: We have something similiar. A new member is first a "candidate" for a trial period. He's then admitted. You have a special dress, we have a special dress. You give the new member a new name, we do the same. You have annual and other occasions which you celebrate, we have the birthday of the Leader and other occasions which we celebrate with marches and banners, just like you.

SHEIKH FARAH: Well, well.

MAN: You have your secret language of "tongues", we have introduced into the tribal language new words and structures and – through keeping foreign words when translating we can speak in a vocabulary that can baffle others. This gives us the same "mystique" and "aura" in which you relish and, which helps you mislead people...

SHEIKH FARAH: We neither lead nor mislead people.

MAN: (CONTINUES) You have blind faith in the Leader of your order "Tariqa", we have conscious faith in our Leader, who is never wrong.

By using your own methods we can replace you effectively. "We fight fire with fire" as he put it.

SHEIKH FARAH: Well. We don't fight others. That would be too easy. We fight ourselves, which is extremely difficult. No weapons are needed unless you call these books weapons.

MAN: These are a pile of useless words. (PAUSE) Is your wife still around or has she deserted you?

SHEIKH FARAH: Gone to the souk. She'll be back soon.

MAN: I'll suggest to the Leader that, whatever your fate, she be given one of the highest medals of the land. She epitomises human endurance. To have lived with someone like you for more than half a century and not to have murdered him – she must be a saint!

SHEIKH FARAH: She's an exceptionally good and patient woman.

MAN: Let's go.

NARRATOR: They went to an underground building, beneath Leader's Square, spacious and dimly lit with oil lamps.

(INSIDE THE BUILDING)

MAN: These were originally caves, which were extended and improved to make these chambers about which very few people know.

SHEIKH FARAH: I see.

MAN: The leader said that he warned you personally about the repurcussions of failure in teaching the camel. Being of a kind and compassionate disposition he has now deemed it fit to give you a glimpse of what you are likely to face. To open a window for you as he put it for a peep inside the closed chambers. The importance of this is that he decided to give you a choice in the method of your punishment. This is a very special privilege granted to you because of your status as a religious man. Other mortals are not treated with such consideration. When you see the "menu" you'll be able to make a good and prudent choice. Come here – please. See. There is the horses' chamber where a criminal will be tied with ropes which are firmly fastened to large leather neck-straps on horses. Four horses, one for each limb. At a certain signal, the blinkers of horses, which are starved for two days are removed and they rush towards the fodder placed in the four different corners of the room, tearing to pieces the four limbs of the criminal. Death follows but it is slow because the head and all the internal organs are left intact.

216

Next, overthere, is the so-called Fish bed. As the name indicates, it is acutally a large frying trough. A criminal is simply pushed into the boiling oil...

Those last three are my favourite – in a manner of speaking. Their design is simple. They are called "Khazoogs". These ten-inch spikes are screwed to the stools. A criminal is held high and made to "sit" on the stool. The spikes are thoughtfully oiled in order not to make things difficult. A criminal is usually left on the "Khazoog" for days. Ha Ha Ha. Actually this Khazoog gave rise to a very interesting incident. One criminal lost consciousness after sitting on the stool for several hours. When he came to, he noticed that his colleague on the second stool, who had been there for two days, had already died. His body was being removed.

He began to shout entreating the guard to move him to the now vacant stool. His request fell on deaf ears. He persisted. In the end the guard explained to him that the two stools and their spikes were identical and that his death was a matter of time, which wasn't likely to be delayed by being on the first or third stool. The desperate man replied "I know". But the time it takes to move from one spike to the other will give me a breather!" Ha Ha Ha! Ha! – (PAUSE) Why don't you laugh? Don't you see the joke? Or has the reading of books blunted your sense of humour?"

SCENE 8

SHEIKH FARAH'S HUT

NARRATOR: Sheikh Farah's wife was alone when the sufi returned from the visit to the torture chambers. She was visibly despondent.

SHEIKH FARAH: What's the matter?

WIFE: Can't you guess? (PAUSE) Today is your last day in this world.

SHEIKH FARAH: Ah – well. That means the few hours left should not be spent in anything but celebration and joy. Cheer up. This is a day to take stock and high-light the best in our life. (PAUSE)

I remember now our marriage ceremony. I was barely eighteen when my father told me he had chosen you as a wife for me. I had only seen you once when you danced in your cousin's wedding ceremony. My father said: your mother has seen her without her "tobe" on. If your mother couldn't find fault with her she must be near perfection – but remember you take a wife the way you buy a water melon, on speculation. Some water-melons turn out to be red and a pleasure to look at; but bitter in the mouth. Others look ordinary and colourless; but are luscious on the plate. You can never know beforehand, or by sight or word-of-mouth. (PAUSE) My verdict, after all these years is a taste of honey that has sweetened my otherwise drab existence. (PAUSE) and still does, unabated (HUGS HER)

WIFE: Stop it! You should respect your old age! Behaving like an adolescent!

SHEIKH FARAH: (LAUGHS) I remember the day I chose the sufi path. I sat opposite sheikh Tajuldin. Our hands clasped. He gave me a particular "word" to recite. He chanted and I repeated after him. He read suras in a cup of Nile water and gave it to me to drink. Then I gave an oath to be faithful to the "Tariqa" and not to have more than one God in my heart. (PAUSE) He then gave me this rosary, this very ragged "jibba" and said: "Go now. He who conceals his learning equates himself with the ignorant." (PAUSE)

Come one – cheer up. It wasn't a bad life after all. Remember the day Rabiha turned six and asked me: "when you light the lamp, where does darkness go?" I'm not sure I know the answer, even now.
She brought her daughter Muna to see me the other day.

WIFE: The day I went to my brothers.

SHEIKH FARAH: The same dimples, the same excessive energy. I couldn't do any work that day. She turned this place upside down; but when her mother came to collect her – I wanted her to stay. The house became as quiet as a graveyard. They'll bring her tomorrow by the way.

WIFE: That'll give the women something to gossip about?

SHEIKH FARAH: Which women?

WIFE: I met Muk's wife at the greengrocer's. You know what she asked me? She said: "when you're a widow – will Rabiha, her husband and their daughter Muna move in to stay with you? You'll need more space. What are you going to do about it?"

SHEIKH FARAH: May God give her an even larger house – and reward you in his own way.

WIFE: Her neighbour said to me (IMITATES) "What are you going to do with the inheritance when your husband dies?"

SHEIKH FARAH: Is that Sheikh Salah's wife? She has every right to be boastful. He left her a great deal.

218

WIFE:	He's still alive.
SHEIKH FARAH:	Because he breathes, eats, drinks and goes to the loo..? He's dead – but not buried! (PAUSE) This reminds me. You'll find my will under that book, Beshshar's collection of poetry. It's short and concise. I leave all my worldly possessions to you.
WIFE:	Have you got any possessions in another town about which I know nothing?
SHEIKH FARAH:	No.
WIFE:	This will mean that you leave me these books and this hut.
SHEIKH FARAH:	Exactly. When Sheikh Tajuldin died, he gave away his hut and his books before he was martyred saying: – I leave as I came. (PAUSE) Well, I'm not as selfless as he. He was killed when he was fifty, and here I am seventy-five-years old and still clinging to life, despite its crises. I still love life:

If my life were a picnic
Oh, how bored I would have been
Constant menace makes me tick tick
and my mind is serene
Some descendant may remember
that I steered a proper course
If we all know tow and whimper
What will happen
to the fountain
of our syllables and words?

WIFE:	Oh – I almost forgot, someone came here. He said he was one of your ex-students. Said to tell you that they now know the site of the Sultan's grave. One of the LD was apparently drunk and he spilled the beans to a young woman whom he wanted to impress.
	(PAUSE) This person who came – was very weird. Almost ghost – like. Had the eyes of that young man, Nadir, who was killed after the demonstration, your late favourite pupil.
SHEIKH FARAH:	How strange. How very strange.

SCENE 9

HALL IN LEADER'S PALACE

NARRATOR:	Sheikh Farah spent the last night of his life receiving visitors who came to say farewell. Some sufis came and went. The tramps

who used to collect some of the food brought from the palace for the camel came to thank Sheikh Farah and the camel. When the sun came out something very exceptional was noticed. On a white wall overlooking Leader's Square someone had written in bold red letters: Our Sultan was not killed while trying to flee the country or hand over power to foreign agents. His grave is by the dune well." People gathered quickly – those who were literate explaining to the others. The LDS went mad. They brought buckets of water and tried to wash the wall clean; but the writing remained clearly legible on the white background. In the end the Leader himself gave the order for the wall to be demolished.

After demolishing the wall, the LDS organised a demonstration in which they chanted:

We follow without question
We firmly believe in you
We tolerate no faction
or independent view.

They marched through the streets in an impressive show of force. There were very few people in the streets. The LDS then got word that many citizens went to the dune well in an attempt to verify what was written on the white wall. When the LDS went there, they found hundreds of on-lookers surrounding a make-shift tomb at the exact site of the old Sultan's unmarked grave. They dispersed them quickly, demolished the tomb, and hastend to the palace in time for Sheikh Farah's audience with the Leader.

Then the moment of truth arrived. Sheikh Farah entered the palace compound where people were waiting, many of whom came straight from the Sultan's tomb.

The Leader appeared with his entourage and sat on the embroidered platform. He began by saying to Seikh Farah:

HALL IN LEADER'S PALACE

LEADER: Well ... Your time is up. How is the camel?

SHEIKH FARAH: He's very well; but has changed a great deal.

LEADER: Only one change concerns me, is it literate now? Can I make it a minister? I need a vizier for culture.

SHEIKH FARAH: He's a very intelligent animal.

LEADER: We know that. We want to hear it speak.

SHEIKH FARAH: Speak? You specifically asket me to teach him to read and write. He speaks by writing and reading aloud.

220

LEADER:	I'm not interested in details. Demonstrate what you have taught it. The reports I got said that your efforts were a success, or were you bluffing?
MAN:	He told me that the camel was ready for any public or private display of erudition.
LEADER:	And you Muk?
MUK:	Well ... He did tell me that his student was making excellent progress.
LEADER:	Did either of you actually test the camel's progress?
MUK:	Sheikh Farah felt quite rightly that the privilege of hearing the camel for the first time should be yours.
MAN:	I didn't even see the camel when I went to the hut. He wouldn't allow it. Instead he told me that our language has 160 words that are synonymous with "camel" (GENERAL LAUGHTER)
LEADER:	Well, Sheikh Farah. Today is your "day of glory". And I hope to share this moment with my loyal subjects who where allowed into the palace compound to mark the occasion. If you succeed this day, the 30th of June, will be a public holiday in all the years to come. The floor is yours.
SHEIKH FARAH:	He is no longer an ordinary camel. He is enlightened and has a mind of his own. He agreed to demonstrate his skills only when you read what he has written. It's not much.
LEADER:	Give it to him. He'll read aloud on my behalf.
MUK:	My leader. The light is not enough and my eyes can't see well.
LEADER:	(TO THE CRIER) You read. Quickly and loudly. Get on with it. Let's call Sheikh Farah's bluff.
CRIER:	(QUICKLY) If a ruler is in power just because he wields a sword What will happen if somebody in a day of no accord Lifted high another weapon and clambered up aboard?
NARRATOR:	There was silence, followed by a wave of loud whispering. Simultaneously the leader turned over the table shouting:
LEADER:	What is this nonsense!

	(HE STRIKES THE GLASS JUG OF WATER IN FRONT OF HIM AND BREAKS IT TO PIECES, WOUNDING HIS HAND IN THE PROCESS.)
MAN:	Quick! Call his mother and physician. The Leader has hurt his hand. (EVERYBODY NOW COMPETING TO SHOW THE LEADER HIS CONCERN)
MUK:	Here! Tie it with this handkerchief. Put some salt first.
MAN:	(TO CRIER) Why didn't you stop reading you fool?
CRIER:	I obeyed the Leader's orders. He didn't say: stop. How could I?
LEADER:	Go away. All of you!
CRIER:	The gathering is over. Go away. All of you.
NARRATOR:	The people were very slow to leave. The camel's words, heard publicly in the presence of the Leader and coming after the demoliton of the wall and the make-shift tomb were like a window that opened in a dark room. It was like a hand that tore off a blindfold. Sheikh Farah led the camel stealthily away in the commotion which followed, humming to himself:

The Leader has a paunch
An army and a rack
I onyl own my torch
my parchment and my stack
But God above (as usual,
meticulous and fair)
to make the forces equal
he gave me this grey hair!

NARRATOR:	Some of his students said: Why don't you ride the camel? He replied:
SHEIKH FARAH:	One doesn't ride a learned camel!
NARRATOR:	He walked past his house to the desert which he knew like the palm of his hand. After taking the leader inside the place, the LDS, led by the "political officer" immediately went to Sheikh Farah's hut. He wasn't there. They pulled down the hut and took all the books to Leader's square where they set them alight.

SCENE 10

HALL IN LEADER'S PALACE –

| NARRATOR: | Some weaks later, in the Leader's Palace |

LEADER: I want to know how it is that this tomb is rebuilt everytime you pull it down?

MAN: As political officer, I saw to it that all preachers discussed the matter in their sermons, which all end now with cursing the devil, Sheikh Farah and ... if you excuse me, the camel.

LEADER: It breaks my heart that the camel has turned against me after all the things I did for it.

MUK: Tradition has it that some camels are descendants of demons. Some evil jinn also take the shape of camels.

LEADER: I was fascinated by the claim that a camel actually weeps when its owner dies. I know better now! If there are 160 words to refer to the camel, maybe it has 160 faces too. (PAUSE) If that camel can betray me as it did, how can I take for granted anybody's loyalty?

MAN: We're working on a second list to purge the army, the LDs and all the civil service. (PAUSE)

LEADER: Is it a coincidence that the crier was so close to me and so eager to read that subversive nonsense to the end?

MUK: A traitor! I wish my eyes were better. I'd have stopped reading.

MAN: He was buried yesterday. Nobody shed a tear for him. His family issued a statement that they had nothing to do with him. His in-laws denounced him.

LEADER: How do we know that he didn't have – some – accomplices? Eh?

MAN: He didn't confess to any.

LEADER: You should have made him confess.

MAN: He was on the "Khazoog" and fainted; we were waiting for him to regain consciousness. I skipped lunch at home and had a snack at the chambers in order to make sure of interrogating him the moment he came to. But he died without regaining consciousness.

LEADER: Anyway. There seem to be many security lapses.

MUK: Indeed. It's shameful. The way Sheikh Farah walked away unchallenged with the camel! I'd be very much interested in more information about the camel's words. After all, the camel is the student – Sheikh Farah is the teacher. How much influence did the teacher have?

LEADER: Indeed.

NARRATOR:	At this point, the maid entered to say that coffee was ready. The Leader didn't want to take it in the garden, so he said:
LEADER:	We'll take it now, here.
MUK:	We shouldn't forget that Sheikh Fadlalla of Astrabad who is admired by Sheikh Farah understood the languages of birds and communicated with them. So – there is a possibility that Sheikh Farah spoke the language of camels.
LEADER:	And put the words in the camel's mouth. Sheikh Farah's guilt is manifest. (PAUSE) (TO MAN)
	You are aware of course that I have dismissed the Head of Security. I'd like you to take over as "Acting Head". Your performance will decide whether you get the job permanently or whether it would be too big for you. (PAUSE) We'll see.
	I want you to concentrate on two things: to arrest and punish those responsible for the writing which made us demolish the white wall, and to track down those who build the bamboo tomb at the site of the cursed traitor's grave.
NARRATOR:	The maid entered with coffee and served each a cup.
MUK:	What about Sheikh Farah?
MAN:	A group is already in the desert, looking for him and for the camel. It's not easy – the desert has a thousand faces. You ride through an area, the wind blows and in a short while all landmarks disappear and the whole desertscape becomes unrecognizable, (PAUSE) But we now face a more urgent problem. That's the reason why I'm here – to seek a directive.
LEADER:	What's urgent?
MAN:	Mysteriously, the camel's words have now appeared on most of the town's walls. Hundreds of LDS have gone out with buckets of water and a special paint remover. Everything should be under control by tomorrow.
LEADER:	My directive is: if you fail to erase the writing from any wall – demolish it!
MAN:	We'll do.

SCENE 11

NARRATOR:	In a desert cave

WIFE:	I was sent by the political officer; he gave me safe passage and a guarantee that no harm will come to me.
SHEIKH FARAH:	What does he want from me?
WIFE:	He says his promotion depends on your giving yourself up – and the Leader's camel. He says you are not wanted for treason; but for theft; because you led away the Leader's camel.
SHEIKH FARAH:	Ha! You know their punishment for theft!
WIFE:	He has arrested all our sons and daughters and our in-laws. He took me to see them. They are treated very well; but he says ... if you don't return voluntarily they'll be taken to the chamber. He says you'd understand. He says the first to be taken there would be our granddaughter, Muna.
SHEIKH FARAH:	Oh God!
WIFE:	He also warns you against any "tricks".
SHEIKH FARAH:	I see.
WIFE:	He says you should give yourself up to the LDS guarding the tomb site. (WEEPS)
SHEIKH FARAH:	Don't worry. I'll hand myself in and no harm will come to anyone. (PAUSE) Go and have some rest. I'll prepare a written reply for you to take. Everything will be alright.

SCENE 12

HALL IN LEADER'S PALACE

NARRATOR:	In the Palace. There are the Leader with Muk, who had officially been promoted to Chief Adviser and the maid who's busy cutting the Leader's fingernails.
LEADER:	All right. Now tie my turban for me.
NARRATOR:	The maid sang:
	They don't deserve a genius
	whose sayings are the source
	of victories and glory
	These ungrateful people
	respond only to force
	They misinterpret kindness
	and are wary of love
	Their main pass-time is gossip
	and fabricated rumours

225

	that undermine the ship
MUK:	Well done – well done!
	(A KNOCK ON THE DOOR. THE MAID ANSWERS)
NARRATOR:	The "Man", the Acting-Head of security, enters, rather agitated but trying to behave normally.
LEADER:	What is it?
MAN:	Sheikh Farah will give himself up the day after tomorrow. I have it in writing.
LEADER:	You must be congratulated. I'll confirm your appointment as Head of Security. When you arrest Sheikh Farah, take him and the camel to the Chamber and let me know immediately. I want to be there after you put him on the "Khazoog".
MUK:	He deserves what he'll get. I want to be there too.
MAN:	We have one minor trouble.
MUK:	Did you say trouble?
MAN:	I said minor.
LEADER:	Minor or major – what is it?
MAN:	The paint-remover didn't work as expected.
LEADER:	No? My orders in this eventuality were very clear.
MAN:	You see Leader ... We did demolish one wall, which turned out ot be the outer wall of a living room. Then – – Then. People armed themselves and stood guarding their houses. Those whose houses were not in danger joined them too.
LEADER:	So what?
MAN:	They outnumber our men. Almost the whole population, Leader.
MUK:	The army, Leader. The army!
LEADER:	You've read my thoughts.
MAN:	The people got their weapons from their sons who are the soldiers of our army. I'm very – worried, Leader.
LEADER:	What a miserable response to the first serious crisis, you face as Head of Security. Worried!! It's time for me to take over command of everything. I'll go to the Army Headquarters.
MAN:	I shouldn't do that Leader. Safety first. You see ... it turned out that the soldier whose fathers' living room was demolished has corrupted the minds of the soldiers of his battalion. They have thrown away their unforms and joined the mob. They plan to demolish several landmarks in Sinnar on which the camel's words

226

	appeared last night. These include ... I can't bring myself to say it Leader ...
LEADER:	Say it. This is an order.
MAN:	Your granite statue which overlooks the town from the top of the hill. The 50-feet-high statue in which you hold high the little yellow book and look upwards towards the future of humanity.
MUK:	Oh – my God!
MAN:	And the tree which you climbed as a boy and which first revealed your potential for inspired leadership and for reaching the top ...
MUK:	That tree is a national monument. 10.000 people visited it last year!! Thousands came from across the borders. Something must be done –
MAN:	I'm afraid there's more to come.
LEADER:	Out with it.
MAN:	The words appeared on the tower; not far from where we're now. It is also targeted by the mob. The palace tower!
LEADER:	This palace's tower? This is an open rebellion. High treason!
MUK:	They're a mad irreligious lot!
NARRATOR:	That evening, the Leader fled to the distant Sultanate of Dar Fur, together with all his courtiers and most top LDS, including the new Head of Security. The people attacked the palace and set the tower on fire. The fire soon reached the top spire. On it the architect of the Sultanate had fixed a sword held by the hand of the Leader and pointing upwards, much higher than the highest minaret in Sinnar. When it caught fire it glowed in the Darkness – like a Tooth of Fire.

Groups of LDS made their way towards the Sultante of Dar Fur to join their leader, chanting:

We follow without question.
We still believe in you.
Historians will absolve us
and see us as the brave
defenders of the New
Society. Of Justice
and of Progress too.

The single-party system
for all the Sinnar folk
denotes the need for Unity,
in action, not in talk.

We will return some day
espousing sacred law
to re-adjust the compass
and educate the crew
and save Sinnar from this
catastrophic impasse

Some of Sheikh Farah's ex-students went to his hiding place in the desert and invited him back on behalf of the population. They rebuilt his hut for him. He was given the key to the locked up palace library, and asked to bring together a group of wise men in order to set down in writing the rules of fair government based on pluralism and a detailed method of the transfer of power in the future:

Delegations were sent to study systems of governments in neighbouring countries. When Sheikh Farah moved back to his hut, one of the first people to come and congratulate was Muk. When Sheikh Farah's wife saw him approaching, she said: You should shut your door in the face of this hypocrite! Sheikh Farah said: "Why should I?". A young woman brought them coffee.

MUK: She's not your youngest daughter, is she?

SHEIKH FARAH: No. She's an ex-student of mine. Quite clever. She volunteered to help my wife on this very busy day.

MUK: Her face is familiar – I must have seen her somewhere.

NARRATOR: The maid, entering said "You saw me at the Leader's palace".

MUK: (GETS UP IMMEDIATELY AND MAKES FOR THE DOOR)

SHEIKH FARAH: Your coffee, Muk. Your coffee.

MUK: Some other time Sheikh Farah! Some other time!

Epilogue

NARRATOR: Well. I've been asked to tutor you in the history of our Sinnar. My choice for this was probably unusual; but it was factual. The grave of Sheikh Farah is in the vicinity of the dam. Some of his descendants still live in the area. Nobody knows where the grave of the Leader is or what his real name was (PAUSE) This aspect of your initiation is over. Tomorrow you will meet an old friend of mine Sheikh Omar who will sum up and round off the week's programme.

	(PAUSE) You may have noticed I have avoided giving answer to the question about the significance of the name of our Sultanate "Tooth of Fire". You should now be in a position to provide at least one answer for yourselves.
SUHA:	(ENTERS): Can I say something?
NARRATOR:	No you can't. You've said more than enough. Everybody – go home. We've finished. (CHASES HER AWAY. SHE STOPS AT A SAFE DISTANCE AND SINGS):

The camel, says our proverb,
sees not its u-shaped neck
It laughs at other camels
and thinks they look like kettles
that thanks to a weird trick –
are moving on four legs!
Should this sort of delusion
amuse us or disturb? (RUNS OUT)

THE END

WOLFRAM FROMMLET and VIRGINIA H. D. WITTS

with participation of Kenneth Khan Asobo, David Chuye Bunyui, Aaron Chiundura Moyo

PALM WINE AND PEANUT SOUP

A Radio-Play

Characters:

Caroline Asobo,	a university student, from a rich urban background
Mr. Asobo,	Caroline's father, a rich businessman
Mrs. Asobo,	Caroline's mother
Atanga Chikiera,	an architecture student, from a poor rural background
Mr. Chikiera,	Atanga's father, a farmer
Mrs. Chikiera,	Atanga's mother
Spencer Kalala,	Atanga's best friend, a university student

SCENE I
(ON CAMPUS)

(CAROLINE GETS INTO HER CAR AND REVERSES AKWARDLY. SHE HITS ATANGA OFF HIS BIKE.)

CAROLINE: (INSIDE THE CAR) Oh, no!

SPENCER: (OUTSIDE) Atanga, are you alright? Can you get up?

ATANGA: Yeah, I think I'm alright, but ... just look at the bike! It's a mess!

(CAROLINE GETS OUT OF HER CAR.)

CAROLINE: Oh, I'm so sorry, I'm really sorry. Are you alright? Hang on just one second. Let me just turn the engine off. I'll be back!

(SHE RETURNS)

CAROLINE: Oh, I'm so so sorry. Are you hurt?

SPENCER: Of course! What do you think he is? Where did you buy your driving license, lady?

CAROLINE: I'm really sorry. I just wasn't looking.

SPENCER: We can see that! If you've got an eye-problem let your Dad drive for you.

ATANGA: Spencer!

SPENCER: Let me help you.

ATANGA: Oh, ah, ... gee, my hip hurts ... careful ...

CAROLINE: Do you think you should see a doctor?

SPENCER: Well, now you've got a bright idea! But there is no doctor around here.

CAROLINE: Well, I realise that. That's what I actually meant – I'll take you to the hospital.

SPENCER: No, no! Don't take that risk, Atanga.

ATANGA: Come on, cool down. I think we should accept that ... Oh, ah, ... we're going to miss our last lecture, Spencer! Make sure you get the notes.

SPENCER: No way, man! I wouldn't leave you alone with that woman! I'll come with you.

CAROLINE: Alright, come, let's go!

ATANGA: What about my bike?

SPENCER: Just leave it here. It's of no use to anybody in that state.

(THEY ALL GET INTO THE CAR.)

(INSIDE THE CAR)

SPENCER: Are you sure you know how to drive?

ATANGA: Come on, Spencer. Please, don't make her nervous.

CAROLINE: I am sorry ... and I am a bit nervous. It's not surprising.

SPENCER: Oh, Atanga, you look beautiful.

ATANGA: What do you mean?

SPENCER: It really suits you – that bump that's coming out of your head.

ATANGA: Oh, I didn't realise.

CAROLINE: You're bleeding!

SPENCER: Please, lady. Concentrate on the road, you can look at him later ... There is the road! Are you a lecturer?

CAROLINE: No, why?

SPENCER: I thought so. You're driving a nice car.

CAROLINE: Well, it's mine.

SPENCER: Oh, hello! Atanga – whom have we got here? Well, well ... should be no problem to pay for the bicycle?

CAROLINE: No, that's not a problem. It doesn't worry me at all. I'm much more concerned about your friend.

SPENCER: How does one get such a nice car as a student?

CAROLINE: My father is a businessman. He bought it for me. Should I have refused it? You both study at the university?

SPENCER: No. My friend is professor in architecture. Don't you know him?

CAROLINE: No, no, I don't actually.

ATANGA: Don't mind him. Don't take him seriously. We're both final year students. We're missing our last lecture, that's why he's so upset.

CAROLINE: What do you study?

ATANGA: Architecture ... And what do you do?

CAROLINE: Sociology.

SPENCER: Oh, very fine, very exclusive.

ATANGA: What's your name?

CAROLINE: Caroline Asobo.

SPENCER: Asobo ... Asobo ... that name rings a bell.

CAROLINE: And you?

ATANGA: Atanga Chikiera and that's Spencer Kalala.

SCENE II
(AT THE HOSPITAL)

(KNOCK ON THE DOOR)

CAROLINE: Hello, can I come in?

ATANGA: Oh, Carol, it's you. Come in.

CAROLINE: Atanga, you've still got that huge bump!

ATANGA: It looks nice, doesn't it? It even changes colour. But, basically, I'm
               fine. Just bruises and this small cut – in fact, I can go home now.

CAROLINE: That's good news.

ATANGA: I saw the doctor half an hour ago. I've been trying to get hold of
               Spencer, but he's in class.

CAROLINE: That's not really a problem! I can give you a lift home.

ATANGA: Thanks, that should solve at least one problem.

CAROLINE: Well, shall we go now or do you still have to see somebody?

ATANGA: No, they've given me a few pain killers. I must only sort out the
               bill.

CAROLINE: You don't have to worry about that because I already paid it. I paid
               it on my way in.

ATANGA: You what?

CAROLINE: I payed it already. That was the least I could do under the
               circumstances. I would also like to pay for your bicycle.

ATANGA: Definitely not! Please, no – I can take care of that myself.

CAROLINE: But it was my fault, so it's obvious I have to pay for it! Why won't
               you let me do that?

ATANGA: Because ..., ah, just leave it.

CAROLINE: No, because of what?

ATANGA: You wouldn't understand that.

CAROLINE: Why not? I knocked you down and so I should pay for the bicycle
               and the hospital.

ATANGA: You see, it's not about the bicycle really, Caroline. There is more to
               it. You, ... forget it.

CAROLINE: Atanga, don't beat about the bush! What do you want to say?

ATANGA:	Well, you see, the way I was brought up would never allow a woman to pay for a man. The hospital bill is enough, but not more.
CAROLINE:	But that's ridiculous! Why halfway? I knocked you down so I should pay for everything.
ATANGA:	No, that's not the point ... you don't understand.
CAROLINE:	Why don't you say what you mean? Are you afraid?
ATANGA:	No, but, you would hurt my pride if you paid everything.
CAROLINE:	But that was not my intention!
ATANGA:	I know, but that's why you don't understand it. Where I come from, things are different.
CAROLINE:	Where do you come from?
ATANGA:	From Kiburi Village. My father is a farmer there. We live with a different set of values.
CAROLINE:	Oh, that's interesting. Will you tell me more about it?
ATANGA:	Maybe...

SCENE III
(IN ATANGA'S ROOM)

SPENCER:	Atanga, the stuff here makes sense to me. Etendu's notes are brilliant as usual. I don't think it was a disaster we missed that lecture – with these notes we'll be able to catch up. It shouldn't be too much of a problem.
ATANGA:	That guy is brilliant. I must say, he shouldn't have any problem finding a job.
SPENCER:	No reason for you to be envious, Atanga. You always did extremely well. I admire your energy. I have the feeling you've got a clear idea of what you want to do after graduation. Quite frankly, I'm not so sure. To think that I might have to sit in one of the government offices and construct another of those horrible fifteen-floor buildings ... oh, boring! You know, these days each building looks just like the other – what sort of creativity is there left for an architect?
ATANGA:	That's the challenge!
SPENCER:	You think so? What are your plans, Atenga? You come from a rural background ... isn't it even more strange and alien to you? What do you want to do? Have you thought about it yet?
ATANGA:	Well, I've got something in mind ...

234

(KNOCK ON THE DOOR)

SPENCER: Let me get it.

(CAROLINE ENTERS)

CAROLINE: Hello.

SPENCER: Oh! It's you!

CAROLINE: Well, I just thought I'd come and see how Atanga is.

SPENCER: Oh, is that so?

ATANGA: Caroline! Come in, come in ...

CAROLINE: Well, just for a moment. I actually just wanted to find out if you're alright. How's your head? Does your hip feel a little better?

ATANGA: I'm fine. Just a few aches and pains here and there. Would you have some coffee?

CAROLINE: Oh, no, thanks. I can't stay ... I just wanted to pop in and make sure that you are alright.

ATANGA: Stay! Have some coffee.

SPENCER: Oh yes, please do. You're welcome. It's covered with the bicycle bill.

ATANGA: Spencer, gosh, ... this guy!

SPENCER: Caroline, you might have a smart idea – before you came in, we were discussing a serious question – "The role of the architect in our society" What projects do you think an architect in this country should get involved in?

CAROLINE: Oh, that's a difficult question. I must say though, I don't think it should be a problem to find work for the two of you. You know, the other day, Atanga told me a lot about the rural areas and where he comes from.

SPENCER: Oh, did he? That's interesting!

ATANGA: Can't you let her finish?

SPENCER: I'm terribly sorry. I didn't know you had already gone that far.

CAROLINE: Oh Spencer, you always confuse me ... yeah, what I really wanted to say was, that I learned from Atanga that there are hardly any schools or hospitals near the villages and the farmers have no storage facilities.

SPENCER: Brilliant idea! But there is only one small problem, would your father provide the funds or where do you think we'll get the money from?

ATANGA: No, Spencer. Caroline isn't too far out. I've applied for a job in that direction.

235

SPENCER:	That's good news!
ATANGA:	I was going to tell you about it before she came in.
SPENCER:	What is it?
ATANGA:	They advertised in the government gazette for an architect who is interested in working on a low-cost housing scheme and that is in the Eastern Province. It's basically about a labour-intensive approach. Well, you know, using local materials and all that stuff.
CAROLINE:	Oh, Atanga, it sounds really interesting. A real challenge! You must tell me more about it ... but, I have to go now – I have a lecture. Please, Atanga, I really would like to know more about it, ok? Good luck to you both. Bye!

(CAROLINE LEAVES)

SPENCER:	Wow, man ... dry season, isn't it? Bushfire ...
ATANGA:	I think she's rather nice.
SPENCER:	Rather nice? She knocks you off your bike, and you think she's rather nice?
ATANGA:	It was an accident, leave it at that. We met afterwards and I think she's thoughtful ...
SPENCER:	Wait a minute! You know what you're into? Atanga, she means trouble with a capital T. You know what I mean.
ATANGA:	No, not really.
SPENCER:	Come on ... they say love is blind, but look – she's rich, beautiful and, I suppose, sexy, but she's not from your class-background. Atanga, no, she's way out of reach.
ATANGA:	I think you're rather taking it too far.
SPENCER:	What do you think she's going to demand in the long run, my dear low-cost architect? How will you settle that bill? Take my advice, forget about her, pretend she doesn't even exist. You're wasting your time!

SCENE IV
(ON CAMPUS/IN THE CAFETERIA)

ATANGA:	Caroline! Caroline!
CAROLINE:	Atanga!
ATANGA:	Hello, Caroline. Have you got time to join me for a cup of coffee in the canteen?

236

CAROLINE: Oh, I'd love to! Yes, I've got half an hour before my next class.

ATANGA: Alright, let's go.

CAROLINE: Your bump is almost gone and the cut is healing well.

ATANGA: I'll be as fit as a fiddle in a few more days.

CAROLINE: And your bicycle? Did you get it fixed? Did it cost a lot?

ATANGA: Slow down, one at a time! My bike is fine. I repaired most of it myself and, no, it wasn't very expensive. And your car? I never asked about that – was it damaged at all?

CAROLINE: Not even a scratch!

(IN THE CANTEEN)

ATANGA: Here we are. What would you like to drink? Coffee, tea or something else?

CAROLINE: I think I'd like a cup of tea, please.

ATANGA: (TO THE WAITER) A coffee and a tea, please.

CAROLINE: There's a place over there where we can sit.

ATANGA: (TO THE WAITER) Thank you ...

CAROLINE: Let me carry the tray. You're still limping, otherwise we won't have anything left in the cups by the time we get there.

(THEY SIT DOWN)

CAROLINE: Do you take sugar?

ATANGA: Yes, three – I have a sweet tooth.

CAROLINE: I only take one, but I like sweet things, too. Chocolates are my weakness.

ATANGA: I must remember that!

CAROLINE: The other day, you started talking about the job you've applied for. Can you tell me more about it?

ATANGA: Wait a minute! It's your turn. You never talk about yourself. I also want to know something about you. What made you decide to study sociology?

CAROLINE: Well, my father is not very happy about it. He wanted me to read economics and go into the family business, and one day take over from him. But I feel there is so much community-work to be done. There are so many areas where I feel we have to change and develop things, so I turned away from economics. Anyway, there are more than enough people in business. To be honest, Atanga, I'm not very interested in my father's business.

237

ATANGA: But ... that's strange to me. How come you developed interest in parts of the society with which you have no contact? You must have grown up in a privileged environment. Would it not be normal to keep your family interests going?

CAROLINE: Well, you're right. It might be the usual way, but for me it was somehow different. In boarding school I had a teacher who gave us a lot of things to read about the other side of life. It opened my eyes to things I never really thought about before. Now I want to do something worthwhile. I still don't know quite what. But, ... I don't want to talk about it now, it's a bit of a touchy issue. Tell me more about your job. What is it?

ATANGA: Well, that job, it's with the Eastern Province municipality, and the best thing is – in the mean time my application has been approved.

CAROLINE: Oh, Atanga, congratulations! That's fantastic news!

ATANGA: Yeah, it's a new housing project and it's based on two principles. I'm supposed to use as many locally available materials as possible. I guess you know why?

CAROLINE: To reduce costs?

ATANGA: That's one aspect. There are no transportation costs involved and the materials are cheaper. But another aspect is that people get involved. Have you ever heard of small-scale industry?

CAROLINE: No.

ATANGA: It's very simple. People learn new skills and rediscover old ones which they have forgotten. In my village, for example, for centuries, we had craftsmen ... if you go there today – nothing left! Many left for town and have been swallowed by modern technology. There is no need for that. We can change the situation.

CAROLINE: What you are saying is that you want to create employment, affordable housing, and – just something people can be proud of because at the end of the day they did it themselves?

ATANGA: Precisely!

CAROLINE: I envy you, Atanga. I wish I had that kind of a perspective on my life. I think you are an optimist.

ATANGA: Why?

CAROLINE: Well, I think you would like to make this world a better place for us all!

ATANGA: I'd like to do as much as one person can.

CAROLINE:	You're amazing, Atanga! You're so humble. That must be your rural background.
ATANGA:	Don't you have to go back to class?
CAROLINE:	Oh, dear! I forgot all about it. Alright then ...
ATANGA:	Alright then ... Caroline? ..
CAROLINE:	What is it?
ATANGA:	Caroline, I'd really like to see you again and ... Have you made arrangements for tomorrow night?
CAROLINE:	No. I don't have anything planned.
ATANGA:	I know a very nice restaurant on Seriala Street. Would you have dinner with me?
CAROLINE:	I'd love to!
ATANGA:	Shall we meet then at seven thirty? In front of the main library?
CAROLINE:	Yes, that'll be fine.
ATANGA:	Okay, bye!
CAROLINE:	Atanga, I'm really looking forward to it!

SCENE V
(IN CAR/ATANGA'S VILLAGE)

(CAROLINE AND ATANGA ARE DRIVING TO ATANGA'S VILLAGE)

CAROLINE:	Oh, this song brings back so many memories. Do you realise it is almost a year since our first date? I remember the evening like yesterday. I don't think I ever told you – I must have changed three or four times before I was happy with the way I looked that night.
ATANGA:	And I was sure you wouldn't come – fifteen minutes late! And there you were ... I felt so ashamed of my old suit and scruffy shoes ... and you looked so beautiful.
CAROLINE:	We were so shy, we hardly said a word to each other, until that waiter spilled the wine. Do you remember?
ATANGA:	Yes, that broke the ice. Accidents certainly have played a role in our relationship. The whole thing started off with a bang, if you remember.
CAROLINE:	Please, don't remind me. By the way, are we almost there? I'm still feeling very nervous about meeting your parents.
ATANGA:	You don't have to, and it's not far now.
CAROLINE:	Your parents must feel very proud of you.

239

ATANGA: Why?

CAROLINE: Oh, you know, with all you've achieved – the housing development and the fact that it has received so much publicity.

ATANGA: I don't know, I'm not so sure about my father. I think he had hoped I'd be more what he thinks is "modern" and have bulldozers, cranes, and so on, on site. He doesn't seem to realise that what often appears to be a simpler method can be the better one. But then it wasn't easy to get the idea across to a lot of the decisionmakers in the beginning either.

             Caroline, what's the matter?

CAROLINE: Nothing.

ATANGA: Why are you so quiet?

CAROLINE: Do you remember what I once called you, when we first met at the canteen? I called you an optimist.

ATANGA: I remember. I am!

CAROLINE: Where do you draw that energy from? Atanga, I asked you a question.

ATANGA: Yes, I know. But it's not so easy to answer. I think basically from my parents. You know, growing up under the harsh conditions of a rural setting, is a permanent lesson about the small steps in life.

CAROLINE: I don't quite get you.

ATANGA: You know, when things change and move in a family like yours, it's always the big things, like a second lorry, another shop somewhere, isn't it like that, Caroline?

CAROLINE: You might be right.

ATANGA: But you know, in the setting I come from, it's the very little things which count.

CAROLINE: For example?

ATANGA: Well, if for one whole season no cow has died of tick-feaver because my father has managed to fill up the dipping tank, then, to us, that is progress, you see?

CAROLINE: I still don't quite know what you mean.

ATANGA: You always want the big results. You're so depressed that there is not a primary healthcare scheme in every little village in the province – one year after you've taken up your job with UNICEF, am I right?

CAROLINE: Yes, indeed you are. But the fact is that every day as I go around the villages, I can see that people do not respond, that they do not set up

240

village health-committees, and when the UNICEF-car arrives for the injection campaign, how many mothers are there? Five out of 200!

ATANGA: How fast do you think these people should change their habits? Let me give you an example: the other day, when I accompanied you to one of the primary health-care meetings, almost the entire village sat there listening to you and your colleagues for two hours. Is that nothing? Nobody walked out of the meeting. That's already something. You must believe in the small steps.

CAROLINE: My optimist. I love you! You're beautiful ... Just changing the subject, are you sure your parents will like the presents?

ATANGA: It's too late to worry about that now anyway. Look, there's the house.

CAROLINE: Which one?

ATANGA: The one on the left. The other one is my uncle's.

CAROLINE: Oh, yes, that's the uncle you always talk about, isn't it?

ATANGA: Yeah, that's him. Well, I'll park under that tree.

CAROLINE: It's shady there.

(THEY GET OUT OF THE CAR)

ATANGA: Can you see them?

CAROLINE: Are those your parents?

ATANGA: Yeah, my Mom has put on so much weight.

Mr. CHIKIERA:
The children have come, the children have come! Mama Atanga! Come my dear children. You're welcome.

Mrs. CHIKIERA:
Atanga ... Atanga, my son! It's so nice to see you. You have brought a daughter!

ATANGA: Mama, I'd like to introduce to you and Papa – Caroline Asobo

Mr. CHIK.: She's welcome.

ATANGA: Caroline, these are my parents.

CAROLINE: How do you do? I'm really pleased to meet you.

Mrs. CHIK.: Caroline, you are welcome to our home!

Mr. CHIK.: Come inside, come and sit. I hear you are a doctor.

CAROLINE: Well, no, not exactly a doctor ...

Mr. CHIK.: Oh, never mind. Just come in.

SCENE VI
(INSIDE THE CHIKIERA'S HOME)

ATANGA: Ah, Pa, this palm-wine is delicious! But then again, you've always made fantastic palm-wine.

Mr. CHIK.: That's the problem with moving to town. How can a person live without palm-wine?

ATANGA: You're right.

CAROLINE: Oh, did you know they now sell palm-wine in bottles in town.

Mr. CHIK.: What did you say, my daughter? Palm-wine in bottles? Ma, did you hear that? ...

Mrs. CHIK.: I heard it.

Mr. CHIK.: Palm-wine in bottles ... that's like eating last week's foofoo!
Our ancestors would turn in their graves a hundred times over if they knew about you modern people. ... My son, is there anything special you want to discuss with me?

ATANGA: Eh, ... Mama, we've come a long way – we're hungry.

Mrs. CHIK.: That's what I thought so.

ATANGA: What about my favourite peanut soup?

Mrs. CHIK.: Atanga, you still remember that?

ATANGA: I remember it very much. Caroline, don't you want to join Mother? She's famous for that.

CAROLINE: I'd love to! That's a good idea.

Mrs. CHIK.: Of course I'll make some. There are lots of fresh ground nuts. I've shelled nearly all of them. Daughter, you can start the rest while I start pounding the others. Let us leave the men to do their business.

CAROLINE: You know that Atanga loves this peanut soup?

Mrs. CHIK.: Did you ever cook some, Carolina?

(THE TWO WOMEN LEAVE)

Mr. Chik.: Let the women go out. My son, that doctor of yours, is that the one you want to marry?

ATANGA: Oh, Papa, I told you she isn't a doctor!

Mr. CHIK.: Whatever it is – is it her?

ATANGA: Yes.

Mr. CHIK.: You know, I had a good look at her. She looks healthy and she's got strong hips for childbearing.

ATANGA: Oh, Pa! You never change, will you?

242

Mr. CHIK.:	Now, listen to me, my son. Good hips are one thing, but that's not all. You know what amazes me? She has painted fingernails! How can she plant yams with those fingernails? Impossible! So, what do you say?
ATANGA:	Papa, look, she went to university with me, we both have a job. She is working for UNICEF now.
Mr. CHIK.:	But I don't know them ...
ATANGA:	That doesn't matter, whether you know them ... What I mean – she's got no time to plant yams. We can buy the food on the market. And, anyway, when we have our own garden, we can plant some vegetables. But we'll do it together and she can learn. There are other things which count today in a marriage.
Mr. CHIK.:	Is it? So if she doesn't grow things, will she have time to have children? What about grandchildren when she is working all day?
ATANGA:	Of course we'll have children, Papa! That doesn't have to interfere with her job. We can arrange for that.
Mr. CHIK.:	Hm, I see.
ATANGA:	So, Papa, what are you saying about the marriage?
Mr. CHIK.:	Hm, it all looks very strange to me. Does a woman not belong to the house anymore?
ATANGA:	Well, Papa, do you remember when Mr. Tamienga, my schoolteacher, came to speak to you and told you I had won a scholarship to go to university?
Mr. CHIK.:	That one I remember!
ATANGA:	He explained to you that it meant I would have to go and live in town. And Mother cried and you were sad and thought you would never see me again.
Mr. CHIK.:	Don't remind me of that.
ATANGA:	And that many bad things would happen to me. Did any of those things happen?
Mr. CHIK.:	I'm sensing something.
ATANGA:	Please, Father, getting married to Caroline is like that. It's a new way. Those things you mentioned were very important when you married Mother, but today they are not as important any longer.
Mr. CHIK.:	Are they not?
ATANGA:	Yeah, Caroline doesn't have to know how to plant crops.
Mr. CHIK.:	Are you saying that the rural way of life is no longer important?

ATANGA: No, no. Of course it still is! But in addition there is also another way.

Mr. CHIK.: But ... there is another thing which worries me. Your new wife, is she not coming from a rich family?

ATANGA: But that's not why I want to marry her.

Mr. CHIK.: Well, remember the saying: "The chameleon changes its colours three times a day before the sun sets behind the mountains."

ATANGA: What do you mean by that, Papa?

Mr. CHIK.: Are you sure you can fullfil her demands with that rich background? What kind of things is she going to ask from you?

ATANGA: Papa, you should not worry about that. We both have our own job. We will not depend on her family at all.

Mr. CHIK.: I see, hm ... We will have to go and see them – did you make arrangements? What was her father's answer?

ATANGA: Well ... in fact they don't know yet.

Mr. CHIK.: How can that be? ... how can that be?

SCENE VII
(IN CAROLINE'S HOME)

(CAROLINE AND HER PARENTS ARE SITTING IN THEIR LIVING-ROOM)

CAROLINE: Mum, how old were you when you married?

Mrs. ASOBO: Let me think ... 24, 25 I think.

CAROLINE: Had you known Dad for long?

Mrs. ASOBO: About a year or so, not so Darling?

CAROLINE: Oh, that's just like me! Just as long as I've known Atanga.

Mr. ASOBO: Atanga, who is he?

CAROLINE: You've met him a few times already.

Mr. ASOBO: Ah! That architect.

CAROLINE: Dad, what do you think of him?

Mr. ASOBO: Pleasant character. What is he doing at the moment?

CAROLINE: He has just finished the first phase of a housing project.

Mrs. ASOBO: That's nice.

Mr. ASOBO: Good for him.

CAROLINE: Didn't you read about it in the paper?

Mr. ASOBO:	When? Was it today?
CAROLINE:	No, not today, but recently.
Mr. ASOBO:	Oh, yes. I remember.
CAROLINE:	Mum, in your days, did you ask your parents about the marriage, or was it Dad who did that?
Mr. ASOBO:	What do you want to say, Caroline? Do you want to say you are getting married?
CAROLINE:	To be honest – yes!
Mrs. ASOBO:	Oh, how beautiful, Caroline! Do we know him?
Mr. ASOBO:	I hope we do! Who is he?
CAROLINE:	Atanga.
Mrs. ASOBO:	Atanga!
Mr. ASOBO:	Why him?
CAROLINE:	We've known each other for over a year and we love each other.
Mrs. ASOBO:	Oh, Caroline, how lovely! Why didn't you mention it before?
Mr. ASOBO:	You keep quiet for a moment! Caroline, what has he got to offer?
CAROLINE:	What do you mean?
Mr. ASOBO:	So – he's an architect at the moment?
CAROLINE:	Hm ...
Mr. ASOBO:	With whom? With the government?
CAROLINE:	Yes.
Mr. ASOBO:	Oh my God! That doesn't promise a prosperous future.
CAROLINE:	He's quite happy.
Mr. ASOBO:	At the moment – because he hasn't got a family around. Isn't he a village-boy?
CAROLINE:	Dad, what sort of language is that – a village-boy?
Mr. ASOBO:	Oh, you know what I mean ... I mean different from us.
CAROLINE:	Different? How? You mean he can't behave or what?
Mrs. ASOBO:	Oh, I think he behaved quite well when he was here. I was very impressed – he's very polite.
CAROLINE:	Thank you, Mum. I taught him how to use a knife and fork.
Mrs. ASOBO:	Oh, you did?
CAROLINE:	Come on! What do you think they are? Of course they use them in the village!

Mr. ASOBO:	That's not the way to talk to your mother! And ... it's not the issue. What I want to know is: is there any financial background?
CAROLINE:	They've got a farm.
Mr. ASOBO:	Oh, you seem to be very well informed.
CAROLINE:	I visited his home village recently.
Mr. ASOBO:	You what?
CAROLINE:	Well, is it a crime?
Mr. ASOBO:	It would be nice to know in what circles my daughter is moving around.
CAROLINE:	But Dad, I'm 24 – same age as Mum when she married you.
Mr. ASOBO:	But she did not marry a village boy!
CAROLINE:	What's the matter with you? What worries you so much, Dad?
Mr. ASOBO:	Well, I tell you – I know the villagers. If you marry one, we'll have the whole family around. We'll be feeding the whole lot. They're all the same.
CAROLINE:	But we both have a job. Atanga can support his family and we don't need your money or your property.
Mr. ASOBO:	That's interesting. All that I've been building up for all these years – that's all going down the drain – for nothing!
Mrs. ASOBO:	Take it easy, darling.
Mr. ASOBO:	For whom did I do all that? If not for you, for your future, to keep things together in the family.
CAROLINE:	Why then, did you allow me to go to university and let me study sociology?
Mr. ASOBO:	Bad enough, it wasn't my choice. At least I would have thought you'd bring a husband home who fits into our setting.
CAROLINE:	Well, in that case, the best would be if you look for a husband for me.
Mrs. ASOBO:	Caroline, don't upset your father so much. He only wants the best for you.
CAROLINE:	The best! But which century do we live in? How does he know what is best for me? I can define for myself whom I love and what is best for me. And in any case, this wouldn't be a problem if I were your son!
Mr. ASOBO:	That's not an issue ... we're your parents. We always know what is best for you. We've got the life-experience – not you, haven't we?
Mrs. ASOBO:	Yes, that's true.

Mr. ASOBO: You will call it off.

CAROLINE: No, Dad. I will not!

Mrs. ASOBO: Caroline, Caroline, where are you going? Don't go away! We want you to be happy!

CAROLINE: That's exactly what I want – to be happy.

Mrs. ASOBO: Oh dear, Caroline. Darling, see what you've done.

SCENE VIII
(AT THE ASOBO'S HOME)

(MR. ASOBO IS LOOKING OUT OF THE WINDOW OF HIS HOUSE)

Mr. ASOBO: Look, look at that. There they are. What did I tell you? The whole village, they're all here, right on our doorsteps!

Mrs. ASOBO: Don't exaggerate, there are only six of them.

Mr. ASOBO: Seven – if you can count properly.

Mrs. ASOBO: Alright, but that's not the whole village.

Mr. ASOBO: Don't let them all in. Only the parents. And make sure they clean their feet. They're filthy! Leave the rest on the veranda.

Mrs. ASOBO: You know they've been driving on that pick-up for hours – of course, they're dusty.

Mr. ASOBO: But one would expect them to have the decency to come in a normal car. Just as I expected.

Mrs. ASOBO: Caroline! They're here, Caroline!

CAROLINE: Okay, I'm coming! Mum, do I look alright?

Mrs. ASOBO: Yes. Oh, you look lovely.

CAROLINE: Hello, welcome Mr.and Mrs. Chikiera, Atanga, it's nice to see you ...

(THE VISITORS ENTER, GENERAL WELCOMING)

ATANGA: Mr. Asobo – my parents, Mr. and Mrs. Chikiera. My aunt and uncle – my father's brother, and my mother's sister and her husband and their eldest son too ...

Mr. ASOBO: Enough, enough, please. Now let's have some order here. We were not prepared for a whole delegation. Mary, take the rest out to the veranda – they can wait there.

(CONFUSION, WHILE MRS. ASOBO TAKES THE OTHERS OUT)

Mr. ASOBO: Mr. and Mrs. Chikiera, you may come through to the lounge, if you must. The rest, out to the veranda.

CAROLINE:	Mr. and Mrs. Chikiera, you must be tired. Wouldn't you like a seat, and maybe something to drink? You must be thirsty from the journey.
Mr. CHIK.:	Thank you very much, my daughter!
Mr. ASOBO:	We have not yet got to that, Mr. Chikiera! Ah ... Mary?
Mrs. ASOBO:	Yes, darling! Oh, I'm sorry. Mrs. Chikiera are you comfortable?
Mr. CHIK.:	Mr. and Mrs. Asobo, thank you for this meeting. We regret the unusual way this has all come about, but my son does things the new way, the "modern" way as he calls it. We do not always agree. Mr. Asobo, your daughter Caroline and my son Atanga wish to marry – we have travelled far and brought some palm-wine, some fresh peanuts and some gifts for you and your family.
Mrs. ASOBO:	Oh, thank you very much, Mrs. Chikiera.
Mr. CHIK.:	May we first share a drink and speak the matters through?
Mr. ASOBO:	Speak through what?
CAROLINE:	Here are the glasses ...

(CAROLINE POURS OUT THE DRINKS)

Mr. Chik.:	To the health of our famiies. To the health of our ancestors.
Mr. ASOBO:	Now, please, let's got on with it! I've got another appointment in half an hour. Let's be quick.
Mr. CHIK.:	Parents of my daughter, we all wish our children to be happy. We had long talks about our two children, and we realised with pleasure that they should make a good couple. We were pleased that our son is in employment and can look after a family, and we are also pleased that he chose a beautiful and healthy girl who can give many grandchildren to all of us. I think we can congratulate ourselves.
Mr. ASOBO:	I don't quite see it that way, Mr. Chikiera.
Mr. CHIK.:	Oh, I know there is something left for discussion, but I think we should be able to look into that.
Mr. ASOBO:	What is that?
Mr. CHIK.:	I think we can find an agreement. We, in the village, are very much aware that a daughter with a rich background and such a good education does not go cheaply.
Mr. ASOBO:	What do you mean?
Mr. CHIK.:	Tradition demands that we talk about the bride price.
Mr. ASOBO:	About what? Now hold it ... we're not on some market place! Anyway, I don't need your money.

Mr. CHIK.:	We didn't have money in mind ...
Mr. ASOBO:	What then? ... Cows?
Mr. CHIK.:	Yes, that's the traditional way.
Mr. ASOBO:	You're asking me to sell my daughter for cattle? Mary, we're probably expected to keep the cattle in the garden.
CAROLINE:	Father, please, do accept that other people have different customs. You know that!
Mrs. CHIK.:	They've abused you!
Mr. ASOBO:	I do! Let them have them! But such people do not have to marry my daughter!
Mrs. CHIK.:	They've abused you again!
Mr. CHIK.:	Such people, Mr. Asobo, as you like to call us, feed you and all the other town people. We do not need your arrogance and we can survive without you. Mother Atanga, and Atanga, let's go.
Mrs. ASOBO:	But you haven't finished your drinks yet!
ATANGA:	Mother, Father, I apologise for the embarassment I have brought to you.
CAROLINE:	But Atanga, it's not your fault. It's me who has to apologise. I'm so sorry. Atanga, what are we going to do?
Mr. ASOBO:	Let them go, let them go ... filthy.

SCENE IX
(AT A STREET CAFE)

ATANGA:	Oh man, the last few months were a nightmare! Sometimes I think it's easier to take bulldozers and cranes and build those skyscrapers instead of trying to get people motivated to take affairs into their own hands.
SPENCER:	What do you expect, Atanga? The rural areas have been neglected for so long. People have to learn not to wait for others, but to trust their own potential.
ATANGA:	There is so much disorientation. It's difficult to get people to see the value of their own roots.
SPENCER:	Yeah, that's a difficult one. By the way, how are you getting on with your parents?
ATANGA:	You mean with Caroline?
SPENCER:	Yes.

ATANGA: They like her, really, but they are not happy we're still not married.

SPENCER: What about Caroline's parents?

ATANGA: Oh, that's another story. Deadlock situation – nothing moves. They have such a narrow idea of how they see the future of their daughter.

SPENCER: Where, do you think, is the bottleneck? Could it be your cultural background, or what?

ATANGA: I'm no longer sure about that. It could be part of the problem, but I think there is more to it. It boils down to money. Their whole value-system is based on business and accumulating property and material things. And they feel this is the only way their daughter can be happy and secure. I don't think he would even mind having me as a son-in-low if I were a businessman and prepared to share his value-system so that it could continue.

SPENCER: You might be right. But is it only an attitude of that class of society? Don't most parents tend to impose their concept of life onto their children, and claim that it's in the interest of their children's happiness?

ATANGA: Good point, Spencer. Are we talking about the generation gap?

SPENCER: I think so.

ATANGA: And what is the way out? Do you suggest that we go our own way and don't turn back? You know, you and I and Caroline, want to realise our choice of lifestyle, but then, is it not cruel to abandon all family bonds? Don't you lose some of the richness of a human society? Can you easily cut yourself off from those that are your flesh and blood and formed your life?

SPENCER: Do you really have to? I still believe that we can bridge that gap. Look at your parents – they've learned to accept that you live a different life, but on the other hand, they're not afraid of you because you've shown them clearly that you still appreciate their values.

ATANGA: Man, stop it ... I'm going to cry in a minute.

SPENCER: No, I'm serious! These things need to be said.

ATANGA: Now what? Any solution?

SPENCER: What do you mean?

ATANGA: I can't go on with Caroline for the next twenty years like this – not being married.

SPENCER: Why do you have to? Why don't you just marry her in your parent's village?

ATANGA:	Funny, we've actually been talking about that.
SPENCER:	So why don't you do it?
ATANGA:	And her parents?
SPENCER:	Invite them! If they come, good for them. If not, they're going to miss something special.
ATANGA:	Come, let's have another beer!
SPENCER:	Am I invited to the wedding?
ATANGA:	Of course, you are! I'd like you to be my best-man.
SPENCER:	Accepted, if it also solves my problem. Up to now I haven't had a lucky number. I only come on one condition: I ride your bike to the wedding and you ask Caroline if she has got a lovely girlfriend who is an appalling driver.

THE END

JOHN ALLEN
ERASTUS HAITENGULA
AIMA IITA
SONIA MAFFEIS
NAPOLEON KANGUEEHI
GERRY HILL

FAMILY BUSINESS

A Play

Characters:

MARTHA, the mother:	like her Biblical namesake: a hard worker – has had a life of uncomplaining submission to God's will, or Fate.
	– uneducated; too busy to concern herself with metaphysical issues or human emotions.
MICHAEL, the first son:	an absent character
	– has already left home; is a travelling salesman, domiciled in Windhoek but "too busy" to visit home very often.
ELIAS:	– the second son, still at school, currently in Standard 10, 17 years old.
REBECCA (Becky):	– only two years younger than her brother, 15.
ERASTUS, called Job:	– third son, last child, about 13,
	– only child without a biblical name.
THE FATHER:	– is not given a name: this is symbolic of his lack of identity to his children.

SCENE ONE

NARRATOR: A house, sparsely furnished. There is a bed in the corner of the room upstage right. To the left of this is a dresser, displaying basic crockery. Immediately in front of this a table with four upright chairs. There are also two armchairs. At the side of the bed is a small table on which there is an asthray, containing cigarette stubs, some magazines and newspapers, poker dice and a picture of a man in a cheap wooden frame. On the walls are pictures: some religious, some purely aesthetic. These are glued directly onto the wall.

Job is lying in the bed asleep.

Elias enters quietly, looks at the boy on the bed, lifts up the ash-tray. He puts down the ash-tray and then goes quietly to the table and puts the books onto the table. He goes back to the table by the bed and picks up a copy of a newspaper, makes a noise and the boy on the bed starts to talk.

JOB: Elias ... is that you? (LIFTING THE BOOK FROM HIS FACE)

ELIAS: Yes, it's only me. I did not mean to wake you up.

JOB: (YAWNING AND STRETCHING OUT HIS ARMS) What time is it? I expected somebody home long ago.

ELIAS: But you knew that I was playing football this afternoon, didn't you? Hasn't Becky been home yet to look after you?

JOB: No, not yet ... unless she came while I was asleep. I haven't seen anybody all day.

ELIAS: But where did you get these cigarettes from, then? And what are these dice doing here?

JOB: (ASHAMED) Janabari got them for me. He came around this morning and we played dice for half-an-hour. You know he comes round every day for mama.

ELIAS: (RISING FROM THE TABLE, HE MOVES TO THE BED AND SITS DOWN AFTER PICKING UP THE DICE)
I don't think mama knows how bad he is else she wouldn't ask him to visit. He is teaching you bad ways, my brother. He is leading you astray. Did you use money for gambling? And where did you get the money for the cigarettes?

JOB: We only used a little money for the gambling. It's no fun without money.

ELIAS: And did you lose all the money? And I still wanna know about the cigarettes.

JOB: I lost today. But I'll get it back next time.

ELIAS: You tell me now about those cigarettes else I'll tell mama about it.

JOB: (FRIGHTENED) Elias, you wouldn't do that. Then you'll get Becky into hot soup as well.

ELIAS: What's Becky got to do with it? Aah, is she the one giving you the money? Tell me. And where does she get money from?

JOB: (GRUMBLING) So many questions. If you tell mama that she is giving me the money, you'll get her into real trouble. You know, she's got a new dress hidden under my bed that mama is not supposed to know about. You mustn't tell her I told you.

ELIAS: (CROUCHES DOWN TO FEEL UNDER THE BED AND TALKS AT THE SAME TIME)
                Becky would sell her soul for a new dress. What's she up to now? This sister of ours only thinks about money.

JOB: That's not fair. It's not true. Becky says that she thinks a lot about me.

ELIAS: That's as maybe but if thinking about you means she gives you money for cigarettes you'd be better off if she only thought about herself.
                (AS HE IS SPEAKING HE HAS FOUND A PLASTIC PACKET AND IS TAKING THE DRESS OUT OF THE BAG)
                My god. What's this? A street-girl's dress ... that's what it is. And when does my sister wear this, I wonder? Mama lets her stay at Aina's house for weekends but she never leaves here looking like this.

JOB: (FINGERING THE DRESS) It's a wonderful dress. She must look lovely in it.

ELIAS: (ANGRY NOW) What do you know? You know nothing, little brother.

                (THEY ARE BOTH HOLDING THE DRESS WHEN THE DOOR SWINGS OPEN AND BECKY ENTERS.)

BECKY: (ANGRY AND FRIGHTENED) What are you doing with that? Why did you tell him about the dress, job? You promised to keep it secret.

                (SHE MOVES OVER TO THE BED AND GRABS THE DRESS AND THE PACKET, THEN MOVES TO THE TABLE AND STARTS TO PACK IT AWAY. ELIAS REMAINS SITTING ON THE BED)

254

ELIAS:	(STILL ANGRY) I'd really like to know where you got the money for that. You could also tell me where and when you intend to wear it. I think you'd better give me some answers quickly.
BECKY:	It's none of your business. Just because you're my brother doesn't mean I must answer all your questions.
ELIAS:	Listen, I know you are giving money to Job for cigarettes. Somehow he finds money for gambling. And now you have this dress. I would really like to solve this problem without involving mama. So please, do tell me.
BECKY:	(SHAKING OFF HIS ARM ANGRILY) Are you threatening me?
ELIAS:	No. I'm just trying to solve the problem because what you are doing for Job is wrong and I think that maybe that's not the only thing that you are doing wrong.
BECKY:	(MOVING TO SIT DOWN AT THE KITCHEN TABLE) I didn't buy the cigarettes. I just gave Job the money. He's got nothing to do all day. And so I was trying to help him ... to make life easier.
ELIAS:	Making life easier! You're an easy sort of girl, aren't you, Becky? That's what you want out of life. Easiness.
BECKY:	Don't lecture me. Don't you lecture me! You've got your football and your guitar. You use sweet words with mama to get permission to play with your band every weekend. You play football when mama thinks that you're here ... with Job ... studying so hard for your matric ... so what makes your life so different?
ELIAS:	(MOCKING) And you've got your fancy dress to make it easy. (HE TURNS ABRUPTLY TO JOB) Who bought the cigarettes for you?
JOB:	(RESENTFULLY) Becky gave me the money for newspapers. But Janabari bought me cigarettes at the shop as well.
	(AT THE MENTION OF THE CIGARETTES, BECKY JUMPS UP AND GOES TO COLLECT THE ASH-TRY. SHE GOES OUT OF THE DOOR AND RETURNS A FEW MOMENTS LATER. SHE PUTS THE ASH TRAY, NOW CLEANED, ON THE DINING ROOM TABLE. IN THE MEANTIME, ELIAS AND JOB CONTINUE TO SPEAK.)
ELIAS:	It was good of Becky to give you money for newspapers but wrong of you to buy cigarettes. Listen, brother, there are many better things you can do with your life, although I know it is difficult for you. You may be physically disabled but life can still be good. You may not have much of a body but a brain ... ah, yes! Don't waste your time and money on smoking

	or gambling. Think. Read. In a way, I envy you, Job ... your choices in life are much simpler.
BECKY:	(HEARING THIS AS SHE RETURNS) Boy, listen to you! Mama would really be proud if she could hear you now. She'd sign you up as preacher at her church for next Sunday! And you could take along your guitar to help her choir along. The perfect son.
ELIAS:	It's not me that's the perfect son. Haven't you forgotten Michael, our big brother? Now there's the perfect son. Mama is forever telling us to be like Michael: he sends money every month but we never see him. He's got a good job but we don't know what it is. And mother loves him but we're all trying to work out why.
JOB:	Be fair, Elias. You know that Michael is a travelling salesman so he's not in Windhoek very much. How would we manage without his money, anyway?
ELIAS:	(AT THE MENTION OF THE MONEY, ELIAS GETS UP FROM THE BED AND WALKS OVER TO THE TABLE, LOOKS AT HIS BOOKS, THEN PULLS AN ENVELOPE OUT OF HIS JEANS) Ah, yes, the money. Then how come that the envelope with the money always has a Windhoek postmark? I'm not blind. (HE WALKS ACROSS TO SHOW JOB) Look at this envelope. See for yourself and then tell me if I'm the one that's blind.
JOB:	Don't give it to me. You might be right, but what's the point?
ELIAS:	You're right '... what's the point? Mama still thinks he's perfect. All I must do with my life for her approval is to send an envelope every month. (BECKY IN THE MEANWHILE HAS PULLED OUT A SUITCASE FROM THE END OF THE BED. SHE TAKES THE PACKET WITH THE DRESS AND STARTS TO PACK THE CASE.)
ELIAS:	What are you doing? Packing your suitcase? Are you going out tonight? Have you asked mama?
BECKY:	(PACKING WITH DETERMINATION) More questions. Don't you ever give up? I'm prepared to give you answers to these questions, though. One – I'm packing; two, yes I'm off to stay with Aina; and three, yes, mama gave me permission four days ago.
ELIAS:	And did mama give you permission to go out in that dress tonight? Did she give you permission to watch T.V. at Aina's house in that dress? And did she give you permission to study with Aina in that dress?

BECKY:	I suppose that my preacher brother would like me to study naked? My brother, the priest has spoken. Amen.
ELIAS:	Aaah ... men. (SLIGHT PAUSE) Many men, I'm sure. All helping you to study and become an expert. Men is a subject always on your mind.
BECKY:	(CLOSING THE SUITCASE LID WITH A BANG) I'm not staying to listen to any more of this. Just because you're my brother that does not give you the right to insult me. I'm off. (SHE TURNS TOWARDS JOB) Tell mama I'll be home tomorrow at about five. She's not to worry.
JOB:	(INNOCENTLY) Becky, you've forgotten to pack your school books.
BECKY:	(TRYING TO STAY CALM) Aina took my books to her house to save me the trouble. You know her uncle picks her up from school in his car. I have to walk everywhere.
JOB:	(TRYING TO KEEP HER THERE) I wish I could see you in your special dress, Becky. I bet you're real pretty.
	(SHE LEANS DOWN TO KISS HIM AND PUTS THE COIN ON THE BEDSIDE TABLE)
BECKY:	One day when preacher brother is converting his friends with his guitar at his nightclub I'll give you a fashion show in my dress, Job. Now, be good, and here's something for some sweets and the "Namibian" tomorrow.
JOB:	You're sweet to me, Becky. I love you.
BECKY:	I love you, too. Take care.
	(SHE PICKS UP HER CASE AND LEAVES)
ELIAS:	Take care. I love you, too. I love you almost as much as I love myself. That's what she means. I can't take this anymore. Life is so easy for her. Life is easy and she is easy.
JOB:	(NOT UNDERSTANDING HIM) You're wrong, Elias. It's hard for all of us. (HE PICKS UP THE PHOTOGRAPH AT THE SIDE OF HIS BED) I often look at this photograph. I don't remember what it was like before father left for the struggle. (HE LAUGHS) That sounds stupid. How could I remember? I wasn't born then. But I've listened to mama's stories. We need a man here don't we? (HE RUSHES ON, WORRIED THAT HE HAS INSULTED ELIAS) ... not that you aren't a man, Elias. But we need a man here bringing money every month, don't we? And someone to suggest the right way to go.

257

ELIAS:	(LIFTING HIS HEAD FROM HIS HANDS WITH A SIGH) I'm not a man because I don't bring money home every month. Michael's not a man because he's not here to guide us. You're not a man because you're too young to know. You're right. We need something ... but I don't know what it is ... except, p'raps, my guitar.
	(AT THE MENTION OF THIS, HE BRIGHTENS AND GOES TO FETCH HIS GUITAR)
	"We need something". That would make a good line for a song. Is there one already? "We need somebody". But that's different.
	(HE PICKS UP THE GUITAR AND STARTS TO STRUM THE STRINGS GENTLY, TRYING OUT THE LINE "WE NEED SO-METHING" IN A VARIETY OF WAYS AT THIS MOMENT THE DOOR OPENS AND MARTHA ENTERS THE ROOM SLOWLY, WITH A LARGE BAG AND SOME SHOPPING.)
MARTHA:	Why is it that every night I come home you are sitting there crying over your guitar and the school books have open arms crying for your attention?
ELIAS:	Ask Job, mama, I was working earlier. I've just started three minutes ago. We were trying to cheer ourselves up.
MARTHA:	(BRISKLY NOW) And why do you need to cheer yourselves up? We should be thankful that the Lord looks after us like he does.
JOB:	(AGAIN, NOT REALLY UNDERSTANDING) We got depressed, mama, 'cause we were talking that if father were here he ... would look after us. If he hadn't gone away for the struggle ...
MARTHA:	(INTERRUPTING HIM WITH A HARD TONE IN HER VOICE) And what is more important to God? That your father stay here to keep you cheerful? Or that he goes away to help his country?
ELIAS:	We weren't discussing what was important for God, mama. Job was depressed 'cause Becky's gone out tonight.
MARTHA:	That's no reason to get downhearted, Job. Be thankful that your sister is a good girl, studying hard with her friend to improve herself in order to help you. She's trying to get good marks like Aina.
ELIAS:	(STIFLING A SARCASTIC LAUGH) Ya, she'll get good marks, alright. She'll really hit the target.
MARTHA:	(MOVING TO THE BACK, BEHIND THE TABLE, TO UNPACK THE GROCERIES) I don't know what is wrong with you these days, Elias. I wish that Michael would come round and give you a talking. I've tried. You've got six months left before your matric. You do

258

	nothing. You see nothing good in anybody or anything. What are you going to do with your life?
ELIAS:	Maybe I'll join the band. The kids at the club think we're good. Moses thinks that he could get us a gig in Angola ... Luanda.
JOB:	(EXCITEDLY) Maybe you could meet father there, Elias. Take his photograph. Tell him about me. Ask him to visit us, maybe.
MARTHA:	(SHARPLY) Enough of such stupid ideas. Nobody else in my family is going to Angola at this moment. Elias must study, get his examinations and then find a job. The municipality is looking for people for next year. Elias can work and help look after you and Becky. When father comes back, then we can think of fancy ideas.
ELIAS:	Mama, a singing plumber, a singing electrician is a fancy idea. I don't want to work for the municipality. I want to do something that I'm good at.
MARTHA:	I haven't got time to argue through this again tonight. Has the bell gone yet? I must be down at the church by eight o'clock. It's the Women's Community meeting tonight.
ELIAS:	But mama, I have to be down at the club by nine o'clock. The band is on for a couple of hours. Moses has given us the O.K.
MARTHA:	Since when does Moses give the "O.K." for what you do with your time? You ask me ... like Becky does.
ELIAS:	Mama, I've stayed home for the last three Fridays to look after Job because Becky wanted to stay out. It's not fair.
MARTHA:	(BRISTLING AT THE SUGGESTION OF UNFAIRNESS) The good Lord knows that I am always fair to my children. Becky asked; you didn't. Anyway, Becky goes out for a good reason ... to improve herself. You want to go out just to waste your life. You will stay here and that is the last word.
ELIAS:	You don't listen to me, mama. You don't see, that I really try for you. (HE PICKS UP HIS BOOKS) Job can see that the books are all on the table. I was working. Ask Job. I'll stay tonight ... but can I go out tomorrow then? You can see my homework before I go. I'm begging you now, mama.
JOB:	(TRYING TO HELP) It's alright, mama. I'm good on my own. I manage all day. He can go tonight if you say yes. P'raps Janabari can come over and read to me.
MARTHA:	Janabari has his own family to worry about at night. The man must be spared our worries; he has enough of his own ... without a job

for eleven months. It's not the same at night ... there are bad people around. Elias must stay with you ... there is no question.

(A CHURCH BELL SOUNDS FROM OUTSIDE)

I must rush, else I'll miss the opening prayers. Do your homework Elias. Teach Job a little reading. Read your bibles. I will be home by half past ten. If your homework looks good, we will talk again about tomorrow night. That's what your father would say to you. Now listen to me.

ELIAS: Yes, mama. I listen to you ... always. I will stay with Job. I will do my homework. I will come to walk with you at half-past ten. And I will ask again about tomorrow night.

MARTHA: Now you speak like Michael. You are a good boy ... you have only lost the way. Do the Lord's will and your prayers will be answered.

ELIAS: I hope so, mama. Maybe the Lord is just a little deaf lately.

MARTHA: (MOVING TO THE DOOR WITH HER BAG) The Lord will not listen if you scorn and mock, my boy. There is some nice fish that I have brought home tonight. Give some to Job while I'm away. Goodnight, my boys. Pray for your father; pray for your sister and pray for yourselves. The right road is sometimes difficult to find. "I am the way" saith the Lord.

(SHE CLOSES THE DOOR QUIETLY BEHIND HER)

ELIAS: (SAYS NOTHING FOR A MOMENT BUT STRUMS HIS GUITAR WITH HOSTILE FEROCITY. HE STOPS AFTER A MINUTE, WEARY AFTER HIS CUTBURST.)

"I am the way, saith the Lord". Life is so easy for mama, it hurts me. Her church meetings ... her bible and her blinded faith. Why is it so simple for others, Job? She works like a dog for those people all day; every day. ... looking after their children, cleaning their house, doing their dirty work ... all for a miserable pittance.

JOB: What's a "miserable pittance", Elias?

ELIAS: I read it in a book at school. It's one of the few things on the English teacher's vocabulary lists that I can be bothered to remember. It means "very little reward", my brother. Remember it. It means your life and mine. We don't have our bibles, or our fancy dresses and we don't put envelopes in the post every month from the Windhoek Post Office. Very little reward.

JOB: The struggle may be over soon, Elias. Then father will come home again. That would be a good reward for both of us, I think. Do you think that he still looks like this?

ELIAS:	He will look like you want him to look, my brother. I hope you're right. One day, in my brother's dream, our father will come through that door and stand there, looking very handsome, and he will say "Come out, Job. Come out and see the world. Come, Becky, I have seen just the dress to make you look like a beauty queen, but you must study a little first before I buy it. Come, mama, look at all this money. You have no need to get up at dawn another day to take the bus to the job with many hours and little money. (HE LAUGHS BITTERLY) And maybe he will say, "Come Elias, here is a new guitar which I have brought for you from Angola. Learn to play it and I shall show you the way ... the way to success and a happy life." Do you think that's what he will say, Job?
JOB:	(WARMING ENTHUSIASTICALLY TO THE FANTASY) I'm sure that he will say just that, Elias. And he will stay on Friday nights while you go and sing your songs. And maybe, sometimes, he and mama will go and listen to you.
ELIAS:	(TAKING UP HIS GUITAR AGAIN AND GENTLY STRUMMING WHILE JOB FINISHES SPEAKING) I've got an idea for "I need something". What do you think of this?
	(SCENE 1 SLOWLY FADES AS ELIAS STRUMS AND SINGS GENTLY)

End of Scene 1.

SCENE 2

NARRATOR:	Saturday evening, about 5.00 p.m. Elias is sitting at the dining room table, writing a piece of music. His school books are lying on the table. Job is sitting on the bed, having a quick cigarette and listening to his brother humming a new tune.

(MARTHA'S VOICE IS HEARD IN THE BACKGROUND. SHE IS SINGING RELIGIOUS SONGS.)

ELIAS:	(SLIGHTLY IRRITATED. HE SIGHS) Is she ever going to stop? My song keeps turning itself into "Onward Christian Soldiers".
JOB:	Neh. (HE STUBS OUT HIS CIGARETTE)
MARTHA:	Elias, tell Becky she'll have to stay home tonight. I have to go to a meeting at the Gospel Outreach Centre. There's an American Evangelist coming to speak to us ...
ELIAS:	(GRINS AT JOB) Certainly, mama. She's just gone next door to Janabari. I'll tell her as soon as she comes back.

MARTHA: Why must she go round there now? She's only just come back from Aina's. Young people today can't seem to sit still for a second. I wanted to tell her myself but I can't wait any longer.

JOB: Not all young people can't sit still for a second, mama.

MARTHA: (LOOKS ASHAMED AND COMES TO THE BED TO KISS HER SON GOOD-BYE) Of course, I did not mean you, Job. You are a special boy ... chosen by the Lord for a special purpose.

ELIAS: Do you want to look at my homework, mama? Remember you promised to let me play with the band this evening if it was finished.

MARTHA: "Promise" is a strong word, Elias. I said no such thing. Show me.

ELIAS: Look, mama, I have finished all my maths. See how neat it is ... and I don't think that there are any mistakes.

MARTHA: (LOOKS AT THE BOOK BUT IT OBVIOUSLY MAKES LITTLE SENSE TO HER) Yes, well, there certainly seems a great deal of writing there, Job. And it is neat. There are no marks, or smudges to show carelessness. (SHE STOPS TO THINK A MOMENT.) You were a good boy last night. Alright, you may go, because Becky will be staying home. But don't be too late.

ELIAS: (THANKFUL) Thank you, mama. I won't be late.

(SHE LEAVES)

ELIAS: (ROLLS HIS EYES SKYWARDS) Thank you!

(MARTHA CAN BE HEARD SHOUTING OUTSIDE THE DO-OR.)

MARTHA: Becky! you must come home now. You are staying to look after Job tonight. I've got to go to the Gospel Outreach Cantre. There's an American Evangelist coming to speak to us ... There's some nice fish from last night ... you can make it for Job and yourself ...

(BECKY'S AGONISED CRY OF PROTEST IS HEARD, BUT CUT OFF BY MARTHA)

BECKY: But, mama, ... Aina is expecting me to go back so that we can finish ...

MARTHA: No buts...

(A MINUTE LATER BECKY BURSTS INTO THE ROOM, VIO-LENT AND ANGRY.)

BECKY: I don't believe this. I just don't believe this. (SHE STARTS TO MOCK HER MOTHER) I have to go to a Gospel Outreach meeting ... please stay with Job tonight. There's an American Evangelist coming to speak to us ... (TURNS ACCUSINGLY TO ELIAS) It's always me.

ELIAS: (CALMLY PACKING AWAY HIS MUSIC AND GUITAR) I stayed last night. Also, I managed to stay without having a heart attack about it.

BECKY: Oh, shut up! Who asked your opinion anyway? I can feel another lecture coming up.

ELIAS: (TURNING TO JOB AND LAUGHINGLY SHAKING HIS HEAD) She's crazy! She's really crazy. Can you believe it? My sister is crazy. She belongs in one of those special places where the people wear white jackets and tie the arms together. Not dresses like that, Becky. Sorry if your plans of studying at Aina's tonight are now finished.

(HE REACHES FOR HIS JACKET AND PICKS UP HIS GUI-TAR)

BECKY: (SHARPLY) And where are you going?

ELIAS: Mama has given me permission to go to the Club tonight with the band. I won't be late. The fish isn't bad, by the way.

BECKY: (HOLDS HIS ARM AND TRIES TO STOP HIM) You can't go, Elias, please, don't go. Stay with Job tonight and let me go out. I am expected. I promise I'll make it up to you. I'll buy you a book of music for your guitar. I'll do your homework for you next week. Anything you want. Please.

ELIAS: (HE HOLDS HER ARMS AND LOOKS DOWN GENTLY INTO HER FACE) Calm down. It's too late, Becky. Too late for you and too late for me to change things. The boys are expecting me and I let them down yesterday. I feel tonight is important for us, Becky. And you, look at you in that dress. Desperate. Is this how you want to spend the rest of your life? Desperate in a dress which does not keep out the cold? Stay here. Do what mama asks. There are many nights ahead and you have many years. Do this for your brother.

BECKY: (BREAKS DOWN CRYING AGAINST HIS CHEST) You don't understand, Elias. I've got to do it now. Life is important now. I'll never have a comfortable life like Aina unless I get it for myself ...

ELIAS: Becky. Stop comparing yourself to Aina. You will never have her life. Be grateful for the one you have. You're young. You're pretty. Be grateful for that.

JOB: Elias is right, Becky. You look better in that dress than I could possible have dreamed of. I'm sorry. It's all my fault. If I weren't the way I am you could go out with no problems.

263

BECKY:	(PULLS AWAY FROM ELIAS AND LOOKS GUILTY) I am a selfish girl. Job, it's not your fault. Don't say that. (SHE SIGHS) O.K. I'll stay. You go, Elias.
ELIAS:	(LOOKING RELIEVED) I won't be late. Bye, guys. (HE PICKS UP HIS GUITAR) Wish me luck.
JOB:	(ONLY JOB ANSWERS) Bye, Elias. Will you sing the new song tonight?
ELIAS:	(AT THE DOOR) No, not yet. The boys haven't heard it yet. (HE LEAVES)
BECKY:	Where's that fish mama talked about? Are you hungry?
JOB:	Naa. Don't worry about food, Becky. That's all I ever seem to do ... think about the next meal. Show me the dress properly now.
BECKY:	(SLIGHTLY IRRITADED) You've been looking at it for the last ten minutes. It's not special. You should see Aina's clothes, Job. Then you'd really be whistling.
JOB:	Aina couldn't possibly look better than you do, Becky. She's not as pretty as you are.
BECKY:	Have you got one of those cigarettes left that Janabari bought for you? I could use one, now.
JOB:	(REACHES FOR THE PACKET AND LOOKS INSIDE) Oh, Becky, there's just one left. Here, you have it.
BECKY:	Oh, no. I couldn't take your last one. It's bad luck. Here, why don't I rush down to he shop before it closes to buy us a new packet? The shop will be shut soon and it won't be safe for me to be out. We might as well have some fun tonight, not so? If you don't want fish, should I buy some food as well? What do you want? A hamburger?
JOB:	(BRIGHTENING AT THE PROSPECT) Becky, that would be great! Elias says that I shouldn't smoke but I'm not very bad, am I Becky? I love hamburgers ... and we don't have them very often. We have fish all the time.
BECKY:	And if the shop is busy, you won't be cross if I'm a bit late, will you, Job? I'll run all the way, because it's dangerous for a girl to be alone in the dark, but if it's very busy, I might take longer than you think. You won't worry? (SHE BENDS DOWN TO KISS HIM) And if you fall asleep while I'm gone I'll wake you up with a hamburger right under your nose.
JOB:	I won't fall asleep, Becky. I'll stay wide awake until you get back. We'll eat the hamburgers and then I'll teach you the game that

	Janabari taught me. Only we won't play for money ... We'll play for cigarettes.
BECKY:	Alright, little brother. I'll buy a big packet of cigarettes.
	(EXIT BECKY WITH A LOVING WAVE)
	JOB LIES BACK ON HIS PILLOWS. HE WAITS. HE RISES ONCE IN THE BED TO LISTEN, THEN FALLS BACK.
	A KNOCK ON THE DOOR IS HEARD. JOB DOES NOT STIR. THE DOOR OPENS AND A MAN APPEARS. HE STOPS IN THE DOORWAY AND LOOKS CAREFULLY AROUND THE ROOM. WHEN JOB STILL DOES NOT MOVE, HE ENTERS THE ROOM CAREFULLY AND CLOSES THE DOOR. HE WALKS TO THE BED AND LOOKS DOWN AT THE SLEEPING BOY.
JOB:	(STIRRING SLOWLY) OPENS HIS EYES AND SEES THE STRANGER. HE MOVES BACK AGAINST THE PILLOWS, LOOKING FRIGHTENED)
	Who ... who are you? Are you one of those bad men mama talks about? Have you come to steal things ... and ... and hurt me?
FATHER:	(SAYS NOTHING, BUT MOVES TOWARDS THE BED AND PICKS UP THE PHOTOGRAPH AND LOOKS AT IT AGAIN)
JOB:	Please don't take that photograph. Take anything else. There's not much. Don't take that.
FATHER:	Who is this on the picture?
JOB:	It's my father. It's of no interest to you. He went away for the struggle. We are waiting for him to come home. Mama says he's working for God and for his country.
FATHER:	You must be pretty proud of him, huh?
JOB:	That's a stupid question. (HE GRABS THE PHOTOGRAPH AND HOLDS IT AGAINST HIM.) Who are you?
FATHER:	Answer me first. You're not Elias, are you? You look young. What's wrong with you? Are you tired or sick?
JOB:	I'm never tired, 'cause I don't use much energy, lying in bed all day, really. I do sleep alot but only 'cause there's not much else to do. It's nice to dream. I really try to dream when I'm asleep. Elias says that's a good thing. He says that he tries to dream, too. I was born funny. I can't walk. Mama says that one day the Lord will help me to walk. But only if I'm good and I'm patient. If I get cross or do bad things then God will punish me by leaving me here.
FATHER:	You're not Elias? What's your mother's name, boy?

JOB:	Do you know Elias? I don't think I should tell you anything until you tell me who you are. What are you doing here?
	(AS HE IS TALKING THE DOOR OPENS AND ELIAS ENTERS, LOOKING TIRED, WITH HIS GUITAR)
	THE TWO MEN LOOK AT EACH OTHER FOR A LONG SILENT MOMENT.
FATHER:	Do you remember who I am, Elias? I've come back.
ELIAS:	(LOOKING CONFUSED) I was four when my father left. He went for the struggle. I don't really remember him. You don't look like the one on the photograph.
JOB:	Elias, I'm glad you're back. This man wanted to take father's photograph but I told him to take anything else.
ELIAS:	What is this? What's going on? Who are you? What are you doing here? Are you trying to frighten Job?
FATHER:	Job? (LOOKS AT THE BOY IN THE BED) Job? I don't remember Job.
ELIAS:	(MOVES TO THE BED, GESTURES HIS FATHER ASIDE INTO THE ARMCHAIR AND SITS ON THE BED) Are you O.K.? Has this guy been bothering you? What's happened?
JOB:	I was waiting for Becky, Elias. She went to get cigarettes. I fell asleep, I think. When I woke up this man was here '... he came and grabbed father's photograph... I got scared ... then you came. I'm glad you're here, Elias. Where's Becky?
ELIAS:	(THROUGH CLENCHED TEETH) I don't know where Becky is, but I'm sure going to find out ... now who are you? (TURNING TO THE MAN)
	(BEFORE THE MAN CAN ANSWER THE DOOR OPENS AGAIN AND MARTHA WALKS IN)
MARTHA:	You!
FATHER:	Yes, Martha. I'm back. Nothing worked out in the end. I made a mistake.
MARTHA:	(STILL STANDING BY THE DOOR) So now you've come back so that we can look after you, I suppose? (TURNING TO ELIAS) Don't you remember your father, Elias?
FATHER:	He doesn't remember me. Where's Becky? and Michael?
JOB:	Becky's just run down to the shop for ... for ... something.
ELIAS:	But the shop was closed hours ago. I'd better go and look for her to see that she's alright.

JOB: Father! Elias said that one day I'd wake up and you would be here. Have you come to stay now, father?

FATHER: (IGNORING THE BOY'S QUESTION) Not much has changed around here, Martha. I see that you have managed well for all these years.

MARTHA: (BITTERLY) We have managed, yes. We have not managed well. As you say, not much around here has changed ... everything is older and a little more worn.

FATHER: That is different. So many religious photographs on the walls. And Job?

MARTHA: (HASTILY) You left before I had a chance to tell you.

FATHER: But I ... I ...

(BEFORE HE CAN FINISH ELIAS AND BECKY ENTER)

Becky! You're a grown girl now. My, but you are beautiful. (HE MOVES OVER TO HUG HER BUT SHE MOVES BACK)

BECKY: After all these years! You have the audacity to come back! What do you want?

FATHER: It was time to come back ... I've come to visit ... I thought ...

BECKY: You thought nothing! Mama, why did he come back?

MARTHA: Becky, it's wicked to be so bitter about the past ... We must look towards the future ...

BECKY: Mama, don't talk to me about the future! We don't need him. Where was he all these years? He left us with nothing, mama. Nothing! Is he staying, mama? Tell me. Is he staying?

MARTHA: (TRYING TO KEEP THE SITUATION CALM) Your father has only just arrived, Becky. Nothing has been said yet. Please don't make things more difficult. Let's sit down calmly and talk.

BECKY: (WITH COLD CONTROLLED ANGER) I am not staying here. There's no room for another person, anyway. I'm going to Aina's. You talk it over, if you want. I don't want to hear.

(SHE BRUSHES PAST ELIAS AND STORMS OUT)

MARTHA: (DESPERATE) It's not safe now, Becky. Come back here and listen to your mama. (TO ELIAS) Go after her, Elias. Make here see sense.

(ELIAS SHRUGS AND THEN LEAVES)

JOB: We haven't managed very well since you left, father. Mama has had many difficulties ...

JOB:	(cont.) And how did it go with the struggle, father? We have worried that life for you has not been safe. Will you tell us about your life in Angola?

End of Scene 2.

Scene 3

NARRATOR:	Sunday evening: the entire family is gathered together. Job is in bed, Elias is sitting on the bed; Father is in the armchair and Becky is sitting at the dining room table. Martha is standing behind the table.
MARTHA:	It would have been better if you hadn't come back. We have really tried to wipe you out of our memories.
FATHER:	Didn't you miss me? I missed you all. There was no alternative.
BECKY:	(JUMPING UP) No alternative? Have you ever considered the pain and suffering we underwent to survive?
FATHER:	Well, Becky, I knew that my family ...
BECKY:	(INTERRUPTING HARSHLY) My family? Ha! Don't waste your breath calling us your family. It is useless and meaningless. All these years mama has had to suffer alone to fill the wide gap you left behind. We're lucky that Michael remembers us always at the end of every month ... otherwise we'd have been feeding out of dustbins. Look at this dress. A gift from the Gospel Outreach Centre. Look at mama. Older than her years. Our struggle has been just as difficult as yours.
FATHER:	There was a good reason to leave you behind ... you were just too young to understand.
MARTHA:	That's enough. What good reason? Maybe it's time they knew a reason. The real reason.
FATHER:	That sounds like a threat, Martha. I've come back now, haven't I? Am I the only one with a secret? Tell me. I have eyes. I have a brain. I have ears. I hear what the sick boy has told me and I don't like it.
ELIAS:	This is going no-where. You both talk in riddles. This is solving nothing.
JOB:	Am I the sick boy he is talking about? What did I say? He only asked about my birthday ... he never sent me anything because he didn't know my birthday.

268

MARTHA: Job, be quiet. These questions are too big for you to understand. Why have you really come back? Has it all gone bad for you and now you come to turn things bad for me as well?

BECKY: I smell the secrets and the small is very bad. You never went to the struggle, did you? You never were a freedom fighter, were you? You just walked out and left us to make your life easier. I know it ... I can tell. You don't look like a man who has been fighting for many years. You don't look as if you've suffered. You don't look like mama.

ELIAS: Shut up, Becky. Why are you causing trouble now? This is not the time for your wild ideas. For God's sake, let mama and ... and ... him sort it out.

FATHER: Why stop her? Why not ask her what else she smells? Well, Becky, if you're so smart, what else do you understand?

BECKY: I understand you've come back here to lean on us ... not lead us. I look at your clothes and understand that you haven't come to save us ... just use us. You don't care about us ... no-one waits for thirteen years before coming home in the middle of the night.

MARTHA: Becky, you understand nothing. Elias is right. You create trouble not understanding.

ELIAS: Everyone is going too far but no-one is finding the way. I do not like the sound of it. It is for mama to solve this family business because if I am not mistaken we are all lost. We must leave them to talk quietly. Becky come for a walk with me.

BECKY: I want to hear the truth. I want to stay. I need to know.

ELIAS: Of course we all need to know. But not like this. Let them talk quietly and than we will come back and hear the truth.

(BECKY AND ELIAS LEAVE)

MARTHA: It is better this way. You must leave before they come back.

JOB: (ANGUISHED) No, mama.

FATHER: Why must I leave? Is it for you only? Because if I stay your secret is no longer safe?

MARTHA: I am at peace now. I have come to terms with my secret and the Lord has forgiven me. I have paid my debts in suffering, in a hard life. I think that you still have debts to pay ... and this is not the way ... to stay here you pay your debts with the suffering of my children. This cannot be.

JOB: Mama, what are you saying? You cannot turn father away like this. We need father.

269

MARTHA: You needed a father thirteen years ago and you have survived without one. Michael needed a father but he had to become one to you, and to Becky and Elias. The need has passed.

FATHER: (ANGRY BECAUSE HE CANNOT FIGHT HER CALM RESOLUTION) Martha, that sick boy needed a father ... Oh yes, but that's not me. Never was, never could be.

JOB: Father, what are you saying?

MARTHA: You are a wicked man to say these things. You were a wicked man when you walked through that door thirteen years ago into the arms of another woman. Without a word, without a tear. Your son was four, your daughter was two. They needed you ... and I needed you. But your needs were different and our needs of little importance.

FATHER: Your faith allows you to talk of wickedness as if right and goodness are yours alone. I walked through that door on January the tenth. That sick boy came into this world on December the fifth, so he tells me. I think that the Lord punished you for that, Martha.

MARTHA: He punished me. He punished me. But now I am forgiven and he helps me. The Lord has shown me the way. And you? If you had found the way why should it point back to this house. There is nothing here for you.

FATHER: I see that now ... a boy who is not mine, a daughter who hates me and a woman who chooses to suffer alone. I will leave before they come back.

MARTHA: And you will leave me with less than you did last time.

(THE FATHER COLLECTS HIS SUITCASE WHICH IS STILL STANDING NEAR THE DOOR – OFF ??:)

FATHER: You always were ... a very hard woman, Martha. You never understood that life could be easier. (HE LEAVES)

MARTHA: (SHE MOVES TO JOB.)

If you could walk with me now, my son, I would ask you to come with me to pray. Will you pray with me, here?

(JOB DOES NOT MOVE AND MAKES NO ANSWER)

Elias and Becky will be coming now. Will you tell them?

(NO ANSWER)

You must do what God tells you, Job. I am going to the Church for a little while ... for help and strength. I have always loved you, my son. And Becky and Elias, they love you too. To know that is to find strength.

(SHE LEAVES QUIETLY AND VISIBLY UPSET)

Scene 4

NARRATOR: Monday morning. Early. Elias is lying asleep in an armchair, still fully dressed. Job is asleep in the bed. Martha is tidying the house. She quietly gets herself organised to leave for work. She puts a hand on Job's head momentarily, takes a long look around the room and then quietly lets herself out.

When she has gone, Elias stirs immediately. He has not really been asleep. He, too, starts packing his schoolbag. He takes out all the schoolbooks and hides these in a cupboard. Then he fills the bag with clothing ... as much as he can pack into the bag. As he closes the bag, Job stirs. He continues to pack up his guitar, even though he knows that Job is awake.

JOB: Elias, is that you?

ELIAS: Yes, it's only me. I did not mean to wake you up.

JOB: I was tired this morning because I could not stop the thinking last night. Is Becky never coming back? That is all that worried me all night. I dreamed that she went far away to a very cold place and I could not follow her.

ELIAS: (SITTING ON THE BED BESIDE HIS BROTHER) You must find a different dream now, my brother. The other dreams, the ones we had before ... they're gone forever. Don't dream of Becky. Your dreams cannot make Becky come back. Perhaps she really wanted to leave ... she just needed a reason to make it seem right.

JOB: What am I going to do if Becky doesn't come back? I miss her already.

ELIAS: Job, you must be strong. This family business has been painful. It has ... caused changes. It may ... cause more. But I can think of one good thing, I think.

JOB: Never. No good things. Only pain.

ELIAS: You're wrong, brother. Don't you see what this must teach us? The dreams, brother. They were wrong dreams. We tried for the dreams that others wanted for us. That perfect world ... it doesn't exist. You must make the dreams for you. That's what Becky has done.

JOB: Elias, I need that perfect world ... I need something to make up for this ... room ... my life. I never wanted other people's dreams. They were all mine.

ELIAS:	I know. I can't explain it easily. Your dreams were wrong ... they didn't work out ... because you needed other people too much. You needed other people to make the dreams work.
JOB:	I only really have other people in the dreams, you see.
ELIAS:	Here. I've got something for you. (HE GOES TO HIS BAG AND TAKES OUT A PHOTOGRAPH)
ELIAS:	I want you to have this photograph. I'd like you to put this on your table instead of the man in the photograph.
JOB:	Elias! You look great ... with your band. So handsome. You look like a real success.
ELIAS:	(QUICKLY) I must be off to school. (HE PICKS UP THE BAG AND HIS GUITAR)
JOB:	Your bag looks heavy today, Elias. There's alot of mathematics homework in that bag? Why are you taking your guitar?
ELIAS:	I might ... I might stay and play with the guys after school today, Job. But I'll come back ... later ... and show you the way, too.
	(HE MOVES TO THE DOOR, THEN REMEMBERS SOMETHING, DROPS HIS BAG AND GUITAR AND RETURNS TO THE BED)
	Mama will need this today. With all the family business I nearly forgot. Here's Michael's cheque. Keep it and give it to mama. One thing. If there's money over tell mama to buy you some school books.
	Bye little brother. Keep the photograph ... I'll be with you all day ... every day. (HE LEAVES)
NARRATOR:	Job studies seriously and slowly takes the frame from the table. He takes out the photograph of Elias's father, tears it slowly into pieces and puts them into the ash-tray. He carefully inserts Elias's photograph and lies in bed looking at it.

End.

DEV VIRAHSAWMY

TANTINE MADOCK

A Play

The Characters:

Tantine Madok: 45 years old.

Vanek: Tantine Madok's son

Jamun: Tantine Madok's neighbour

Police Inspector

Janik: Tantine Madok's daughter

Valmika: Janik's fiancé

Fleki: Vanek's friend

Dalan: Jamun's husband

Scene I

IN TANTINE MADOK'S KITCHEN. SHE IS A 45 YEAR OLD WOMAN. SHE IS
VERY BUSY. WHILE DOING HER HOUSEHOLD CHORES SHE SINGS. HER
25 YEAR OLD SON VANEK COMES IN.

VANEK: Is tea ready? I'm thirsty ... What's the time?

TANTINE MADOK:
Very early, almost noon. What tea do you want my love? Seven
o'clock tea, ten o'clock tea, midday tea or three o'clock tea?

VANEK: Has Fleki come to see me?

TANTINE: Neither Fleki, nor Platab, nor Muraf. Eh! There's a letter for you.

VANEK: What's in it?

TANTINE: Don't know. The postman came early. It's on the table in the other
room ... Don't you want to know what's in it? Maybe it's important
... Maybe there's a job for you.

VANEK: A job! Do you think it's that easy?

TANTINE: Have a look at least!

VANEK: Later. Give me some tea ... What have you cooked for lunch?

TANTINE: Guess! You're good at it.

VANEK: Oh Lord! Don't tire my genius ... You tell me!

TANTINE: Look here Vanek! I've been running about since five o'clock this
morning. If you want to know, see for yourself. Here's your tea.

VANEK: Ma, why ask me to waste my precious energy when you can so easily,
so beautifully tell me ... I bet there's aubergine curry again.

TANTINE: What more do you want? ... Thank God there's at least these precious
aubergines. It's a miraculous plant. Yesterday I sold quite a few ...
There's still enough for us. Eat what we've got.

VANEK: Ma, haven't any of your precious hens laid a teeny-weeny egg? I bet
you've sold every single one of them. You should have kept at least
one for me.

TANTINE: And with what would I buy chicken feed?

VANEK: Heavens! Picking on me again. No consideration for my misery. Do
you think it's all that easy to get a job?

TANTINE: Help me to lift this pail of water. The taps are dry. Luckily I've got
this pailful (VANKE DOES NOT MOVE) That's all we've got for
the whole day ... When will this drought stop!

VANEK: Did you collect some water for my bath?

274

TANTINE:	(SHE LIFTS THE PAIL HERSELF, PUTS IT IN A CORNER OF THE KITCHEN AND PUTS A LID ON IT) Water for your bath! To drink, to cook there isn't enough ... Go to the river.
VANEK:	The river! You're out of your mind, ma! It's polluted water. Do you want my skin to itch all over ... Have you washed my shirt?
TANTINE:	Not yet ... This afternoon if there's water ... Why don't you wash it yourself?
VANEK:	It's woman's work, ma? You don't expect a man to do that.
TANTINE:	Why don't you sell aubergines, clean the chicken coop, tidy the yard ... Is that also woman's work? Why can't you do that?
VANEK:	You won't like it, ma, I know. What will the neighbours say. You sent me to college, I have my higher school certificate. Doing such things will downgrade my status, ruin my standing. Ruining my status means ruining your status. I'm always thinking of you, ma. Your good and loving son is here only to please you and think of your happiness.
TANTINE:	Don't think of me. Think of yourself ... Take your food, then get out of here. I've still a hell of a lot to do. I have to get the order of dalpuri ready. The customer will soon come to collect it.
VANEK:	Ma, last night I dreamed I won the national lottery.
TANTINE:	Last night or this morning?
VANEK:	You're at it again. I'm serious and you think it's a joke. When I win the national lottery ma, you'll no longer have to keep chickens, grow vegetables, sell dalpuri, gato pima or samoosa. I'll give you everything. I'll employ a servant. You'll be my princess. (TRIES TO HUG HER).
TANTINE:	Leave me alone Vanek. I've got work to do ... Have you bought a lottery ticket?
VANEK:	Maybe it won't even be necessary.
TANTINE:	Stop dreaming. You're in my way.
VANEK:	Ma, I'm serious. I've got great plans for us.
TANTINE:	Vanek, what's that you want?
VANEK:	Me, ma? Nothing! That is ... Forget it!
TANTINE:	Well, if there's nothing you want take your food and let me get on with my work. (VANEK GOES TO HELP HIMSELF) Eh Vanek! Don't wipe out the "caraille". Leave some for others.
VANEK:	Others? Who else?
TANTINE:	Me for one.

VANEK:	Don't worry, I'll only take my share ... You're sure there's not an egg to get this stuff down.
TANTINE:	Take a few fresh chillies. That will do.
VANEK:	Hell! Chillies. Think of my delicate stomach. You don't want me to get sick, do you?
TANTINE:	I suppose booze is good for your stomach.
VANEK:	Booze! What booze?
TANTINE:	Last night you were completely drunk again.
VANEK:	Some friends treated me to a few tots. They love me. They help me to forget my sorrows.
TANTINE:	(REMOVES A HUGE POT FROM THE FIRE) Can't they help you find a job?
VANEK:	We're all in the same mess.
TANTINE:	But where the hell do you get the money to buy all that piss?
VANEK:	That's my business! ... When will you people learn to respect us ... This cheap ration rice is disgusting.
TANTINE:	Don't eat it, if you don't feel like it. Nobody's forcing you (SHE STARTS KNEADING FLOUR).
VANEK:	You're right! That shit they sell has an awful after taste ... Isn't there some pickles?
TANTINE:	See if there's some in the cupboard ... I doubt it! Every time you and your friends get drunk you come to me for pickles.
VANEK:	Don't be so mean ... If they come to you, it's because they appreciate your stuff.
TANTINE:	Tell them I don't want them to appreciate it anymore. Anyway I can no longer afford to make pickles. Oil and spices are now too expensive.
VANEK:	But what will you do then with all the "bilainbi" fruits on that tree?
TANTINE:	You just have to eat plain bilainbi when you have a hangover.
VANEK:	Ma, I have an idea ... I think you'll like it. Why don't you specialise in making pickles and selling them. You can make a lot of money in this way.
TANTINE:	Good! Why don't you do it. You've got plenty of time.
VANEK:	Time? Me? Never! Anyway I have no skill. You see what college education has done to your poor little son. He can't even make pickles.
TANTINE:	You're wasting all that food.

VANEK:	I'm not hungry.
TANTINE:	No. Don't throw it away. Put it in the cupboard.
VANEK:	Where's Janik?
TANTINE:	At work.
VANEK:	What day is it today?
TANTINE:	Thursday. Why?
VANEK:	I thought it was Sunday.
TANTINE:	Everyday's Sunday for you.
VANEK:	Ma ... Ma... Haven't you a teeny-weeny ten rupees note to lend me. I'll pay you back tomorrow.
TANTINE:	Where do you think I'll get that ... Pay back ... If only! Do you think I pick money off trees?
VANEK:	Don't be so mean! Always counting rupees and cents ... Hasn't Janik left you some? I need only ten rupees. If you're good to me, this evening, if I'm lucky, I'll give you ten times more back. Cross my heart!
TANTINE:	Janik's money is not your problem. Leave that girl alone. She's getting her things ready for her wedding.
VANEK:	That's what I wanted to tell you. She's exaggerating! New dress, new shoes. Always going out with that boy. What a waste!
TANTINE:	That's not your business. Let her live her life. She works hard. She's not a sponger.
VANEK:	Her business is my business. She's my sister after all. Why is she in such a hurry to get married? What's the fuss? She must realise that her elder brother is unemployed.
TANTINE:	(SILENCE) ... Vanek can you go to the shop to get me a bottle of oil ... There's some money in the box on the cupboard ... I badly need the oil. Hurry up!
VANEK:	(GOES TO THE CUPBOARD, LOOKS INTO THE BOX, WHIST-LES WITH SURPRISE) E, ma... You're rich.
TANTINE:	All right! All right! Take your ten rupees. Hurry up. Get me the oil.
VANEK:	Ma, I've got urgent business to attend to ... Ask Tantine Jamun's son to get you what you need. I really must go ... (TANTINE JAMUN ENTERS. SHE IS ABOUT THIRTY). ... Tantine Jamun, you're a godsend. Is your son home?
JAMUN:	No Vanek, he's at school.

VANEK:	At school! What a waste! He is just being prepared for idleness. Get him out. There's no hope at school.
JAMUN:	Why do you want him?
VANEK:	The old bag needs a bottle of oil. She needs someone to go get it. I'm in a hurry. Important rendez-vous!
JAMUN:	Never mind! I have to do some shopping. I'll get it for you, Tantine Madok.
TANTINE:	You spoil him!
VANEK:	I'll leave you to your intellectual preoccupations. I must push off. Bye. My best regards to Tonton. (HE GOES OUT).
JAMUN:	Tantine Madok, today's Thursday. There's a good Indian film on t.v. ... Our t.v. is not working.
TANTINE:	Come to our home to watch. I'm watching it too. It's such a good film. The end is too sad. Last year, remember we saw it at the pictures. Ayo! When the lights went on again I had to hide my face. I was crying. I was so ashamed to be caught crying by the young ones there. You know them. They lose no chance to tease.
JAMUN:	Same here ... But you know. The young ones were too busy hiding their tears to notice us.
TANTINE:	The film always reminds me of Vanek. I fear he may end up in the same way.
JAMUN:	Tantine! Why worry? It's only a film. In life it is different.
TANTINE:	How can a good boy change in such a way?
JAMUN:	Wrong choice of friends. But can we really blame him?
TANTINE:	Often, they make the wrong choice.
JAMUN:	I don't know. Life is like a fisherman in a rough sea. His boat is rocked about. One tiny mishap and ... The fisherman may well know the sea. Only one tiny mishap and everything is upside down. At times we are just sucked in by a strong current.
TANTINE:	Some are really unlucky.
JAMUN:	Don't know. Maybe there's no such thing as luck. Maybe we get what we deserve. It's tough.
TANTINE:	No, Jamun. There is good luck, there is bad luck.
JAMUN:	Maybe. Sometimes I think we reap what we sow.
TANTINE:	You speak just like Janik. She thinks like you. She believes that I spoil Vanek.
JAMUN:	Janik is very concerned by what is happening to her brother.

278

TANTINE:	I am worried. He has changed so much. He's no longer the same ... He's my only son ... I like to think that when I will be old ... never mind. He lacks seriousness.
JAMUN:	He is young. He'll change. You remember my husband. He went haywire. He has settled down now.
TANTINE:	Vanek is not all that young. He's twenty-five. When I was his age I already had two children.
JAMUN:	Times have changed.
TANTINE:	This one does not want to work. He's a lazy bones. He roams about without a purpose. He looks for food, for booze, for money ... He shows no interest in anything. Remember when he had just left school after his exams. He used to help in the house, do odd jobs. He went to his club, he was active in the village. He played for the local football team ... Now ... Now he is a wreck. He lies idle ... No sense of time ... no sense of date ... He just drinks. He's drunk everynight. Everynight he comes home with his friends ... all drunk ... They play cards, swear, laugh ... I can't say anything. They go to bed late ... get up late ... This is not life.
JAMUN:	Why worry Tantine Madok. The moment he gets a job he likes he'll become another person. He's only going through difficult times.
TANTINE:	This one will not change. A bolt has gone loose inside. What if I find a wife for him? That may help. What do you think?
JAMUN:	I don't know.
TANTINE:	He's taken after his father. They say he was just like this before he married me.
JAMUN:	Did you know that?
TANTINE:	You're nuts. Had I known that I don't think I would have married him.
JAMUN:	There you are! Who in his right mind would give his daughter ... See your lot. He's left you for another. Do you want this to happen to somebody else's daughter?
TANTINE:	Me, I was born under a rotten star. It may not happen to another.
JAMUN:	What he needs is a job he likes ... Then he'll change. See my husband! Who thought he would change? But he has.
TANTINE:	Vanek won't change. He's taken after his father. Always thinking of a good time ... lazy ... doesn't like work ... Just like his father ... Just the same.
JAMUN:	Give me the money. I'll go get the oil.

279

TANTINE:	Just a minute. (SHE TAKES THE BOX). The bastard!
JAMUN:	What's up!
TANTINE:	He's pinched all of it. Ayo Bondié! Oh God! What am I to do with that son of a bitch?
JAMUN:	Never mind! I'll get it for you. You'll pay me later.
TANTINE:	Wait ... There must be some money in my spice box. (SHE OPENS A BOX, RUNS HER FINGERS IN IT AND TAKES OUT SOME CREASED NOTES). I have to hide my money in different odd places. Otherwise there would never be a cent in the house. Take this.
JAMUN:	I'll have your oil sent to you. See you this evening for the film.
TANTINE:	Watch the shopkeeper. He's dishonest!
JAMUN:	Don't worry. I know all his tricks ... Do you badly need the oil?
TANTINE:	I think I can manage. Bring it when you come for the film.
JAMUN:	Salam! (SHE GOES OUT BUT RETURNS IMMEDIATELY).
TANTINE:	Ho! Weren't you going?
JAMUN:	What has gone wrong?
TANTINE:	Where?
JAMUN:	There's a police car in front of your house.
TANTINE:	A police car! Why?
JAMUN:	Don't know. The police inspector is coming.

(A POLICE INSPECTOR COMES IN.)

POLICE INSPECTOR:

	Good day madam. Is this the house of Vanek Vayling?
TANTINE:	Yes. Why?
INSPECTOR:	We need him at the police station. Where's his room? We have instructions to search everywhere.
TANTINE:	Search everywhere! Look here, Sir, what right have you got to come into my house and search everywhere? Where do you think you are?
INSPECTOR:	We have reason to believe ...
TANTINE:	Leave my house at once!
INSPECTOR:	Look here madam! Don't stand in our way. You'll be sorry for it. There'll be trouble for you.
TANTINE:	Don't mind me. My troubles are mine. But you'll not search my house. There's no criminal here. I know my rights.
JAMUN:	Have you a warrant?

280

TANTINE:	Yea, have you a warrant?
INSPECTOR:	There's no need for one.
JAMUN:	The law says you need a warrant to search a house.
INSPECTOR:	OK, OK, ladies. But I'll be back. You'll see! (GOES OUT)
TANTINE:	Eh, Jamun! What's a warrant?
JAMUN:	A paper signed by a magistrate giving the right to the police to search a private house.
TANTINE:	How do you know that?
JAMUN:	When my husband was in his wild days, I learnt many things. Why is the police looking for Vanek?
TANTINE:	Do you think he got drunk and misbehaved?
JAMUN:	Perhaps! You must ask him when he comes back. He must be careful. Misfortune never knocks on the door.
TANTINE:	He's just left. You were here weren't you? He can't possibly have had time to do anything wrong. No. It must be for some other thing. Perhaps they have come to offer him a job in the force.
JAMUN:	A job! Search his room to give him a job? He is suspected of something, I'm sure.
TANTINE:	Suspected! Why?
JAMUN:	At what time did he come back last night?
TANTINE:	He normally comes late.
JAMUN:	Was he drunk?
TANTINE:	He drinks everyday.
JAMUN:	Was he drunk?
TANTINE:	Slightly! ... As usual. He and his friends were quite normal. They sang, laughed, played cards ... as usual.
JAMUN:	Where does the money come from?
TANTINE:	Heaven! You think they use ...
JAMUN:	Use stolen money to drink. Quite possible!
TANTINE:	I don't think so! It may bo money he pinches here in the house. Not money pinched outside. In the house, maybe, not outside. I'm sure my son will never do such a thing ... I'm sure.

Scene II

(EARLY EVENING. STILL IN TANTINE'S KITCHEN. JANIK IS EATING).

TANTINE: But if there's really something against him, what must we do?

JANIK: Let him sort out his own mess. Nobody asked him to do it.

TANTINE: He's your brother, Janik. You're not being fair!

JANIK: Big deal! My brother! Has it ever occurred to him that his stinking bullshit may stick on other's lives.

TANTINE: He's going through a tough time. We must help him.

JANIK: Look here mother, I'm fed up with him. When will he start helping himself.

TANTINE: You're too young to understand.

JANIK: I've had a rough day. All I want is some peace.

TANTINE: Where's Valmika? Why hasn't he come?

JANIK: I don't want to hear his name again.

TANTINE: You've had a row?

JANIK: I don't want to see him again.

TANTINE: What's the matter Janik?

JANIK: Forget it!

TANTINE: Have some curry. Janik you have not touched your rice.

JANIK: I'm not hungry, Mother. I think I'll break my engagement.

TANTINE: What is the matter with all of you? The police is after Vanek, you want to break your engagement.

JANIK: Mother, what will I do with a man who is unable to make any decision. "I must ask my mother". Just like a baby.

TANTINE: Don't be harsh to him. He loves his mother.

JANIK: There's a limit. Breaking off is the best solution.

TANTINE: Ayo Bondié! My house is going topsy-turvy.

JANIK: It is topsy-turvy. A brother who refuses work, spoilt by his mother, a fiancé who is tied to his mother's apron strings. I feel like kicking the hell out of here.

TANTINE: You keep on saying that I pamper him. I pamper you too. I have no favourite.

JANIK: Mother, it's not a question of preferring one to the other. You know that when he left school with his Higher School Certificate he got a job as shop assistant. You told him not to go. You told him he deserved something better. At home he does nothing. You won't allow him to do any menial work. You find it normal that after a week's work I help you in the kitchen, to clean the house. You find it normal that I wash my clothes myself. But your son, this superior being, this prince ... Now you find it strange that he has become a parasite. Mother, can't you see what you've done to him ... Can't you see, mother?

TANTINE: I have always loved you both the same.

JANIK: Mother, you have been wonderful to us. I appreciate it. You've gone out of your way always, to please us. But you have not been able to control him.

TANTINE: No matter what I do, I'm always blamed. I have no one to fall to. If I had a mother to ... No one cares for me.

JANIK: Mother, forget it ... Forgive me ... Let's talk of something else.

TANTINE: Janik, promise me you'll not break your engagement.

JANIK: Mother! That's my life, my business.

TANTINE: See! You do choose your time ... Your brother may go to jail and you're talking of ...

JANIK: Don't you think that a short stay there will definitely help to stabilize that piece of cork. See what happened to Tantine Jamun's husband. That's a good example.

TANTINE: It's not true. You yourself told me that in most cases prison life makes them worse.

JANIK: Oh hell! Do what you want. I have enough to cope with.

TANTINE: A car has stopped. Go see if it's not Valmika's car.

JANIK: I'm going to my room. Tell him I'm not home.

TANTINE: Why do this? If he's come it's because he loves you. Stay here. Greet him. Make it up. (VALMIKA COMES IN)

VALMIKA: Good evening Tantine Madok. Is Vanek in?

JANIK: You've come for him or for me?

VALMIKA: Where's Vanek?

TANTINE: He's out. Not back yet. Anything the matter?

JANIK: Mother, you know what's the matter. He is wanted by the police.

VALMIKA: How do you know?

JANIK: The police came here this morning.

TANTINE: I gave them a piece of my mind. They had no warrant.

VALMIKA: Did you listen to the news last night?

JANIK:	No.
VALMIKA:	There was an attempted hold-up. The police suspects some people ... Vanek is one of them.
TANTINE:	Vanek. They must be crazy. They will not touch my son. I will not let them.
VALMIKA:	Maybe he was not involved. He is only suspected. A friend, a lawyer, gave me the information. He is appearing for one of the suspects. He has told me that the police is looking for Vanek. I must find out where he is, to prevend any rash behaviour.
TANTINE:	What right have they got to suspect my son?
JANIK:	Mother, hold on. Anyone can be a suspect.
TANTINE:	Anyone but not my son.
VALMIKA:	Janik, go ask Tantine Jamun to come keep your mother company while we go out to look for Vanek. (JANIK GOES OUT).
TANTINE:	Is it serious?
VALMIKA:	If there is proof, yes.
VALMIKA:	Valmika, do you honestly believe Vanek can do such a thing?
VALMIKA:	I don't think so ... but you know many good people have been known to get caught in things they never intended to do ... It's difficult to know what goes on in the minds of people.
TANTINE:	Vanek is a good boy. He has passed his Higher School Certificate ... He wouldn't do such a thing.
VALMIKA:	I agree Tantine, I agree. He's not a bad sort. Let's find him first, and then find out ... Can't you remember anything he said before he went?
TANTINE:	No, nothing odd. Nothing special. He was quite normal ... (A GIGGLE). You know the usual Vanek ... Oh yes! He said he had a very important appointment.
VALMIKA:	What appointment?
TANTINE:	He didn't tell me. None of my business he said.
VALMIKA:	Did he mention anything about money?
TANTINE:	He's always after my money. He pinched everything I had in the box up there.
VALMIKA:	So he was badly in need of money then.
TANTINE:	He is always badly in need of money. For his bus fares, his cigarettes, to go to the pictures.
VALMIKA:	Does he drink a lot?

TANTINE:	Why do you ask?
VALMIKA:	If he drinks a lot, he needs a lot of money.
TANTINE:	You see Valmika, he's a good boy. All he needs is a job.
VALMIKA:	I'm not blaming him.
TANTINE:	He's always being blamed. He's not a bad sort I tell you. My family is honest. Take Janik for example ... (JANIK AND JAMUN ENTER)
JANIK:	What about me! Val, let's go look for him. Tantine Jamun will keep mother company. Mother, if anything happens call Tonton Dalan.
VALMIKA:	If he comes back before us, tell him to wait here.
TANTINE:	If the police comes?
VALMIKA:	If the police comes ...
JANIK:	Tell him to go hide at Tantine Jamun's place, to wait there until we come.
VALMIKA:	That's it. Tantine Jamun, is it ok with you?
JAMUN:	Yes. Dalan knows what to do. Eh! Somebody's coming!
TANTINE:	(GOES TO THE DOOR) Who is it? (A VOICE OUTSIDE "IT'S ME TANTINE"). Fleki, it's you! Come in! Come in!
FLEKI:	Where's Vanek?
JANIK:	I thought he was with you?
FLEKI:	I've been looking for him since this morning.
VALMIKA:	So is the police.
FLEKI:	The police? Why?
VALMIKA:	Don't you know? You were together yesterday?
FLEKI:	Man, no problem. We were together, the whole day. Then in the evening we tried that new rum. Man, that's great stuff.
VALMIKA:	You know that the police is looking for you lot.
FLEKI:	The police? Us? No. Not at all, man. We are looking for Vanek, not the police.
TANTINE:	The police came here this morning looking for Vankek.
FLEKI:	Here? For Vankek? Ha! Ha! Tantine, again trying to pull my leg. You won't get me this time.
VALMIKA:	Vanek is one of the suspects.
FLEKI:	Man, suspect for what?
VALMIKA:	Yesterday's hold-up.

FLEKI: All the suspects have been arrested. What has Vanek got to do with all that crap. That's crazy, man, crazy. Vanek, Platab, Muraf and myself spent the whole day together. We've got witnesses. What's you talking about. Shit! False accusation. False and malicious.

TANTINE: I knew all the time he was innocent. I know. I know my son.

JANIK: Mother, don't get carried away please. We must find Vanek first. If he hears of the police looking for him, he may panic and do something stupid.

VALMIKA: You two ladies stay here. Fleki, Janik and myself will go out to look for him. (THEY GO OUT).

TANTINE: See how those bastards torture people!

JAMUN: Never mind dear. It's all over now... Shall we go see our film?

Scene III

(LATE AT NIGHT. TANTINE'S KITCHEN. SHE IS MAKING TEA.)

JANIK: Eleven! He's still not back. We looked everywhere, everywhere we could think of.

TANTINE: Janik, it's very late. Go to bed. You work tomorrow.

VALMIKA: Tantine is right. Have some rest. I'll stay and keep watch.

JANIK: It's o.k. I'm all right.

TANTINE: You want some warm milk?

JANIK: Don't worry, Mother. I'll have some tea like the rest of you.

TANTINE: Don't take tea. It makes you nervous. Then you won't sleep.

FLEKI: Me, man, nothing gets me. Black coffee makes me sleep like a log.

JANIK: Fleki you don't have to wait. Go if you want.

FLEKI: Man, don't mind me. I am a creature of the night. During the day I sleep. I live like a bat.

JAMUN: That's why you are always hanging around on people's fruit trees, especially lichees!

FLEKI: Lichees are God's gift. They are there to be enjoyed by God's children.

VALMIKA: Until the day you drop down like a rotten fruit.

FLEKI: Have you seen a monkey fall from a tree, man? Have you?

TANTINE: (WITH A TRAY FULL OF MUGS) Have your tea. I've already put sugar.

286

JANIK:	How was the film Tantine Jamun?
JAMUN:	Very sad. I've already seen it three times. It's so sad ... Your mother cried.
TANTINE:	So did you.
JANIK:	You're both the same. You love those melodramatic films ... You love to cry, don't you?
VALMIKA:	So does my mother! She needs her regular crying session. (JANIK LOOKS AT HIM SILENTLY ... THEN SMILES LIGHTLY) Jan, I'm sorry. You're right. There's a limit.
FLEKI:	Fuf! It's burning hot ... The tea, I mean.
JAMUN:	You want me to cool it?
FLEKI:	No. Never mind. Blow and bite like a musk-rat! (HE SINGS) ..."When the wind blows"... (HE BLOWS INTO HIS CUP).
JAMUN:	As usual! Blowing his own trumpet.
TANTINE:	Tantine Madok, do you want me to make another round to look for him?
TANTINE:	No, no dear boy. He'll be back soon. I know it.
JANIK:	Val, you've done everything you could. It's getting very late. You have to work tomorrow.
VALMIKA:	No problem. I'm used to going to bed late.
JANIK:	Your mother will worry for nothing. She's on her own.
VALMIKA:	Don't worry, I tell you. She's all right. She likes to be on her own from time to time.
JANIK:	Mother, we have decided to have a room for Val's mother in our new house.
TANTINE:	You are right, children. You are both good children. God will bless your home.
FLEKI:	Can't I have a place in the garage?
JANIK:	There will be a lichee tree. You can hang yourself on it.
FLEKI:	Where do you get money to have a new house built? Have you won the lottery?
TANTINE:	You're just like Vanek. Living in hope. Win a lottery! To get money we must work. Jamun, do you know what he told me this morning? He dreamed that he had won the first prize. I asked him whether he had bought any ticket. Do you know what he said? ... The funny boy! ... He said it was not necessary to buy a lottery ticket to win.
VALMIKA:	When did he say that?

TANTINE:	Today, just before he left.
JANIK:	Val, are we thinking the same thing?
VALMIKA:	I think so.
TANTINE:	What's the matter?
VALMIKA:	Did he say anything else?
TANTINE:	No.
VALMIKA:	What was the police looking for?
TANTINE:	They wanted Vanek.
JAMUN:	They wanted to search his room. I asked them if they had a warrant.
JANIK:	Search his room!
VALMIKA:	Jan, go see if ... you know ... in his room.
TANTINE:	No, don't. He'll be furious if he finds out.
JANIK:	Mother, we just want to see if there's anything there to help us to understand what's happening.
TANTINE:	Don't remove anything. You know what a temper he has.
JANIK:	Don't worry, mother.
VALMIKA:	Fleki, you know him better than us. Please help us.
FLEKI:	Man, there's nothing. Nothing I tell you.
VALMIKA:	Any illegal activity?
FLEKI:	Everything we do is illegal ... but petty things. The do-it-yourself sort of things, you know!
VALMIKA:	Like what?
FLEKI:	What do I know man! Say petty transactions, harmless business, illegal betting. You know, that sort of crap. Nothing serious.
VALMIKA:	What business?
FLEKI:	Travelling by bus without paying the fares, gate crashing here, gate crashing there ... You know.
VALMIKA:	Cannabis?
FLEKI:	We do not smoke. We are not addicts, man. We're clean.
VALMIKA:	Drug pushing?
FLEKI:	Now and then ... You know for a few rupees.
VALMIKA:	That's all?
FLEKI:	Yap!
JAMUN:	They love to borrow permanently a lot of stuff. Last week Fleki wanted to sell me a stolen radio set.

FLEKI:	Not stolen ... smuggled goods.
TANTINE:	I think he is coming. There's someone in the yard ... No, it's not him. It's not his footsteps.
JAMUN:	It's my husband's steps. (DALAN COMES IN)
DALAN:	He's not back yet?
JAMUN:	You left Tifis alone?
DALAN:	He's o.k. He's done his homework and has gone to bed. He's fast asleep ... Any news?
TANTINE:	He's not yet back, Mr. Dalan. Heaven knows what has happened to him.
DALAN:	Stop worrying sister. Nothing has happened. He's young, that's all. Things will get better. I know what I am telling you.
VALMIKA:	Tonton Dalan, what do you think has happened?
DALAN:	Valmika, the unemployed's world is a nightmare. You are surrounded by a huge trap. Each step leads you to it. Then all of a sudden, clap! You're in it ... I was a drug pusher, soft stuff, cannabis ... How did it happen? One day I was terribly hard up. A pal gave me some cannabis to sell. Little by little I sized up the business, got new contacts. Profits grew, appetite grew ... (JANIK RETURNS)
JANIK:	Mother, can't you tell him to clean his den? How can he live in such filth.
TANTINE:	I'm not allowed it.
VALMIKA:	Did you find anything?
JANIK:	Nothing in his room. But on the table in the other room I found this letter – an official letter, not yet opened. Can I open it?
VALMIKA:	Of course. Read it.
JANIK:	(OPENS THE LETTER) He had to appear in court today.
TANTINE:	The letter came only this morning.
VALMIKA:	What's the date on it?
JANIK:	14th September.
VALMIKA:	The letter was written 10 days ago. The post office is really not serious.
JANIK:	Not only the post-office. Very often civil servants make a miserable mess of everything.
VALMIKA:	Now I understand why the police is looking for him. He was summoned to court and didn't go. They wanted to search his room to make sure that he was not hiding there.

DALAN:	All that quickly? He didn't turn up in court at ten and by noon the police was looking for him. That's quick. Too quick if you ask me ... No, there's something else.
JANIK:	What else?
DALAN:	The ghettos are full of snares. You know who conned me? My own wholesale dealer. The bugger!
VALMIKA:	Why?
DALAN:	Time to time, some people must be caught. Always the small fry.
JANIK:	But why?
DALAN:	We all know that drug selling is a very prosperous business. If from time to time no one is arrested and sentenced to a term of imprisonment, the public gets worried, loses faith in the law and the police. But if a few small fry are punished everybody is happy. It's good for society's morale. The big tycoons get peace, business keeps on flourishing ... I fear for Vanek.
JANIK:	It's all so complex!
DALAN:	You're right. Life is not all that easy. You have to be in it to know.
JANIK:	Mother, you are staying up for nothing. Go to rest. Val and myself will wait for him.
TANTINE:	What have we done to deserve this?
JAMUN:	Tantine, these things happen. Nobody's to be blamed. We just have to face it.
TANTINE:	No, Jamun, things cannot happen just like this. Janik is right. I must have spoilt him.
JANIK:	No, mother. It's not true. You did what you thought right.
DALAN:	By trying to do too much we undo everything. Shit! What a life!
JANIK:	I no longer know what's right. What's wrong. At times Vanek irritates me, at times I blame him, at times I feel so sorry for him.
VALMIKA:	Darling, don't be so upset.
FLEKI:	Eh! I've got a brilliant idea. I told you I was brilliant, man. What if I declare myself guilty of the charge ...
DALAN:	Fleki, shut up! It's not time for joking.
FLEKI:	You're too thick to understand. I'm serious. I have many previous offences. I'll go to the Police Station, tell them I'm a drug pusher and that Vanek is innocent ... I dragged him into it. He didn't know what he was doing. They will then have to drop the charge against him.

TANTINE:	No, Fleki. Each one must bear his own cross.
FLEKI:	His cross is mine as well. I really dragged him into it.
VALMIKA:	It's not possible. You'll both be locked up.
JANIK:	Can't a good lawyer get him out. I have my savings.
TANTINE:	It's for your wedding.
VALMIKA:	We'll not need a big wedding. A simple intimate one will do.
JAMUN:	We too can help, not Dalan?
DALAN:	Yes, let's go and see Mr. Malink. He's a good lawyer. I know him well.
TANTINE:	It's him this time, I know his steps. I'm sure he's drunk ... He has the cheek to sing – wait my boy! You lose nothing to wait. (VANEK COMES IN. HE'S CLEARLY MORE THAN TIPSY). Is it a time to come back home? Have you seen your face, you rascal?
VANEK:	Eh! What's wrong with you all? You've been driven off your beds ...
TANTINE:	Aren't you ashamed Vanek?
VANEK:	Ashamed ... Ma. can't you hear the dogs howling. They've eaten my pride ... Mother, mother dear beloved mother, your son is proud to be your son ... Your faces are all pulled down. Cheer up. Is there a funeral? You know what time it is? You beautiful people, God bless you. Sleep well.
FLEKI:	Eh! Pal where have you been? We've been looking for you.
VANEK:	Fleki, keep quiet. You're disturbing my thoughts. Tu m'empêches de rêflechir. That's bad, boy.
VALMIKA:	We've been looking for you all over the place.
VANEK:	Looking for me? Why look for me? I am here. I am there, I am nowhere, I am everywhere. I am on O without a figure. I am the world's bad conscience.
TANTINE:	Stop it Vanek! Be serious for a change!
VANEK:	Ay, ay, Madam. Your wishes are my commands. You want me to drop the anchor. Ay, ay, Sir. I'll drop the anchor ... The sea is rough captain.
JANIK:	The sea is rough for all of us, Vanek. Let us help you...
VANEK:	Jan, you're weeping. Wipe your eyes my angel. There's no cause for sorrow. All's fine.
VALMIKA:	The police is looking for you.

VALMIKA:	I know, sonny boy. I know. I've been duly informed. I have my contacts, you know.
TANTINE:	Why are they looking for you?
VANEK:	Don't worry ... Nothing serious. They wanted to know where I was when those stupid twits tried to rob the bank. These nincompoops! Incompetent idiots!
DALAN:	What did you do?
VANEK:	Tonton Dalan ... You are as experienced as I am. I went to the station, I made a declaration. I have proofs, alibis, and what not. Eh! Fleki ... How are you boy? ... You are my main witness ... Anyway the debutants have all been caught and what more, they have confessed. Eh – Fleki, why gape at me? You've seen a miracle.
TANTINE:	You had us all on tenterhooks. You can't go on like this. You must change.
VANEK:	Change! Why change? Vankek knows what he's doing. Vanek is an irresistible elusive butterfly. I am Fantomas, I am He.
VALMIKA:	I have to go. Goodnight everybody. Goodnight darling.
VANEK:	Goodnight! Goodnight! (BLOWS A KISS TO VALMIKA)
JANIK:	I'll see you to your car, Val.
JAMUN:	We have to go too. See Tantine! You've worried yourself out of your wits for nothing. Vanek will not end up as in the film.
DALAN:	Vanek, believe me boy, you must change course. The shit world holds no promise. There's no future in it.
VANEK:	There's no future for beginners and amateurs. Only professionals succeed.
VALMIKA:	You're right. We'll help you to be a professional.
VANEK:	(LOUD LAUGHTER) You don't understand a shit. Ma, this morning I borrowed thirty rupees from your kitty ...
TANTINE:	Forget it. We'll talk about it tomorrow. We'll start anew, along new lines ... The sea may be rough my son, but together we'll face it ... I love you Vanek. We'll get out of it.
VANEK:	Don't keep on interrupting me! ... Take these 300 rupees. Capital and interests. All bills have been paid. No bad debts. Business can only but flourish.
TANTINE:	Vanek, where did you get that?
VANEK:	I've won the lottery, ma.
TANTINE:	Vaneeeek! Oh God, no! (SHE FAINTS)

JANIK: Ma....!
END.

MOHAMED SHERIFF

THE CROOKS AND THE FOOLS

A Play

Characters:

MAMUDU,   a crook

JENNEH,   his sister

FLOMO &

SAKPA,   friends of Mamudu

BLINDMAN,   a beggar

A POLICE OFFICER

A TAXI DRIVER

A LITTLE GIRL

OLD WOMAN,   Musa's grandmother

MAMMY,   daughter of old woman

MUSA,   a young boy, mammy's son

THE LITTLE GIRL'S MOTHER

A CROWD NEAR THE BLIND MAN'S HOUSE

ACT I

JENNEH:	Mamudu, what's wrong with you this morning. You do not look happy.
MAMUDU:	My sister, I am not. I owe two of my friends some money. I don't have one cent to pay them back now. They are both coming here to collect their money at eight o'clock this morning; it's already twenty past seven. I looked through the window a few minutes ago, and I saw the two of them keeping watch at the gate. I am sure they've been there since five o'clock this morning. And that is the only way out of the yard. Those bastards are taking no chance. If I could send them away without any trouble, then I would go out and hustle. I am sure that by the end of the day, I shall have made enough money to pay them back.
JENNEH:	Mamudu, why can't you find a job and stop this practice of yours.
MAMUDU:	Jenneh, let's not go over that again. You know that it's not easy to get a job in Monrovia.
JENNEH:	But you should keep on trying, Mamudu. The life you live now is not decent for any respectable person.
MAMUDU:	I know, Jenneh; but while I am trying very hard to get a job, what shall we live on? Fresh air and water? Besides, even if I get a job, will the salary be enough for us to live on?
JENNEH:	We shall manage, Mamudu. I shall supplement what you would earn with whatever I get from selling food at the market place at week-ends. And even if you have no job, Mamudu, this does not justify your way of earning a living.
MAMUDU:	Jenneh, since mother died five years ago and joined father in the grave, you've never been sent home from school even once for failing to pay your school fees; you've never asked me for anything that I could not provide; and I have never failed to pay your hospital bills or to buy your medicines. My dear little sister, do I need any more justification? Don't you realise that all what I am doing is for your sake? You are to take your West African School Certificate examination this year. Where am I to get money to pay your fees? Another thing, Jenneh, you've accepted the way I've been providing for you all these years without any question. Why have you started objecting lately?
JENNEH:	Mamudu, when our parents died, I was only a little girl, I took everything you did as the right thing; I felt you were earning your

living just like any other honest person. But now I can see that this is not what you're doing. Brother, I know you are doing all this for my sake. I know you love me greatly and want me to live a happy and comfortable life. For the past five years, you've been sleeping on this mat on the floor and allowed me to sleep on the only bed we have.

You're always in debts because of me, and making life comfortable for me, you're forced to say things that are not true, to make promises you cannot keep.

MAMUDU: I can't help it, Jenneh. This is a dog eat dog world – kill or be killed. And I do not regret anything – as long as you are happy, Jenneh. I promised mother that I would take good care of you.

JENNEH: But you don't have to ruin your life, your selfrespect, just to please me. People speak ill of you everywhere. I can't bear to hear people making unpleasant comments about my brother.

MAMUDU: Jenneh, I have seen girls, younger than you, ruin their lives, prostitute themselves because they have nobody to support them. I would rather be called a crook or a thief than have people label you a prostitute. It's a quarter to eight now, Jenneh; since I have no way of escaping, I might as well go out there and meet those two.

JENNEH: Okay, Mamudu, take care. We'll take more on this later. (GOES TOWARD THE DOOR.)

Mamudu, just one question: suppose you were to get into trouble and go to jail, what would happen to me? Who would take care of me?

MAMUDU: (AFTER A PAUSE) Jenneh, to tell you the truth, it has never occurred to me that I might get into trouble and go to jail. But now that you've told me, I shall think about that seriously.

JENNEH: Please, do brother.

A KNOCK COMES ON THE DOOR

MAMUDU: Either one of both of them are here! I'll lie down on the bed and put a blanket over me as if I were ill.

JENNEH: None of them will believe you.
(THE KNOCK IS REPEATED)

MAMUDU: I know, but I must give them some excuse. Go and open the door.

JENNEH OPENS THE DOOR AND FLOMO ENTERS.

JENNEH: Hello, may I help you.

296

FLOMO:	Is Mamudu in? Even if you were dead Mamudu, you would cough up my money. I have no patience for your tricks today. Mamudu! Mamudu!
JENNEH:	My dear, act like a gentleman. Why are you behaving like this? You walked in here without a word of greeting to anybody and now you begin to shout like someone who has seen an evil spirit. What's all the fuss about.
MAMUDU:	(MOANS) Don't mind the bushman, Jenneh. That's the only way he has been taught to behave.
FLOMO:	You call me a bushman with my ten dollars on you? Vomit it before I turn this place into hell for you.
MAMUDU:	Don't point your dirty fingers at my face. You ought to be ashamed of yourself, playing the fool for only ten dollars.
FLOMO:	My people come and hear what the ungrateful dog is saying. For only ten dollars? When my ten dollars saved you from being dumped into a cell, it was not "only ten dollars" then, was it? And now you open that goal post of yours which people take for a mouth to tell me that I should be ashamed of asking for what is mine? (A KNOCK)
MAMUDU:	My good friend, do you expect me to run all over this city looking for you to give you your money? What did we arrange yesterday? (KNOCK, KNOCK, KNOCK)
FLOMO:	That you should go to my house with my money at ten o'clock, that if you failed to do so I should come here this morning and collect it. And that's exactly what I have done. (KNOCK, KNOCK, KNOCK)
MAMUDU:	And what do you think I did last night? When I found your house in darkness, what do you think I should have done? Sat down there and waited until you turned up? (KNOCK, KNOCK, KNOCK)
FLOMO:	Mamudu, you are the biggest liar in the whole world. Look here, I'm not going to waste my breath on you. You didn't meet me last night; I agree with you. Now that I am here, can I have my money?
MAMUDU:	Last night, I had trouble with some policemen while I was returning home from your place. I had to give them your ten dollars before they released me. I have no money now, but I promise you faithfully that you will get your money at ten tonight.

297

FLOMO:	Mamudu, I'm not a stupid fool. I'll get my money. You never went to my house yesterday. (VIOLENT POUNDING ON THE FRONT DOOR)
MAMUDU:	You'll get your money; there is no doubt about this. But it will be only tonight. Jenneh open the door; there is someone knocking.
FLOMO:	I'm leaving you now, Mamudu, but I'll be back. And when I return I will not be alone. If you are not locked up in a cell today, don't you ever call me Flomo again (GOES OFF, STAMPING HIS FEET)
JENNEH:	Mamudu, there is noone at the door.
SAKPA:	I am here. Nobody opened the front door for me, so I came in through the back door.
JENNEH:	But you are not supposed to do that.
SAKPA:	I'm sorry young girl, but your brother owes me something, and I just can't go back without it. I told my wife before I left home to put a pot of water on the fire, and I must return with rice and other ingredients that make this hard life of ours a bit bearable. My children ate uncooked cassava for breakfast yesterday, and they kept on drinking water for the rest of the day. Therefore I'm not going back without my money.
MAMUDU:	I'm sorry to hear that Sakpa. Since we parted yesterday, I have not been myself. It seems as if it is malaria. I was unable to go out and find any money, but I promise you that you'll get your money at 2 p.m. today.
SAKPA:	You cheap crook, you good-for-nothing animal, you son of a worthless mother ...
JENNEH:	How dare you turn your foul mouth on my mother. You ill-bred creature.
MAMUDU:	You unruly thing, do you have the audacity to abuse my mother because I owe you ten dollars? I, who picked you up from the gutter when you did not know your way about this city?
SAKPA:	I meant every word I said.
MAMUDU:	Sakpa, get out of my house! you bastard!
SAKPA:	Send me out of your house and call me a bastard with my money in your belly? (SLAPS MAMUDU) I'll beat you up and drag you to the police station. (SLAPS HIM AGAIN) Give me my money. (SLAP)
JENNEH:	(SLAPS SAKPA ON HIS BACK) How dare you attack my brother. Take that (SLAPS HIM AGAIN) Mmm!

298

MAMUDU:	Stop it, stop it, Sakpa; I don't want to fight, stop!
	(JENNEH CONTINUES TO HIT SAKPA REPEATEDLY, SAYING "LEAVE MY BROTHER")
SAKPA:	(HOLDS HER HANDS AND THEY STRUGGLE, JENNEH SAYING "LEAVE MY HANDS" REPEATEDLY IN A BREATHLESS TONE)
	Look here, young girl, I didn't want to do this, but I must give you some good slaps to get you off my back (SLAPS HER; SHE SCREAMS.)
MAMUDU:	(HIS VOICE RAISED IN ANGER) Take your dirty hands off her before I kill you. You wait till I come back (RUNS OFF AND RETURNS IN A VERY SHORT WHILE) Take your dirty hands off her and get out before I cut you with this knife. You'll get your money at two. Get out! or I'll kill you!
JENNEH:	No, Mamudu, don't do that! I have ten dollars; I'll give it to him. Give me the knife. (GOES OFF FOR A SHORT WHILE AND RETURNS WITH SOME COINS JINGLING IN HER HAND) Here, take your money and get out!
SAKPA:	I'm leaving. Mamudu, you know that for all your cunning, your sister is far more sensible than you are.

JENNEH AND MAMUDU: Get out!

SAKPA GOES OUT LAUGHING AND SLAMMING THE DOOR BEHIND HIM WITH A LOUD BANG.

JENNEH:	Mamudu, this is what I was saying. What a life!
MAMUDU:	My sister, in this jungle, survival is the word. I know those very well. No amount of smooth talk would have sent them away. You shouldn't have given him your money. I know that was about all your capital in your small business.
JENNEH:	Don't worry, brother, I still have some more foodstuff for sale. I didn't want you to hurt him and get yourself involved with the police.
	Mamudu, please stay home and don't get yourself into anymore debts and trouble. I'm certain that by the end of the day, I shall have made enough money from selling cassava so that you can pay Flomo his money.
MAMUDU:	Okay Jenneh, I'll just call on my friend down the road. I won't be long.
JENNEH:	Please, Mamudu, take care. Look for a job. We shall survive by the power of the Almighty.

MAMUDU:	InShaAllah. So see you later. (GOES OFF)
JENNEH:	Oh Mamudu, now I can see clearly why mother used to call you Wolf. Yet he loves me so dearly. And I love him too – very much. O Allah, please save my brother from the Satan and guide him to the right path.

SCENE II

A STREET LEADING TO A BEACH. THE MURMUR OF THE WAVES IN THE BACKGROUND

MAMUDU (TO HIMSELF):

I've been on the streets now for over two hours without making a cent. Jenneh has made me nervous with that talk about going to jail. May Allah protect us from that type of misfortune. But if I quit this game, how are we going to survive? Nobody gives you a cent for nothing these days. Relatives? They will tell you that the load they carry in one day is heavier than all what you've carried on your little head since you were born. Find a job, she said. Job? Even the degree-holders with so-called good jobs are complaining of hard times. I am only a high school graduate. What would any salary do for me? And even our big men take here and there. Of course, they steal differently from the way I steal. But stealing is stealing. Whether it is done in a big office or in a small street, like this one, does not matter; we're all thieves, stealing to satisfy our selfish desires. If you are caught – jail! Jail? Protect me, o God.

LITTLE GIRL:	Kool-aid, Ice-cream Kool-aid. Come and wet your throat and satisfy your thirst with ice-cream kool-aid. If you don't buy, you will remain hot. Buy and be cool. It's only ten cents. If it is not iced, don't buy.
MAMUDU:	Here comes my bread and butter, my breakfast. I'll use formula A5 for this one. She's only a little girl – about ten. (CALLS HER) Em ... em ... em ..., I'm thirsty. Come here, little girl. What's the cost of your icecream kool-aid?
LITTLE GIRL:	Only ten cents, Sir.
MAMUDU:	Only? You girls know how to talk, eh? Let me see if I have small change; I'm very thirsty. Oh, too bad. I've only five-dollar coins. Do you have change for that amount?
LITTLE GIRL:	No, I have sold only twenty cents worth of icecrem since I left home. How much do you want?

MAMUDU:	Fifty cents' worth.
LITTLE GIRL:	Oh, I don't have change for that amount and I don't know where I can find change around here.
MAMUDU:	Hmm, take the money and go down to the beach; the fish mengers will change it for you.
LITTLE GIRL:	Okay, I'll do that. It seems as if today will be my lucky day. Yesterday was a bad day for me.
MAMUDU:	Look here, don't keep me waiting. I'm in a hurry.
LITTLE GIRL:	I won't be long, Sir. I'll be back here in the time it will take you to shut your eyes and open it again.
MAMUDU:	You just go ahead and stop talking like a parrot (GIRL GIGGLES AS SHE GOES AWAY) Ah say, small girl, come back here!
LITTLE GIRL:	What is it, Sir?
MAMUDU:	I don't trust you with my five dollars. You children born in Monrovia are very cunning and dishonest. Even a child born yesterday could wash a toothless, grey-haired Oldman's face with pepper and water without him knowing it until it is too late.
LITTLE GIRL:	But what will I do with your five dollars? I have about fifteen dollars worth of ice-cream in that cooler. And the cooler itself is worth over five times the value of your money.
MAMUDU:	Little girl, your mouth has grown older than your little self. Let your mouth rest a little. And put down the cooler. What will I do with fifteen dollars worth of ice-cream? Eat it and get married to diarrhoea?
LITTLE GIRL:	But errr ... it's ... it's ... not that I don't want t-t-t-to leave it but if anything happens, my mother ...
MAMUDU:	Look here, let me have my money; you are wasting my time. Hurry up! If you do not want to do business, you let me know. You'll make a poor business woman when you grow up. And that would be a pity, for you are such an intelligent and pretty little girl.
LITTLE GIRL:	Okay, let me put it down. But please take care of it, sir. Yesterday, after sales, the money I took home was two dollars and fifteen cents short of what I should haven taken home. My mother beat me and beat me until I thought I was going to die. So she threatened that if I lost even ten cents today, she would remove the skin from my body just as the muslims do to the sheep during pray day.
MAMUDU:	Don't worry, small girl; I'll sit right beside it on this rock, and I'll watch it until you come back. Now go. No, no, no be careful!

Don't run lest you fall down. (A PAUSE AS THE GIRL GOES AWAY) What a sharp little girl. Her eyes are open. But not wide enough to see through the tricks of Mamudu – the master of the game. Hm. Strange, though, that I should feel a bit guilty about what I'm going to do just because of what she said her mother did to her yesterday. I'm beginning to get soft, if I begin to feel sorry for this girl, where will I get Flomo's money. He has threatened to bring in the police. This girl's family is probably having no difficulty in cracking the hard nuts of life. From what I've learnt from her, her mother is in business, and her father ... ? No doubt, he is employed in a well paid job. So they live well; they are not merely surviving hardship like us. And that woman has no right to send such a small girl to sell in the streets. There comes a small boy. SSSS! sss! small boy! Yes, you. Please come. Here, take the ten cents. I want you to take this cooler to the car road for me.

BOY:	What part of the car road.
MAMUDU:	Right there, at the junction. Let me put in on your head. Mhm! Is it alright? Good. Now go ahead. I'll be right behind you. Go! Go on! Walk fast. Good. Don't turn round! Just go ahead I'm right behind you. Keep on moving. (THE SOUND OF MOVING CARS CAN BE HEARD NOW AS THEY GET NEAR THE MAIN ROAD) Okay, set it down here on the side walk and go away, yes, there!
LITTLE GIRL:	(FROM A DISTANCE, HER VOICE IS COMING FAINTLY.) Thief, thief! please stop him! He's a thief!
MAMUDU:	What! so soon? What shall I do now? Leave everything and run away? No, not yet. Here comes a taxi; Taxi! Taxi! Good! (SOME PEOPLE HAVE JOINED THE GIRL IN RAISING THE ALARM. THE CRY OF THIEF! THIEF! IS GETTING LOUDER.) Driver, please take me to Bannersville; I have a cooler with me; I'll give you a buck. Good. (THE CAR DOOR OPENS, A PAUSE, SLAMS SHUT.) Let's go (THE CAR ROARS OFF) Hmm! Alhamdullillah Thanks to God. That was a narrow one.
TAXI DRIVER:	What did you say?
MAMUDU:	I was only thinking aloud (CRY OFF "THIEF, THIEF" STILL IN THE AIR)
TAXI DRIVER:	Oh, I see. Domestic problems, eh? I wonder what that noise is about.
MAMUDU:	Oh, that? Just a little boy. They say he stole some fish down at the beach.

TAXI DRIVER: (LAUGH) Must have been hungry. (THEY BOTH LAUGH.)

SCENE III

THE BACK YARD OF A HOUSE

AN OLD WOMAN, A YOUNG LADY AND A SMALL BOY ARE IN THE YARD.

MAMUDU: (STANDING AT GATE OF THE YARD) This is the way to earn quick money. I invested about six dollars on operation Ice-cream Kool-aid and sold it for twenty-six dollars – a profit of twenty. This is not bad for a start and its not yet twelve o'clock. I'll now go for the main course. But I'll have to be very alert; I almost underrated that tiny mosquito of a girl. But where will I start ?? Em, em ... And come to think of it, why not here? This backyard is very filthy, and from what I see, those people in there are just the right type to apply formula 3. (HE PUSHES THE GATE) Good morning to this house (MAKES THE TONE OF HIS VOICE SOUND FORMAL) Good morning ...

OLD WOMAN: Morning my son. Are you well?

YOUNG LADY: Morning Sir. How's your body.

MAMUDU: I thank God.

OLD WOMAN: Yes, papa, what's the matter?

MAMUDU: Give me a minute, Oldlady; let me take out my file from my bag. No, no, no young lady, don't touch anything. Put down that container with urine and stool in it, and don't touch that dustbin. Leave everything! You people have been warned before. I need not introduce myself anymore. I take it you know that I'm a sanitary inspector. Now tell me who is the owner of this house?

MUSA: But, Mister, when have you people started inspecting houses on Saturdays?

MAMUDU: What did you say? Look here, I'm doing the questioning, not you. Besides, I am talking to your elders, so shut up and listen.

MUSA: All I'm saying is that I've never seen sanitary inspectors going to people's houses on Saturdays.

MAMUDU: Old woman, will you please tell your son to keep quiet? Or else I'll walk out of this place, and when I return it's not going to be easy for you.

OLD WOMAN:	Musa, shut up and go away, or I'll beat you with this stick. Don't mind him son; he's always like that, opening his big mouth when nobody wants him to do so.
MUSA:	Very good, Gramma. Very good. You'll never learn. This is what brother Abraham always tells you about. As soon as you see these people with pen and paper and neck-tie, you become so confused and frightened that you're ready even to kill your first born to please them.
OLD WOMAN:	See what I'm saying? He's a foolish boy. Hear what he says. Even a cow has better sense than you.
MAMUDU:	Oldma, I have come neither to be abused by a little maggot nor to be kept here the whole day by you.
OLD WOMAN:	(THWACKS MUSA WITH A WOODEN SPOON) My son, I don't think we need to prolong this talk. We've done wrong; there is no doubt about that – the yard is filthy. All we can do now is to ask for pardon. Of course, we shall attend to your pains – the time you've taken to come here.
MAMUDU:	No, no, no, oldma, don't get this whole thing wrong, I'm not here for money; I'm only doing my duty. I will not take money from you. Although this is my first time meeting you, I feel I've known you for years, for I can see my old mother in you.
OLD WOMAN:	May God bless you for what you've said. My son is just your age. As soon as I saw you, I knew you came from a good home. What is your name child?
MAMUDU:	I'm Mathew Samuels. But good ma, let's not waste time; I have to cover this whole area. Will you answer these questions, please? Who owns this house? Don't snatch my pen from my hands like that; I have to write.
OLD WOMAN:	No son, you can't do that to your mother. Let me keep the pen until you're ready to leave. Almighty Allah will reward you for your kindness to me. Oh! son, how can you do that? I've just called on the Almighty God to bless you, yet you've snatched the pen from my hand again?
MAMUDU:	Don't worry, Ma. This is all in the line of duty – to keep the records straight. Everything will be alright.
YOUNG LADY:	Mister, you say everything will be alright, yet you're busy writing? I haven't said anything up to this point because I felt that my oldmother would be able to persuade you.
OLD WOMAN:	Hmmm! My child, don't do this to us. Don't let an old lady down.

MAMUDU:	Who owns the house, please? I've told you not to worry.
OLD WOMAN:	I'm the owner.
MAMUDU:	Name? Your name.
OLD WOMAN:	Mabendu Kama-ra.
MAMUDU:	Who is responsible for the accumulation of rubbish over there?
OLD WOMAN:	I am.
MAMUDU:	Hmmm, so you are responsible for everything?
OLD WOMAN:	Yes, son, everything.
MAMUDU:	You know that the fine is at the Pulic Health Department, not so?
YOUNG LADY:	I thought you said everything would be alright?
MAMUDU:	That was what I said, but I want you to know how much offenders pay at the office so that, if it is possible for me to help you, you will know the real value of what I shall have done for you.
OLD WOMAN:	May the Almighty bless you. As soon is I saw you I knew you were a good child. Mammy, go inside and bring my bag. My child, I will attend to your pains. It's not much, but that's all your old mother can afford now. May God bless you my child, May God bless you. I wish my son were here so that you could meet him. Just like you. Anyway, he'll be back soon. He went to one of their club meetings, and he told me he wouldn't stay long.
MAMUDU:	He'll be back soon? (ALARM IN HIS VOICE) I'd like very much to meet him, but I'm in a hurry now. I'll definitely come back here again. What is keeping this young lady in the house? I'm in a hurry.
OLD WOMAN:	Mammy, hurry up, you tortoise; the inspector wants to go.
MAMMY:	I'm coming, Mama. The bag was not where you usually keep it. Here it is.
OLD WOMAN:	Give it to me. Oh, where did I put my money? Ah, here it is. Please take this, my son. Don't forget to visit us, anytime.
MAMUDU:	Thank you, oldma, I'll surely come.
OLD WOMAN:	(RAISING HER VOICE AS HE GOES AWAY) You're always welcome. (A PAUSE). Chai! He has taken ten dollars from me. Thanks to you, Mammy. Its seems as if dust blocked your ears. Since early this morning I have been telling this Mammy girl to get Musa and the other children to throw the rubbish away.

MAMMY:	I've been after them since morning; Musa didn't even look at me. What else must I do.
OLD WOMAN:	You don't know what to do? Can't you whip Musa?
MAMMY:	Whip him? So that he'll whip me too?
MUSA:	Listen to what she says. That's now you spoil people's name. Did you tell me anything this morning about throwing away the rubbish? A big woman like you telling lies to her own son!
OLD WOMAN:	Shut up, both of you: between you, you've cost me ten dollars. Ten dollars! That's what that child of hell took from me, and that was all the money we had in the house.
MUSA:	That's good for you, Grandma, since you'll never learn. I'm happy! I'm going after that man, Grandma; I'll find out where he lives.
OLD WOMAN:	Go and bring trouble on yourself, you hear? If I look at you then, don't call me Mabendu. You good-for-nothing boy.
MUSA:	I don't care; I'm going after him!

SCENE IV

A STREET WITH HEAVY TRAFFIC

NOISE OF MOVING VEHICLES IN THE BACKGROUND.

MAMUDU:	(WHISTLING A CHEERFUL TUNE): By God, I've made good business today. Now I have thirty-six dollars and ten cents on me, more than enough to pay that fool Flomo three times over. And it's just two o'clock. Yet my darling sister, Jenneh, says I should quit this noble profession. Anyway, we shall discuss that later. The market place is about a hundred yards from here, why not call at her stall so that we can go home together. We'll buy some cassava, plantain and fish and she'll prepare a delicious dish for us. But wait, here comes a blind beggar. Am I to leave him alone and go straight to my sister? Or should I shoot the game and add to my ever increasing stock. If I leave him alone, won't I be kicking a blessing with my left foot? I've heard that these people amass enough wealth to send them on pilgrimage to Mecca, yet they pay no income tax. Has the government budget ever included income tax for beggars? Let me collect the tax for the government. Hey, Mamudu. But the Old folks say: That thing which goat enjoys most is what brings her diarrhoea. Well, I've never experienced it.

BLINDMAN:	(HIS WALKING STICK, WHOSE BASE IS CAPPED WITH METAL, MAKES HEAVY NOISE ON THE PAVEMENT AS HE WALKS):
	Fisabidillah, Fisabillah. I beg in the name of Allah and the prophet. Give freely and you shall receive. Nothing is too big, nothing is too small.
MAMUDU:	Oldman, have ten cents.
BLINDMAN:	Albarrkah. May Allah bless. May you have a long life.
MAMUDU:	Amina.
BLINDMAN:	Goodhealth ...
MAMUDU:	Amina
BLINDMAN:	Riches
MAMUDU:	Ameeena.
BLINDMAN:	May you follow the right path and the footsteps of the holy prophet ...
MAMUDU & BLINDMAN:	
	May the peace and blessing of Allah be with him...
BLINDMAN:	And his followers, so that you may go to heaven.
MAMUDU:	Ameena. But excuse me Oldman, don't you have anybody to accompany you home? (PAUSE)
	Don't you stay with anybody at home? (PAUSE) I only want to help you, Oldman. Can't one of your children or your wife accompany you whenever you go out? Old man, I only want to help you – if you don't mind. I'll accompany you to your house.
BLINDMAN:	Son I can take care of myself. I've been doing this all by myself for the last fifty years. Thank you for the offer son; may Allah bless you.
MAMUDU:	Never mind, Oldman, I'll still accompany you.
BLINDMAN:	Son, I thank you! I'm staying just round the corner near to the market place. Don't bother ...
MAMUDU:	Ah, just as well. That's exactly where I'm going – to see my younger sister. You see, Sir, my father died when I was only a little child and I never had the opportunity to receive blessings from him. Therefore whenever I get an opportunity to find some blessing, I never let is slip from me.
BLINDMAN:	Then let's go, son. May Allah bless you.
	THEY WALK IN SILENCE EXCEPT FOR THE SCRUND OF THE BLINDMAN'S STICK ON THE PAVEMENT.

THE LITTLE GIRL AND HER MOTHER A LITTLE BEHIND
THE BLIND BEGGAR AND MAMUDU.

MOTHER: Oh baby love, I don't know what sort of child you're. Almost everyday you go out to sell for me, you have to bring me one kind of loss or the other. See what you've done today again. This new cooler costs forty dollars ... plus fifteen dollars of ice-cream kool-aid which has gone in vain.

But as your father often says, I am to be blamed, for I ought to have stopped sending you out to sell for me long ago. Let's pass by the market; maybe we shall see some good fish to buy for supper. I also want to ...

GIRL: Mama! Mama! Do you see that tall slim man walking ahead of us with the blindman? He is the man who stole the cooler this morning. He's the man! Look at the shirt and the trousers! The tie! He had on a tie this morning!

MOTHER: Shh, don't get so excited. If he becomes aware of your presence, he will disappear. Are you sure he is the man?

GIRL: Yes, I'm sure. I swear by my mother.

MOTHER: In that case, we shall walk behind him quietly and watch him closely to see what business he has with that beggar. If he is your thief, then there is no doubt only he is accompanying a blind beggar.

GIRL: To steal from him?

MOTHER: Certainly. To cut his throat just as he did to you this morning.

GIRL: Can't he spare even a beggar.

MOTHER: Thieves don't spare even their dead parents. Let's move faster; they've just turned around the corner leading to the market.

MAMUDU: So this is the street in which you live Oldman?

BLINDMAN: Yes son.

MAMUDU: For how long have you been living here?

BLINDMAN: For over thirty years. (THEIR CONVERSATION IS ACCOMPA-NIED BY THE RHYTHMIC SOUND OF THE BLINDMAN'S STICK AGAINST THE PAVEMENT.)

MAMUDU: Hmm! That's a long time. You first came here atleast five years before I was born.

BLINDMAN: It's clear from your voice, son, that you're only a child. My house is on your left, a little away from the street. A narrow path leads to it.

MAMUDU:	Isn't that convenient.
BLINDMAN:	Convenient? How?
MAMUDU:	I mean its ... its ... its away from the noise of the traffic and people, particularly the troublesome children.
BLINDMAN:	I understand son. I understand very much what you mean.
	(THE BLINDMAN WHISTLES THREE TIMES, TAKING A SLIGHT PAUSE EACH TIME)
MAMUDU:	Why did you do that?
BLINDMAN:	Did what? Whistle? Ah, that's to drive away evil spirits. Evil spirits are afraid of the sound of whistling.
MAMUDU:	Africa will never be free from superstition.
BLINDMAN:	What did you say?
MAMUDU:	Oh, I was only thinking aloud.

****

GIRL:	Mother! Mother! They've taken that narrow path on the left.
MOTHER:	I know, Baby Love. I've seen them. We shall go after them. That's probably where the blindman lives. Your thief won't escape this time.
GIRL:	They've entered that little wooden house.
MOTHER:	We shall wait for him right here. When he comes out than will be the time to give him the biggest shock of his life. Whatever he steals from the blindman will be enough proof that he is indeed a thief. And that will lend support to our charge against him.
GIRL:	Mother! Mother! Do you hear that? They've caught him! (A CONFUSED NOISE IN THE BACKGROUND! AMIDST WHICH THE CRIES OF THIEF! THIEF! THIEF! ARE HEARD REPEATEDLY) They've caught him mother! And here they come! Oh mother, they are beating him mother! (THE NOISE IS GETTING LOUDER)
MOTHER:	We shall wait for them right here. God the Almighty never sleeps. And thank God, here comes a policeman. Officer!
Officer:	What's the matter? A thief?
MOTHER:	Yes, a man stole something from a blind beggar. And officer, I too have a complaint against that same man.
Officer:	Okay, give me a minute. Let me keep this situation under control, or else they'll kill that man. Hey! stop! stop! Stop beating him! Hand him over! Stop this, I say. (BLOWS HIS WHISTLE

REPEATEDLY UNTIL THE NOISE SUBSIDES, MAMADU IS MOANING) Now. Keep quite everyone. I want the people involved to come forward and explain. You come here and stop crying. Are you not a man? Stand right beside me here. Can't you stand up? Okay, sit on the ground. Now, who will come forward and tell me what you people have against this young man. Ah, ah, ah, ah, one person at a time. (BLINDMAN COMES FORWARD, THE SOUND OF HIS STICK DISTINCT AMID THE EXCITED MURMURS) Oldman, what do you have to say?

BLINDMAN: This young man met me on my way home and gave me ten cents. After that he started asking me many questions. This is unusual. You know, People normally have very little to do with us beggars besides droping a few coins into our palms as if we were lepers. And we are not.

Officer: Never mind that for now. Get straight to the point.

BLINDMAN: Forgive me son, I forgot that you're a busy man. Well, I became suspicious. You know, I have been blind for more years than most of you have lived. And I've been living in this city, in that house there, for over thirty years.

CROWD: Hmmm!

BLINDMAN: I've had a great deal of experience with thieves in this city. They are real children of hell. He offered to accompany me home. I told him not to bother, that I would find my way. He would not hear. To make a long talk short, and not to waste your time, he accompanied me home. He is not the first good angel of Allah who has offered to accompany me home and in the end turned out a thief. You know, although I can find my way home without much difficulty, I still find it more convenient when I'm guided by somebody, particulary when the traffic is heavy. At first these good angels succeeded in getting away with my money. Then my neighbours advised me that whenever I had any suspicious person accompanying me, I should give them a signal. And we agreed that I should whistle three times when I get close to warn them that we are coming. This has turned out to be a useful scheme. Apart from the fact that it has discouraged many who might have tried to steal, it actually has made us catch some who did try, including this young man. As soon as I placed my bag down when we entered, he took it. By then some of my neighbours were watching his actions through the window. And the bag he took did not even contain any money. I always keep my money in the pocket of my gown. The bag he took contained only a few stale loaves of bread.

(THE CROWD BURSTS INTO LAUGHTER) Finally this good angel said good-bye nicely and walked out into the waiting hands of my neighbours. (THE CROWD BURST INTO CRIES OF THIEF THIEF, THIEF.)

Officer: (BLOWS HIS WHISTLE UNTIL NOISE DIES DOWN): Thank you, Oldman. May God bless you.

MOTHER: Officer, I also have a complaint against this man. This morning he stole a cooler and about fifteen dollars worth of Ice-cream from my daughter ...

JENNEH: Lord have mercy. Laillah haillah allah... It's Mamudu! Mamudu, what have you done? Officer, he is not a thief; he's my brother (THE CROWD BURST OUT LAUGHING) Officer, I beg you to let him go. He didn't steal.

MOTHER: Young girl, don't let me get angry with you. What do you mean by "He is not a thief, let him go?" He stole something worth fifty dollars from my daughter this morning.

You see, young girl. It's a pity that you should have such a useless person as your brother.

JENNEH: Please let him go; he is badly hurt already. I'll pay back all your money. I sell right over there at the market place. Some of these people know me. I am Jenneh Summaray. I promise I'll pay you all back. Please let him go officer.

(BREAKS INTO SOBS; MAMUDU IS MOANING. SOME PEOPLE IN THE CROWD ARE LETTING OUT SYMPATHE-TIC SIGHS; OTHERS ARE GIGGLING)

O Mamudu, see what you have done. What a shame! What a disgrace! I've been warning you against this all along. Officer, please let him go. I'll pay them back. I'll give these people my name and address (SOBS) And they can collect their money.

Officer: Young girl, I do pity you; it's a terrible thing to have such an elder brother; but there is nothing I can do here for you. We just have to go to the police station; maybe you can settle the matter there ... But by the time your brother will be out of this trouble, I don't think he will even dream of stealing.

THE CROWD JEERS AT HIM AS HE IS CARRIED ALONG BY THE POLICE-MAN.

Biographical notes

ACHOLONU, Catherine Obianuju Born 1951, Nigeria. Studied English Literature at Düsseldorf University, Germany, PhD in Igbo Literature. Published short stories, children's poetry and essays in literary criticism. She is a lecturer in the English Department of Alvan Ikoku College of Education, Owerri, Imo State, Nigeria.

ADEPITAN, Titi
Born 1959, Nigeria. When he wrote "Adieu Innocence" in 1984 he was post-graduate student in English at the University of Ibadan. He now teaches at the English Department of Ogun State University, Ago-Iwoye, Nigeria. He writes poems, and is presently working on his first novel "Kiyoola".

AIYEJINA, Funso
Born 1949, Osaso, Bendel State, Nigeria. Graduated at Ile-Ife University, post-graduate studies in Canada and Trinidad. For over a decade he taught African and Carribean Literature and Creative Writing at Ile-Ife. He presently lives and works in Trinidad. Published short stories, radio plays and poems. For his collection of poems "A letter to Lynda" he received the poetry prize of the 'Association of Nigerian Authors' in 1989.

ALLEN, John Born in Namibia. Former student of St. Paul's College, Windhoek. Studies B. Communications at the moment. At TUCSIN (The University Campus for Studies in Namibia) he was a member of the creative writing drama group.

ASOBO, Kenneth Khan
Born 1960, Pinyin-Bamenda, Cameroon. He works for Cameroon Radio & Television, CRTV, at Yaoundé. He is Deputy Head of Cultural Radio Programmes.

AYUK, Augustin Ayuk
Born in Cameroon 1956. University studies in linguistics at Yaoundé and Montréal. He works as translator and journalist at CRTV Yaoundé, where he produces his own extremely popular children's story telling programme, based on his own "modern adaptations" of Cameroonian and West African oral literature. His main writing interest is in African oral literature.

BALOGUN, Odun F.
Born 1946, Oka, Nigeria. Studied under a scholarship programme at Leningrad University, thereafter at the University of Illinois, USA. PhD in Slavic Languages. Taught at the English Department of Benin University, Benin City, Nigeria. At present he is professor in the English Department of Southern University, Baton Rouge, USA. Published several short stories and academic studies, e.g. "Tradition and Modernity in the African Short Story."

BUNYUI, David Chuye
Born 1961, Ndu-Nkambe, Cameroon. Producer of cultural radio programmes at CRTV Provincial Station Maroua. He has participated as actor in several theatre productions.

CHEKOL, Messeret
Born 1957 at Yedrawratch, Gojjam Region, Ethiopia. Due to smallpox he became blind in 1962. Completed university studies in English and Literature at Addis Ababa in 1981. Worked for the National Broadcasting Station as producer of cultural programmes. He is presently studying on a scholarship in the USA. "Fetters Gone" was one of his first narrations, 1984.

DEDJENE, Megdelawit
Born 1968, Addis Ababa, Ethiopia. Visited the German School until Government take-over in 1976. In 1983 she won an award in a United Nations Information Service Competition with her first short story. "It had a destiny", a contribution for Radio Deutsche Welle "Africa Competion" in 1985 was her second attempt at writing at the age of sixteen. She is presently studying in Bonn, Germany.

FELLOWES, Ernest Sidney
Born 1916, England, moved with his parents to the then "Southern Rhodesia" at the age of three, spent his childhood on a diamond field; was in any and every possible field of employment in England and Rhodesia, from taxi driver, factory worker, restaurant owner, from Royal Army, the police force to Rhodesian Railways clerk. Married to a Shona wife. Together with his wife and son he had to leave Rhodesia for political reasons in 1974 and returned to Zimbabwe in 1982 where he now lives in Ruwa."Serpents in the Sunshine" has strong autobiographical elements and was his first attempt towards writing in 1984.

FROMMLET, Wolfram
Born 1945 in Ravensburg, Germany. Studies in Art, Theatre, Music and Literature. As stage director and dramaturg at various German theatre houses; community development art projects with working class children in the Ruhr area; author, director and journalist of features, documentaries, children's and educational programmes for German radio and TV stations; project manager of media communications training project in Lusaka/Zambia. Principally involved as producer and dramaturg in the development of African and Asian radio drama, as well as in educational and rural broadcasting at Radio Deutsche Welle Training Centre, Cologne. Numerous publications on North-South issues, children's literature, African literature, media development. Edited and compiled "African Radio Plays", Nomos Publisher, Baden-Baden 1991.

HAITENGULA, Erastus
Namibian. Former student of Preciss College, Zimbabwe. As a member of the TUCSIN drama group he took part in the collective writing of "Family Business". Studies B.A. Law at the moment.

HILL, Gerry
British. Studied in Zimbabwe. She taught English at TUCSIN, Windhoek, Namibia, where she, due to her interest in drama and novel writing, initiated a "drama society" of which creative writing was a part. In her capacity as English lecturer she guided the collective writing experiment of "Family Business". She is presently living in Johannesburg.

IITA, Aina
Namibian. Received her high school education at Preciss College, Zimbabwe. Member of the TUCSIN drama group. She is presently studying in Switzerland.

ISAAC, Christian
Born 1949, Sierra Leone. BA in English and Philosophy, Diploma in Education. Taught in various schools in Sierra Leone and Liberia. The three narrations were his first publications.

KAHIGA, Samuel
Born 1944, Nairobi, Kenya. Writer and journalist. He wrote several short stories. With his brother, Leonard Kibera, he wrote "potent ash", a collection of political short stories on the period of Kenya's "Emergency" at the dawn of British rule; East African Publishing House, 1968.

KALU, Okpi
Born 1947, Ndi Oji, Imo State, Nigeria. Graduated in film and television from New York University; Television Training Institute, London. He has been employed as principal TV producer since 1980 by Nigerian Television Authority. He is presently chief script writer for NTA, Lagos.
"The Champion Wrestler" won a first prize at Radio Deutsche Welle "Africa Literature Competition", 1985. Seven novels were published by Macmillan, London, i.e. "The Smugglers", 1977, "Crossfire", 1981, "Biafra Testament" 1982, "South African Affair", 1983, "The Politicians", 1984.

KAMKONDO, Dede
Graduated with BA in Sociology and Literature at Malawi University. He teaches Communication at Bunda College, University of Malawi, Lilongwe. He writes radio plays ("The Mission of the Hyena", "Mother to the Child", in: "African Radio Plays, Baden-Baden 1991); short stories and several novels for children and young people. "The Flying Saucer", "Sivo and the Cruel Chief", Popular Publications, Limbe, Malawi, 1989; "Truth will out", MacMillan, London 1986; "Children of the Lake", Limbe, 1988; "For the Living", Dzuka Publishers, Blantyre, 1989.

KANGUEEHI, Napoleon
Born in Namibia and educated at Martin Luther College, Omaruru, Namibia. Was a member of the TUCSIN drama group. He is hoping to become a human rights lawyer in Namibia.

314

MAFFEIS, Sonia
Born in Namibia. Received her high school education at St. Paul's College, Windhoek. Was a member of the TUCSIN drama group and intends to study graphics design.

MAK'OLOO, Omondi
Born 1960, Nairobi, Kenya. He worked as journalist and editor for "Drum" , True Love" and the Kenyan "Sunday Times".
Published two novels "Too young to die" , Macmillan, London 1986; "Times Beyond", Heinemann Kenya, 1991. He is currently Secretary of the Writer's Association of Kenya.

MASAGBOR, Richard Abekhe
Born 1940, Nigeria. University studies in Nigeria, England and France. Taught at primary and secondary schools, before joining Benin University, Benin City, as lecturer in English and Literature. His writing is influenced by his strong interest in folklore studies.

MNGUNI, Herbert Mbukeni
Born 1946, KwaZulu, South Africa. A teacher by profession, he also studied radio and television broadcasting at the Catholic RTV Centre, Hatch End, England. He writes radio plays, poems and short stories. Four of his plays were broadcast by Radio Bantu, South Africa. He is presently attached to the Free University, Berlin, Germany, conducting a research programme on "Zulu children's moonlight games". Co-editor of the African literature journal AWA-FINNABA, Berlin.

MOLLEL, Tololwa Marti
Born 1952, a Maasai of Northern Tanzania. University studies in Drama in Dar es Salaam and Alberta, Canada. For some ten years lecturer in the Department of Art, Music & Theatre, University of DSM. He was strongly involved in Paukwa Theatre Group, DSM, and has been performing as actor and story teller in Tanzania, Europe and North America. He writes short stories, plays, children's stories and books, both in English and Suaheli. Many of his stories have been published and broadcast in Tanzania, England, USA, Denmark and Norway. The cultural traditions and the wealth of oral literature of his Maasai people form a strong background in several of his stories and books.
"Rhino's Boy", Outrigger, New Zealand, 1988; "Matembezi Msituni" (Suaheli, 'a walk in the forest'), Tanzania Publishing House, Dar es Salaam, 1987; "Rhinos for Lunch and Elephants for Supper", Oxford University Press, 1991; "A Promise to the Sun", Little, Brown & Company, 1992; "The Orphan Boy", Clarion Books, NY 1990.

MOYO, Aaron Chiundura Born 1954, Gweru, Zimbabwe. Writes novels, radio and television plays in Shona. He recently joined Zimbabwe Broadcasting Corporation,

Harare, as producer and playwright. He has also acted in a number of television plays.

MSENGEZI, Chiedza
Born 1953, Zimbabwe. High school teacher, presently working at a Teacher Training College. She started writing short stories and poetry, both in English and Shona, after joining the "Zimbabwe Women Writers", ZWW, at its inauguration in 1990.

MUBARAK AL, Khalid Mustafa
Born in Sudan. University studies in Drama in Sudan and England. Dean of the Institute of Music and Drama (once famous far beyond the Sudanese borders before it was run down by the Military and Fundamentalists); Director of Khartoum University Press; Professor for English and Arabic Literature at Khartoum University.
Sudan's leading playwright, both in English and Classical Arabic. His second play, "Station Street" was a runner-up in the BBC African Service' "Playwright Competition" in 1972 and published in Heinemann Writers Series, London 1973; "The Desert Crocodile or Why Allah stopped sending Prophets" received a first award in Radio Deutsche Welle "Africa Literature Competition", 1985 (in: "African Radio Plays", Baden-Baden, 1991). Several of his plays were broadcast both on Radio Omdurman, Khartoum and Sudan TV and performed at the National Theatre. Due to the political situation in his home-country he is presently living in Bristol, England.

OBI, Joseph Enuenwemba Born 1954, Isoka, Bendel State,Nigeria. MA and PhD in Social Sciences. Worked as a teacher and Social Welfare Inspector until 1977. He now lectures Sociology and Anthropology at the University of Benin, Bendel State, Nigeria. Published academic essays on Sociology & African Literature, and short stories.

RAMLOUL, Soonderlall
Born 1944, Mauritius. Works as a banker at Quatre Bornes. He has written several short stories.

SHERIFF, Mohamed
Born 1960, Sierra Leone. Lives in Freetown. Since 1984 he has worked as teacher of English and Head of Language Department at various Muslim High Schools. He has written several radio plays, mainly on the socio-economic situation and the cultural disintegration of the urban youth and the generation gap within the urban sector of his country. Wrote a dissertation on "Recent trends in Sierra Leonean drama."

VIRAHSAWMY, Dev
Born 1942, Mauritius. University studies in Linguistics at Edinburgh University. Senior Lecturer at the Mauritius Institute of Education. In 1984 he was Cultural Adviser to the Government and a leading member of the Alliance Party. Author of several collections of poems and radio plays. The radio play "Li" won a prize at the 11th "Concours Théatrale Interafricain" by Radio France Internationale.

WITTS, Virginia H.D.
Born 1948, Pershore, England. She has been living in Namibia for the last 17 years. She works as announcer and producer of radio programmes for the NBC, the Namibia Broadcasting Corporation, Windhoek. "Palmwine and Peanut Soup" was her first experience in creative play writing during a radio drama course at Radio Deutsche Welle Training Centre, Cologne, 1991.

Editorial notes:

The narrations and plays in this anthology represent different writing techniques, literary styles and thus, to varying degrees approaches towards the English language as a means of sovereign, authentic communication from within an African context.

One of the editorial deliberations was to give a forum to a wide facette of mostly unpublished African literature . A good number of the writers had, at the time they wrote the pieces of work printed here, little or no experience in writing. Others had already published several collections of stories, novels or plays.

To illustrate that both different styles and different stages of writing professionalism can contribute to the cultural and literary scene in Africa and ought to be made public, Literary master-pieces such as "His Excellency's Visit" or "Tooth of Fire" stand alongside a (then) 16 year old Ethiopian school girl's "document", together with a "political memory note book" such as "Serpents in the Sunshine" or folk- and documentary-based first writing attempts like "Dendi" and "Fetters Gone".

While some have never been regularly exposed to literary styles and traditions, others have had a constant challenge to their own writing due to their professional backgrounds as lecturers in English, Literature or Drama.

Although many of the stories were contributed to the Radio Deutsche Welle ""African Literature Competition" in 1985, thus with the intention of future broadcasting, editorial adjustments at varying degrees had to be made in order to reach higher radio suitability.

All editorial changes were done with painful care and under the following principles:

* in same cases words, verbs or phrases sounded too stilted, deliberately "picked" and literary ambitious; they stood out from the socio-cultural context of the story, the characters or the narrator. These were exchanged for culturally more credible ones.

* due to the anthology's main aim – i.e. the provision of literary material for radio broadcasting to an African audience – the audibility of some of the texts had to be enhanced:
i.e. unnecessary repetitions, long winded descriptions, psychological side-tracks or unimportant details were polished and shortened; in certain cases both epic and dramatic elements were smoothened in order to enhance clarity of dialogues, flow of scenes or description of events, a person's psychology or habits.

* language corrections were made exclusively on the characteristics of the narration, the characters, the cultural setting the literary piece is intended to reflect. Language correction was only made where it helped shape and polish a writer's authentic style or where authentic style lapsed. No abstract ideals or rules of "correct

English" were applied. On the contrary. The editor hopes to have done the utmost to strenghten and support authentic, and sometimes quite unorthodox forms of African English.

April 1992   Wolfram Frommlet

Acknowledgements

For a second time I have been able to compile and edit a collection of African writing due to the active support of two German institutions and their understanding of inter-cultural aid: The Deutsche Welle Radio Training Centre (DWAZ), Cologne and The Cultural Department of The German Foreign Office, Bonn.

Due to this financial and administrative support the literary works in this anthology will find their way back to where they came from: the African continent. Through the distribution channels of DWAZ, German Embassies and Goethe Institutes the lion's share of this edition will reach writers, libraries, broadcasting stations and cultural institutions who otherwise have no access to these works.

In particular I would like to thank the Director of the Deutsche Welle Radio Training Centre, Mr. Winfried-Illo Graff and Mr. Wolfgang Ernst from the Department of Preservation of Culture within the Foreign Office for enabling this second anthology.

I am very grateful to the German UNESCO Commission for having listed both this anthology as well as the previous one, "African Radio Plays", Nomos Publisher, 1991, under the German contributions for the UNESCO World Decade for Cultural Development.

Finally my thanks to Ms. Christiane Schifferdecker from Nomos Publisher, Baden-Baden, who spontaneously backed the idea of a second anthology of African literature.

Cologne, May 1992   Wolfram Frommlet